Rethinking G.K. Chesterton and Literary Modernism

This book comprehensively rethinks the relationship between G.K. Chesterton and a range of key literary modernists. When Chesterton and modernism have previously been considered in relation to one another, the dynamic has typically been conceived as one of mutual hostility, grounded in Chesterton's advocacy of popular culture and modernist literature's appeal to an aesthetic elite. In setting out to challenge this binary narrative, Shallcross establishes for the first time the depth and ambivalence of Chesterton's engagement with modernism, as well as the reciprocal fascination of leading modernist writers with Chesterton's fiction and thought.

Shallcross argues that this dynamic was defined by various forms of parody and performance, and that these histrionic expressions of cultural play not only suffused the era, but found particular embodiment in Chesterton's public persona. This reading not only enables a far-reaching reassessment of Chesterton's corpus, but also produces a framework through which to re-evaluate the creative and critical projects of a host of modernist writers—most sustainedly, T.S. Eliot, Wyndham Lewis, and Ezra Pound—through the prism of Chesterton's disruptive presence. The result is an innovative study of the literary performance of popular and 'high' culture in early twentieth-century Britain, which adds a valuable new perspective to continuing critical debates on the parameters of modernism.

Michael Shallcross is an independent researcher, based in York, UK.

Literary Texts and the Popular Marketplace
Series Editors: Kate Macdonald, Ann Rea
Editorial Board: Kristin Bluemel, David Carter,
Stella Deen, Christoph Ehland, David Finkelstein,
Jaime Harker, Nick Hubble, Elizabeth Maslen,
Rebecca N. Mitchell and Victoria Stewart

Titles in this Series

1 The Business of the Novel
  Economics, Aesthetics and the Case of Middlemarch
  Simon R. Frost

2 Fashioning the Silver Fork Novel
  Cheryl A. Wilson

3 Comedy and the Feminine Middlebrow Novel: Elizabeth von Arnim and Elizabeth Taylor
  Erica Brown

4 John Buchan and the Idea of Modernity
  Edited by Kate Macdonald and Nathan Waddell

5 Women's University Fiction, 1880–1945
  Anna Bogen

6 William Clark Russell and the Victorian Nautical Novel
  Gender, Genre and the Marketplace
  Andrew Nash

7 Modernism, Middlebrow and the Literary Canon
  The Modern Library Series, 1917–1955
  Lise Jaillant

8 Rethinking G.K. Chesterton and Literary Modernism
  Parody, Performance, and Popular Culture
  Michael Shallcross

Rethinking G.K. Chesterton and Literary Modernism

Parody, Performance, and Popular Culture

Michael Shallcross

LONDON AND NEW YORK

First published 2018
by Routledge
2 Park Square, Milton Park, Abingdon, Oxon OX14 4RN

and by Routledge
711 Third Avenue, New York, NY 10017

Routledge is an imprint of the Taylor & Francis Group, an informa business

© 2018 Taylor & Francis

The right of Michael Shallcross to be identified as author of this work has been asserted by him in accordance with sections 77 and 78 of the Copyright, Designs and Patents Act 1988.

All rights reserved. No part of this book may be reprinted or reproduced or utilised in any form or by any electronic, mechanical, or other means, now known or hereafter invented, including photocopying and recording, or in any information storage or retrieval system, without permission in writing from the publishers.

Trademark notice: Product or corporate names may be trademarks or registered trademarks, and are used only for identification and explanation without intent to infringe.

Library of Congress Cataloging-in-Publication Data
CIP data has been applied for.

ISBN: 978-1-138-67873-6 (hbk)
ISBN: 978-1-315-55875-2 (ebk)

Typeset in Sabon
by codeMantra

Contents

List of Figures vii
List of Abbreviations ix
Acknowledgements xi

Introduction: Sublime Vulgarity, Fanatical Play 1

1 The Chesterbentley: A *Fin-de-Siècle* Nonsense Friendship 18

2 The Ethics of Travesty: Chesterton's Ludicrous Performance on the Edwardian Literary Stage 55

3 A Hundred Visions and Revisions: Chesterton Refracted through the Avant-Garde of 1910 103

4 We Discharge Ourselves on Both Sides: The Parodic Commerce of Chesterton and the Men of 1914 142

5 *Le Mob c'est Moi*: 1920s Modernism as Monstrous Carnival 195

6 Audacious Reconciliation: The Human Circulating Library of Late Modernism 235

Works Cited 267
Index 285

List of Figures

1.1	Letter sent from E.C. Bentley to G.K. Chesterton, January 1894, with illustrations by Chesterton	48
2.1	Caricature of Oscar Wilde by Max Beerbohm, 1894	60
2.2	*Mr. G.K. Chesterton giving the world a kiss*, Max Beerbohm, 1904	74
2.3	*A true Victorian cuts a disreputable author*, G.K. Chesterton, 1932	83
3.1	Wyndham Lewis photographed by George Charles Beresford, 1913	130
4.1	Caricature of G.K. Chesterton by Max Beerbohm, 1912	166
4.2	Caricature of G.K. Chesterton by Edmund Kapp, 1919	166
4.3	Caricature of Wyndham Lewis by Edmund Kapp, 1914	175
4.4	Caricature of Alfred Beit by G.K. Chesterton, 1905	187
5.1	*Mr Wyndham Lewis as a Tyro*, Wyndham Lewis, 1921	209
5.2	T.S. Eliot photographed by Henry Ware Eliot, 1926	215
6.1	*G.K. Chesterton Esq.*, Wyndham Lewis, 1932	247
6.2	*Self-Portrait*, Wyndham Lewis, 1932	247

List of Abbreviations

BL MS   Manuscript held in the British Library, London. Indexed in *The British Library Catalogue of Additions to the Manuscripts: The G.K. Chesterton Papers*. Ed. R.A. Christophers. London: British Library, 2001.

Bod MS   Manuscript held in the Bodleian Library, University of Oxford. Catalogued as Bod MSS.Eng.misc.e.861–870. 'Diaries of E. C. Bentley, 1894–1905'.

CDN   G.K. Chesterton. *G.K. Chesterton at the Daily News: Literature, Liberalism and Revolution, 1901–1913*. 8 vols. Ed. Julia Stapleton. London: Pickering & Chatto, 2012.

CFB   G.K. Chesterton. *The Complete Father Brown Stories*. Ed. Michael Hurley. London: Penguin Books, 2012.

CW   G.K. Chesterton. *The Collected Works of G.K. Chesterton*. 37 vols. to date. Gen. eds. George J. Marlin, Richard P. Rabatin, and John L. Swan. San Francisco: Ignatius, 1986—.

DN   *Daily News*

ILN   *Illustrated London News*

PTSE   T.S. Eliot. *The Poems of T. S. Eliot*. 2 vols. Eds. Jim McCue and Christopher Ricks. London: Faber and Faber, 2015.

Acknowledgements

This book began life as a PhD studied at Durham University from 2010 to 2013. I am very grateful to the English Department at Durham for offering me the studentship that made this possible, and to my supervisor, John Nash, for his invaluable support and guidance. I would also like to thank the generous readers who have more recently taken time to comment on the book's final draft: Kostas Boyiopoulos, Patrick Crozier, Ellen Renner, Julia Stapleton, and Nathan Waddell. Grateful thanks are also due to my excellent editors at Routledge, Michelle Salyga and Tim Swenarton, and production manager, Assunta Petrone, for their diligence and professionalism in guiding this project to completion.

Portions of the text have previously been published in *English*, *English Literature in Transition*, *Essays in Criticism*, and the *Wellsian*, and are reprinted here in amended form with the kind permission of the editors. Excerpts from Richard Aldington's *Soft Answers* are reproduced by kind permission of the estate of Richard Aldington c/o Rosica Colin Limited, London. Quotations from the works of E.C. Bentley are by permission of Curtis Brown, quotations from T.S. Eliot by permission of Faber and Faber Ltd, quotations from Wyndham Lewis by permission of the Wyndham Lewis Memorial Trust (a registered charity), and quotations from Ezra Pound by permission of New Directions. I am grateful to the British Library for permission to quote and reproduce an image from the manuscripts of G.K. Chesterton, and to the Bodleian Library for permission to quote from the diaries of E.C. Bentley. My thanks to Berlin Associates for permission to reproduce images of the work of Max Beerbohm, to the Chris Beetles Gallery for the same permission in relation to Edmond Kapp, and to Bridgeman Images in relation to Wyndham Lewis.

I would like to salute the brilliance of my friends Chris Beckett, Paul Bignell, Kostas Boyiopoulos, Yoonjoung Choi, Graham and Kate Durant, Tom Helsby, Lee Horner, Patrick Jones, Avishek Parui, Val Pearson, Lou Richards, James Spinney, Ben Thorpe, James Vaughan, Don Walls, Jamie Wilson, and Mark Wootton. My thoughts are always with my dearest pal and scholarly inspiration, Oliver Grant. I am deeply indebted to the love and support of my wonderful family: Alice, Edmund, Hattie, and Susan Fisher; Terry Fisher (*in memoriam*); Ellen, Kit, and William Richardson;

and Jeffrey, Richard, and Val Shallcross. Most importantly, I would like to thank my wife, Tracy, for her kindness, encouragement, and patient accommodation of the third who walks always beside us, wrapped in a black cape and brigand's hat.

Finally, this book is dedicated, with profound love and gratitude, to my grandmother, Doris Shallcross, from whose bookshelves I first borrowed a copy of *Father Brown* a decade ago, thinking it might offer a little light reading to pass an hour or two. I owe her immeasurably more than the somewhat belated return of that book.

Introduction
Sublime Vulgarity, Fanatical Play

> "These opposites won't do. They don't work. They don't fight. If it's white instead of black, and solid instead of liquid, and so on all along the line—then there's something wrong. [...] Things made so opposite are things that cannot quarrel."
> —Father Brown, in 'The Duel of Dr. Hirsch' (*Pall Mall Magazine*, Aug. 1914; CFB 214)

> "Do you know," said Lord Beaumont [...] "I can never quite make out which side you are on. Sometimes you seem so liberal and sometimes so reactionary. *Are* you a modern, Basil?"
> "No," said Basil, loudly and cheerfully, as he entered the crowded drawing-room.
> —Chesterton, 'The Painful Fall of a Great Reputation' (CW 6:96)

To set out on a sustained exploration of G.K. Chesterton's relationship to literary modernism might seem a wild-goose chase worthy of one of his own quixotic protagonists. After all, the majority of critics who have given the matter any consideration have concluded that no meaningful correspondence existed between the two. John Coates considers Chesterton's engagement with modernist aesthetics 'cursory' (*G.K. Chesterton*, 8), while Colin Cavendish-Jones claims that he 'never made the slightest attempt to understand the aims and ideas of the modernist movement' (86). For Samuel Hynes, Chesterton's habitual use of '*modern* as a term of opprobrium' meant that he 'could not be just to its writers' (86), while David Lodge reports that he 'either opposed or ignored [... the] Modern Movement in literature' (145) throughout his career. The responses of modernist writers to this apparent embodiment of unreflective intransigence have gone almost completely undiscussed in critical literature on the period. The contemporary reader is left to assume a dynamic of mutual hostility and incomprehension: the targets of Chesterton's disdain met his nugatory grasp of modernist aesthetics with haughty disregard, and an unbridgeable impasse was permanently established.

In addition to Chesterton's assumed intolerance of all things aesthetically modern, this schism is often considered to derive from his staunch advocacy of popular culture, which set him irreconcilably at odds with the 'high' cultural programme of modernist standard-bearers such as

2   Introduction

T.S. Eliot, Wyndham Lewis, and Ezra Pound. In his 1959 study, *The Centre of Hilarity*, Michael Mason neatly summarises the distinction at hand, situating Chesterton and Eliot as such pristine opposites that it would be 'almost ludicrous to compare them' (13), since Chesterton had represented the 'popular bowels' of British culture, while Eliot stood for its 'clerkly head' (14–15). More recently, Lee Oser has reemphasised this divide: 'Chesterton is comical, democratic, and orthodox. Eliot is ironic, aristocratic, and a priest of art' (39). In the binary terms of this narrative, the leading exponents of 'high modernism' formed an aesthetically radical, though culturally elitist, vanguard, while Chesterton led a culturally democratic, if aesthetically retrograde, counterinsurgency.

This view has derived much of its pertinency from the willingness of critics to trust in the pronouncements of the protagonists themselves. Pound's proposal that the house magazine of high modernism, the *Little Review*, should bear the blustering subtitle, 'Making No Compromise with the Public Taste', is complemented by his complaint that Chesterton's populism created 'an atmosphere in which art is impossible' (Pound, *Letters*, 171), while Lewis's assertion that his debut novel, *Tarr* (1918), was conceived for a 'publique d`élite' (Lewis, *Letters*, 552) is offset by his pithy dismissal of Chesterton's corpus as the outpourings of a 'dogmatic toby-jug' (*Time*, 387).[1] In a comparable vein, Eliot's obituary of Chesterton in the *Tablet* (20 June 1936) guides the reader's attention away from his possible aesthetic merits, while projecting a self-evident authority to arbitrate on such matters: to 'judge Chesterton on his "contributions to literature," [...] would be to apply the wrong standards of measurement' ('Obituary', 531).

As Russell Kirk observes of Eliot's imperious tone, it is rather 'as if the obituary of William Cobbett had been written by the Primate of All England' (192). Kirk's reference to Cobbett, the radical populist, is apt. In his lifetime, Chesterton was more than happy to collude in such reductive representations, because they corroborated his self-image as a champion of unrefined popular culture over what he considered an oligarchy of effete aesthetes and privileged dilettantes. As he argues in 'The Case for the Ephemeral',

> [t]he real objection to modernism is simply that it is a form of snobbishness. It is an attempt to crush a rational opponent not by reason, but by some mystery of superiority, by hinting that one is specially up to date or particularly 'in the know'.
>
> (*All Things*, 4)[2]

The grafting of the term 'high' to 'modernism' further compounded the offence: Chesterton argues elsewhere that in cultural terms '[t]he horrible word "High" [...] logically means nothing, but morally means priggishness' ('Women, Worrying, and the Higher Culture', *ILN* 12 May 1906; *CW* 27:189).

In a bid to debunk this projection of superiority, Chesterton peppered his journalism with bluff denunciations of 'the nonsense of the Ezra Pound period' ('The Spirit of the Age in Literature', *Bookman* Oct. 1930; CW 21:605–606) and turned to light verse to convey the news that he was 'getting rather tired of D.H. Lawrence' ('Ballade of a Morbid Modern', *G.K.'s Weekly* 9 Nov. 1933; CW 10.2:477). While such raillery successfully situated him as the arch-representative of the popular market of his day, the legacy of these low-level skirmishes has been a considerable depreciation in Chesterton's subsequent critical standing, as the two-dimensional caricature of 'the medieval Merry Englander with his spear tilted against modernity' (Hurley, 70) has calcified into a critical truism.[3] Much as Basil Grant, the hero of Chesterton's short story, 'The Painful Fall of a Great Reputation', bursts obtrusively into the genteel drawing room, a very deliberate bull in a china shop, the critical consensus presents us with a vision of Chesterton blundering his way around a hyper-refined aesthetic realm, swinging his swordstick indiscriminately, while failing to knock a single exquisite modernist artefact from its pedestal. In this sense, the title of Chesterton's story possesses an unwitting irony, since the tale operates partially as a satire of Oscar Wilde, whose subsequent elevation to the canon has derived in large part from a critical sense that he embodies a radical 'ultra-modernity' ('Importance', 195), as George Bernard Shaw put it. Conversely, Shaw unconsciously prophesised the decline of Chesterton's formerly substantial reputation in the course of a local controversy in 1916: 'Mr. Chesterton, as an anti-Modernist, compromises himself' ('Case', 327).

There is an additional irony in this development, since the young Chesterton was frequently likened to Wilde; indeed, a contemporary reviewer of his critical study, *Charles Dickens* (1906), confidently announced that 'Mr. Chesterton is a literary disciple of Oscar Wilde' (Douglas, 'Signed', 126). Margaret Canovan has discussed how this confusion might have come about, highlighting Chesterton's simultaneous mimicry and manipulation of Wilde's rhetorical techniques: having learned the 'mode of paradoxical witticism from Oscar Wilde [...] he deliberately used [...] the paradoxical style of the intellectual elite, in order to defend against that elite the common sense of the common man' (21). If this manoeuvre implies an arch subversion on Chesterton's part, it also reflects a more painful act of extrication from the culture that he was criticising. His lifelong friend, E.C. Bentley, later reported that in their schooldays, Chesterton's literary preference was for the Victorian classics and he 'did not care [...] for lighter reading' (qtd. in Clemens, 3), a contention supported by a letter sent from Chesterton to Bentley in 1890, in which Tennyson's *In Memoriam* (1849) is contrasted favourably with the popular adventure novels of 'that interminable ass Kingston' (Ward, *Gilbert*, 34–35).[4]

4   *Introduction*

These sentiments are a far cry from those with which Chesterton announced himself to a startled bourgeois readership a decade later. His foundational statement of sympathy with populist aesthetics, 'A Defence of Penny Dreadfuls' (*Speaker*, 16 Mar. 1901), anathematises his own 'class' for its deviation from mass taste: 'it is we who are the morbid exceptions; it is we who are the criminal class' (*Defendant*, 26). If, as Canovan argues, this cultural *volte-face* is suggestive of 'the *reformed* intellectual, whose views about his former vices are often as severe as those of the reformed drunkard' (37), it is instructive to note the insistent repetition of the collective pronoun—'it is *we*'—which draws both essayist and audience into the sphere of criticism. Although Chesterton would no doubt have met the question posed by Lord Beaumont to Basil Grant—'*are* you a modern?'—with an equally emphatic 'No', the same shift in orientation recurs periodically throughout his critical writing in glancing references to '*we* moderns' (*CW* 4:141; my emphasis). As A.R. Orage noted in the *New Age* in 1913, 'Mr. Chesterton, though a critic of our days, is its most complete incarnation' ('Readers and Writers', 25 Dec., 241). This duality helps to account for Chesterton's later contention that the ongoing 'debate about new forms in art interests me, because my reaction to it is not that of the ordinary reactionary' ('A New Theory of Novelty', *ILN* 6 Oct. 1928; *CW* 34:606). When Chesterton has Beaumont express confusion over Grant's cultural politics—'I can never quite make out which side you are on'—he exposes a kernel of multivalence that Grant shares with his creator.

Beaumont's disorientation might stand as an equally apt gloss on readers' responses to figures such as Eliot and Lewis, whose poetry and prose often combine radically avant-garde aesthetics with deeply reactionary cultural sentiments. In puzzling out this apparent contradiction, Kevin Rulo has argued that the 'high modernism' of the fabled 'Men of 1914'—Eliot, Joyce, Lewis, and Pound—is best understood as a local manifestation of Antoine Compagnon's wider grouping, the 'antimodern' (254).[5] Compagnon's analysis lends the term a greater nuance than had been implied by Shaw when attributing the same outlook to Chesterton. As Rulo explains, Compagnon distinguishes the 'antimodern' from the 'non-modern' because 'the antimodern has a Janus face' (260); its 'ambivalence' manifested in the work of writers who possess a consciousness of their absorption within, and occasional affinity with, the conditions of cultural modernity, but remain 'able to reflect critically upon modernity', rather than being 'slaves to the novelty of the modern' (255). As with Chesterton's rebounding between the self-implicating 'we' and self-extricating 'No', the antimodern temperament is characterised not so much by an affectation of pristine critical distance from the age, as a more-or-less subterfuge sense of identification, offset by an ostentatious enactment of resistance.

My interest is in exploring the ways in which this multivalence manifests itself through forms of parody and performance in the individual writings and group interactions of Chesterton and a variety of literary modernists—primarily Eliot and Lewis, but also a wider cast of loosely aligned figures of the avant-garde—so as to rethink these relationships in more productive terms, centred upon various interconnected forms of dialogic play. One might say that these writers performed a *traversal* of modernity in two distinct senses—both in the legal sense of refutation, conducted through satire, and in the ambulatory sense of boundary transgression, achieved through imitation. In the process, they also traversed one another's writing—a compound of opposition and identification is traceable not only throughout Chesterton's textual sparring with modernist literature and the ambivalent responses of modernist writers to his cultural influence, but also the rivalrous engagements that took place between fellow modernists.

These textual traversals were frequently conducted through forms of parody, which is appropriate, since this discursive practice conjoins a projection of difference with an inscription of similarity. Linda Hutcheon summarises the operation of parody as a 'repetition with critical distance' (6), while Margaret Rose explains that an 'ambiguity' pertains to 'the prefix "para"', deriving from 'its ability to describe both nearness and opposition' (8)—both 'beside' and 'contrary to' (Barnhart, 754). As these accounts suggest, the indefinite admixture of collusion and opposition characteristic of the antimodern finds an aesthetic corollary in parodic discourse. Parody always operates somewhere on a sliding scale between adversarial satire and imitative pastiche, rebounding intractably between a subversion and retention of *author*ity, acceding neither to unreflective rejection nor uncritical emulation.

The intrinsically playful ethos of the form also mediates the agonistic confrontation of cultural voices by staging it as a rumbustious wit contest, composed of various modes of textual cross-dressing. These qualities make parody an equally useful means of rethinking the interplay of 'high' and 'popular' discourse in modernist practice. Malcolm Bradbury observed long ago that with the advent of 'modernism the arts of parody took on a far more central role' (57) as a structural tool upon which serious literary merit might be conferred. Eliot's *The Waste Land* (1922) famously begins with a parody of Chaucer and proceeds through a magpie trawl of literary history, scavenging materials from canonical sources and contemporary popular culture alike. Joyce's *Ulysses* (1922) is 'built out of parody' (Dentith, 15) on both a macro and micro level: a thematic burlesque of Homer's *Odyssey*, incorporating one chapter—'Oxen of the Sun'—composed entirely of pastiches of historical texts and literary styles 'from Latin prose to fragments of modern slang' (Gifford, 336n1).

Nonetheless, the parodic energies of the period extended far beyond the serious-minded structural experiments of its totemic works, to encompass a cornucopia of facetious missives, skits, and asides conceived primarily to amuse or provoke, often by travestying the very masterpieces that were offered up to the public as objects of veneration. Take, for example, a letter sent in August 1925 from Joyce to Harriet Shaw Weaver, whose editorship of the *Egoist* from 1914 to 1919 was instrumental in the inception of the high-modernist project, leading to the serialisation of extracts from *Ulysses* and the publication of Eliot's *Prufrock and Other Observations* (1917), Joyce's *A Portrait of the Artist as a Young Man* (1917), and Lewis's *Tarr*. While informing Weaver of his recent activities, Joyce breaks into a sprightly parody of *The Waste Land*:

> Rouen is the rainiest place getting
> Inside all impermeables, wetting
> Damp marrow in drenched bones.
> Midwinter soused us coming over Le Mans
> Our inn at Niort was the Grape of Burgundy
> But the winepress of the Lord thundered over that grape of Burgundy
> And we left in a hurgundy.
> (Hurry up, Joyce, it's time!)
>
> (Joyce, *Selected*, 309)

Dennis Brown has argued that the interactions of the 'Men of 1914' should 'be considered less in terms of individual stylistic development than as a series of moves within an overall intertextual group-game' (*Intertextual*, 1). Joyce's playful *communiqué* can be read as a minor move in this game, performing his difference in front of the influential modernist patron through a genial pastiche of Eliot's more sobering account of the regenerative effects of rain. In doing so, Joyce advertises a rather more accommodating relationship with the material world than that which results either from the poet's temperamental mordancy or his enduring, if qualified, adherence to T.E. Hulme's view that the 'properly classical poem' must be 'dry and hard' (Hulme, *Collected*, 66). Joyce's skit demonstrates the unnerving capacity of parodic discourse to get inside all impermeables, fecundating the sacrosanct *urtext* into a boisterous new life. However, the aggression implied by the incursion is mediated by the burlesque insertion of his own biography into the text, in a manner that emphasises identification, and finally locates him in the less than dignified company of Eliot's sottish 'sweet ladies' (*PTSE* 1:61).

Chesterton complements Joyce's wine with cheese in his picaresque satire, *The Flying Inn* (1914), in which the hero, Patrick Dalroy, offers up a derisory parody of W.B. Yeats's 'The Rose of Battle' (1892): '"Cheese of all Cheeses, Cheese of all the world", as my compatriot, Mr Yeats, says to the Something-or-other of Battle' (238). Elsewhere, Chesterton notes that '[b]ad cheese symbolises the startling prodigy of matter taking on vitality' ('Popular Jokes and Vulgarity', *ILN* 21 Mar. 1908; *CW* 28:67). Dalroy's parodic recourse to cheese draws attention to parody's comparably uncanny investment of an apparently stable textual entity with new vitality, a trick pre-empted by Chesterton's much-anthologised parody of Wordsworth, 'Sonnet to a Stilton Cheese':

> Stilton, thou shouldst be living at this hour
> And so thou art. Nor losest grace thereby;
> England has need of thee, and so have I –
> [...]
> my digestion, like the House of Lords,
> The heaviest burdens on herself doth lay
>
> (*CDN* 7:120)

In reimagining the poet's heady appeal to Milton in burlesque, corporeal terms, Chesterton not only anticipates Joyce's implied deflation of the parodic target's stately self-importance, but also his implantation of the parodist within the sphere of mockery, here via a carnivalesque invocation of his groaning digestive system.

As these exhibitive acts suggest, if the figures upon whom I will focus are inveterate parodists, they are also incorrigible performers. This was an age of personality writ large, in which broad caricature was as much the mode as painstaking depth psychology, and the exuberant means through which these writers staged their literary identities, often in terms of a figurative embodiment of their texts, filtered through to their reception. Hugh Kenner writes of 'the Wyndham Lewis repertory company' ('Mrs.', 91); V.S. Pritchett views Eliot as a 'company of actors inside one suit' (qtd. in Ackroyd, 118); Robert Blatchford considers Chesterton 'an actor [who] played a part, and dressed for a part' (qtd. in Ward, *Return*, 80). Although this imagery suggests the centrality of self-dramatisation to each writer's navigation of the modern literary marketplace, a more disruptive performance of cultural outlawry is also at play: think of Chesterton suddenly brandishing an alarmingly proportioned knife at a public debate, only to use it to sharpen his pencil (see Ward, *Gilbert*, 218–19), or Lewis placing his service revolver amidst the cutlery during dinner with the Prince of Wales, an action calculated to 'draw dramatic attention to himself' (Meyers, 82), but also to breach social convention in a more subversive sense. The writer-performer, like the antimodern and the parodist, is a double-figure, both arch spectator of, and engaged player in, the comedy of the age.

The penchant of Chesterton and Lewis for implanting sinister incongruities within genteel settings might seem a far cry from Eliot's exorbitant reticence in matters of propriety, as satirised in Virginia Woolf's famous account of his attendance of literary gatherings 'in a four-piece suit' (qtd. in Gordon, *Eliot's*, 84) and Lewis's observation to a visitor that Eliot 'doesn't come *in here* disguised as Westminster Abbey' (qtd. in Kenner, *Pound*, 444). However, these visions of sartorial superabundance might also be viewed in a different light, informed by Chesterton's

8 *Introduction*

account of festive revelry: 'really vigorous and exultant men [want] to wear more and more clothes when they are revelling. They want worlds of waistcoats and forests of trousers and pagodas of tall hats toppling up to the stars' ('The Mummers', *DN* 30 Dec. 1911; *CDN* 7:274). The 'wopsical hat' worn by 'Mr. Eliot' in his self-parodic skit on Edward Lear, 'Lines for Cuscuscaraway and Mirza Murad Ali Beg' (Jan. 1933, *Criterion*), might be imagined as such a vertiginous contrivance, mutely ironising the poet's poker-faced 'mouth so prim' (*PTSE* 1:143). Time and again in these writers' lives and work, we find this spirit of play operating alongside, and productively complicating, more pragmatic concerns with cultural self-projection, and introducing subtle intimations of similarity within ostentatious performances of peculiarity.

Sublime Vulgarity

The conceptual ties of parody and performance that linked these writers operated in tandem with numerous prosaic cross-threads that connected Chesterton and modernism on a day-to-day level in the early years of the century. These are traceable throughout the personal and professional interactions of the close-knit world of literary London, as well as the overlapping network of periodicals to which writers of the era contributed. Chesterton's friendships with ideologically proto-modernist, if aesthetically populist, figures such as Shaw and H.G. Wells are only the most conspicuous illustration of this crossover. Wells took particular delight in reporting an anecdote involving the 'quarrelling' (qtd. in Ward, *Gilbert*, 322) James brothers, which serves as an apt metaphor of the competing views of Chesterton circulating at the time. The philosopher, William James, was very much a Chesterton fan, sending an ebullient letter of praise on the publication of *Charles Dickens*: 'O, Chesterton, but you're a darling! I've just read your Dickens—it's as good as Rabelais' (Ward, *Gilbert*, 323). Consequently, James was 'immensely excited' (Ward, *Gilbert*, 322) one day to learn that Chesterton was staying at an inn near the Rye residence of his brother, Henry. The austere novelist did not share his brother's enthusiasm—he once assured an enquiring journalist that modern writers 'do not think of Chesterton' (qtd. in Ward, *Gilbert*, 322) at all—and was mortified when William shinned up a garden ladder to spy at Chesterton's window, ordering him to climb down, while quizzing Wells anxiously over whether such things were 'done' (Ward, *Gilbert*, 322).[6]

William James's interest was reciprocated: Chesterton praised him for 'popularising philosophy', employing a typically burlesque analogy to endorse James's knack of making 'metaphysics' perform 'an undignified dance of common-sense', a methodology that Chesterton considered to mark 'a turning point in the history of our time' ('The Philosophy of William James', *ILN* 17 Sept. 1910; *CW* 28:599).[7] Of course, James's primary claim to such a status is now located in his coining of the phrase 'the stream of consciousness' (180), which later became synonymous with Joycean aesthetics. For his part, Joyce wished 'kicks up the arse' (*Selected*, 141) to both Chesterton and Henry James in a letter to his brother, Stanislaus, in December 1906. In Chesterton's case, this hostility might have been inspired by the recent publication of *Heretics* (1905), a critical survey of the Edwardian literary landscape, in which the titular apostates include two of Joyce's formative influences: Henrik Ibsen and George Moore.

Having been arraigned in *Heretics* for his 'solemn folly' and 'dusty egoism' (72), Moore later displayed an admirable equanimity in attesting that Chesterton's dramatic debut, *Magic* (1913), commanded his 'artistic sympathies': 'I am not exaggerating when I say of all modern plays I like it the best' (Ward, *Gilbert*, 315). Moore's sympathies would seem to have been shared in at least some measure by Joyce, since his violent feelings towards Chesterton later cooled sufficiently for him to take time out from writing *Ulysses* to assist in a plan to bring *Magic* to the Swiss stage in May 1918 (see Ellmann, R., *James*, 439–40). Although interference from the British consulate finally caused the project to founder, Joyce's attempt to enlist Pound to intervene in a related dispute prompted an irritated dispatch from the latter, alleging possession of 'documents proving that a company of players [has] put on a Chesterton play (for which they ought all to be poisoned until dead of gangrene)' (May 1919, Pound, *Pound/Joyce*, 154).

Despite Pound's murderous urges, it was by no means a truth universally acknowledged in cultivated circles that Chesterton's aesthetic methods were inimical to the avant-garde. In an article for the *Egoist* ('Schönberg, Epstein, Chesterton, and Mass-Rhythm', 16 Feb. 1914), the arts commentator, Huntly Carter, draws Chesterton together with the serialist composer, Arnold Schönberg, and the modernist sculptor, Jacob Epstein, as exponents of what he terms 'mass-rhythm', citing *Magic* as evidence that even 'the most conservative form of mind [is beginning] to put the cosmos on the stage in an individual way' (76). Although it might be argued that Carter's juxtaposition illustrates the very epistemological confusion that Chesterton insistently ascribed to his contemporaries, it also speaks once more to a genuine ambivalence at the heart of his creative work. Indeed, insofar as *Magic* portrays a Faustian magus figure with a distinct authorial resemblance, presented in ambiguously monitory and celebratory terms, it is appropriate that the play should briefly have found association with the author of *A Portrait of the Artist as a Young Man*.

Similarly, Chesterton's frequently reactionary politics did not blind more progressively minded authors to his aesthetic merits, nor was this valuation always framed in terms of a shoehorning into the avant-garde. Although Rebecca West excoriated Chesterton's social polemics as 'a study in prejudice' ('Mr Chesterton', 5) in a blistering attack in the

Clarion (14 Nov. 1913), she warmly praised his comic novella, *Manalive* (1912), in the *Freewoman* (14 Mar. 1912), as an 'intoxicating and delicious fairy tale' ('Manalive', 292). West's only complaint was that Chesterton insisted upon adulterating pure farce with satire, 'preach[ing] the gospel when heaven has sent him down a comic song' ('Manalive', 293). A year later, Virginia Woolf set forth a converse view of his merits in an approving account of Chesterton's short fiction in the *Times Literary Supplement*, praising the 'genial gusto' of his tales, which 'point a moral or possess a sting which take[s] them out of the province of farce into that of satire' ('Les Copains', 7 Aug. 1913; *Essays* 2:17).

More practical considerations also played a part in complicating cultural boundaries. D.H. Lawrence's friend, Jessie Chambers, recalled that he 'often read and discussed' Chesterton's articles in the *Daily News*, and sent Chesterton a sample of his work in 1908, asking 'his opinion of its merit' (Lawrence, 43) with an implicit view to publication. Although another of Lawrence's sometime friends, Katherine Mansfield, can be found dismissing Chesterton as 'an old wind bag' (*Collected*, 101) in a 1918 letter to John Middleton Murry (1 Mar.), three months later she writes again, wondering if she might get something published in the *New Witness*, a periodical then under Chesterton's editorship (6 Jun. 1918; Mansfield, *Collected*, 222).[8]

The *New Witness* ran regular parodic skits on highbrow culture, and Mansfield might perhaps have had a similarly comic contribution in mind, since she had first distinguished herself as a writer on the 'Pastiche' column in Orage's idiosyncratic periodical, the *New Age*. 'Pastiche' operated both as a vehicle for satire and as a testing ground for inexperienced contributors, whose displays of wit would mark them down as a writer of potential. One of Mansfield's entries from 25 May 1911, composed jointly with Beatrice Hastings, is a parody of Chesterton's popular journalism, with its occasionally predictable formula of exalting the commonplace. In an implied satire of his advocacy of female domesticity, the underappreciated merits of the broomstick are set forth in a manner that finally leads Chesterton to identify with that least domesticated of feminine archetypes, the witch: 'I find myself regretting my complete abandon to my English dinner, and I long to leap from my wadded wrappings and straddle the broomstick for the one, great, simple adventure' ('A P.S.A.', 95).[9]

Although Mansfield's parody sets out to reinforce a sense of cultural disparity between Chesterton and the enlightened constituency of the *New Age*, the targets of 'Pastiche' were often precisely those marginal avant-garde groups that the journal might have been expected to defend against the slings and arrows of the popular press. Immediately after the publication of Lewis's self-consciously incendiary journal, *BLAST* (1914), Carl Erich Bechhöfer's 'Pastiche' column was devoted to a lampoon of 'WYNDY LEWIS', combining a formal parody of Lewis's expressionist drama, *Enemy of the Stars*, with mimicry of the journal's notorious blasting of eclectic phenomena—'grammar', 'spelling', 'reason', and 'sense' are all denounced on this occasion (30 July 1914; 308). Similarly, while the *Egoist* ran a largely favourable review of *BLAST* by the Imagist poet, Richard Aldington, the piece was accompanied by a cartoon by Horace Brodzky, irreverently captioned 'THE LEWIS-BRZESKA-POUND TROUPE. Blasting their own trumpets before the walls of Jericho' (Aldington, 'Blast', 15 July 1914; 272).[10]

As these examples suggest, the literary journals of the day were often characterised by a much more irreverent juxtaposition of 'high' and 'low' discourse than might be anticipated from their forbidding reputation. Even *BLAST*, which might be thought the final word in avant-garde experimentation, incorporated a 'strange mixture of seriousness and facetiousness, common sense and absurdity', as P.G. Konody put it (qtd. in Black, 33). This duality derives from an ambivalence at the heart of its chief contributors. Few modernist writers were more vociferous in their dismissal of the products of popular culture than Lewis, whose severe satirical persona was intimately wedded to an assumption of personal responsibility for maintaining standards in the ever-expanding mass market of modern literature. Nonetheless, he carried out his satirical ministrations in prose 'egregiously alive' with 'galvanic energy' (*Intertextual*, 32), in Brown's words—a riot of physical grotesquery and low farce, as evocative of the pantomime stage as the lecture hall. Exorbitantly desirous of attaining classical austerity yet temperamentally incapable of such elegant restriction, Lewis presents a one-man exposition of Eliot's laconic observation in 'Ulysses, Order, and Myth' (1923): '[i]t is much easier to be a classicist in literary criticism than in creative art' (166). As his 'showman' (*Wild*, 1) avatar, Kerr-Orr, explains, with a note of exasperation, 'I simply cannot help converting everything into burlesque patterns' (*Wild*, 6).

Pound was equally anxious to instil a sense that the new literature represented a locus of learned authority. In 1911–12, the *New Age* ran a series of his 'expositions and translations in illustration of the "New Method in Scholarship"', portentously titled 'I Gather the Limbs of Osiris' (see 30 Nov. 1911; 107). As Michael Coyle notes, although Pound 'delighted in excerpting snippets from the mass-circulation dailies and reprinting them in the more "highbrow"' journals, his purpose was 'to embarrass popular opinion by placing it into elite context' (1), rather than to interrogate the validity of such cultural segregation. Not for nothing does Bechhöfer's satire of *BLAST* include a Poundian poem berating the hapless reader: 'You rubberneck, roughneck, redneck, lowbrow' (308).

Nonetheless, Orage aptly characterised Pound's own 'style [as] a pastiche of colloquy, slang, journalism and pedantry' ('Readers and Writers', *New Age*, 23 Oct. 1913; 761), and the capering salesmanship of

Pound's private correspondence occasionally deploys distinctly 'lowbrow' language to mock the very endeavour for which he was publicly propagandising. Writing to Lewis, he conjures a characteristic eruption of Learesque linguistic travesty to scoff at a publisher who would 'like to do a bit-er-igh-Brow stuff. (He used much more dignified langwidge)' (Pound, *Pound/Lewis*, 146). Elsewhere, in a letter to Eliot concerning his editorial work on *The Waste Land*, Pound pre-empts Joyce's burlesquing of the poem's generative motifs, as well as his textual cross-dressing, placing both himself and the fertile yet recalcitrant author in a posture conceived to compromise their dignity: 'Ezra performed the Caesarean', assisting in the birthing of Eliot's 'printed Infancies' (Pound, *Letters*, 234).

A persistent ricocheting between gravity and levity pervades the modernist landscape, from Conrad Aiken's assessment of his friend Eliot as a 'clown', who '[f]or all his liturgical appearance [was] capable of real buffoonery' (qtd. in Gordon, *Eliot's*, 32), to Murry's approval of the 'transcendental buffoonery' (Untitled, *Nation & Athenaeum,* 22 Apr. 1922; 197) of *Ulysses*. When Pound eventually moderated his advocacy of Joyce during the long gestation of *Finnegans Wake* (1939), he turned to a comparable juxtaposition of the sacred and profane to express his impatience: only 'divine vision or a new cure for the clap can possibly be worth all the circumambient peripherization' (15 Nov. 1926; Pound, *Letters*, 276). Each account turns upon the same 'deification of the ludicrous' (*CW* 6:275) that Chesterton had activated in his debut novel, *The Napoleon of Notting Hill* (1904), a comingling of 'sublimity' with 'absurdity' (Chesterton, *Varied*, 183) that he discusses as essential to the construction of parody in a near-contemporary encomium to the American popular parodist, Bret Harte.[11]

Although Pound took a somewhat contrary view of his countryman—he consigns 'Bret Harte to the dung heap' (Mar. 1915; *Letters*, 99) in a letter to another modernist patron, Harriet Monroe—his frustration at Joyce's methods aligned him with Chesterton, who observed that while 'Homer manages to be very pure in very plain language [...] Joyce manages to be very coarse in very esoteric language' (*CW* 21:608). One might say that Chesterton strived after a converse effect: to convey esoteric ideas in coarse language. Nonetheless, the formal consequences were not entirely dissimilar—when Chesterton approvingly compares the verbal ingenuity of street slang to 'the literary doctrine of the symbolists' ('A Defence of Slang', the *Speaker* 27 Apr. 1901; collected in *The Defendant*, 145), he anticipates the ethos of aesthetic plurality that vitalises *Ulysses*. Likewise, when Ronald Knox describes Chesterton's novel, *The Man Who Was Thursday* (1908), as having been 'written as if the publisher had commissioned [...] the Pilgrim's Progress in the style of the Pickwick Papers' (qtd. in Ward, *Gilbert*, 169), his suggestion that Chesterton has merged the playful techniques of popular parody with a structural seriousness of intent not only mirrors Joyce's methods, but does so by citing texts later pastiched in *Ulysses*.

In 'A Defence of Farce' (*Speaker*, 16 Feb. 1901), Chesterton notes that 'two thousand years have beaten as vainly upon the follies of the "Frogs" as on the wisdom of the "Republic"' (*Defendant*, 127).[12] Both *Thursday* and *Ulysses* pursue a peculiarly comprehensive rendition of this vision of classical art, compacting each strand into a single text. In Chesterton, this approach reaches its apogee in the epic 'detective comedy' (Chesterton, *Autobiography*, 323) of *Father Brown*, in which detective fiction—a genre produced and consumed by all categories of 'brow'—is imbued with elements of nonsense, farce, satire, and the grotesque, which become the formal means of conveying Chesterton's most cherished theological beliefs. When the narrator of the opening story, 'The Blue Cross', prefaces the first direct appearance of the heroes, the priest, Father Brown, and the trickster-thief, Flambeau, with an account of 'the sublime vulgarity of man' (*CFB* 13), we discover a comparable compacted duality embedded within the core of his existential vision.[13]

Chesterton's priest is a far-from conventional model of the sublime: this 'grotesque figure' (*CFB* 172) is portrayed variously in vegetative terms as a 'turnip' (*CFB* 118), 'stagnant as any vegetable' (*CFB* 661), and 'a big, black mushroom' (*CFB* 421), and in folkloric terms as 'a quadruped with a very comic human head' (*CFB* 172), 'a goblin' (*CFB* 24), and a 'short bolster in the semblance of a guy' (*CFB* 365). Chesterton's litany of extravagant slights inhabits the terrain of Francois Rabelais, the exemplary practitioner of sublime vulgarity in the Western canon and the inspiration for Mikhail Bakhtin's famous exposition of the carnivalesque in European literature and culture. Perhaps unsurprisingly in view of his account of being 'soused' by 'the winepress of the Lord', Joyce has long been discussed as the twentieth century's nearest equivalent to Rabelais, from Valery Larbaud's contemporaneous review, which Joyce cited approvingly (see Anspaugh, 149, n.2), to the more recent work of critics such as M. Keith Booker.[14] Less well-documented has been Chesterton's rivalrous claim to this distinction. The first word in all of his published fiction is 'Rabelais' (in 'The Tremendous Adventures of Major Brown', *Harper's Weekly*, 19 Dec. 1903; *CW* 6:52), and comparisons recur thereafter throughout his reception, from William James's seemingly eccentric appraisal of *Charles Dickens*—'it's as good as Rabelais'—to Shaw's affectionately mocking account of Chesterton and Hilaire Belloc in the *New Age*, 'The Chesterbelloc: A Lampoon' (*New Age* 15 Feb. 1908), which contends that 'France did not break the mould in which it formed Rabelais. It got to Campden Hill in the year 1874' (136).

Shaw's vision of a mould that turns out new satirists at periodic intervals posits a family tree to which Chesterton also drew repeated attention. In *William Cobbett* (1922), he traces the antimodern temperament

14 *Introduction*

back to antiquity in the 'splendid scurrility' of Aristophanes: 'a mighty mocker and derider of the details that were modern in his day; the wild hats and whiskers of ancient progress [...] Aristophanes was an enemy of modernity, and indeed of modernism' (34). In an essayistic definition of 'Humour' composed for the *Encyclopaedia Britannica* (May 1928), Chesterton charts a later dynastic line of humourists extending from Chaucer, Cervantes, and Rabelais to Swift, Sterne, and Dickens (*Spice*, 28), while elaborating Rabelais's role in the thread that runs 'from Pantagruel to Pickwick' ('Prohibition and the Press', collected in *Fancies*, 84): he 'opened a new chapter by showing that intellectual things could be treated with the energy of high spirits and a sort of pressure of physical exuberance, which was itself humorous in its very human abandon' (*Spice*, 27–28).

Chesterton's accounts closely anticipate Simon Dentith's critical exposition of the 'comic and destabilising' tradition of European parodic literature, which passes 'from Rabelais, Sterne's *Tristram Shandy* and on to Joyce's *Ulysses*' and finds expression in texts that are 'wildly inclusive of discursive styles drawn from all directions, high and low, academic and popular' (78). In drawing attention to this trans-generic, diachronic tradition of 'serio-comical' (Bakhtin, *Problems*, 106) discourse, these complementary readings suggest a means of rethinking the relationship between Chesterton and literary modernism in terms that transcend the limitations of periodisation. Rather than conceiving these writers principally as figureheads of a time-specific elitist/populist, or avant-garde/reactionary, stand-off, we might more profitably situate them as participants in a cross-pollinating dialogue between academic and folk cultures that has informed the practices of carnivalesque literature for centuries. In this light, the publishing world of early twentieth-century London might be reimagined as a bustling metropolitan update of Bakhtin's medieval public square, in which values and vaunts are brought together to wrestle before an astonished public by authors who delight in bringing 'together ideas and worldviews, which [... are] absolutely estranged and deaf to one another, and forc[ing] them to quarrel' (Bakhtin, *Problems*, 91).

Fanatical Play

Dentith's reference to destabilisation might be extended beyond these writers' irreverent blasting of cultural convention, to convey the disruptive effect of their carnivalesque methods upon the dogmas that have accreted to their own critical receptions. Hugh Kenner, the eventual documenter-in-chief of *The Pound Era* (1971), gestures towards the desirability of such a disruption in his critical debut, *Paradox in Chesterton* (1948). Within a discussion of analogy and myth, he pauses to reflect on the philosophical affinity of Chesterton and Joyce: 'It is surely a demonstration of the contemporary critical muddle to find the most advanced experimenter of his time building upon the same first principles, and exploiting the same kind of analogical perception, as the man whom avant-garde critics decry as the very type of hearty Toryism' (127–28). Four years earlier, Graham Greene had drawn attention to an equally marked stylistic correspondence, noting the curious fact that 'a generation that appreciates Joyce finds for some reason Chesterton's equally fanatical play on words exhausting' (105).

Kenner's 'analogical perception' and Greene's 'fanatical play' offer a suggestive pathway through the 'critical muddle' at hand. Analogy derives etymologically from the Greek *analogia*, meaning 'relation' (Barnhart, 32), and is based upon the principle of simultaneous similarity and difference. Accordingly, analogy is a further connotation of the 'para' embedded within parody: 'beyond or distinct from, but analogous to' (Thompson, 989). Chesterton bases his understanding of parody upon the same principle: 'Parody does not consist merely of contrast; at its best it rather consists of a superficial contrast covering a substantial congruity' ('The Pantomime', collected in *Common*, 54). Meanwhile, if we adhere to Chesterton's attentiveness to the 'original life in a word' ('Spelling Reform and Hidden Meanings', *ILN* 29 Sept. 1906; *CW* 27:291) and peel back Greene's phrase to its etymological kernel, 'fanatical play' becomes 'temple dance' (from the Latin *fanum* and the Middle Dutch *playen*; see Barnhart, 368/804), an activity that brings to mind Chesterton's definition of parody: 'the worshipper's half-holiday' (*Varied*, 186).

Poised upon a hair-splitting 'half', Chesterton's epigram displays a semantic fastidiousness worthy of his satirical vision, elsewhere, of 'Mr. Henry James in an agony of verbal precision' (*Orthodoxy*, 22). In taking pains to emphasise a counterweighted balance of adherence and departure, the phrase corresponds to Bakhtin's argument that the function of the medieval carnival in relation to the authority of the church was to provide a brief respite, during which the citizenry was free to mock the very institution that it conventionally revered. As Bakhtin explains, the game-playing of carnival draws 'the players out of the bounds of everyday life, liberating them from usual laws and regulations' (*Rabelais*, 235). Accordingly, another way of interpreting 'the worshipper's half-holiday' would be to think of parody as opening up a carnivalised textual space in which the cultural fanatic is granted an interregnum of play, whether guying admired allies or aping antagonists, on the tacit understanding that deeper congruities underlie the placarded contrasts.

In willingly entering this arena of inversions, the parodic artist engages in an act of self-destabilisation, designed to throw a spoke into the mechanisms of criticism. As John Docker observes, while carnivalesque writers 'parody conventionality', they simultaneously 'parody themselves and their own claims to truth' (143), thus enacting a resistance to what Eliot terms the urge to 'dragoon [...] the delicate and evasive truths of

16 *Introduction*

historical and literary criticism [...] into the goose-step of dialectic' (qtd. in Perl, 79). A comparable valuation of nuance informs Lewis's practice of 'deliberate self-contradiction' (Klein, 113–14), which arises from an urge to establish a space 'beyond action and reaction' (Lewis, *BLAST*, 1:30). In the second issue of *BLAST*, the reader is encouraged to join in: 'Hurry up and get into this harmonious and sane duality'; learn to 'talk with two tongues', to 'be a duet in everything' (2:91). Chesterton neatly summarises the ethos at stake in his autobiography: 'the agreement we really want is the agreement between agreement and disagreement' (*Autobiography*, 338).

Sublime vulgarity, fanatical play... If a conjoining of ostensible contraries seems to amass around Chesterton's corpus, this suggests that we might gainfully apply the same principle to his controversies. Much as Rose finds the critical value of parody to lie in 'forc[ing] the reader to make associations between texts not normally placed together' (*Parody*, 77), Chesterton observes that when one idea 'meet[s] another idea [...] two opposite cords of truth become entangled in an inextricable knot' (CW 11:449). Likewise, Bakhtin's reference to the quarrelling of ideas in the crucible of 'dialogic interaction' (*Dialogic*, 279) echoes Father Brown's complaint that things made pristinely 'opposite [...] cannot quarrel'. The protracted conflict detailed in the pages that follow illustrates the validity of Brown's intuition. As with the boisterous atmosphere of Bakhtin's public square, this histrionic contest for cultural authority is rarely a genteel, well-mannered affair, not least because these writers conceive the issues at stake to be of the greatest professional, cultural, and even existential urgency. Nonetheless, the final outcome was an unlikely salvaging of mutual understanding, subsequently lost to a critical audience more invested in underlining the opposition than in negotiating the complication.

However, before exploring the progress of this public confrontation across almost half a century of British culture, let us first turn to Chesterton's earliest private skirmish with a modernist, begun in a school playground in North London in the late 1880s.

Notes

1 For the assertion that Pound made this suggestion to the periodical's founder, Margaret Anderson, see Wetzsteon, 311.
2 This is the introductory essay in *All Things Considered*, 1908.
3 Michael Hurley, who coins this phrase, offers a refreshing antidote to this caricature. His study, *G.K. Chesterton* (2012), is the best critical work on Chesterton's aesthetics produced in recent years.
4 A reference to W.H.G. Kingston.
5 The phrase was coined by Lewis in his 1937 memoir, *Blasting and Bombardiering* (249).
6 Wells also relayed this anecdote to Virginia Woolf, as she reports in her diary (4 July 1926, *Diary* 3:92).

7 Chesterton goes on to demur that he finds James's own philosophical 'system (or denial of a system) [...] insufficient' (CW 28:600).
8 The *New Witness* was founded in 1912 by Cecil Chesterton to supersede Hilaire Belloc's periodical, the *Eye Witness*. Though disagreeing with his politics, Chesterton termed Murry 'a very distinguished modern writer' ('On Fate and a Communist', collected in *All I Survey*, 101), while Murry reported that 'I liked [Chesterton] immensely and [found him] a very honourable opponent' (Ward, *Gilbert*, 508).
9 Two decades later, Chesterton proved Mansfield prescient, arguing that 'a broomstick does not strike me as being intrinsically a dull subject, but rather a romantic one', since it conjures the contrasting images of 'George Herbert' and 'witches' ('On Jonathan Swift', collected in *All I Survey*, 70–71).
10 'BRZESKA' refers to the sculptor, Henri Gaudier-Brzeska, a signatory of the Vorticist Manifesto published in *BLAST*.
11 Responding to the 'Bret Harte' essay, the contemporary reviewer E.C. Marsh remarked that hitherto 'the delicate, elusive art of the parodist has been grossly misunderstood [...] I know of no critic who has done anything toward elucidating the philosophy of parody save Mr. Chesterton' (193).
12 First published as 'The Philosophy of Farce'.
13 'The Blue Cross' was first published on 23 June 1910 as 'Valentin Follows a Curious Trail' in the American periodical, *The Saturday Evening Post*. It was renamed for British publication in *The Storyteller*, in September 1910.
14 See *Joyce, Bakhtin, and the Literary Tradition* (Michigan: Michigan UP, 1995).

1 The Chesterbentley

A *Fin-de-Siècle* Nonsense Friendship

> It is a joke, meeting your other half.
> —E.C. Bentley on Chesterton, diary entry, 2 Oct. 1895
> (Bod MS Eng.misc.e.864)

> It is a terrible thing to be always admiring people and always differing from them.
> —Chesterton, 'Nothing' (*DN* 2 July 1904; *CDN* 2:251)

When Chesterton and Bentley met for the first time, they physically assaulted each other. As Chesterton later recalled in his autobiography, '[w]hen I first met my best friend in the playground, I fought with him wildly for three-quarters of an hour' (59). Finally, lying exhausted in the mud, Bentley 'happened to quote Dickens or the Bab Ballads' and 'we plunged into a friendly discussion on literature which has gone on, intermittently, from that day to this' (59). Although Chesterton affirms that '[t]here is no explaining' (59) such behaviour, Bentley affects to try in his memoir, *Those Days* (1940), adopting a rather different rhetorical register to authorise Chesterton's account, through an arch parody of anthropological discourse:

> I have not the least doubt that we did signalize our instinctive liking for each other in the way that is usual among mammals of tender years [...] by struggling and tumbling about in imitation of a hostility that only the death of one of us could terminate.
>
> (46)

The discordant styles of the two accounts offer an initial hint of the temperamental differences that would mould, and sometimes imperil, the development of their friendship. By reframing Chesterton's burlesque anecdote in a mock-academic register, Bentley delivers a superficially spritely rendition, which simultaneously serves to withdraw from emotional investment into defensive irony. If the formal mode of delivery tells us something about Bentley, the thematic context is equally revealing of Chesterton. The dynamic of the vignette, in which male interaction swings vertiginously from atavistic antagonism to intellectual camaraderie, would set a template for the vacillation between opposition and identification, antipathy and affinity, that consistently characterised Chesterton's later responses to the dominant thought of the age. With this in mind, in order to properly understand the nature of his public struggles with leading literary modernists—and the deep emotional investments that underscored these ostensibly ideological disputes—it is essential to begin by bringing to light the private progress of his relationship with the figure he termed 'my first and in every sense original friend' (*Autobiography*, 67), whose proto-modernist temperament had a decisive, visceral impact upon Chesterton's early literary and philosophical development.

One Hope, One Toil, One Pair of Boots

In their respective reminiscences, Bentley and Chesterton are equally effusive in discussing the importance of their friendship. As Bentley notes,

> [f]or years we were as near to each other as it is possible for friends to be [...] I first met [Chesterton] at that time of life when personal influence counts for most, and one's nature is in the making for good or evil. His friendship was the best thing that ever happened to me.
> ('Introduction', ii–iii)

In *Those Days*, he submits that their youthful 'relationship did not mean so much to [Chesterton]. For one thing, it did not change his life as it changed mine' (45). Nonetheless, he goes on to assert that 'if I have anything to be proud of, it is that to him our friendship mattered a great deal' (*Those*, 45), a contention supported by the fact that Chesterton refers to Bentley as his 'best' friend in works spanning thirty-six years—from his first publication, *Greybeards at Play* (1900), to the valedictory *Autobiography* (see CW 10.2:353; *Autobiography*, 59).

Fortunately, much of the detail of the pair's early relationship has been preserved in their correspondence and in Bentley's contemporaneous diaries.[1] When carefully examined, these archival records suggest that the Chesterbentley may be a still-more significant composite creature than Shaw's famous portmanteau creation, the 'Chesterbelloc' ('Chesterbelloc', 137), in pursuing a proper understanding of the maturation of Chesterton's thought. This should be unsurprising, given that Shaw intended his burlesque hybrid image to convey the essential temperamental misalliance of Chesterton and Belloc, whose public self-juxtaposition he compared to the comic disjunction of a 'pantomime elephant' (138). As Shaw explained, 'Chesterton and Belloc are so unlike that they get frightfully into one another's way' (138). Conversely, in dedicating the nonsense-verse collection, *Greybeards at Play*, to Bentley,

Chesterton conceived the Chesterbentley as a genuine composite creature. His preface echoes Bentley's vision of Chesterton as his 'other half' in the diary of 1895, adapting Aristotle's conception of the highest form of friendship as '[o]ne soul abiding in two bodies' (qtd. in Laertius, 188) to produce an image of the pair as a nonsense creature possessing 'two hearts with single hope / Two faces in one hood' (*CW* 10.2:353).

Garry Wills observes that in Chesterton's juvenile sketches, Bentley 'is described in terms that a Copperfield would hesitate to use of Steerforth' (*Chesterton*, 13), thus corroborating A.N. Wilson's contention that Chesterton was disposed to hero-worship his friends (99). This view is backed up by Maisie Ward's assessment that in his youth 'Chesterton not only admired [Bentley]—as he was to do all his life—but wanted to be like him, to say the kind of thing he thought Bentley would say' (*Gilbert*, 36). Ward argues that in their earliest correspondence, Chesterton tended to adapt his own mode of expression to the more detached, ironic style of Bentley, in a pastiche of his friend's rhetorical tone. This certainly seems true of Chesterton's highly uncharacteristic remarks in an unpublished, undated letter, most probably composed in 1891: 'as far as personal taste and instincts are concerned, I share all your antipathy to the noisy Plebian excursionist. [...] I think that the lower orders are seen unfavourably when enjoying themselves' (BL MS Add. 73191 fol. 11). As Ward notes, such sentiments were 'not in the least like either the Chesterton that was to be or the Chesterton that then was. But [they were] very much like Bentley' (*Gilbert*, 36).[2]

Chesterton later summarised the basis of such dynamics in an essay fittingly titled 'The Snob' (*DN* 4 Apr. 1908): 'idealisation implies imitation' (*CDN* 5:49). This implicitly pejorative equation illustrates the distrust of rhetorical conflations of sublimity and synthesis that Chesterton consistently displayed in his maturity, here framed by a concern over the ethical and psychological compromises to one's integrity that might arise from an abnegation of selfhood. He seems to recognise that if the ideal classical friendship posits the hybridisation of a single spirit within two bodies, this excessive identification offers neither party a distinct individuality. In a discussion of pastiche in *Charles Dickens*, Chesterton suggests that such relations are structured upon uncritical deference to the other party: 'youth in actual experience is the period of imitation and even of obedience' (35).

As each participant in the relationship seeks to resolve this tension between submissiveness and self-assertion, the dynamic of friendship comes to hinge upon what Sandra Lynch terms a 'balance between identity and difference' (106). This scenario mirrors the ambivalence of the antimodern and of parody, vacillating between intimacy and distance—one might say, between worship and half-holidays—in a manner that challenges the stability of the bond, by undermining the possibility of a perfect symmetry between the expectations that each friend brings to the relationship. Despite the apparently idealised, amalgamative terms of the *Greybeards* dedication, a comparable tension is detectable in the partially unpublished drafts of Chesterton's preface. In an illustrated draft, he expands upon the theme of spiritual and physical unity of purpose:

> One hope, one toil
> One pair of boots
> Joined us eternally.
>
> (BL MS Add.73242 A fol. 4)[3]

Here, the incantatory repetition of 'one' again enacts a unification of the two friends, while the juxtaposition of the sublime and the material—hope, toil, and boots—serves to conjoin mind with body. However, the bathos of the descent from top to bottom, or head to toes, also guards against any hint of grandiloquence, deflating the sublime rhetoric of one soul in two bodies with the burlesque image of two bodies awkwardly occupying one pair of boots. This engenders a delicate critical distance, which is stressed further by the final phrase—'Joined us eternally'—in which a subtle semantic disjunction causes a permanent avowal to be rendered in the past tense. An earlier draft contains another farcical juxtaposition of the material and the sublime—'I often ate his dinner up / To prove that we were one'—along with another confusion of tense: 'He *was* my nearest friend / We *wear* one hat: smoke one cigar / (one standing at each end)' (BL MS Add.73242 A fol.1; my emphases).

In this earlier draft, the underlying grounds of Chesterton's anti-sublime rhetoric and tense-based implications of rupture become clearer when he begins to stray free-associatively from the eulogistic tone of the public dedication into an airing of more private grievances: 'If I should make the Welkin ring— / (A thing I never tried) / Exclaiming "She would grace a King!" / Would he be satisfied?' (BL MS Add.73242 A fol.1). Chesterton's reluctance to make 'the Welkin ring' perhaps alludes to Bentley's irritation at Chesterton's failure to discuss Violet Boileau, Bentley's fiancée, in sufficiently exalted terms, since the phrase refers to a sublime invocation of the celestial sphere.[4] The hint of critical distance in these lines is then rendered startlingly explicit on the following page, as the orientation switches from passive rumination ('would he') to direct second-person address ('you are'), while Chesterton's tone switches from frustrated departure to explicit enmity:

> For snobs and sinners are to me
> Like gases to Professor Dewar
> Be comforted: I never knew
> A more oppressive snob than you are.
>
> (BL MS Add.73242 A fol. 2)

Since Dewar's particular scientific innovation was to freeze gases, Chesterton would appear to be threatening to freeze Bentley out of his affections here. In a subsequent revision to this stanza, he crosses out 'snob' and replaces it with 'cad'—perhaps the gravest insult in his vocabulary.[5] The uncharacteristic rancour of these lines is attributable not only to Bentley's snobbish attitude towards his love interests—in the diary of 1898 he notes his approval of Violet's 'caste', in which regard 'she is rather an improvement on any other lady I know' (14 Apr. 1898; Bod MS Eng.misc.e.867)—but perhaps also to Bentley's intense dislike of Chesterton's own fiancée, Frances Blogg. This antipathy comes to light in several of Bentley's partially self-censored diary entries. For example, on 10 December 1898, Bentley records that

> I was [?] on by Frances Blogg's manner today. She is not—I won't mince [section cut out] too free and easy. She doesn't study, I suppose, to be young-ladyish [section cut out] she did. Unconventional camaraderie in a woman is a thing that I could live without.
> (Bod MS Eng.misc.e.869)

Over a year later, Bentley's opinion remains unmodified: 'Called with [Violet] on Chestertons. Frances Blogg was there; whom I cannot bring myself to be enthusiastic about' (15 Mar. 1900; Bod MS Eng. misc.e.869).

While it seems likely that some sort of verbal expression of this distaste may have provoked Chesterton's outburst, his accusation of snobbery should also be understood in relation to a more long-standing schism between the pair, fostered by their differing attitudes towards camaraderie in a wider cultural sense. This schism was particularly sharpened by their divergent responses to the culture of *fin-de-siècle* Decadence, which Chesterton had come to passionately oppose by the late 1890s, but which Bentley responded to rather more ambivalently.[6] For example, while Chesterton reacted with profound disquiet to the amorality preached by the Decadent 'blackguards' ('The Diabolist', *DN* 9 Nov. 1907; *CDN* 4:339) whom he encountered while studying at the Slade School of Art, Bentley enthuses, in a diary entry composed at Oxford, over having recently met a 'Merton Decadent [...] a wonderful man, all Oscar Wilde and Yellow Book' (3 Feb. 1895; Bod MS Eng.misc.e.863). In view of this temperamental divergence, it is telling that in the first draft of the *Greybeards* preface, Chesterton ends his attack on Bentley as follows:

> And ten years hence I feel that you
> Will be a replica of Hankin.
> (BL MS Add.73242 A fol. 2)

This is almost certainly a reference to the playwright, St. John Hankin, a close predecessor of Bentley at Merton College, and a figure whom Chesterton singles out in his autobiography as the quintessence of Decadence:

> He was a pessimist [and] a fundamental sceptic, that is a man without fundamentals; he was one who disbelieved in Man much more than he did in God; he despised democracy even more than devotion; he was professedly without enthusiasms of any kind; [and] in all this he was [...] very near to the centre of the culture and philosophy of London at that time.
>
> (146)[7]

Earlier in the memoir, Chesterton recalls that by the late 1890s he 'was full of a new and fiery resolution to write against the Decadents and the Pessimists who ruled the culture of the age' (95). Chesterton's rejection of this perceived cultural oligarchy arose from a sincere belief in the importance of being earnest, a quality that he felt to be embodied by his devoutly Christian fiancée. At the same moment, Bentley was pulling in the opposite direction, a dynamic evoked by a sardonic reference to the '[v]ery earnest' Bloggs in the diaries:

> If society is to be maintained alive, Bloggs must, I think, be kept within limits. [...] I am willing—I am anxious to know and value them and to admire and love them; but not to become as them. They are not my ideal.
>
> (28 Mar. 1897; Bod MS Eng.misc.e.866)[8]

The implicit stress upon the 'my' in the final clause suggests that Bentley's animosity may have derived from an irrational annoyance at his friend's acquisition of a new, discordant object of idealisation. Meanwhile, Chesterton's belief that Bentley was pursuing a converse trajectory that would ultimately render him Hankin's 'replica'—a term suggestive of identity confusion brought about by uncritical emulation—implies Chesterton's comparable irritation at discovering in his other half a detached, sceptical temperament, drawn to the fathomless ironies encrypted within the implicitly mocking title of Wilde's play and the linguistic trapdoors unbolted by the inhabitants of Lewis Carroll's Wonderland. A more detailed analysis of Bentley's ostensibly playful preoccupation with nonsense demonstrates that there is much to back up this supposition.

Going to Jericho to Throw a Jabberwock

Chesterton and Bentley each emphasised the importance of nonsense literature in binding their friendship. In Bentley's obituary of Chesterton, he recalls that a 'collaboration in the producing of oceans of nonsense with pencil and paper [...] was the favourite amusement in [our] schoolboy circle' ('G.K.C.' 526), a context which perhaps informs Chesterton's conjecture that their brawl might have been brought to an end by a quotation from W.S. Gilbert's *Bab Ballads* (1869). However, Bentley's subtraction of Chesterton's popular-cultural touchstones—Dickens and Gilbert—from his academically couched exposition of that first meeting is suggestive. With his scholarly progress to Oxford in 1894, Bentley took his place within a lineage of nineteenth-century academic parodists, satirists, and/or nonsense-writers—from Charles Stuart Calverley to Carroll, Wilde, Beerbohm, and Hankin—with whom he felt a strong temperamental affinity. In contrast, the anti-academicism that would later colour Chesterton's response to literary modernism was already hardening around this time—when he visited his friend at Oxford in 1894, Bentley paused to note in his diary that the university was unknowingly 'nourishing the adder in its bosom' (17 Nov. 1894. Bod MS.Eng.misc.e.862).

In *The Origins of English Nonsense* (1997), Noel Malcolm outlines two enduring, parallel seams of nonsense in English culture: a popular strain, composed of 'folk materials: drinking songs, humorous ballads, folktales, nursery rhymes', and an academic form, which finds expression in the 'parodic routines and in-jokes' characteristic of 'comic University dramas' (4–5). Of the two strains, Bentley evinced a marked preference for the latter, while Chesterton went on to propagandise forcefully for the former. Bentley's bias is already apparent in his adolescent innovation in nonsense literature, the clerihew, which he conceived while studying with Chesterton at St. Paul's School. Structurally, the clerihew takes the form of a single quatrain with an AABB rhyme scheme in which any of the lines may differ drastically in length from any of the others, producing a formal incongruity aptly described by Chesterton as a 'severe and stately form of Free Verse' (*Autobiography*, 61). Thematically, the clerihew typically enacts an irreverent and often flagrantly fictitious manipulation of the biographical details of a 'stately' historical or contemporary public figure, whose name must formally dictate the terms of the initial rhyme. Bentley's inaugural clerihew on Humphrey Davy offers a representative sample:

> Sir Humphrey Davy
> Abominated gravy.
> He lived in the odium
> Of having discovered sodium.
>
> (*Complete*, 38)[9]

Elizabeth Sewell identifies four principal 'ideas' of nonsense: 'inversion or upside-down turning', 'rhyme, the gift of a particular language in providing *un*fitting pairs', 'disproportion: "A grasshopper stepped on an elephant's toe"', and the 'most important' attribute: 'muddling things up' ('Nonsense', 141). The Davy clerihew displays each of these elements. Davy's principal claim to fame counterintuitively leads to his infamy, an 'inversion' directly enabled by the '*un*fitting' rhyme of odium and sodium, while the juxtaposition of his alleged aversion to gravy and his greatest academic achievement produces a radical 'disproportion' in the selection of relevant biographical material, framed by an incongruous conflation of the material and the intellectual. The effect of the whole is to 'muddle things up', in the sense that an apparently trivial quirk of temperament, which no conventional biographer would be likely to mention, is given anecdotal precedence over the one apparently indispensable fact of Davy's biography, his discovery of sodium, which is then claimed to have blackened his name, rather than made it. In summary, all the conceptual ties that conventionally unite to provide an objective framework for biographical assessment are splintered in a miasma of referential derangement.

Bentley's comic disregard for biographical verity is reconfirmed by a discursion on Davy's alleged biography in *Those Days*. In a mockportentous parody of the sense of elective affinity that draws the biographer to her/his subject, Bentley alleges that Davy was expelled from Oxford for a series of outrageous, Rabelaisian pranks:

> Adolescent myself, it was with a wistful interest that I had learned how Davy, as a youth, had been indulged in his passionate fondness for cock-fighting, trout-tickling, and brawling in church. When I found that, in his second term at Oxford, he had been gated for cutting off his tutor's ears, my enthusiasm knew no bounds.
>
> (154)[10]

Bentley's apocryphal tale of Davy's disgrace gestures towards the genuine biography of Calverley, who was expelled from Oxford in 1852 for committing insubordinate practical jokes. Of the school of 'scholarly frivolity' that Calverley fathered, Chesterton argued, with considerable ambivalence, that 'it is enduring in the sense that it is detached. They have got outside life, if only to laugh at it. In their frivolity [is] a somewhat sad philosophy' ('A Book of the Day: College Fireworks', *DN* 5 Oct. 1905; *CDN* 3:205). Chesterton's later assessments of Bentley and Hankin strikingly mirror this analysis. In his autobiography, he asserts that the young Bentley had been 'too detached and ironic to become conspicuous in connection with a cause, or any of the things in which youth is generally both communal and combative' (67), while elsewhere he describes Hankin as an inscrutable 'omnivorous observer' who 'had a slight smile always on his face' ('The Evil Day', *DN* 26 June 1909; *CDN* 5:344).

This imagery of detachment also inflects Chesterton's remarks on the two most significant former Oxonians to influence his relationship with Bentley: Carroll and Wilde. In an article for the *Daily News* ('Books of the Day: The Works of Oscar Wilde', 19 Oct. 1909), Chesterton deprecates the 'airy detachment' with which Wilde 'and his school professed to stand as solitary artistic souls apart from the public' (*CDN* 6:98–99). Elsewhere, he discusses Carroll's work as 'purely intellectual folly' ('George MacDonald and His Work', *DN* 11 June 1901; *CDN* 1:102) characterised by a lack of humanity that produces a conceptual imbalance: 'there is nothing but nonsense in his nonsense. There is no sense in his nonsense; as there is in the more human nonsense of Rabelais' ('Lewis Carroll' *New York Times*, 1932; collected in *Handful*, 118). Similarly, the 'Humour' essay includes a complaint that '[e]verything in Lewis Carroll is part of what he called the Game of Logic', abstracted from everyday life, delivered within a critique that connects nonsense to the programmatically unengaged 'art for art's sake' doctrine of Decadence: 'Jabberwocky is not a parody on anything; the Jumblies are not a satire of anybody; they are folly for folly's sake on the same lines as art for art's sake' (*Spice*, 29).

Bentley's Oxford diary praises Carroll's 'splendid book' (10 Apr. 1896; Bod MS Eng.misc.e.865), *The Game of Logic* (1887), noting that he had read it with Chesterton, who presumably demurred at his friend's unqualified approval. In 1930, Chesterton asserted in a public lecture that his youthful literary conversations with Bentley had first convinced him that there was no 'allegorical' element in Carroll's nonsense world to connect it to the shared contexts of objective reality (Connolly, 295). In 'A Defence of Nonsense' (*Speaker*, 2 Feb. 1901), Chesterton posits a comparable distinction between 'the completeness of' Edward Lear's 'citizenship in the world of unreason' (*Defendant*, 66) and the nonsense of previous eras, which he conceives as a rhetorical device mobilised in the service of earth-bound satire:

> some of the greatest writers the world has seen—Aristophanes, Rabelais and Sterne—have written nonsense; but [...] in a widely different sense. The nonsense of these men was satiric—that is to say, symbolic; it was a kind of exuberant capering round a discovered truth.
>
> (*Defendant*, 64)[11]

In convincing Chesterton that an element of ontological rupture inhered in Carrollian nonsense, Bentley was also signalling a temperamental rupture from his friend. This tension is illustrated by a letter sent to Chesterton in January 1894, in which Bentley alludes to a prior conversation on the subject of chess, a suggestive context in the light of the chess-game conceit of *Through the Looking Glass, and*

What Alice Found There (1871), which imbues Carroll's narrative with the abstract principles of a logic puzzle. It transpires that Bentley considers certain forms of game playing to be 'unhuman' and, therefore, 'unmoral', a conviction that appears to have caused a disagreement between the pair. Bentley's explanation is emollient, yet reiterative:

> Of course, you did not take quite seriously what I said the other evening about games like chess: to do myself justice (my favourite game) I think that the games in which you are in lively conversation with the rest of the world worth mentioning, like Pool or Billiards, are not to be included in the category of quite unhuman games. One talks and enjoys oneself; while chess and those silent, rapt kind of wit-contests are [...] a spiritualized fight. One plays them [...] but one loathes them, for all that. Now billiards may be regarded as a means of promoting intellectual conversation [...] it is distinctly a human game. [But where chess is concerned, the] word 'unhuman', corresponding in ethical phraseology to the artistic 'unmoral' ought, I think, to be used.
> (BL MS Add.73191 fol. 39)

While Bentley's terms imply an element of self-disgust in the 'unhuman' act of withdrawal—'one loathes' these games—they also indicate an urge to attain this condition: 'one plays them' all the same.[12] The comparable act of psychic withdrawal conducted by the nonsense writer is evoked in Sewell's account of another of the 'characteristics of Nonsense': while '[p]eople are not excluded from the nonsense game [...] it has a tendency to whittle down their humanity, to make them chessmen rather than men' (*Field*, 137). In this way, 'people tend to be turned [...] into playthings' (*Field*, 137–38). Sewell's observation might be applied to the clerihew, in which public figures become puppets in a detached game of referential derangement, the formal and thematic rules of which encourage an arbitrary conflation of the proper noun with a random character trait, location, object, etc., so as to heighten the comic effect. This attribute of Bentley's invention corroborates Susan Stewart's assertion that the purest forms of nonsense radically disrupt commonsense notions of relation: 'Nonsense does not undermine the idea of causality so much as it undermines the sense of contingency and necessariness underlying the everyday sense of causality. In nonsense, anything can cause anything else' (138). As Stewart explains, this deranging action is frequently accompanied by a withdrawal from critical commentary upon objective reality: 'the danger of nonsense' lies not only in its status 'as a valueless activity, but as an activity "without values"' (209).

One thinks of the insistently negating refrain of William Archer's contemporary review of *The Importance of Being Earnest* (1895): it 'imitates nothing, represents nothing, means nothing, is nothing' but a beguiling *jeu d'esprit* (*World*, 20 Feb. 1895; 190). Chesterton's imaginative connection of nonsense and Decadence in the 'Humour' essay also anticipates Sos Eltis's discussion of Wilde's Carrollian approach to dialogue: 'Wilde transformed standard nonsense into the more systemic and disconcerting illogicality which characterises *Earnest*'s dialogue' (177). Reviewing Wilde's play for the *Speaker*, A.B. Walkley wrote approvingly that it showed the author to be 'an artist in sheer nonsense' (23 Feb. 1895; 196), while Shaw evinced less enthusiasm, considering it Wilde's 'first really heartless' play (qtd. in Shaw, 'Importance', 194). Chesterton chose the same term to describe the work of Wilde's acolyte, Hankin, whose 'world of cool and almost heartless comedy' (*CDN* 5:344) conjures a vision of an amoral nonsense universe, dictated by a blind self-interest and arbitrary violence not far removed from the motiveless animus of Carroll's Wonderland or the inexplicable brutality of Lear's limericks.

Hankin's comedies subvert Chesterton's morally-centred view that '[s]atire may be mad and anarchic, but it presupposes an admitted superiority in certain things over others; it presupposes a standard' (*Orthodoxy*, 34). The nihilism of plays such as *The Charity That Began at Home* (1906) suggests that far from positing an ethical ideal against which the dramatised conduct falls short, Hankin's worldview is closer to that of 'the grotesque writer', as defined by Philip Thomson, who 'does not analyse and instruct in terms of right or wrong, or true or false, nor does he attempt to distinguish between these. On the contrary, he is concerned to demonstrate their inseparability' (42). For Chesterton, Hankin's plays are the work of 'a very fastidious judge' (*CDN* 5:344) who damns the world *in toto*, mocking all moral values and social conventions equally, while positing no alternative framework to take their place. William H. Phillips backs up this reading, arguing that Hankin typically 'satirize[d] the sacred cows of earnestness, duty, work, and marriage, while suggesting the probable meaninglessness of human endeavours' (97). One thinks of Chesterton's assessment of Swinburne, who 'set out to break down without having, or even thinking he had, the rudiments of rebuilding in him' (*CW* 15:505).

Wolfgang Kayser associates the grotesque with an anti-ethos of 'disintegration' that possesses an 'abysmal quality' (52). In this light, it is instructive to consider the distinction between wit and humour that Chesterton draws in the 'Humour' essay, which turns upon the relative resemblance of the two forms to pure nonsense: 'Nonsense may be described as humour which has for the moment renounced all connection with wit', since wit represents 'reason on its judgement seat' (*Spice*, 29), a self-distancing satirical exposure of rejected folly.[13] For Chesterton, nonsense trips the lever that converts the judgement seat into a ducking stool: grotesque humour, if completely divested of satirical intent, consists in 'passing the borderland, in breaking through the floor of sense and falling into some starry abyss of nonsense far below our ordinary human life' (CW 15:387). It is no coincidence that in *The Man Who Was Thursday* the narrator's account of Gabriel Syme's apprehension of 'that final scepticism which can find no floor to the universe' comes just a few pages after the Marquis's baleful assessment of the progress of the plot—'"[g]oing to Jericho to throw a Jabberwock!" cried the other, tearing his hair' (CW 6:577)—a proposition that conflates Carrollian nonsense with a descent into hell (for which Jericho is a colloquial synonym).

In *Greybeards at Play*, Chesterton turns to light verse to depict this state of ontological disarray. His introductory dedication to Bentley is immediately followed by a satire of Decadence—'On the Disastrous Spread of Aestheticism in All Classes'—which employs apocalyptic terms to articulate an anxiety over the proliferation of pessimistic detachment and sceptical derangement in British *fin-de-siècle* culture. In the process, Chesterton introduces elements of moral satire into the 'clear and *unadulterated* nonsense' (*Autobiography*, 61; my emphasis) that he identified as Bentley's *metier*:

> The sea had nothing but a mood
> Of 'vague ironic gloom,'
> With which t'explain its presence in
> My upstairs drawing-room.
>
> The sun had read a little book
> That struck it with a notion:
> He drowned himself and all his fires
> Deep in the hissing ocean.
>
> Then all was dark, lawless, and lost:
> I heard great devilish wings:
> I knew that Art had won, and snapt
> The Covenant of Things.
>
> (*Collected Nonsense*, 16)

Malcolm argues that for centuries, 'one of the standard building-blocks of nonsense literature' has been the 'category-mistake' and identifies this as a central feature of academic nonsense, citing the example 'to take Tobacco in Ramus Method' (11) as an absurd conflation of the physical and intellectual planes. In the case at hand, Chesterton turns academic nonsense against itself, combining a category mistake—the material world conversing and studying literature—with a clerihew-like manipulation of disproportion and incongruity—the sea entering a drawing room—to bolster his satirical critique of the deranging drive of Decadence, which finally ruptures the 'Covenant of Things' when the sun is annihilated by Art.

This is just one of many examples of Chesterton employing apocalyptic rhetoric when discussing Decadence. For example, the famous exchange between Lord Henry Wotton and Lady Narborough in

The Picture of Dorian Gray (1890)—'"*Fin de siècle*" murmured Lord Henry. "*Fin du globe*" answered his hostess' (Wilde, *Complete*, 137)— lurks behind Chesterton's protestation in 'Milton and Merry England' that '[i]t is now almost impossible to bring home to anybody, even to myself, how final that *fin de siècle* seemed to be; not the end of the century but the end of the world' (collected in *Fancies*, 220). Elsewhere, Chesterton recalls that 'I used to think at one time that between the pessimists and the praisers of God, between Schopenhauer and Whitman, there must be a war without any truce till the stars fall' ('Lines by a Noble Lord', *DN* 16 Dec. 1904; *CDN* 2:344–45).

In 1901, Chesterton argued that 'the popularity of Schopenhauer [...] far surpasses the popularity of any of his contemporaries in philosophy' ('The Great Pessimist', *DN* 7 June 1901; *CDN* 1:94). This was not a situation of which he approved. In *The World as Will and Idea* (1818), Schopenhauer argues that existence is essentially characterised by a perpetual rebounding between suffering and boredom, stemming from the individual's subjection to the uncontrollable exigencies of the abstract 'will to life', a 'blind, irresistible impulse' that finds human expression in an endless striving after the possession of extrinsic phenomena (*World*, 176–77). Schopenhauer argues that if possession is achieved, the result is merely a profound ennui, which can only be stanched by the pursuit of further objects of desire, in a perpetual cycle of competition with other subjective manifestations of the will, in pursuit of goals that are fundamentally inconsequential.

In *George Bernard Shaw* (1909), Chesterton summarises the theory thus: 'The intellect, if it could be impartial, would tell us to cease; but a blind partiality, an instinct quite distinct from thought, drives us on to take desperate chances in an essentially bankrupt lottery' (*CW* 11:455). In this sense, Schopenhauer's vision of existence not only entails an extreme ontological scepticism that resembles the nonsense writer's undermining of commonsense notions of objective relation, but also anticipates the ontological pessimism of Decadence in its conception of human endeavour as at best meaningless and at worst maleficent. As Chesterton concluded, in another uncharacteristically rancorous judgement, insofar as Schopenhauer encouraged the inference that 'all good and happiness is an illusion [... he] appears to me the most contemptible [...] of all men whose souls have influenced the world' (*CDN* 1:95).

Schopenhauer's preferred solution to the cycle of suffering and boredom that he diagnosed was a withdrawal into a state of artistic dispassion that would enable the individual to escape the pain of desire and overcome the loss of volition caused by slavery to the will by learning to witness life as a detached observer (see *World*, 102–103). As Rafey Habib explains, 'Schopenhauer had envisaged the artist as stepping outside the human drama, a live person among the puppets' (75). Although Schopenhauer considered his espousal of pristine artistic detachment to be a more subversive and philosophically cogent 'denial of the will to life' (*World*, 250) than suicide, he contended, nonetheless, that suicide was a perfectly rational response to the conditions of existence (see *Essays*, 78–79). As Chesterton notes with bitter irony in *Orthodoxy*, at the *fin de siècle* an argument consequently arose as to 'whether it was not a very nice thing to murder one's self' (64).

Commentators have occasionally raised a sceptical eyebrow at Chesterton's apocalyptic rendition of Decadence. William Blissett argues that there is a 'note of melodrama' in the 'exaggerated picture of Wilde's Nineties' ('G.K. Chesterton', 104) that he paints, while Sewell claims that Chesterton 'prefers a chimera of his own inventing' to the reality and then 'blames Wilde for it' ('G.K. Chesterton', 572). However, the suicidal conceits of Decadence were not mere rhetorical abstractions extrapolated by Chesterton with a feverish literalism, but the artistic expression of an urgent existential reality. A disproportionately large number of Decadent writers suffered mental breakdowns and/or committed suicide, including Hankin, who ultimately drowned himself in 1909, convinced that he was doomed to inherit his father's mental frailties and invalidism. For Chesterton, this cultural pattern made Bentley's temperamental leaning towards Decadence a cause of alarm. The influence of Schopenhauer's precepts upon his friend begins to be implied by Bentley's urge to step outside the human drama into the 'unhuman [...] unmoral' realm of the chess game, as well as his taste for the destabilising mechanisms of the clerihew, through which the objects of his disconnected gaze become puppets to be manipulated with a whimsical irreverence. This influence is also discernible in the consistent rhetoric of detachment and derangement found in Bentley's correspondence with Chesterton in the mid-1890s and by the increasingly fatalistic determinism that began to permeate his diary entries in the years that followed.

You must think I am going mad: I daresay I am

Between the summers of 1893 and '94, Bentley underwent a period of psychological distress, conveyed in his correspondence in terms that combine studied, ironical detachment with intimations of lost volition before inscrutable forces beyond his control. In an exchange in the summer of 1893, he recalls having recently passed 'the most miserable night I ever remember to have had', before seeking to reassure Chesterton with the suspiciously extravagant claim that 'my existence has never been marred by a shadow of doubt or uneasiness on any subject whatsoever. In fact, I am at this moment hardly able to hold the pen on account of a paroxysm of light hearted merriment' (19 Aug. 1893; BL MS Add.73191 fol. 36). Bentley's protestations of pristine intellectual certitude are somewhat undermined by the repeated suggestions of incapacity that suffuse his letter. Earlier, he speaks of an inability to 'imitate my own style', before relating the 'paroxysm' of laughter that hinders his physical mastery of the pen, details that employ playful rhetoric to hint at a sense of combined mental and physical loss of control.[14]

A further hint of subjective disorientation is discernible in another of Bentley's letters, dated 28 March 1894: 'The above paragraph, which my pen wrote of its own accord, I take to be of the nature of an imitation of somebody's style; but I don't know whose' (BL MS Add.73191 fol. 43). There is an air of Schopenhauer being viewed through the prism of Wonderland in these accounts. As Elizabeth Sewell notes, apropos of Chesterton's own work, nonsense writing 'may not be merely a clever exercise in wit; it may be an unconscious distress signal' ('G. K. Chesterton', 556). Sure enough, several months later Bentley confesses to '[h]iding my feelings behind a sickening mask of gaiety,' through which 'I endeavour fruitlessly to dissemble the state of mind I am in' (BL MS Add.73191 fol. 39). Another of his letters begins '[t]hank you for replying to my last two; I almost expected you to refuse to notice them. You must think I am going mad: I daresay I am' (25 Aug. 1893; BL MS Add.73191 fol. 37). In the margins, Chesterton has sketched a stormy-browed, despairing figure.

On the unpublished second page of the illustrated draft of the *Greybeards* dedication, Chesterton addresses Bentley's period of mental disturbance at length. Page two follows directly on from the line, 'joined us eternally', expanding upon the hint of temporal disjunction in the proceeding line:

> But a time came when he was changed
> He wept & tore his clothing
> And foamed & rolled upon the floor
> (The others noticed nothing)
> But I, with Friendship's keener view
> Watching him writhe & yell
> And turn a vivid blue, conceived
> That all might not be well.
>
> I said 'Cease rolling in the grate'
> 'Relax this stoic pride'
> He hurled the fire-irons at my head
> And dreamily replied
> 'To you, O friend this mask of calm
> Can scarce conceal my pain'
> He idly stood upon his head
> And seemed himself again.
>
> (BL MS Add.73242 A fol. 5)[15]

These stanzas were excised from the published version and replaced with a briefer, sanitised version.[16] As will be noticed, the lines attributed to Bentley in quotation marks closely paraphrase his remarks in the correspondence, while Chesterton's reference to watching Bentley 'writhe and yell', and the combination of sudden violence and implied somnambulism that permeates the draft is suggestive of Bentley's consistent rhetoric of abnegated self-control. When Chesterton refers, in the published dedication, to himself and Bentley as 'Dolls living' (*Collected Nonsense*, 3), one thinks of Sigmund Freud's account (after Ernst Jentsch) of the air of uncanniness provoked both by 'dolls and automata' and by 'epileptic fits and [...] manifestations of insanity' (*Uncanny*, 135). Such phenomena are disturbing because they imply that 'mechanical [...] processes may lie hidden behind the familiar image of a living person' (*Uncanny*, 135), much as Schopenhauer argues that the apparently freely willing individual is actually the dupe of existential forces beyond her/his control.

If the allusion to classical philosophy in Chesterton's exhortation to 'relax this stoic pride' perhaps hints at his friend's attempted projection of stoicism in constructing a 'mask of gaiety', Bentley's broader rhetoric is more precisely suggestive of the tenets of Greek sceptic philosophy, to which Schopenhauerian pessimism is also indebted. For example, Pyrrhonist scepticism posits a philosophy of withdrawal in which scepticism is rendered an absolute principle, resulting in a total suspension of judgement, or withholding of assent (*epoche*), a strategy pursued with the aim of achieving mental imperturbability, or *ataraxia* (see Mates, 61–62). Some possible explanations for why the young Bentley might have been attracted to the prospect of imperturbability are suggested by the diaries. In *Those Days*, he recalls that Chesterton 'had an ideally happy home', blessed with parents who also 'made their home a place of happiness for their two boys' many friends' (46/49). To judge by the diaries, Bentley's parental home was considerably less idyllic. On 19 January 1899, he reflects that

> I should face [my future], I really believe, with a light heart, if we were happy in our home. But the most that home is to me now is a material resource; there is no spiritual comfort there; never has been any.
>
> (Bod MS Eng.misc.e.869)

Later in the same year he wonders, anxiously, 'if I shall ever be as violent as my father. I don't think I ever could. But I am distressed by this' (7 July 1899; Bod MS Eng.misc.e.869). On Christmas Day, 1898, he writes of the recent death of a dissolute uncle from an 'overdose of Chloral': this baleful figure 'had far less principle than anybody I ever knew [and] was the worst and most hopeless of modern types of character'; nonetheless, he

> had a great influence on me at a very plastic period [...] I don't know if I shall ever get rid of the results of that influence [...] I cannot forget, though it's long since I saw him last, that he and I were very good friends.
>
> (Bod MS Eng.misc.e.869)

These anxieties seem to have invested Bentley with a fatalistic view of genetic inheritance—the diaries attest that 'I am a determinist' (24 Feb. 1895; Bod MS.Eng.misc.e.863), and elsewhere he reports that he has been reading the work of the genetic determinist, August Weismann (9 Nov. 1894; Bod MS.Eng.misc.e.862). Bentley's fears of genetic association with his father's violence and his uncle's depravity find expression in diary entries that often depict him as a veritable Roderick Usher, ruminating on his tainted bloodline, or 'my family curse' (1 Aug. 1899; Bod MS Eng.misc.e.869), as Bentley puts it.[17] Elsewhere, he asserts that '[w]e are, all the Bentleys I know are, a kindred of brutes' (15 Sept. 1898, MS.Eng.misc.e.867).

The influence of Weismann's theory of 'germinal selection' is particularly suggestive in the context of Bentley's admiration of the pessimistic biological determinism of Emile Zola, whose *Rougon-Macquart* (1871–93) novel-sequence stressed the unavoidable, malefic consequences of genetic inheritance.[18] As Bentley writes on 23 April 1899, '[r]eading Zola's Debacle, a splendid work. Wonderful man' (Bod MS.Eng.misc.e.869). Chesterton detested the work of Zola in equal proportion to that of Ibsen, whose fatalistic family tragedies were esteemed by Bentley: '[went] to a matinee of The Doll's House; which I thought a fine play' (2 Sept. 1897; Bod MS.Eng.misc.e.866).[19] In later years, Chesterton affectionately parodied Bentley's detective novel, *Trent's Last Case* (1913), in the form of a mock-Ibsenian drama scripted for domestic performance: 'Mr G.K. Chesterton presents the modern and compelling problem drama Trent's Last Cottage', a wry conceit that serves to establish ironic distance from Bentley's influences (see BL MS Add.73309D. fol. 48).

However, in their youth, Chesterton was more deeply immersed in his friend's troubles, and was viscerally alarmed by Bentley's confessions of mental disturbance. In an undated letter of 1893, which arose from the pair's prior discussion of a 'suicide controversy' (BL MS Add.73191 fol. 33) in the press, Chesterton drops the tone of adolescent flippancy that often served as a distancing mask of gaiety in their correspondence and adopts an uncharacteristically earnest mien. Referring to an earlier conversation, he reminds Bentley that 'the real remedy for such faddists [as pessimists] is, as you said, genuine friendship' (BL MS Add.73191 fol. 33). Chesterton reports that he has discarded a letter 'in which I summoned up all my powers of spiritual consolation in the hope of fixing your state of mind, your hints of which worried me' (BL MS Add.73191 fol. 33). He then offers the following anti-Schopenhauerian advice: 'Face for a moment the conception of the world being a sham, of the sum of all things being barren, and you will feel it is impossible' (BL MS Add.73191 fol. 33).

These underlinings emphasise a recourse to intuitive, sensory experience that is entirely new to their correspondence and would ultimately become Chesterton's primary defence against the temptations of scepticism and pessimism in his maturity. The peroration ends on a rhetorical note that is immediately recognisable as the future journalistic voice of 'G.K.C.', in a discussion of his recent holiday game-playing that differs radically from the 'unhuman' form of game-playing discussed by Bentley: 'I sally out in the evening and play with children on the sands: coastguards' and visitors' children alike, except that the coastguards' are rather the more refined' (BL MS Add.73191 fol. 33).[20] The final remark could be considered to represent the birth moment of Chesterton's strident populism, conceived in an attempt to impress a more healthy outlook upon his friend, while signalling a telling divergence from his previous, Bentleyan remarks that 'the lower orders are seen unfavourably when enjoying themselves'.

If Chesterton was beginning tentatively to construct a worldview distinct from that of his friend, it is significant that Bentley's period of psychological instability formed a point of convergence with Chesterton. In the summer of 1894, Bentley writes that 'I have not been for some time quite normal. There was a time in your own experience when you had something of the sort' (BL MS Add.73191 fol. 63). This time has long been discussed by Chesterton's biographers as the period of crisis that he endured while studying at the Slade School of Art between the autumn of 1893 and the summer of 1894—a timespan that almost exactly coincides with Bentley's period of disturbance.[21] In his autobiography, Chesterton explains that an extended spell of solitary reflection induced a 'mood of unreality and sterile isolation' that led him to doubt the existence of external reality: 'It was as if I had myself projected the universe from within' (92). Curiously enough, Chesterton depicts *himself* as a replica of Hankin here. If the latter 'disbelieved in Man much more than he did in God', Chesterton confesses that while atheists would tell him 'so pompously that [they] did not believe there was any God [...] there were moments when I did not even believe there was any atheist' (*Autobiography*, 92).

Despite Chesterton's testimony that 'my morbidities [...] sounded the most appalling depths of fundamental scepticism and solipsism' (*Autobiography*, 341), William Oddie has argued that Chesterton's malaise was probably not as serious as he claimed:

> the evidence is that his morbid state of mind was never at any point wholly debilitating, and that his struggle against the blight of what he termed 'pessimism' [was] seen as an external and cultural threat rather than as a personal problem [...] there was probably never a time when he was wholly engulfed.
>
> (90)

Similarly, Oddie claims that Chesterton had safely passed through this phase by the time that he left the Slade. He draws this inference from another letter sent from Chesterton to Bentley, which is undated, but which Ward speculates may have been sent in the 'Long Vac., 1894' (*Gilbert*, 48). Here, Chesterton appears to be speaking of a crisis that has been fully resolved:

> Inwardly speaking, I have had a funny time. A meaningless fit of depression, taking the form of certain absurd psychological worries, came upon me, and instead of dismissing it and talking to people, I had it out and went very far into the abysses, indeed. The result was that I found that things, when examined, necessarily spelt such a mystically satisfactory state of things, that [... I was made] certain that it is all right.
>
> (*Gilbert*, 48)[22]

Again, the tone here is pedagogic, seeking to reassure Bentley, through a projection of similarity, that Chesterton has recently discovered a means of surmounting the depression with which both men were struggling. Oddie cites this letter as proof that by the summer of 1894, 'the nightmare through which' Chesterton had passed was 'ended [...] forever' (124). As Oddie (over-)stresses, at this stage Chesterton's troubles were '*already over*' (132). However, a series of entries in Bentley's diary of late 1896 directly contradict this assertion, instead demonstrating that Chesterton's debilitating neuroses continued at least up to the time of his first courting of Frances. These diary entries indicate that Chesterton's psychological problems were not pristinely left behind in a manner both reassuring to the biographer and preferable to Chesterton in his construction of a pedagogic autobiographical narrative. Far from being disturbing emotions later recollected in tranquillity, these were difficulties with which he battled on an ongoing basis.

On 12 October 1896, Bentley writes, 'Gilbert, returning, was very nervous and unwell. It appears [... that] he gets into a state of nervous frustration and terror, and gets overwhelmed by his imagination' (Bod MS Eng.misc.e.865). The following day, Bentley records that

> Gilbert had a very bad attack this evening—when I had gone to bed, and almost to sleep, he suddenly turned up in my room—as far as I could gather, unable to face the thing alone, and only finding relief in talking to somebody. I did my best to converse, and kept on dropping asleep and dreaming short dreams between the sentences—awful work! He really ought to be seriously taken in hand. It would never do—few things would so seldom do—to have him breaking himself down for good.
>
> (13 Oct. 1896; Bod MS Eng.misc.e.865)

With its weariness and wordplay, this account retains a curiously detached tone. Bentley interrupts the flow of his recollection to police his use of rote phraseology, employing the archetypal nonsense trick of literalising a figure of speech ('never do'; 'seldom do') to inject an arch emotional distance into the account. This trait is mirrored in the ironical turn of phrase, 'relax this stoic pride', with which Chesterton responds urbanely to Bentley's loss of volition in the abandoned *Greybeards* preface. It is as though each man retreats into self-preserving detachment upon encountering an objective manifestation of his own mental state.

However, on 17 December 1896, Bentley adopts the note of unguarded earnestness that had emerged earlier in Chesterton's correspondence:

> I love, and can't help loving, a man who has been to me all that he has been; but it only makes my fear and sorrow for him the more acute. I am afraid, deeply afraid for this man's future; for he has made his bed.
>
> (Bod MS Eng.misc.e.866)

The meaning of Bentley's final, enigmatic remark is difficult to determine, though one plausible context is Chesterton's increasingly strong attachment to Frances at this time. Another possibility is his increasing sense of literary purpose, which is brought to light by a slightly earlier entry, in which Bentley records that, on another visit, 'Gilbert toiled away at his story of the man who would be God. I wonder if it will be good. It should be, by the pains he's taking with it' (21 Sept. 1896; Bod MS Eng.misc.e.865). It seems likely that a nascent version of *The Man Who Was Thursday* is the text to which Bentley is referring here. Chesterton later asserted that he first began to draft the novel in the early 1890s, a project that he pursued throughout the following years in a variety of titular guises, including 'The Picture of Tuesday' in 1896.[23]

Bentley's diary entries shed an illuminating light upon what Evelyn Waugh later intuited to be the 'night-fears' (74) that inform the novel, suggesting that its subtitle—'A Nightmare'—was more than a merely metaphorical conceit. Chesterton's fictional reconstruction of his psychological struggles—which had taken the form of a delusion 'of being God' (*Autobiography*, 92)—may have initially exacerbated his sense of psychological disturbance as he struggled to establish a more constructive, creative means of 'project[ing a] universe from within'. As he argues in *Orthodoxy*, '[i]magination does not breed insanity. Exactly what does breed insanity is reason. Poets do not go mad; but chess-players do' (9). Nonetheless, Bentley's account of his friend being 'overwhelmed by his imagination' suggests a traumatic grappling with the exchanges of existential perspective that Chesterton would later refine within the final text. Since Bentley was not always on hand in the next room, he perhaps found the 'relief in talking to somebody' that he needed through this opening up of textual dialogue. If so, the precise nature of the dialogues that he chose to establish in his most intimately self-revelatory novel warrant more sustained examination.

A Man Constantly Changing into Other Men

In an article for the *Listener* on 'Both Sides of the Looking-Glass' (29 Nov. 1933), Chesterton posits a distinction between popular and academic versions of the modern fairy-tale. In expressing a preference for the fairy-tale worlds of Hans Christian Andersen over those of Lewis Carroll, he explains that Andersen 'remained in touch with the enormous tradition of the earth in the matter of mystery and glamour—he did not have to make a new and rather artificial sort of fairy-tale out of triangles and syllogisms' (collected in *Spice*, 69). Although this argument corroborates Sewell's view that Chesterton's populist aesthetics constituted an 'attempt [...] to move from Nonsense, with its isolation, to Fairy tale with its identification' ('G.K. Chesterton', 571), having appraised the relative merits of each approach he prefers to retain both: 'I only know that if you try to deprive me of either of them, there will be a row' (*Spice*, 69). *The Man Who Was Thursday* exemplifies this urge to establish a dialogue between the popular and the academic by grafting the bracingly untethered irrationalism of Victorian nonsense to the grounding communitarian ethos of folk- and fairy-tale convention. As the narrator explains of the 'huge masquerade' that takes place at the novel's conclusion, 'it was, somehow, as absurd as Alice in Wonderland, yet as grave and kind as a love story' (*CW* 6:630).

In the bulk of the narrative, the reader apprehends an array of physically improbable characters through the prism of Gabriel Syme's disorientated gaze as he attempts to comprehend the nature of the anarchist cell that he has infiltrated, much like Alice attempting to get to grips with the baffling motives and mannerisms of the inhabitants of Wonderland. At the height of Syme's disarray, he experiences a terrifying vision of the *corps morcelé*, perceiving the anarchist dubbed 'Friday', Professor de Worms, to be 'in the last dissolution of senile decay', a state that 'did not express decrepitude merely, but corruption', so that 'Syme's quivering mind [...] could not help thinking that whenever the man moved a leg or arm might fall off' (*CW* 6:523). When rational explanations for such nightmarish visions are revealed, the secondary characters' assumption of more reassuring dimensions is repeatedly described in terms of the fairy-tale 'transformation scene' (*CW* 6:560/578), while the disturbing rhetoric of bodily corruption is replaced with the joyously burlesque imagery of 'the Marquis, recklessly throwing various parts of himself right and left about the field' (*CW* 6:756) as he strips off his disguise.

In *Orthodoxy*, Chesterton explains the appeal of the traditional fairy-tale thus: 'I have not found any modern type so sanely radical or so sanely conservative' (50). Jean-Jacques Lecercle argues that this dualism is also a defining quality of more contemporary forms of nonsense: 'nonsense is on the whole a conservative-revolutionary genre' since it is 'structured by the contradiction [...] between over-structuring and de-structuring, subversion and support' (2–3). This duality applies equally to the merger of moral policeman and merry relativist that Chesterton identified in the single entity, Dodgson/Carroll, who possessed 'one life in which he would have thundered morally against any one who walked on the wrong plot of grass, and another life in which he would cheerfully call the sun green and the moon blue' (*Defendant*, 66).

Chesterton's retention of measured affiliation with Carroll was based partially upon a similar duality—his sense that the latter's brand of nonsense was not only a symptom, but also a potential cure of the intellectual maladies of Decadence. Consequently, Chesterton went so far as to argue that the *Alice* stories were not children's books at all, but a kind of self-help manual for academics: 'the very best of Lewis Carroll was not written by a man for children, but by a don for dons [...] it may be questioned whether the little girls he wrote for were tortured by relativist scepticism' (*Spice*, 68). While this reflection might be thought to somewhat underestimate the inner life of little girls, Chesterton's key point is that Carroll's knack of giving 'mathematics a holiday' enables the intellectual to view ontological scepticism from a comic perspective: much as Bentley seemed 'himself once more' when 'stood upon his head', Carroll was 'teaching dons to stand on their heads' (*Spice*, 68).

Chesterton's tacit affinity with Carroll's imaginative landscape is perhaps explicable in psychogenic as well as philosophical terms. Although he claimed that in the mid-1890s he 'was not mad, in any medical or physical sense' but 'was simply carrying the scepticism of my time as far as it would go', the specifics of Chesterton's condition—a 'calm horror of detachment' (*Autobiography*, 92)—strongly resemble the psychological disorder of derealisation, in which the individual's perception of the external world becomes distorted in a manner that causes her/his immediate environment to appear unreal or dreamlike. Rather than a considered, philosophical espousal of solipsism, this condition should be understood as an involuntary psychiatric state in which the subject becomes unable to conceive the world as possessing a meaningful existence external to her/his consciousness. Those who experience derealisation frequently suffer from 'panic disorder' (Johnson and Kring, 179), a condition evoked in Bentley's diary accounts of Chesterton in 1896.

One form of derealisation is a clinical condition that has come to be known as 'Alice in Wonderland syndrome' (Magalini, 28). The sufferer from derealisation often experiences Alice's sense of sudden physical diminution and gigantism, a sensation caused by perceptual distortions in the size or shape of objects (see Johnson and Kring, 232). Familiar locations are experienced as alien or surreal, with features of the landscape undergoing a dolly-zoom effect that causes a disorientating enlargement ('macropsia') and/or shrinking ('micropsia') of objective phenomena. This syndrome is particularly common amongst migraine sufferers (see Magalini, 28), and it is perhaps telling that Chesterton later recalled experiencing severe headaches in his late adolescence (see Ward, *Gilbert*, 45).

These early traumatic experiences inform much of the imagery of Chesterton's later fiction. As his contemporary, Dixon Scott, noted of the early *Father Brown* stories,

> dreadful is the way some peaceful secondary thing—a group of trees, or a distant passer-by, or a quiet country church—will suddenly writhe out of its place and rush into the foreground, waxing horribly, like a face in a fever, as though struggling to express something too monstrous for speech
>
> (267)

A comparable waxing of the object world is evoked in *The Man Who Was Thursday* in Syme's account of his initial conception of the apparent anarchist ringleader, Sunday, as a terrifyingly enormous figure: 'the face was so big, that one couldn't focus it or make it a face at all. The eye was so far away from the nose that it wasn't an eye' (*CW* 6:620). This alarming nonsense vision is again scrupulously balanced with imagery that Chesterton associated with more benign forms of nonsense; elsewhere, Sunday is portrayed in Rabelaisian terms as a comically gluttonous Gargantua: 'he ate like twenty men; he ate incredibly, with a frightful freshness of appetite,' so that before long, 'he had swallowed a dozen crumpets [and] drunk a quart of coffee' (*CW* 6:527). Not for nothing does 'A Defence of Farce' place Rabelais at the head of the 'old masters of a healthy madness' (*Defendant*, 127).

The movement of *The Man Who Was Thursday* between motifs of derangement and reconstruction finds expression in the symbiotic relationship of its nonsense-title to the narrative itself. The riddle of Chesterton's titular category mistake necessitates detective work on the part of both Syme and the reader, as the initially disorientating narrative progresses through a process of conservative restructuring towards its harmonious conclusion.[24] As a result, the word 'Thursday' comes to play a decisive symbolic role in the novel. Chesterton considered the moon to be 'the mother of lunatics' (*Orthodoxy*, 21) as well as 'the patroness of nonsense' (*Defendant*, 69); therefore, it is allegorically significant that Thursday is the fourth day of creation, on which God created the moon, a context that suggests that the title might be considered a circuitous way of reframing the statement 'The Man Who Was a Lunatic'.

Of course, the title is initially made to logically cohere through Syme's accession to the anarchist council, an organisation in which each conspirator is named after a day of the week. However, Chesterton deliberately establishes the council as a nonsense construct that vexes Syme's sense of discrete subjectivity, initially compounding his lunacy. As Sunday explains, this 'branch has always had the honour of electing Thursdays for the Central European Council. We have elected many and splendid Thursdays' (*CW* 6:497). By accepting this role, Syme submits to a voluntary abnegation of subjecthood, thus initiating the nightmarish central section of the novel in which Chesterton presents a comprehensive survey of the 'horrible fairy tale of a man constantly changing into other men', which he considered 'the soul of decadence' (*Defendant*, 33–34): a 'world where men took off their beards and their spectacles and their noses, and turned into other people' (CW 6:583).

Syme's madness is finally dispersed by an allegorical reorientation of his personification of Thursday during the culminating 'carnival' (CW 6:629), in which he is literally dressed as the fourth day of creation. This conceit serves to transmute his internalised lunacy into an externalised emblem of the act of creation, thereby re-establishing coherent individuality: Syme 'seemed to be for the first time himself and no-one else' (CW 6:628). If we consider this movement to mirror the process through which Chesterton sought to overcome his psychological traumas through the act of creating the novel itself, the carnival setting becomes central to a proper understanding of his intent in juxtaposing academic and folk nonsense in counterpoint. In Bakhtinian terms, the plot's progress from disarray to order represents a simultaneous shift between differing modes of the grotesque, from the Romantic to the carnivalesque. As Bakhtin explains, whereas the carnivalesque is 'directly related to folk culture [...] the Romantic genre acquired a private "chamber" character [...] marked by a vivid sense of isolation. The carnival spirit was transposed into a subjective, idealistic philosophy' (*Rabelais*, 37). Consequently, for Bakhtin, 'the world of the Romantic grotesque is [...] a terrifying world' in which 'that which was habitual and secure [...] suddenly becomes meaningless, dubious and hostile' (*Rabelais*, 39).

Bakhtin situates this fault line in the grotesque as a historical development, with the carnivalesque mode representing a pre-Enlightenment standard and the Romantic grotesque being explained as a product of post-Enlightenment culture. The dyadic movement of *The Man Who Was Thursday* sets out to reverse this historical process, reinstating the immersive materiality of the 'folk' grotesque in the form of the final carnival, which follows on from the terrifying, hostile atmosphere of the central section. The novel ultimately ends where it began, with a dialogue between Syme and his erstwhile antagonist, the sulphurous nihilist Lucien Gregory, albeit with the key distinction that the pair are no longer locked in mutual suspicion, but are now 'walking like old friends, and [...] in the middle of a conversation' (CW 6:635). This footstep-retracing process of repetition with deviation complements the wider movement of reversal that the novel undertakes on a historical level, through which the cultural misadventure, as Chesterton perceived it, of post-Enlightenment Romantic subjectivism is cancelled out by a spooling back of time to recover a medieval mode of communitarian folk grotesque.[25]

In *Rabelais and His World*, Bakhtin argues that the two historical strands are distinguished further by their contrasting deployment of an identical symbol: the mask. For Bakhtin, the mask 'reveals the essence of the grotesque' in both its 'folk carnival' and 'Romantic' manifestations (40), but with a crucial distinction: the former 'is connected with the joy of change and reincarnation [...] with the merry negation of uniformity and similarity' (39), while the latter 'loses almost entirely its regenerating and renewing element and acquires a sombre hue. A terrible vacuum, a nothingness lurks behind it' (40). At the height of Syme's disarray, this vacuum opens up when the thought occurs to him: 'was he wearing a mask? Was anyone wearing a mask? Was any one anything?' (CW 6:583). The climactic pageant replaces this disturbing vision with the benign spectacle of the *dramatis personae* clad in vibrant carnival disguises, which emblematise the 'inexhaustible and many-colored life' that Bakhtin finds 'behind the mask of folk grotesque' (*Rabelais*, 40). As the narrator explains, 'these disguises did not disguise, but reveal' (CW 6:627), a phrase almost exactly echoed in John Lechte's analysis of Bakhtin's account of the carnivalesque mask as a symbol 'which does not hide but reveals' (9).

Of course, this imagery is also closely aligned to the dictum famously coined in Wilde's 'The Critic as Artist' (1890), in which, by curious coincidence, a character named Gilbert affirms that men 'will tell you the truth' if given 'a mask' (*Complete*, 1045). The thematic echo of Wilde's text in *Thursday* points towards a further subtle dialogue that the novel sets up with an ambivalently beheld forebear, complementing Chesterton's adaptation of Carrollian nonsense by engaging with the man whom he considered the embodiment of Decadence. In the early years of Chesterton's public career, he consistently sought to position himself as the anti-Wilde, an urge no doubt exacerbated by the frequency with which critics linked their names. His efforts to counteract this association reach their apogee in *Orthodoxy* and *Thursday*, both published in 1908. In the former, he arrives at a formula for expressing a transactional engagement with one's debt of gratitude to existence: 'we can pay for sunsets. We can pay for them by not being Oscar Wilde' (50). Meanwhile, the verse preface to *Thursday* projects a clear-cut divide between himself and Bentley on one hand and the Decadent forces of the 'Green Carnation' (CW 6:473) on the other, employing carnivalesque imagery of merry buffoonery to emphasise the distinction:

> Science announced nonentity and art admired decay;
> The world was old and ended: but you and I were gay;
> [...]
> Fools as we were in motley, all jangling and absurd,
> When all church bells were silent our cap and bells were heard.
> (CW 6:472)

As we have seen, this carefree characterisation is unrepresentative of Bentley and also far from the whole story where Chesterton was concerned: the verb 'jangling' is aptly chosen, with its evocation of irritated nerves as much as playful fooling. In a letter sent to Bentley in 1892, Chesterton discusses Wilde in terms that encapsulate his youthful tendency to vacillate between adherence to his friend's tastes and self-assertive departure. Chesterton reports his father's reading of '*your friend* Oscar Wilde's book on Lying, bound up with some other equally amusing and equally paradoxical discourses', only to modify the possessive note: 'I am developing a power of reasoning out nonsense quite after the heart of *our friend* Oscar' (BL MS Add.73191 fol.21; my emphases). Notwithstanding the terms of the *Thursday* preface, it seems that both Chesterton and Bentley 'admired decay' in their youth, in the shape of their 'friend' Wilde's essay, 'The Decay of Lying' (1889).

Almost half a century later, Chesterton evinced a renewed willingness to address the ambivalence of his relationship to Wilde, frankly acknowledging *Thursday* to have been the invention of a 'young *half*-pessimist of the '90s' (*Autobiography*, 102; my emphasis) and explaining the dedication as a note to a friend 'who had been through the same period and problems' (92–93). This measured readmission of resemblance is emphasised by his alterations to the manuscript copy of the autobiography. Having disassociated his own 'madness' from Wilde's homosexuality, asserting that he never felt 'the faintest temptation to the particular madness of Wilde', Chesterton crosses out the subsequent line—'but I could at this time have imagined many disproportioned' passions—and replaces it with 'I could at this time imagine the worst & wildest disproportions' (BL MS Add.73268A fol.98). Having initially projected difference, Chesterton's revision re-inscribes identity via a pun that confers upon himself the *wild*est disproportions.[26]

If Chesterton's imaginative disproportions recall Sewell's account of the salient features of Carollian nonsense, they also accord with another immoderate vision that afflicted Chesterton's younger self: an apprehension of the cultural *size* of Wilde, who 'filled up more room, both in mind and body, than anybody else on that stage' (CW 18:75), much as the body of the father-figure, Sunday, is conceived to occupy an unmanageable quantity of space in the nightmare section of *Thursday* (see CW 6:620). Chesterton conjures a similar image of Wilde's cultural centrality in *The Victorian Age in Literature* (1913), contending that the

> movement of those called Aesthetes (as satirised in *Patience*) and the movement of those afterwards called Decadents (satirised in [...] *Autobiography of a Boy*) had the same captain; or at any rate the same bandmaster. Oscar Wilde walked in front of the first procession wearing a sunflower, and in front of the second procession wearing a green carnation.
>
> (CW 15:516)

While pausing to note Chesterton's insertion of superfluous references to satires of each movement into this account of Wilde's progress, almost as an incantatory psychological *aide-mémoire*, we might also observe that the pageant leader bearing a metaphorical sunflower in Chesterton's novel is Sunday, whose name combines Christian and Apollonian connotations and who begins the novel as a dreaded father-figure who seems to augur annihilation and ends it by leading the detectives on a benignly nonsensical procession through the capital towards the idyllic conclusion. In this way, the novel's historical footstep-retracing conceit accrues an additional dimension via a subtle symbolic allusion that serves to rewind the biographical progress of Wilde. If Bakhtin's account of the decay of the regenerative element of the mask in post-Enlightenment Romantic culture correlates to the chronology of Wilde's swapping of the sunflower for the un-generative green carnation, Chesterton's novel sets Wilde's biography on a process of enforced reversal, catapulting him back to the unworldly, lower-case romanticism of his earliest theorising.

Appropriately enough, this tacit gesture of reconciliation was inspired by the assistance in 'reasoning out nonsense' that Chesterton had derived from 'The Decay of Lying', specifically the essay's famous account of life imitating art. Wilde's avatar, Vivian, begins by explaining that 'Schopenhauer has analysed the pessimism that characterises modern thought, but Hamlet invented it. The world has become sad because a puppet was once melancholy' (*Intentions*, 32). In pursuing this line of argument, Vivian identifies a further example of the 'imitative instinct' in a context that conflates childhood innocence with the tropes of popular fiction, discussing

> silly boys who, after reading the adventures of Jack Sheppard or Dick Turpin, pillage the stalls of unfortunate applewomen, break into sweet shops at night, and alarm old gentlemen [...] by leaping out on them in suburban lanes, with black masks and unloaded revolvers.
>
> (*Intentions*, 32)

Chesterton later applied a comparable moral to Wilde himself: he 'sometimes pretended that he was more important than morality, but that was mere play acting' (*CDN* 6:98).

Wilde's puckish juxtaposition of analogies drawn from Schopenhauerian philosophy and the popular adventure novel not only suggests a model for the existentialist picaresque of Chesterton's fictional universe, but also implies that Wilde had assisted him in reasoning out the nonsense of his formerly snobbish attitude towards writers such as 'that interminable ass Kingston'. In this light, it is with some chutzpah that Chesterton's foundational attack upon the anti-populism of post-Wildean culture, 'A Defence of Penny Dreadfuls', activates the same conflation of 'gutter-boys' and 'German professors' (*Defendant*, 25–26) initiated in 'The Decay of Lying'. Elsewhere, Chesterton explains the parodic relationship of *Thursday* to the conventional animus of detective fiction in terms that tie Wilde's imagery of innocent play to the revelatory mask motif of 'The Critic as Artist': 'In an ordinary detective tale the investigator discovers that some amiable-looking fellow who subscribes to all the charities [...] has murdered his grandmother [...] I thought it would be fun to make the tearing away of menacing masks reveal benevolence' (qtd. in Ward, *Gilbert* 168). Through such conceits, *Thursday* incorporates both an explicit rejection—in the verse preface—and a tacit assimilation and accommodation—in the body of the text—of the arch-priest of Decadence.

As this dynamic suggests, Syme's plot-level escape from solipsism—a process literally riddled with covert conversations—is mirrored in the novel's dialogic play with Carroll and Wilde, which functions to subvert the isolation of the text itself. By piecing together fragments from the literary artefacts that had imaginatively framed his friendship with Bentley as a means of assembling his own nascent identity, Chesterton sets out to establish an internal forum within which to argue his way out of the ontological crisis that he had experienced at the *fin de siècle*. If this polyvocal textual dialogue suggests that finding one's own literary voice is finally a matter of establishing the right balance between a multitude of mutually correcting influences, it is appropriate that a third shadow-presence in the novel is the very figure with whom Chesterton was in most intimate dialogue during its initial conceptualisation: Bentley.

The Moon and the Monocle

In his autobiography, Chesterton discusses the confusion caused in some quarters by the novel's verse dedication, in which he speaks directly 'to my friend Bentley [...] asking rhetorically: "Who shall understand but you?" In reply to which a book-reviewer very sensibly remarked that if nobody understood the book except Mr. Bentley, it seemed unreasonable to ask other people to read it' (102). This humorous suggestion that Chesterton had contrived a curiously alienating *roman à clef* hints at the deeper duality within this and other texts of his maturity, in which the raw materials of his youthful dialogues with Bentley are interwoven with explorations of more recent public controversies. Nonetheless, the explicit invocation of Bentley in the dedication has led critics to overlook his clandestine implantation within the narrative itself. This can perhaps be explained by the counterintuitive, viscerally disturbing context in which he appears, which further complicates Chesterton's dedicatory evocation of the pair as anti-Decadent partisans, who 'held the fort' doggedly until 'the Green Carnation withered' (*CW* 6:473).

Amongst the anarchists whom Chesterton's fictional avatar, Syme, initially conceives himself to be battling, the most vividly nightmarish is Professor de Worms, a figure whose name combines academia with decay—here the title of Professor Dewar undergoes a literal process of corruption—and whose features bear a marked resemblance to Bentley. The narrator notes that de Worms's scholarly spectacles jar incongruously with his spritely body: 'the head upon that bounding body was still pale, grave and professional, like the head of a lecturer upon the body of a harlequin' (CW 6:540). This is almost precisely how Chesterton describes Bentley in his autobiography: 'I used to say that he had the head of a professor on the body of a harlequin' (61). Professor de Worms is reputed to be a 'German Nihilist philosopher', almost certainly an allusion to Schopenhauer, whose theory of the primacy of the will is evoked in an irreverent explanation of de Worms's philosophy: '"Energy, he said, was the All. He was lame, short-sighted, and partially paralytic"' (CW 6:549).

Syme eventually discovers that the apparent anarchist before him is actually a fellow policeman, who has been physically parodying the original de Worms all along. After having broken character, the undercover agent implies that his *modus operandi* involved a burlesque rendition of the central conceit of *The Picture of Dorian Gray*: '"I am a portrait of the celebrated Professor"' (CW 6:549). If the audacity of the policeman's actions contrasts sharply with Chesterton's view of Schopenhauer's philosophy as 'a mere nightmare induced by lack of nerve' (CDN 1:95), it would seem that Chesterton has set out to persuade himself that he had mistaken the teenage Bentley for a *bona fide* sceptic when he had simply been putting on a particularly accomplished performance. Chesterton later credited Bentley with 'conceal[ing] a very powerful sense of humour under [an] almost impenetrable disguise' (*Autobiography*, 61); in *Thursday*, Bentley's impenetrable persona is reconceived as a consequence of acting a perilous part that ironically conveyed his animus towards the figures whose 'replica' he appeared to resemble. As the policeman explains to Syme, in terms that closely resemble the motive of the satirical parodist, 'I disliked [de Worms] so much that I resolved to imitate him' (CW 6:549).

In a reversal of the dynamic that structures the novel's dialogue with Wilde, the unmasking of de Worms represents an attempt on Chesterton's part to reconcile the differences with Bentley that he had *effaced* from the prefatory verse, by sloughing off the elements of his friend's personality that he found antipathetic. To quote Whitman, the staunch anti-pessimist invoked in the *Thursday* dedication, 'what I assume you shall assume' (*Complete*, 63). There is something a little despotic about this endeavour, suggestive of Lynch's account of the Aristotelian friend as a 'reflection of [...] one's own narcissism', rather than 'a challenge [...] a genuine other' (101), a curious irony given that the novel's dialogic ethos was conceived partially as a strategy for escaping the same insular condition.[27] This irony is reinforced by Bentley's own comments on their friendship. In *Those Days*, he expands upon his seemingly counterintuitive remark that the pair's 'relationship did not mean so much to' Chesterton, explaining that his friend displayed a tendency towards creative withdrawal: 'a poet—as I think he has himself written somewhere—can always do without other people, much as he may enjoy their society' (45).

In contrast, Bentley's diaries occasionally focus upon the much-needed reassurance that he found in the conversational familiarity of Chesterton's correspondence: '[r]eading Gilbert's letters one always feels he is talking to you, and one almost converses' (1 Nov. 1895; Bod MS Eng.misc.e.864). If it seems surprising to find the apparently aloof Bentley complaining of Chesterton's withdrawal and attesting to an emotional reliance on his conversation, there is also a rather sad irony in Bentley's later account of a philosophical dispute between the pair. On 15 December 1896, he records that they recently 'fought the battles of the past two months over again; and I felt more than ever how widely our respective ways of looking at things are diverging. But the curious thing is, it makes not the least difference' (Bod MS.Eng. misc.e.866).

The evidence suggests otherwise: Chesterton was now beginning to distance himself from Bentley in increasing frustration at his non-committal personality and seemingly contradictory espousal of a dogmatic rationalism that Chesterton found antipathetic. Chesterton's autobiographical account stresses that Bentley's youthful writing 'confined itself to being critical or flippant' (67), while finding his broader demeanour to be characterised by a 'rigid flippancy' (*Autobiography*, 77). In an early article on 'Critics and Conversation' (*DN* 21 May 1901), Chesterton terms 'flippancy, the blackest of all the enemies of joy', because it is 'an extinguisher' of 'dialogue' (*CDN* 1:86). In 'E.C.B.', a dedicatory verse written in the late-1890s and collected in *The Wild Knight and Other Poems*, the focus of Chesterton's criticism progresses from the inveterate flippancy to the dogmatic rigidity. In a further failed attempt to contain his irritation, he begins the poem with an acclamation of Bentley as a 'good man through and through' before building to a bitter air of reproach: 'for thy sake I even faced / The knowledge that is worse than hell; / And loved the man I saw but now / Hanging head downwards in the well' (*CW* 10.1:274). This strongly implies that Chesterton considered his descent 'very far into the abysses' to have been occasioned by an attempt to commune empathetically with his friend and, worse, that this suffering had been futile, since Bentley had finally chosen to close himself off in an unilluminating realm of bottomless philosophical speculation.

This frustration is subtly encoded in the illustrations with which Chesterton adorned the offending section of Bentley's epistolary account of the 'unhuman' chess-game as a 'silent, rapt kind of wit-contest' (Figure 1.1, overleaf).

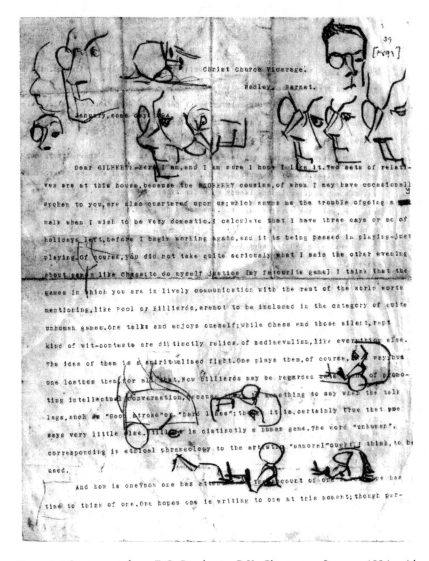

Figure 1.1 Letter sent from E.C. Bentley to G.K. Chesterton, January 1894, with illustrations by Chesterton (BL MS Add.73191 fol. 39) © The British Library Board.

These sketches bear a marked resemblance to Bentley, though Chesterton's reason for placing a prominent monocle on each image of his friend is initially unclear. Mark Knight's discussion of Chesterton's fictional symbolism offers a first clue to the explanation: 'For Chesterton, spectacles offer a terrifying instance of the grotesque because they involve the possibility that behind the appearance of the grotesque there might be nothing at all' (103). Knight's analysis is corroborated by these sketches, in which no eye is depicted behind the monocle, but rather a perfectly circular void. The specifically 'mono' element of Chesterton's visual symbolism is also significant in the context of Bentley's increasingly obsessive espousal of determinism, since the loss of one eye implies a monoscopic, rather than stereoscopic, mode of vision, with attendant loss of perspective. In *Orthodoxy*, Chesterton employs this ocular distinction to differentiate between the 'morbid logician' and the 'healthy [...] ordinary man' (20) in an account that centres upon the latter's intuitive willingness to accept inexplicable contradictions, in contrast to the systematising drive of the rationalistic intellectual. For Chesterton, the

> ordinary man [...] has always cared more for truth than for consistency. If he saw two truths that seemed to contradict each other, he would take the two truths and the contradiction along with them. His spiritual sight is stereoscopic, like his physical sight: he sees two different pictures at once and yet sees all the better for that.
> (*Orthodoxy*, 20)

Chesterton then cites the cross as a positive emblem of this vein of existential contradiction: 'though it has at its heart a collision and a contradiction, [the cross] can extend its four arms for ever without altering its shape. Because it has a paradox in its centre it can grow without changing' (21). By way of contrast, he employs the circle as 'the symbol of reason and madness' (20). Discussing the rationalistic certainties of the intellectual, he notes that 'the circle of the moon is [...] clear and unmistakable [...] as the circle of Euclid on a blackboard' (21), much like the pristine circle of the monocle that he affixes to his caricatures of Bentley. Chesterton concludes that '[d]etached intellectualism is (in the exact sense of a popular phrase) all moonshine; for it is light without heat, and it is secondary light, reflected from a dead world' (21).

In Chesterton's fiction, monocles are invariably worn by characters who represent aloofness, worldly success, and social conformity. For example, a politician in 'The Red Moon of Meru' (*Storyteller* Apr. 1927) possesses a 'monocle that was the only gleam in his hard, legal face' (*CFB* 618), while the Honourable James Barker in *The Napoleon of Notting Hill* is a 'rigidly official' government figure with 'a monocle screwed into his eye' (*CW* 6:229–30). Perhaps most tellingly, the rationalistic 'criminological expert' in *Manalive*, Dr. Cyrus Pym, not only sports a 'dandified monocle', but also possesses a physical bearing closely reminiscent of the discordantly professorial head and harlequinesque body of de Worms: Pym's 'dress and gestures' are 'bright enough for a boy's; it was only when you looked at the fish-bone face that you beheld something acrid and old' (32).

As the very 'incarnation of Scientific Theory' (39), Pym is called upon to make a professional judgement upon the distinctly Chestertonian protagonist, Innocent Smith, who is suspected to be criminally insane, thus producing another scenario, first sketched out in the 1890s, in which a Chestertonian protagonist encounters a threatening Bentleyan antagonist.[28] Pym's analysis is delivered in a parody of the excesses of determinist jargon, of the kind popularised by Cesare Lombroso: Smith is a 'lunatico-criminal' type with 'incurable [...] criminal perversities' (37), whose incapacity to control his seemingly untoward behaviour renders him 'a monstrosity, something that oughtn't to be at all' (33). If the least approved aspects of Bentley's personality find their way into the character of Pym, his more sympathetic attributes are apportioned to Michael Moon, an ironical, disillusioned journalist. As the lunar appellation suggests, Moon represents Bentley's simultaneous capacity for cool detachment and a more creative lunacy. In an exact replication of Bentley's career path, Moon is discussed as a 'flippant journalist [... who] had once been hazily supposed to be reading for the bar' (8) and is found, at one stage, in an 'absurd attitude, with his elbow on the grate' (37)—recall the *Greybeards* dedication, 'I said "Cease rolling in the grate"'.

Since 'Cyrus' translates as 'the sun', Pym is conceived as Moon's antipode—whereas *Thursday* had embodied Bentley's contradictions within a single disguised individual, *Manalive* partitions the contrasting elements of his personality between two distinct characters. When Moon finds himself compelled to challenge Pym in order to defend Smith in the burlesque domestic courtroom scene that dominates the novel's second section, a scenario emerges in which the legal and ontological innocence of the surrogate Chesterton becomes intimately wedded to the triumph of the preferred Bentley. Pym is finally worsted in debate by Moon, who succeeds in demonstrating the fallacious grounds of Pym's materialist methodology. Moon's increasing indignation at Pym's mean-spirited interpretations of Smith's behaviour finally causes his tone to alter 'from the *mock heroic* to the *humanly* indignant' (91; my emphases), a switch from aloof irony to worldly engagement that enacts Chesterton's desired resolution of Bentley's dualistic character.

The diaries suggest that Chesterton had some grounds for hope in this respect. On 8 October 1895, Bentley analyses his feelings towards Chesterton in terms that progress from an arch, self-reflexive parody of Lombroso's pseudo-academic rhetoric to a straightforward, unguarded statement of emotional attachment:

> to be friends in the way that we are is on the face of it absurd.—I am an egoist, I have long been aware; and probably "have for my characteristics a nebulosity of mental representation, a confused and motley ideation, too much eroticism, an abnormal emotional fabric", and so on, like the men in Lombroso. Certainly I felt a good deal sorrier than, apparently, many people do at leaving their friends'.
> (Bod MS Eng.misc.e.864)

In *Manalive*, Pym is not so much driven off as converted—amid the general merriment of the festive resolution, '[e]ven Dr. Pym, though he refrained from dancing, looked on with real benevolence' (95). In this light, it is notable that Chesterton's courtroom confrontation activates the same symbolic triad—sun, moon, and monocle—invoked in a contemporaneous essay, 'The Dulness of Cliques' (*DN* 11 May 1912), in which he articulates the dangers of ontological scepticism:

> [W]hile men are and should be various, there must be some communication between them if they are to get any pleasure out of their variety. [...] If we all start with the agreement that the sun and moon exist, we can talk about our different visions of them. [... But] if once it be held that there is nothing but a silver blur in one man's eye or a bright circle (like a monocle) in the other man's, then neither is free, for each is shut up in the cell of a separate universe.
> (*CDN* 8:77)[29]

As this suggests, Chesterton considers excessive subjectivism to breed alienation by dispensing with the shared objective contexts that foster mutual understanding, whereas communication offers a means of evading solipsism and encouraging community cohesion, while safeguarding plurality of perspective. Moon's intervention in *Manalive* has a similar effect, validating Smith's eccentric perspective, while remedying Pym's tunnel-visioned dogmatism, in a sanguine exposition of the courtroom as an ethically effective dialogic arena.

It is a foundational paradox of Chesterton's philosophical development that his dialogic sensibility was sharpened through a process of self-extrication from the confines of his closest friendship. In replacing the principle of one soul occupying two individual bodies with that of two distinct souls collaborating in one collective body-politic, Chesterton arrived at a cogent ethics of interpersonal relation that entailed a rejection of the original terms upon which the friendship had been based. In W.H. Auden's account of the psychological reassurance derived from the preservative quality of caricature, he argues that we 'enjoy caricatures of our friends because we do not want to think of their [...] dying', but also that 'we enjoy caricatures of our enemies because we do not want to consider the possibility of their having a change of heart so that we would have to forgive them' (383). Bentley comes to stand in the same dialogic relation to Chesterton as that in which Turnbull stands to MacIan in *The Ball and the Cross* (1909): his simultaneous 'friend and enemy' (*CW* 7:236), preserved indefinitely in the detached, 'unmoral' role articulated in the letter of 1894—a document that Chesterton had compulsively covered in caricatures of Bentley.

Nonetheless, while Chesterton's autobiographical pen portrait insists that 'of all men I have known, [Bentley] is the man whose mind has least changed', this is partly because it 'has least lost its balance' (67). Chesterton's replacement of the amalgamative conceit of '[t]wo faces in one hood' with a stress upon a 'duplication of mentality' (*Manalive*, 52) within the distinct individual suggests a more reconciliatory moral drawn from the perplexingly contradictious personality of his friend. As Innocent Smith finally testifies, together with the reformed 'student of Schopenhauer' (53), Emerson Eames, in a jointly composed text embedded within *Manalive*, '[t]here is a mystical, even a monstrous truth, in the statement that two heads are better than one. But they ought both to grow on the same body' (52). In *The Napoleon of Notting Hill*, the final *rapprochement* of the mismatched protagonists discloses the necessary constitution of this twin consciousness: 'the pure fanatic [and] the pure satirist' are really 'two lobes of the [same] brain' (CW 6:379).

In possession of this hard-won lesson in dual-mindedness, Chesterton burst in upon the proto-modernist public arena of 1900 and was quickly accused both of 'undue flippancy, [and] undue earnestness' (Scott, 265) by baffled critics. To borrow another of Chesterton's punning assessments of Wilde, '[l]ike a many-coloured humming top, he was at once be*wilder*ment and balance' (*CDN* 6:100; my emphasis). These are the necessary attributes of an accomplished wrestler. Having suspended his bout with Bentley, Chesterton now turned his attention to the Edwardian public at large. As a bruised correspondent to the *Daily News* later complained,

> [w]hile you are off your guard, he tightens his embrace, and presently in his burly arms you are floating among the clouds in some unearthly ballet of masked ideas. The pace quickens, and, dizzy with the gliding motion, the capricious steps, Mr. Chesterton suddenly flings you down.
> (H.N.B., 'A Last Word on Blind Spots', *DN* 26 Nov. 1907; *CDN* 4:350)

This riotous metaphysical masque is the subject to which I will now turn.

Notes

1 The correspondence can be found in the British Library's holdings of Chesterton's manuscripts. Bentley's diaries are housed at the Bodleian Library, University of Oxford. See List of Abbreviations for bibliographical details of both. The diaries are bound in ten volumes and are in good physical condition, although they have been tampered with by Bentley over what appears to be a number of years, from pages apparently torn out contemporaneously to sections more carefully excised, presumably when re-reading the diaries as research for *Those Days*. Occasional pencil markings would also appear to have been made by Bentley, or perhaps by his son, Nicolas, who read the diaries as research for his own memoir, *A Version of the Truth* (1960).
2 Ward appears to be alluding to this letter, though she does not cite it directly.

3 The first page of this draft is published in Chesterton, *Collected Nonsense, 2*, but the second page, quoted on p.32, remains unpublished.
4 The draft ends with the line, 'would it rhyme to Boileau?' (BL MS Add.73242 A fol. 3).
5 The revision reads: "Snobs are my joy: I never [knew?] / A more oppressive [aggressive?] ~~snob~~ cad than you. / Think me not flattering or fond / Nay do not blush: it is your due" (BL MS Add.73242 A fol. 2). The text is written on T. Fisher Unwin headed paper, which indicates that it almost certainly must have been composed between 1898 and 1900, in the period between Bentley's first meeting with Violet and the end of Chesterton's tenure at the publishing house.
6 When referring to decadence, I employ capitalisation in relation to writers and philosophies conventionally connected to the Decadent movement of the 1890s, and lowercase in relation to decadence in its wider cultural and ontological senses of degeneration and entropy.
7 At the time in which the *Greybeards* dedication was composed, Hankin was best known as a drama critic for the *Times*, where he worked from 1897 to 1899, as well as for writing short satirical pieces for *Punch*, from 1898 to 1903. For further details, see Phillips, 23–24. Hankin was a talented parodist, later producing two well-received collections, *Mr. Punch's Dramatic Sequels* (1901) and *Lost Masterpieces and Other Verses* (1904). In his autobiography, Chesterton acknowledges that Hankin's 'amusing literary travesties' showed him to be 'a man of real talent' (146).
8 Bentley judges the Bloggs 'what shall I say?—the least little bit neurotic. [...] My own belief is that if society were all Bloggs society would come to an abrupt conclusion' (Bod MS Eng.misc.e.866).
9 This is one of several versions of the rhyme. The second line of the illustrated manuscript version reads 'Was not fond of gravy' (*First*, 7). Bentley later asserted that the original composition had favoured 'Detested' (*First*, xv). Having given the matter careful consideration, the present author finds 'Abominated' to be the most satisfactory of the three.
10 The scholarly context of the clerihew is equally evident in a mock-confrontational clerihew, in which academic achievement is confused with moral rectitude, in a biographical context that throws an interesting light upon Chesterton's reference to dispatching snobs via the Dewar method:

> Professor Dewar
> Is a better man than you are.
> None of you asses
> Can condense gasses.
>
> (*Complete*, 39)

11 First published as 'Nonsense'.
12 In the diaries, Bentley later claims to have forced himself to take up chess against his temperamental inclinations: 'This plan of compelling myself to play chess, for which I have absolutely no taste, is amusing to me' (4 Jan. 1897; BL MS Eng.misc.e.866).
13 See Martin (25–46), for an account of the enduring distinction drawn historically between wit and humour.
14 Bentley seems also to be referring to an attempt on Chesterton's part to initiate a parodic correspondence: he demurs at the 'notion of writing things to people in imitation of the styles of other people' (BL MS Add.73191 fol. 36).
15 The lines perhaps also allude to the dialogue of the King and Queen of Hearts in *Alice*:

> "...you never had fits, my dear, I think?" he said to the Queen.
> "Never!" said the Queen, furiously, throwing an inkstand at the lizard as she spoke.
>
> (*Annotated*, 160)

16 'I marked the absent-minded scream, / The little nervous trick / Of rolling in the grate, with eyes / By friendship's light made quick. / But youth's black storms are gone and past...' (Chesterton, *Collected Nonsense*, 3).
17 In contrast, Chesterton archly informs readers of his autobiography of his 'regret that I have no gloomy and savage father to offer to the public gaze as the true cause of all my tragic heritage' (29). *Father Brown* stories such as 'The Doom of the Darnaways' (*Nash's Magazine*, June 1925) satirise this kind of fatalistic genetic thinking.
18 *Germinal* (1885) is the thirteenth novel in Zola's series.
19 In *Heretics*, Chesterton refers ironically to the culture of the 1890s, in which 'genial old Ibsen filled the world with wholesome joy, and the kindly tales of the forgotten Emile Zola kept our firesides merry and pure' (30).
20 William Oddie quotes from this letter, but suppresses all references to Bentley's mental condition, thus withholding the context that directly prompted the correspondence so as to imply that the pair were simply discussing the perils of pessimism in a detached, theoretical sense. See Oddie, 102–103.
21 See Oddie, 89/123, for further details.
22 This letter is not collected in the British Library's holdings of Chesterton's correspondence. It is first referred to in Ward, from which later biographers have perhaps taken it.
23 See Oddie, 329, for Chesterton's assertion, and Oddie, 160–61, for a more full account of the connection of this sketch to the final novel.
24 I discuss this aspect of the novel in more detail in 'G. K. Chesterton's Assimilation of *Fin-de-Siècle* Voices in *The Man Who Was Thursday*: The Dialogic Sensibility' (*English Literature in Transition, 1880-1920*, 59:3, 2016, pp. 320–40), in an account of the text's dialogic relation to the nursery rhyme, 'The Man of Thessaly', and Rudyard Kipling's short story, 'The Man Who Was' (1890).
25 Throughout these pages, I follow Bakhtin's capitalisation of Romanticism when referring to post-Enlightenment 'subjective, idealistic philosophy' (*Rabelais*, 37) in a wider sense, while employing lowercase romanticism to denote the aesthetic movement of the nineteenth century.
26 Chesterton was fond of this pun. In 'Books of the Day: The Works of Oscar Wilde', he praises the 'wild truth' and 'wild intellect' of the dramatist's greatest wit (*CDN* 6:98).
27 Chesterton describes his period of solipsism in his youthful poem, 'The Mirror of Madmen', as a nightmare of 'Vast choirs of upturned faces' in which 'every face was mine' (*CW* 10.1:232).
28 See, for example, 'The Man with Two Legs' (*CW* 14:769–71). This sketch was most likely composed in the late 1890s and also contains themes later incorporated into *The Man Who Was Thursday* and *The Club of Queer Trades* (1905).
29 This analysis bears echoes of Walter Pater's celebrated advocacy of Impressionism in the 'Conclusion' to *The Renaissance* (1873). Despite his implied demurral at Pater's philosophy, elsewhere Chesterton terms the conclusion of *The Renaissance* a 'splendid peroration' (*CW* 15:451).

2 The Ethics of Travesty
Chesterton's Ludicrous Performance on the Edwardian Literary Stage

[T]he costume must be an argument[.]
—Roland Barthes, 'The Diseases of Costume' (46)

"I am the Last Liberal," said Murrel. "In fact I've escaped from Madame Tussaud's."
—Chesterton, *The Return of Don Quixote* (CW 8:220)

Discussing his first entry into public life in his autobiography, Chesterton recalled that at this threshold moment 'my wife [...] disguised me as far as possible in the large hat and cloak familiar to caricaturists' (164). This intervention has conventionally been assigned a utilitarian rationale: Frances's notoriously absent-minded and physically cumbersome husband could not be relied upon to dress himself appropriately to dine with fellow writers or deliver public lectures unless he was supplied with a single, easily manageable, and capacious uniform. Nonetheless, Chesterton's insistent corroboration of this burlesque scenario suggests that his interest in adopting the outfit extended beyond sartorial pragmatism to a more performative self-dramatisation, as illustrated by his augmentation of the diaphanous black cloak and wide-brimmed 'brigand's' (Chesterton, *Autobiography*, 137) hat with an extravagantly flourished swordstick. These seemingly contradictory qualities—the enthusiastic confession of bumbling incompetence and the self-aggrandising performance of swashbuckling bravado—are curiously entangled throughout Chesterton's biography, each aspect a consciously proffered gift to the caricaturist, yet also a literal and figurative cloak for the persona beneath.

The continuous factor in the two elements is travesty, the etymological root of which—the French *travesti*—means 'dressed in disguise' (Barnhart, 1162). By the seventeenth century, the term had accrued an implicitly rhetorical, debasing connotation: to be 'dressed so as to be made ridiculous, parodied, burlesqued' (Barnhart, 1162). The two definitions come together in Chesterton's merging of his proclivity for rhetorical burlesque—in the modern sense, unclothing or revealing—with his taste for sartorial travesty—or costuming, camouflaging—to produce a curiously equivocal striptease, combining self-exposure and self-concealment, rather as the costumes adopted in the climactic pageant of *The Man Who Was Thursday* function as a 'disguise [that does] not disguise, but reveal'.

While Chesterton would have found sympathy with Barthes' theatrical dictum, he might have gone on to execute one of his characteristic switchbacks: the costume must be an argument, and the argument must be costumed. By consistently dressing his rhetoric in the self-deprecating tones of the public buffoon, while dressing his body in such a way as to pass off the whole performance as a playful masquerade, Chesterton's multilayered self-travestying enabled him to carve out a distinctive role amongst the panoply of literary practitioners who paraded their profession ostentatiously before the gaze of the Edwardian public. Nonetheless, his disquiet over the commercial expedients that drove this 'display of his own persona' (Coates, *G.K. Chesterton*, 145) in the modern cultural marketplace also led him to mistrust the peculiarly literal corporate body that he had constructed. The histrionic construct of the fugitive from Madame Tussaud's was not always a performance that sat harmoniously with the private individual. Consequently, as the decade progressed, he increasingly strived to assemble a coherent ethics of travesty through which to navigate an era that he termed, with considerable ambivalence, the 'age of publicity' (qtd. in Ker, 616).

A Licensed Jester

Having been offered a regular contributory role on the Liberal periodical, the *Speaker*, in 1900, Chesterton's first major journalistic success came with his series of cultural 'Defence' essays, composed and collected the following year as *The Defendant*. The contents of this series break down broadly into two categories—aesthetic defences of popular forms (detective stories, penny dreadfuls, nonsense, farce) and ethical defences of undervalued cultural and existential phenomena (slang, skeletons, ugly things). The most famous antecedents of Chesterton's format are, of course, Sir Philip Sidney's 'Defence of Poesy' (1595) and Percy Bysshe Shelley's 'A Defence of Poetry' (1840). However, Chesterton inverts the advocacy of the sublime that underpinned these earlier models. As with his defense of popular parody in the 'Bret Harte' essay, rather than recruiting 'high' forms of culture to defend the legitimacy of the subjects under discussion, Chesterton focuses upon forms conventionally considered frivolous, scurrilous, or unrefined, which he re-evaluates as 'high and legitimate forms of art [...] worthy of moral reverence and artistic ambition' (*Defendant*, 123/125).

This critical method takes inspiration partially from the embrace of the vulgar that Chesterton had discovered in the work of Walt Whitman and

Samuel Johnson. Whitman's importance in sustaining Chesterton through his youthful traumas has long been recognised, primarily because Chesterton directs the reader of the *Thursday* preface to the correct source. If Wilde is the villain of the novel's dedicatory verses, then Whitman is unquestionably the hero—the textual helpmeet to the Chesterbentley, whose *Leaves of Grass* (1855) first sent out a 'cry of cleaner things' from the poet's home in 'fish-shaped Paumanok' (*CW* 6:472). Chesterton termed Whitman 'the greatest man of the nineteenth century' ('Conventions and the Hero', *DN* 15 Oct. 1904; *CDN* 2:313) and projected his sense of identification in the binary terms of a battle line with his vision of a 'war without any truce [...] between Schopenhauer and Whitman'.

Chesterton's view that the bonds of friendship formed the antidote to pessimism derived much of its ardency from Whitman's visionary evocation of the 'new city of Friends' (164). Cecil Chesterton recalled that his brother ecstatically embraced Whitman's vision of 'the redemption of the world by comradeship' (qtd. in Oddie, 135), while Chesterton argued that Whitman's most valuable lesson had been the principle that 'comradeship [... is] the permanent foundation of democracy' ('Summer Festivals and Ceremonies', *ILN* 19 May 1906; *CW* 27:190). This utopian conjunction was decisive in shaping Chesterton's later 'mystic passion' (O'Connor, 88) for democracy, which finds cultural expression in *The Defendant*. Freya Johnston argues that one of the chief distinctions of Whitman's verse is its 'enumerative method of assembling high and low materials precisely in order "to enlarge" the literary empire's "limits"' (65). As Chesterton later expressed the principle, this form of cultural egalitarianism should not be thought of as a 'dull levelling but an enthusiastic lifting' (*CW* 3:148).

This ethos derives equally from the influence of Samuel Johnson, whose 'prefaces and dedications are [often] written in defence of transparently low subjects [such as] the game of draughts' (Johnston, 96), a principle of 'enlarging trifles' (Johnston, 94) that finds a close parallel in Chesterton's choice of the title *Tremendous Trifles* (1909) for a later essay collection. Although Johnson often exploited the juxtaposition of '"official verbal machinery" and "colloquial phrases"' for comic purposes, this was invariably in the more fundamental service of 'confronting high ideas with "inelegant applications" to common life' (Johnson qtd. in Johnston, 11) with the aim of demonstrating that 'there is, on Christian terms, no definitively mean subject: "in the Christian context humble everyday things [...] become compatible with the lofty style"' (Johnson qtd. in Johnston, 15). This account could be applied word for word to Chesterton's intent in the 'Defence' essays. As he asserts elsewhere, in the 'vast metaphysical democracy of things', all phenomena are equal: 'Not only are all men brothers, but all ideas are brothers. All things are equal, and therefore in the whole wide world there is no such thing as a bathos' ('A Good Miscellany', *DN* 10 Oct. 1903; *CDN* 2:137).

Notwithstanding this idealistic precept, there is also a more confrontational dimension to this advocacy of the quotidian, which Chesterton shares with Whitman and which expresses itself precisely in the satirical identification of bathos in the rejected cultural other. Whitman's accumulative ethos inevitably set him at odds with those who embodied the opposing principle of discrimination and refinement in nineteenth-century culture. Ironically, this caused Whitman to inject a certain discriminatory exclusivity into his own rhetoric. For example, he asserts, with a self-checking equivocation, that 'I accept the world—most of the world—but somehow draw the line somewhere on [the] great army of critics, parlour apostles' (qtd. in Trilling, 397). A comparable kernel of ambivalence is discernible in his utopian 'city of friends'. Whitman explains that this establishes 'a city invincible to the attacks of the whole of the rest of the earth' (105), a gathering of forces to defeat a worldly opponent, rather than a truly idealistic unification of humanity. The nature of the forces against which Whitman sought to position himself is illustrated by his rather Rabelaisian enumeration of the evils of a world 'rich, hefted, lousy, reeking, with delicacy, refinement, elegance, prettiness, propriety, criticism, analysis' (qtd. in Trilling, 397).

Whitman's invincible city is evoked in the *Thursday* dedication when Chesterton recalls that he and Bentley 'held the fort, our tiny flags unfurled' (*CW* 6:472) against the tide of Decadence, a movement that comes under implicit fire in *The Defendant* for its excessive delicacy. Whereas the crude realm of popular literature 'is always on the side of life' *Defendant*, (27), Chesterton considers contemporary high culture to be characterised by 'a decadent and diseased purity' (59), an oxymoronic juxtaposition that echoes the quasi-nonsensical category mistake of Whitman's 'reeking [...] refinement'. In 'A Defence of Slang', Chesterton articulates the issue at stake as a contrast between rhetorical vitality and atrophy:

> The aristocracy [has lost its] function of standing to the world for the idea of variety, experiment, and colour, and we must find these things in some other class. [...It] is to certain sections of the lower class [...] with their rich and rococo mode of thought, that we must look for guidance [...] Nothing is more striking than the contrast between the heavy, formal, lifeless slang of the man-about-town and the light, living, and flexible slang of the coster.
>
> (*Defendant*, 142)

Chesterton's sublimation of the unrefined consequently becomes bound up with an exposition of the bathos of the sophisticated. In a discussion of Maurice Maeterlink in 'The Failure of the Aesthetes' (*ILN* 25 Dec. 1909), he emphasises the air of equivalence between 'low' and 'high' aesthetic forms that results from choosing to view the author's work in a burlesque light: 'Once shift your sympathy by an inch, and "Pelleas and Melisande" becomes a roaring farce' (*CW* 28:450).[1] Discussing Wilde in similar terms in *The Victorian Age in Literature*, he argues that this shift of sympathy draws the critic into line with the position of the populace at large: a sense of the poet's absurdity will arise if 'the reader [should only] move his standpoint one inch nearer the popular standpoint' (*CW* 15:518).

This perspectival adjustment enables Chesterton to refine his knack for pinpointing unintentional self-parody in Wilde's work, ironically turning the latter's earnestness against him with a critical laughter that Chesterton claims to have evaded the unconsciously comical poet:

> In Wilde's poetry we have particularly a perpetually toppling possibility of the absurd; a sense of just falling too short or just going too far. [... One feels] that Wilde is poised on the edge of a precipice of bathos.
>
> (*CW* 15:518)

To illustrate the point, Chesterton cites the lines, 'These Christs that die upon the barricades / God knows that I am with them—in some ways', before going on to conjure an irreverent image of 'Wilde lolling like an elegant leviathan on a sofa' while composing his complacent paean to popular insurrection 'between the whiffs of a scented cigarette' (*CW* 15:518).[2]

Despite Chesterton's stress upon the populist sympathies that enable him to make such leaps of critical distance, his knack for identifying bathos in Wilde was substantially inspired by a figure whom Chesterton considered to possess 'every merit except democracy': Max Beerbohm ('Popular Jokes and Vulgarity', *ILN* 21 Mar. 1908; *CW* 28:66). Writing of this relationship, Cecil Chesterton sought to complicate the question of who had influenced whom, in another account that takes inspiration from Wilde's precept in 'The Decay of Lying' that life imitates art: 'I am prepared to uphold that Nature, in an hour of terrible joy, fashioned Mr Beerbohm after taking note of what was written in a tattered exercise-book of Mr Chesterton's school days' (Unsigned, 92–93). If this is the case, Nature had cribbed Chesterton's papers in order to do his bidding, since, as Terry Caesar notes, 'a good part of [Beerbohm's] early career was spent hoaxing, parodying, and generally making fun of [Wilde]' (24). Beerbohm's methods included the composition of ever-more monstrously inflated caricatures of Wilde in which the latter's would-be sublime dandyism is reimagined as a ridiculous clash between the will-to-artifice and the exigencies of nature (Figure 2.1, overleaf).

Figure 2.1 Caricature of Oscar Wilde by Max Beerbohm, 1894.

Beerbohm's gargantuan imagery might perhaps have contributed to Chesterton's apprehensive view of Wilde as occupying a disproportionate amount of space on the late-Victorian stage; if so, it also suggested a paradoxical means of cutting Decadence down to size, which Chesterton later refined textually in the bathetic image of the lolling leviathan. Beerbohm's simultaneous building up and knocking down of Wilde reflects his singular ability to project both proximity to, and distance from, Decadence, a skill that does not seem to have been lost on the young Chesterton. *The Defendant* operates not merely as a parody of the sublime perorations of Sidney and Shelley, or a sympathetic adaptation of the cultural precepts of Whitman and Johnson, but also as a series of pastiches of the essay that provided Beerbohm's *entrée* to the literary world, 'A Defence of Cosmetics' (1894), published in the Decadent house-magazine, the *Yellow Book*.

'A Defence of Cosmetics' was a deliberate 'hoax' (Beerbohm qtd. in Felstiner, 15) on conventional late-Victorian essayistic practice, taking the form of a 'mock-encomium' (Felstiner, 11) to a seemingly trivial facet of Decadent fashion. The mock-encomium is an academic nonsense-form that proverbially 'combine[s] a low subject with the rhetorical techniques appropriate to a high one' (Malcolm, 96), thus producing a humorous 'contradiction between form and content, the form being that of an oration arguing strenuously about high matters, and the content being perversely inconsequential' (Malcolm, 11). Beerbohm's methodology prefigures Chesterton's conceit of discussing apparently trivial subjects in the loftiest of mock-*belles-lettristic* tones, exploiting a comic mode of rhetorical reverse-travesty openly acknowledged by Chesterton in the introduction to *Tremendous Trifles*: 'If anyone says that these are very small affairs talked about in very big language, I can only gracefully compliment him upon seeing the joke' (6). Nonetheless, while Chesterton borrows Beerbohm's playfully parodic style and method of defending 'low' subject-matter by referring the reader to the authority of the ages over the vagaries of contemporary taste, his 'Defence' articles are tonally quite distinct, shying away from the inveterate flippancy and non-committal character that Beerbohm shared with Bentley. In contrast, Chesterton protests that his own essays are 'ethically sincere' (*Defendant*, 8) in their promotion of the subjects under discussion.

In *Heretics*, Chesterton draws upon a fourth antecedent of the *Defendant* method in order to refute the conventional notion that 'funny is the opposite of serious' (121): 'Mr. Bernard Shaw is funny and sincere' (122). Chesterton invested much time and energy in projecting himself as Shaw's antithesis; nonetheless, their relationship was again based upon a complex interplay of similarity and difference. Although Shaw's ornamenting of his sincerely held views with a tone of playful paradox influenced Chesterton's journalistic voice, *Heretics* sets out to emphasise their ideological opposition, devoting a chapter to the demerits of Shaw's philosophy—chiefly that 'Shaw is not a democrat' (*CW* 11:400). Even in doing so, Chesterton apes the comical impudence of Shaw's rhetorical tone in controversy, explaining that the title of his collection applies to any 'man whose view of things has the hardihood to differ from mine' (*Heretics*, 13). In the preface to *George Bernard Shaw*, Chesterton has fun parodying this 'amusing trick of self-praise' (*CW* 11:479), explaining that rather than producing the smooth, unobtrusive prose of the conventional journalistic leader-writer, Shaw might declaim obstreperously,

> "[t]he element of religion, as I explain religion, in the Puritan rebellion (which you wholly misunderstand), if hostile to art—that is what I mean by art—may have saved it from some evils (remember my definition of evil) in which the French Revolution—of which I have my own opinion, involved morality, which I will define for you in a minute."
> (*CW* 11:363–64)

Chesterton employed this rhetorical insight to distinguish himself verbally in the staged seriocomic wit contests that punctuated his public engagement with Shaw. As he later recalled, the pair 'met more in public than in private; and generally upon platforms [...] especially upon platforms where we were put up to fight each other, like two knock-about comedians' (*Autobiography*, 228). Though they always remained on friendly terms, Shaw's verbal approach to Chesterton was characterised by a relentless insolence, to which the latter responded with a comically incongruous surfeit of civility. In the transcript of 'Do We Agree?', a public debate between the pair in 1928, Chesterton attests meekly to the 'vast superiority' of his opponent's 'powerful intellect' (*CW* 11:547) shortly before Shaw blusters that 'Mr. Chesterton's speech tempted me to get up and smite him over the head with my umbrella' (*CW* 11:552). Chesterton responds to this physical threat with mock-abjection: 'When Mr. Shaw refrains from hitting me over the head' it is a consequence of 'his real kindness of heart, which makes him tolerant of the humblest creatures of God' (*CW* 11:553).

Although Chesterton might seem to be getting a raw deal in such exchanges, elsewhere he implied that he was playing a more canny game of subversive mirroring: 'When Mr. Bernard Shaw tries in a genial way to bully me, I am merely moved to bully him back, with an even more brutal geniality' ('Books of the Day: The Religion of H.G. Wells', *DN* 6 Nov. 1908; *CDN* 5:202). Chesterton's performance pitches him as the wise fool to Shaw's philosopher-king, fending off the latter's blows with a capering dexterity, while acting as humble truth-teller to the imperious cultural personage. In setting up this dynamic, Chesterton again took inspiration from Beerbohm's relationship to Wilde. Beerbohm had consistently undermined Wilde's attempts to project exquisite detachment, playing paradoxically urbane jester to the lordly figure whose aesthetic movement Chesterton considered to have '*ruled* the culture of the age' (my emphasis).

In a verse tribute to Beerbohm, Chesterton ascribes to him 'a shameless impudence / As shameless a humility' (qtd. in Ward, *Gilbert*, 135). If this sounds like an apt epigram on the court jester, Beerbohm's broader demeanour also accorded with Chesterton's dictum on the wit and the buffoon: 'Do not fancy you can be a detached wit and avoid being a buffoon; you cannot. If you are the Court Jester you must be the Court Fool' ('The Flat Freak', *DN* 8 Jan. 1910; *CDN* 6:178). Beerbohm's consistent self-deprecation countered any misapprehension that he perceived his own position to be uniquely dignified. John Felstiner cites Beerbohm's instruction to a would-be biographer to critically undermine him wherever possible, observing that the 'personal myths [that Beerbohm] established are always in some sense designed to lessen himself' (26). A similar story is told by Chesterton's colleague at *G.K.'s Weekly*, W.R. Titterton, who recalled that it was 'a martyrdom' for his editor to be the face of the paper, but that he finally agreed to the use of his image on the proviso that it should take the form of a 'highly satirical, insulting and otherwise unflattering' caricature (qtd. in Ker, 512). As Michael Asquith has pointed out, Chesterton's 'willingness to make himself ridiculous in public' made him seem 'so far the reverse of pompous that you might almost say he was always standing on his *in*dignity', glorying 'in his failures and fiascos' (120).

Ian Boyd observes that 'the fool figure [...] seems to have held a permanent fascination for Chesterton' (140); certainly, this was the prism through which many of his contemporaries viewed him, both for good and ill, although the praise and blame did not always come from the directions one might expect. Whereas a reviewer of *The Ball and The Cross* in the progressive *Freethinker* approved Chesterton's cultural role as a 'licenced jester [...] Attired in motley and banging a bladder' (Smith, 'A Licensed Jester', 16 Oct. 1910; 242/240), the Dean of St Paul's, William Inge, dismissed his journalistic output as 'the elephantine capers of an obese mountebank' (qtd. in Shaw, 'Tribute', 539). These conflicting responses reflect a cultural ambivalence over the buffoon-figure as deeply ingrained as that which attended to the parodist. If the latter had frequently been conceived by the late-Victorians as 'some sort of scrofular, scurrilous second-rater who failed to make the grade himself and now indulges his spleen by jeering [... at] his helpless subject' (Kiremidjian, 'Aesthetics', 232), George Eliot ventriloquised a comparable view of burlesque buffoonery through her critical alter ego, 'Theophrastus Such', who laments

> the sadly confused inference of the monotonous jester that he is establishing his superiority over every less facetious person, and over every topic on which he is ignorant or insensible, by being uneasy until he has distorted it in the small cracked mirror which he carries about with him as a joking apparatus.
>
> (95)

There is a trace of this disposition in the taunting titular irony of Chesterton's satire of the Wildean dandy, 'The Painful Fall of a Great Reputation', which hints at the pleasure that the manufacturer of bathos takes in the spectacle of the cultural other being brought down low. As Eliot's 'Such' argues, this attitude contributes to a 'Debasing' of 'the Moral Currency' (95). Conscious of these potential criticisms, Chesterton sought doggedly to advance a contrary interpretation of buffoonery based upon moral elevation. Much as the 'Bret Harte' essay stresses the humility upon which successful parody depends—'real parody [is] inseparable from admiration [...] Mere derision, mere contempt, never produced or could produce parody' (*Varied*, 184)—his journalism sets out to ethically legitimise buffoonery, justifying the jester role as a means of challenging authority: 'I can say what I feel about the politicians, as the Fool in the old Court could say what he felt about the King' ('Liberty, Liberalism and the Libertarians', *ILN* 3 Mar. 1928; *CW* 34:482).

In 'An Apology for Buffoons' (*London Mercury*, June 1928), Chesterton observes that 'I myself, who am a very minor buffoon [...] do regularly as a matter of business make a multitude of bad jokes. I do it for reasons of demagogy' (*CW* 3:355). Contrary to the commonly held pejorative view of the demagogue as a sower of discord and demoralisation—'a political agitator appealing to the basest instincts of a mob' (Thompson, 357)—Chesterton claims demagogic buffoonery to be a force for social cohesion, forging connections in an otherwise schismatic society: the 'whole case for buffoons is that jokes ought to be obvious [... today] a chasm has opened in the community of beliefs and social traditions, which can only be spanned by the far halloo of the buffoon' (*CW* 3:355).

Chesterton's demagoguery derives from a willed identification with the 'mob', a socio-political extension of the culturally 'populist standpoint' that he advocates as a means of disclosing the absurdity of Wilde's aesthetics. The private prehistory of his psychological struggles is central to this public performance—in *Thursday*, Syme's mental recovery is accompanied by a revelation of the benignity of '"the mob"' (*CW* 6:604). In the year of the novel's publication, Chesterton commented that it was 'painful to notice that at the present time mobs are not properly admired' ('The Hysteria of Mobs', *ILN* 18 Jan. 1908; *CW* 28:26). On another occasion, he notes that 'to appreciate the virtues of the mob one must [...] be on a level with it (as I am)' ('The Garden of the Sea', *DN* 20 Aug. 1910; *CDN* 6:313). However, as he explains in 'The Suffragist', the demagogue is not only at one with the people, but also stands apart in the role of ethical standard-bearer: '"demagogue," in the good Greek meaning, does not mean one who pleases the populace, but one who leads it' (collected in *Miscellany*, 7). By using his journalistic position to act as an advocate for the masses, Chesterton posits himself as a cultural loudhailer at the disposal of a silenced majority, in opposition to the cloistered coteries that he considered to overwhelmingly dominate the cultural conversation of the age. He strives to become the public's representative in the press, a disruptive fifth-column columnist: 'the only quite uncultured person in England who writes articles' ('The Orthodoxy of Hamlet', *DN* 18 May 1907; *CDN* 4:222).

However, the 'matter of business' that Chesterton uses to signify 'regularly' in 'An Apology for Buffoons' also hints at the more prosaic considerations that underpinned his performance of buffoonery. Inge's term, 'mountebank', connotes both a 'clown' and a 'swindler [...] appealing to an audience from a platform' (Thompson, 889), thus hinting at another of the accusations conventionally levelled at the buffoon: that of debasing the moral currency in pursuit of more literal coin. The clown at the medieval dining table was considered a '[p]arasite' (Welsford, *Fool*, 8) who must sing for his supper: *parasitos*, another derivation of the prefix 'para', translates literally as 'beside food', so that the original meaning of the social parasite was one 'who eats at the table of another, earning meals by flattery' (Barnhart, 756). When Chesterton first achieved celebrity with his journalistic work on the *Speaker* and the *Daily News*, he was a young, recently married man with no private means. His ability to financially support his household was directly connected to the relative popularity of his journalism. In a letter designed to financially reassure Frances, he writes that 'everything depends just now [... on] keeping wide awake to the turn of the market [...] getting the feelings and tendencies of other men' (Ward, *Gilbert*, 128).

The journalistic culture that Chesterton was entering thrived upon controversy: rather than making one's way by *flattering* the feelings and tendencies of other men, the crucial question was how one might set oneself up in viable opposition. In the case of the Chesterton/Shaw double-act, the resulting projection of pristine difference prompted consistent sidelong critical glances. The pair's endlessly protracted duel was viewed in certain quarters as a mutually beneficial 'sham fight' (*Gilbert*, 191), as Ward puts it: 'when Shaw reviewed Chesterton on Shaw, more than one paper waxed sarcastic on the point of royalties and remuneration gained by these means' (*Gilbert*, 205). Desmond Gleeson argued that 'G.K.C. and G.B.S. contrived to make one another' (qtd. in Ward, *Return*, 224), while Wills recurs to imagery suggestive of a *Father Brown* mystery: 'Even in their obvious contrasts there was a certain symmetry, like the precise reversal of a man's image in a mirror' (*Chesterton*, 116). Vivian Carter even mooted the jocular possibility that 'Chesterton' was an elaborate disguise adopted by Shaw for intertwined psychological and commercial purposes:

> Shaw, it is said, tired of Socialism, weary of wearing Jaegers, and broken down by teetotalism and vegetarianism, sought, some years ago, an escape from them. His adoption, however, of these attitudes had a decided commercial value, which he did not think it advisable to prejudice by wholesale surrender. Therefore he, in order to taste the forbidden joys of individualistic philosophy, meat, food and strong drink, created "Chesterton".
> (*Bystander*, Sept. 1909; qtd. in Ker, 248)

Shaw was tickled by such trapdoor conceits, affirming nonchalantly that 'I have never pretended that G.B.S. was real: I have over and over again taken him to pieces before the audience to shew the trick of him' ('Chesterbelloc', 137), as though he were his own ventriloquist's dummy. In contrast, Chesterton experienced considerable disquiet over the depersonalising drift of these public personae, an unease compounded by the fusion of commercial promotion and personal demotion bound up with his buffoonish self-branding. On his first lecture tour of America—a money-making exercise that followed the example famously set by Wilde—he complained that the crowd seemed content for the speaker 'merely [to] exhibit himself on a stand or platform for a stipulated sum; or be exhibited like a monster in a menagerie' (qtd. in Ker, 436). These stresses come to a head in a letter sent to Ronald Knox in the early 1920s following the death of Chesterton's father, in which an air of extreme dissociation between the private self and the public image emerges:

> I am in a state now when I feel a monstrous charlatan, as if I wore a mask and were stuffed with cushions, whenever I see anything about the public G.K.C.; it hurts me; for though the views I express are real, the image is horribly unreal compared with the real person [...] public comments about my religious position seem [...] as if they are about somebody else – as indeed they are. I am not troubled about a great fat man who appears on platforms and in caricatures, even when *he* enjoys controversies on what *I* believe to be the right side.
>
> (qtd. in Ker, 470; my emphases)

In order to navigate the self-alienating conditions of modern celebrity, Chesterton set about constructing a still-more sophisticated vision of the ethical parameters of public buffoonery.

The Half-Conscious Buffoon

The performance of abjection that punctuated Chesterton's public engagements with Shaw finds a corollary in Enid Welsford's account of the buffoon who is made to pay for the licence to criticise by accepting a debased social status, 'earn[ing] his living by an openly acknowledged failure to attain to the normal standard of human dignity' (3). As early as 1907, J.A. Hammerton observed that some critics accused Chesterton of attempting 'to conceal his mental deficiency' through paradox (255). Chesterton's intuitive response seems to have been: if you can't beat 'em, join 'em. From the 'Ballade of the Grotesque', into which he inserts himself as a case study (see Ward, *Gilbert*, 139), to the numerous epigrams of bodily self-deprecation that attained a legendary status in his own time, Chesterton's insistent documentation of his shortcomings bears a striking resemblance to Welsford's account of the 'court-fool' who

> causes amusement not merely by absurd gluttony [...] but by mental deficiencies or physical deformities which [...] put him in the paradoxical position of virtual outlawry combined with utter dependence on the support of the social group to which he belongs.
> (55)

Chesterton alludes opaquely to this state of dependency in a privately circulated parody of Shelley's 'An Exhortation' (1820), which begins with mockery of his own physical infirmity (he was recovering from a bout of whooping cough at the time) before deflating the sublime rhetoric of the antecedent defence counsel via imagery that commercially debunks the target while placing the parasitic parodist beside food:

> Shelley, the ethereal bard, who had
> A tidy income from his dad,
> Sang (as his month's allowance came)
> That poets live on love and fame:
> The poet who has penned these lines
> On more material matter dines.
>
> (Ward, *Return*, 150)

Chesterton's financial dependence upon the journalistic forum within which he paraded his deficiencies made the power dynamic of this performance queasily ambivalent. This resulted in a curiously vexed relationship between jobbing writer and audience, complicated further by the fact that his principal readership was not so much the populace at large for whom he thought to intercede, as a progressive subsection of the middle class whom he was attempting to re-educate.[3] An illustration of the resulting tension occurs at the beginning of *The Flying Inn*, in the seemingly un-Chestertonian guise of an atheist tub-thumping at the seaside: '"Hypocrites!" he would say; and then they would throw him money. "Dupes and dastards!" and then they would throw him more money' (8). In a review of *The Napoleon of Notting Hill*, Bentley discusses Chesterton's relationship to his readership in strikingly comparable terms: he 'hurls himself upon [...] the hyper-aesthetic, ultra-literary' members of his audience, 'fells them and grinds them to powder; and they clamour for a repetition of the treatment' ('Novel', *Bystander*, 27 Apr. 1904; 97).

Chesterton's unusually frequent application of the second person pronoun in his journalism exemplifies the adversarial dynamic at hand. In drawing the reader into the frame of the text, so as to break down the sense of clear distinction between speaker and auditor, this carnivalesque device enables Chesterton to tread an ambiguous line between arch acerbity and obsequious flattery, whether implicating the reader in his abjection—'quite stupid people (like you and me)' ('The Daisy as Imperial Symbol', *ILN* 8 June 1907; *CW* 27:482)—or deploying physical and intellectual praise with an extravagance that edges towards the ironic—'with your well-known Herculean strength' ('The Falsity of Statistics', *ILN* 18 Nov. 1905; *CW* 27:60), 'in the words of Aristotle (the Greek of which you have on the tip of your tongue)' ('Public Houses', *ILN* 9 Dec. 1905; *CW* 27:77). Of course, this conceit was not his own invention—it extends from the 'familiarity with the spectators' (Welsford, 288) evinced by the Elizabethan stage-fool back to antiquity. As Chesterton observes in the 'Humour' essay, in Aristophanes 'Dionysus asks to see the wicked in hell and is answered by a gesture pointing at the audience' (*Spice*, 26).

This confrontational buffoonery also brings to mind a more modern and less intuitive influence: Charles Baudelaire. Few would think to place the two men together, not least since Chesterton refers to the father of modernist verse as 'loathsome' (*G.F. Watts*, 17) on one of the few occasions upon which he acknowledges his existence at all. Nonetheless, Baudelaire's critical writing finds a place in the family line of seriocomic encomia to which *The Defendant* contributes: Felstiner notes that although 'Beerbohm seldom mentioned him, it is striking how close Baudelaire's claims and his style' (9) come to Beerbohm's in his essay, 'In Praise of Cosmetics', from *The Painter of Modern Life* (1863). Compagnon discusses Baudelaire as a pioneer of the antimodern temperament (see Rulo, 255), and his 'defiant self-distancing from and complicity with his bourgeois public' (Habib, 237) finds a close echo in Chesterton's mocking accounts of the 'insignificant corner of the world which forms the educated society of which *you and I* are the sparkling ornaments' ('The Blank State of the Modern Mind', *ILN* 3 Apr. 1926; *CW* 34:71; my emphasis).

The Painter of Modern Life includes a treatise on 'The Essence of Laughter' (1855), in which Baudelaire strikingly anticipates the methods through which Chesterton managed his public persona. Here, Baudelaire develops the principle of *dédoublement*, a phenomenon exemplified by the 'philosopher [who has] acquired by habit a power of rapid self-division and thus of assisting as a disinterested spectator at the phenomena of his own ego' (154). When applied in a literary context, this scenario posits a heightened self-mastery in which the performing writer/actor is kept under constant surveillance by the critical police officer at the artist's shoulder. Baudelaire summarises this dynamic as a counterbalance of immersion and self-distancing, in a phrase immediately suggestive of the operation of parody: the comic performer has attained 'the power of being oneself and someone else at one and the same time' (165).

Baudelaire's exemplary practitioner of *dédoublement* is the comic actor, or stage clown. As he explains, the amateur philosopher first discovers the skill 'of rapid self-division' in the act of tripping over, at which point her/his apprehension of the self-as-spectacle is rendered painfully lucid. This fleeting insight is refined and rendered programmatic by the professional comedian, who makes 'a business of developing in themselves their feeling for the comic, and of dispensing it for the amusement of their fellows' (165). Baudelaire's account corresponds to Chesterton's distinction between the 'unconscious buffoon', who is merely 'a blockhead', and the 'conscious buffoon', who is 'a humorist' (*CW* 15:487), a parallel that accords, in turn, with Malcolm's account of the enduring historical 'dual-category' of the 'fool', 'which spanned lunatics and mental defectives on the one hand ("natural fools") and witty entertainers ("artificial fools") on the other' (113–14).

For the modern public figure, consciousness of this dynamic offers a means of warding off a humiliating absence of self-possession. Chesterton could be pitilessly forensic in locating and exploiting the 'blind spot[s]' in fellow writers, which he considered to be caused by a 'sudden inaccessibility to laughter' (*William Blake*, 28). Despite his admiration of Whitman's merits, he claimed to have uncovered 'his only defect, that he never does see the fun of himself' ('The Great Simplicity', *DN* 27 July 1907; *CDN* 4:269), much as he pictured Wilde stumbling unknowingly towards a 'precipice of bathos'. In contrast, Gary Saul Morson identifies '*pre-emptive self-parody*' (78) as a mode of ironic address that serves to second-guess criticism, thereby rendering it superfluous. Anthony Burgess noted that Chesterton was particularly adept at deploying this strategy—in refusing to take 'himself seriously', he consistently 'anticipated the parodist and the satirical cartoon' ('Level', 251). As Chesterton puts it himself, 'You can say anything against a man who praises himself; but a man who blames himself is invulnerable' ('The Faults of the Press', *ILN* 26 Oct.1907; *CW* 27:576).

Accordingly, Chesterton's second-person journalistic assaults are not only characterised by offence, but also defence, in the form of explicit pre-empting of criticism: '[w]hen I came down to breakfast I looked at the morning paper; not (as you humorously suggest) at the evening paper' ('Hamlet and the Psycho-Analyst'; collected in *Fancies*, 21); 'this is not, as you are at this moment saying that it is, a mere fancy' ('The Unintelligence of Our Civilisation', *DN* 21 May 1904; *CDN* 2:230). Think also of the journalistic article that originally housed his 'Sonnet to a Stilton Cheese' ('The Shy Town', *DN* 29 Apr. 1911), in which the mockery of the parodist's corpulence is accompanied by a nod to the reader's assumed foreknowledge of his mental frailties. As Canovan notes, in *Robert Browning* Chesterton 'misquoted a great many of Browning's lines; staggeringly, he [...] even unconsciously invented a new line for Browning's poem "Mr. Sludge the Medium"' (13). Conscious that he had become renowned for such lapses, Chesterton prefaces the skit by alluding to his absent-mindedness as a paradoxical means of advertising his self-awareness: 'I feel myself as if some literary influence, something that has haunted me, were present in this otherwise original poem; but it is hopeless to disentangle it now' (*CDN* 7:120).

Nonetheless, there is an unaddressed danger in Baudelaire's argument that the knack of *dédoublement* is 'acquired by habit'. While Chesterton's performances of self-consciousness suggest that a complex mixture of the parody of others and of oneself may be an effective way of managing one's sense of self on the public stage, this interrogation of the reader ironically ends by becoming a predictable mannerism in itself, recurring in article after article. As John Gross observes, '[l]ike all platform performers, [Chesterton] runs the risk of being trapped by his own style' (241). In this sense, the job of the parodist is to highlight the degeneration of a character actor into self-typecasting. Think of Henri Bergson's view of the 'practical joke' as an ethical intervention, designed to identify a lapse into 'mechanical inelasticity [...] where one would expect to find the wide-awake adaptability and the living pliableness of a human being' (10). As Bergson summarises, the exploited quality is a certain rigidity of body, mind and character, that society would [...] like to get rid of in order to obtain from its members the greatest possible degree of elasticity and sociability. This rigidity is the comic, and laughter is its corrective.

(21)

A playful instance of this urge to police rigidity is presented by Beerbohm's response to the dozens of encomia to Christmas that Chesterton produced, year in, year out, for his various journalistic employers. Beerbohm parodies this activity in 'Some Damnable Errors about Christmas', a mock-essay in his collection, *A Christmas Garland* (1912). While Beerbohm's title skewers Chesterton's occasional over-enthusiasm for correcting his readers' assumed subscription to idiotic fallacies, he has 'Ch*st*rt*n' end his article with the ominous threat, 'I shall return to the subject of Christmas next week' (22). Beerbohm inscribes an ambiguity over whether 'Ch*st*rt*n' is joking or in earnest here—the implication arises that self-reflexivity does not preclude the repetition of a predictable tic. Likewise, when Chesterton advises the readers of the *Daily News* 'I will enlighten your barbaric blindness next week' ('A Dilemma about Demons' (*DN* 18 Jan. 1913; *CDN* 8:227), his advertisement of the danger of lapsing into hubristic demagoguery does not alter the fact that this is precisely the course that he intends to pursue in seven days' time.

In *Robert Browning*, Chesterton diagnoses unintentional self-parody as arising, paradoxically, from an unproductive form of self-consciousness that derives from the peculiar nature of modern literary celebrity. He argues that unswerving self-resemblance is 'the result of the self-consciousness and theatricality of modern life in which each of us is forced to conceive ourselves as part of a dramatis personae and act perpetually in character' (142). One thinks of Beerbohm's satire of Wilde, 'The Happy Hypocrite' (1897), in which the mask worn by the protagonist slowly melds into his person: 'No longer did he feel it jarring on his face. It seemed to have become an integral part of him' (*Happy*, 52). R.C. Churchill has argued that a similar calcification began to grip the 'performance' of Chesterton and Shaw under the Edwardian public spotlight: 'The more "GBS" Bernard Shaw became, the less, some people felt, there was left the original Shaw, and Chesterton was, apparently, swallowed up by "GKC" long before he wrote The Man Who Was Thursday' (300).

The nearest approach to a satisfactory solution is somehow to combine the arch and the ingenuous within a single *ludic*rous self: both unconscious object of ridicule and conscious agent of play (from the Latin *lūdere*, to play; Barnhart, 613). This is precisely the balance that Chesterton sets out to achieve in the 'Humour' essay, bringing another instructively prevaricating 'half' to bear in his contention that humour 'originate[s] in the half-conscious eccentric' (*Spice*, 22). Like the wit engaged in satirical controversy, this figure 'also discovers a contradiction, but it is in himself' (*Spice*, 24) and hones a capacity to exploit this consciousness for comic purposes. If this premise appears to closely echo Baudelaire's account of *dédoublement*, Chesterton sets out to invest the theory with a more subtle ethical dimension. Whereas Baudelaire argues that for the skilled comic artist, 'there is not one single phenomenon of his double nature of which he is ignorant' (165) and ascribes laughter, as a general principle, to pride—'it is the consequence in man of the idea of his own superiority' (153)—Chesterton argues that the necessary imperfection of the humourist's self-awareness 'corresponds to the human virtue of humility' (*Spice*, 22).

This immersive conception of humour 'involves some confession of human weakness' (*Spice*, 22), embracing the 'idea of the humourist himself being at a disadvantage and caught in the entanglements and contradictions of human life' (*Spice*, 23). If these terms return us to the positive vein of 'contradiction' that Chesterton perceived both in the symbol of the cross and the stereoscopic dual-vision of the 'ordinary' man, his ethical stress upon a cognisance of weakness accords with the grounds upon which he distinguished himself from Shaw: 'there is nothing really problematic in Shaw's mind [...] his wit is never a weakness; therefore it is never a sense of humour' (*CW* 11:380/447). Elsewhere, he implicitly draws Shaw into the critique of monoscopic vision developed in *Orthodoxy*, comparing the monocle of Joseph Chamberlain to the 'single eye of Mr. Bernard Shaw' ('A Glimpse of My Country', *DN* 9 Mar. 1907; *CDN* 4:175).

For Chesterton, the exemplary model of the half-conscious eccentric is a Shakespearean figure to whom he was frequently compared:

> when Falstaff (a model of the humorist become or becoming conscious) cries out in desperate bravado, "They hate us youth," the incongruity between the speech and the corpulent old humbug of a speaker is present to his own mind, as well as to ours.
>
> (*Spice*, 24)

While Falstaff 'really did bemuse himself with youthful companionship', he simultaneously 'knew [this] to be like a drug or a dream' (*Spice*, 24) and so was at once 'half unconsciously and half consciously humorous' (*Spice*, 22). Chesterton concludes that there is 'in the origins of humour, something of this idea of the eccentric caught in the act of eccentricity and brazening it out; something of one surprised in disarray and become conscious of the chaos within' (*Spice*, 24). Rather than an impervious comic professional for whom no banana skin goes unnoticed, Chesterton's self-spectating philosopher remains imperfectly vigilant yet also aware of this imperfection: a reflexivity infused with humility, which guards against the potential for complacency to set in through an assumption of invulnerability.

72 The Ethics of Travesty

In this sense, the urge of the humourist to 'open the guard or confess [...] inconsistency' (*Spice*, 23) can be understood to function as a perverse method of self-defence. By confessing archly to the mental defect, the self-parodist conjoins artificiality and authenticity, projecting a self-aware identification as a 'natural fool', which subtly precludes the possibility of truly being one. A similar duality is present in the title of 'An Apology for Buffoons', which represents a personalised variation on the defence format. As Johnston observes, 'the word "apology" [...] harbours strains of humility and defiance, vulnerability and resistance, covering the plea of "guilty" and "not guilty" simultaneously. [... It is] a single word whose meanings contradict one another' (76–77). The curiously misapplied title of Chesterton's debut collection is equally instructive. In his 'Defence of a New Edition', Chesterton addresses the publisher's malapropism, while conceiving *himself* as an indefensible phenomenon: 'speaking legally, a defendant is [...] one who defends himself [...] a thing which the present writer [...] certainly never dreamed of attempting' (*Defendant*, 6). Nonetheless, Chesterton had implanted this ambiguity in the original text, employing both connotations within a single sentence: 'when worldlings despise the world' what is required is 'a defendant [...] a counsel for the defence' (*Defendant*, 16).

Despite his protestations, in cultural terms, *The Defendant* is as much an act of self-defence as dispassionate advocacy, a pre-emptive riposte to an intellectual atmosphere in which certain aesthetic forms with which the writer identifies are deemed culturally invalid, with the further implication that the society will consider the author himself invalid unless it is educated in an alternative approach to culture. Chesterton's early criticism takes its cue from Wordsworth, who famously argued (after Coleridge) that the 'great and original writer [...] must himself create the taste by which he is to be relished; he must teach the art by which he is to be seen' (103). Bentley hints at the necessity for Chesterton to pursue a comparable strategy in a diary entry concerning the early drafts of *The Napoleon of Notting Hill* that Chesterton was working on when the pair began their careers in public life:

> Sat up with him planning an absurd story of a London war that he is busying himself with just now. The kind of thing that never can be published until he has educated the public up to liking anything he writes—then they would be capable of seeing the good in his frantic, fanciful tales.
>
> (4 Feb. 1900; Bod MS Eng.misc.e.869)

As we have seen, the commercial expedience of this wider project was a source of unease for Chesterton. As early as 1901 he writes of the 'literary antics which are, unfortunately, necessary to procure' food for his table ('What Our Readers Think', *DN* 24 Oct. 1901; *CDN* 1:243). In this sense, his parodic affirmation that he dines on more material matter than the transcendent Shelley conveys a subtly fiscal pun: the journalistic buffoon dines out on essays composed in praise of the material. However, the same skit stresses that in his work for 'the Nation, the New Age, [...] I played the fool to play the sage' (Ward, *Return*, 149). Chesterton's urge to invest buffoonery with moral heft is illustrated by the existential ethics of materialism that he began to construct in the Edwardian era as a further justification of the fool-figure. In 'The Unpopularity of the People' (*DN* 18 Dec. 1909), he advocates a quasi-Dionysian dissolution of the self within the immersive public body: in this scenario, the individual

> has given himself away; that is, he has lost his proud and lonely personality [...] the man in the mob has been melted in a monstrous furnace; he has a lurid and almost loathsome transformation; he has become merely human.
>
> (*CDN* 6:164)

Chesterton expands upon this premise a year later, in *What's Wrong with the World* (1910):

> No one has ever begun to understand comradeship who does not accept with it a certain hearty eagerness in eating, drinking, or smoking, an uproarious materialism [...] You may call the thing an orgy or a sacrament; it is certainly an essential. It is at root a resistance to the superciliousness of the individual. Nay, its very swaggering and howling are humble. In the heart of its rowdiness there is a sort of mad modesty; a desire to melt the separate soul into the mass of unpretentious masculinity. It is a clamorous confession of the weakness of all flesh [...] This sort of equality must be bodily and gross and comic. Not only are we all in the same boat, but we are all seasick.
>
> (*CW* 4:95)

The queasy, subjectivity-undermining terms of this analysis acknowledge that this condition of social immersion is not uncomplicatedly psychologically reassuring, but it is nonetheless posited as a healthier option than withdrawal into the existential divorce of abstract intellection. Chesterton's account conforms to Bakhtin's explanation of the efficacy of carnival in reconceiving the world as 'one great communal performance', thereby 'liberating one from fear, bringing the world maximally close to a person and bringing one person maximally close to another' (*Problems*, 160). Bakhtin links this overflowing of physical limits to a disintegration of social boundaries:

74 *The Ethics of Travesty*

> all that is bodily becomes grandiose, exaggerated, immeasurable. This exaggeration has a positive, assertive character [...] Manifestations of this life refer not to the isolated biological individual, not to the private, egotistic "economic man," but to the collective ancestral body of the people.
>
> (*Rabelais*, 19)

Consider, in this light, Beerbohm's earliest caricature of Chesterton, from 1904, an image of 'Mr G.K. Chesterton giving the world a kiss', in which the subject's grandiosely exaggerated body is brought into maximal proximity to the world (Figure 2.2):

Figure 2.2 Mr. G.K. Chesterton giving the world a kiss, Max Beerbohm, 1904.

Chesterton's vision of 'seasick' camaraderie boldly embraces a foreknowledge of the subject's journey towards a more fundamental dissolution, a point elaborated in an article on 'The Secret Society of Mankind', in which death is figured both as a levelling and unifying phenomenon: 'We are all in a boat which will certainly drown us all, and drown us equally [...] we sail to the land of an ogre, *edax rerum*, who devours all without distinction' (collected in *Fancies*, 120). Bakhtin's account of 'the gaping jaws' of festive laughter, which leave the individual 'not impenetrable but open' (*Rabelais*, 339), suggests that with the open laugh, the individual unconsciously mimics, and thereby mocks, the ogre on the far horizon. By way of contrast, Chesterton frequently employs the sneer or smirk as a symbol of the unconstructive, inward-facing laughter of the wit, or 'judge', who is unwilling to be 'touched at all' (*Spice*, 23) by life: laughter literally lays open the defences, while the sneer closes communication. In *Chaucer* (1932), Chesterton employs this distinction to establish his titular subject as a positive antitype of Matthew Arnold, who, 'for all his merits, did not laugh but only smiled—not to say smirked' (*CW* 18:161). Again, this dualistic symbolism anticipates Bakhtin's account of the distinction between the Romantic and folk grotesques. In the Romantic form, 'laughter [was] cut down to cold humor, irony, sarcasm. It ceased to be a joyful and triumphant hilarity. Its positive regenerating power was reduced to a minimum' (*Rabelais*, 38).

In Chesterton's parodic series of 'answers to the poets' composed for *G.K.'s Weekly*, there occurs a particularly labyrinthine example in which 'The Sea replies to Byron (As it might have appeared to Wordsworth)' (21 Mar. 1925). Here Chesterton returns the repressed voice of the material world, which promptly declares that it will have the last laugh at the solipsistic poet's expense: 'Thy songs are speeches, void of all save Thee [...] Till nature blows the man-hater sky-high [...] And dashes him against the Truth' (*CW* 10.2:333). Chesterton's material buffoonery posits his status as a comparable force of nature. By making himself the cracked mirror through which society might view its own corporality, he conveys a moral articulated eloquently in his late novel, *The Return of Don Quixote* (1927): 'the vast shadow of caricature pursues our desperate dignity and beauty' (*CW* 8:236). Thus, the 'far halloo of the buffoon' becomes the tool through which to convey a rather more sombre vision of the brotherhood of man: the final moral of 'The Secret Society of Mankind' is that 'men seem to be the only cosmic conspirators who have been let into the joke' of mortality; '[t]hat is what the equality of men means to me' (*Fancies*, 122–23).

Kenner remarks upon the consistent interplay of 'verbal' and 'metaphysical paradox' (*Paradox*, 17) in Chesterton's work: these 'paradoxes arise either out of our own confusion, which thinking can more and more nearly resolve, or from the nature of Being which is unresolvable'

(*Paradox*, 23). These terms might be compared to Baudelaire's exposition of the satirical *comique significatif* and grotesque *comique absolu*—the former emphasising cultural discrimination, the latter existential intractability (see Hannoosh, *Baudelaire*, 40)—and to Chesterton's distinction between wit and humour: 'wit is always connected with the idea that truth is close and clear. Humour, on the other hand, is always connected with the idea that truth is tricky' (*CW* 11:447).

In a similar dynamic, the themes of *The Defendant* extend from the local cultural sparring of 'A Defence of Penny Dreadfuls' to encompass the more existential territory of 'A Defence of Skeletons' (*Speaker*, 20 Apr. 1901), in which the human frame performs a rather gruesome 'practical joke' upon its temporary inhabitant: the skull becomes a 'grinning mantrap' (*Defendant*, 47) embedded within the self. Here we encounter a motif that Chesterton will return to many times, that of the pantomime 'Transformation Scene', in which 'the front scene is still there, but the back scene begins to glow through it' ('The Peasant', *DN* 8 July 1911; *CDN* 7:163). As he explains, the skeleton is a kind of mordant buffoon, not only harbouring a painful 'fall' (*Defendant*, 47) for the future, but also performing a capering parody at the expense of self-regard in the interim: 'however much my face clouds with sombre vanity [...] the bones of my skull beneath it are laughing for ever' (*Defendant*, 49).

The personal pronoun repeated emphatically in the passage above is the self-implicating 'my', while it is 'we' who are repeatedly impugned for failing to conform to mass taste in 'A Defence of Penny Dreadfuls'. There are no instances of 'you' being used as direct address in *The Defendant*—this gesture of simultaneous intimacy and detachment infiltrated his journalistic prose incrementally over the subsequent decade, culminating in the stern admonishment to the reader discussed earlier, which is also couched in the second person: 'Do not fancy *you* can be a detached wit and avoid being a buffoon; *you* cannot' (my emphases). Nonetheless, Chesterton once more attempts to infuse this antagonistic textual relationship with a more constructive ethical dimension, using his finger-jabbing at the sedate reader as a carnivalesque means of engendering a sense of active participation and empathetic relation. The dialogic address breaks down mutual alienation while promoting a reciprocal heightening of consciousness: the writer becomes more acutely self-aware through consciousness of the presence of the audience, while the audience is made more self-conscious by being forced to confront its ethical relation to the writer. This immersive principle again corresponds to Bakhtin's account of the democratic laughter of the carnival, which is 'universal in scope; it is directed at all and everyone, including the carnival's participants [...] he who is laughing, also belongs to it' (*Rabelais*, 11–12).

This ethics of immersive buffoonery perhaps finds most intriguing expression in a later article on 'The Innocence of the Criminal', in which Chesterton refines his taxonomy of buffoonery to incorporate the '*half-*conscious buffoon' (collected in *Fancies*, 145; my emphasis), while extending the analogic context from the cultural and existential to the social. In conjuring a carnivalesque vision of the plight of the poor in modern 'Upsidonia' (*Fancies*, 142), Chesterton defines the innocent criminal as 'a sort of comic acrobat, a knockabout comedian who does as many things as possible on his head. He is, both by accident and design, a tumbler' (*Fancies*, 143). In other words, we are dealing with a further type of the Baudelairean comic actor, whose bathetic descent is reconceived as the mechanism of a social trap that the criminal is powerless to avoid, but equipped to commentate upon through a 'reaction into ridicule, and even self-ridicule' (*Fancies*, 144). In the process, the innocent criminal begins to sound remarkably similar to the journalistic buffoon—recall Welsford's account of the fool's 'outlawry combined with utter dependence on the support of the social group to which he belongs'.[4] As Chesterton explains, 'this half-conscious buffoon who is the butt of our society is also the satirist of it. He is even the judge of it' because he is a representative of 'historical humanity' (*Fancies*, 145). A more detailed examination of Chesterton's use of sartorial travesty to perform cultural outlawry in the Edwardian era will reveal just how far he took his sense of identification with this criminal archetype.

A Legend in the Flesh

In Christopher Hitchens's final journalistic dispatch—a review of Ian Ker's biography of Chesterton—the latter-day clown-prince of controversy offers a largely negative assessment of Ker's subject, punctuated by an implicitly disparaging reference to Chesterton's 'vastly draped and histrionic form' ('The Reactionary', *Atlantic*, Mar. 2012). Ambiguously poised between the textual and sartorial, Hitchens's phrase neatly encapsulates an enduring critical disquiet over Chesterton's theatricality, 'histrionic' implying both exuberant self-exhibition and a more stilted air of affectation. As Wills notes, for some his '*persona* has seemed deliberately artificial; they suspect something hidden and sinister which had to be cloaked in such gigantic pantomime' (*Chesterton*, 2). As we have seen, his Edwardian adversary, Robert Blatchford, labelled Chesterton 'an actor' who 'played a part, and dressed for a part', a criticism reframed in commercial terms in Dudley Barker's inference that Chesterton's mode of dress functioned principally as a 'publicity device' (132).[5] In response, biographers have often seemed anxious to defend Chesterton against the imputation that his appearance was consciously manufactured. Ward insists that 'those who knew Gilbert best believed him incapable of posing' (*Gilbert*, 142), while Ker seems to anticipate Hitchens's disapproval, protesting that although Chesterton 'was well aware of his public image [...] that does not necessarily mean that it was "put on"' (96).

These rather timid appeals to a conventional post-Enlightenment model of authenticity are outflanked by Chesterton's more radical rebuttal, which he developed from an early stage in his career and founded precisely upon an authentication of artifice. As with his attempts to counter the venal associations of buffoonery by advancing a pedagogic agenda on behalf of 'historical humanity', Chesterton argued that deliberately putting on a sartorial performance might represent a deeper form of authenticity than slavishly acceding to the diktats of convention. For Chesterton, the man of fashion is merely clothed 'in the ridiculous disguise of a gentleman', a performance that 'tells one nothing at all, not even whether he is one' ('Modern and Ancient Pageants', *ILN* 3 July 1909; *CW* 28:350–51). He turns to a pre-Enlightenment standard to illustrate the value of a contrary model: in medieval society, 'vivid and heraldic costume was meant to show everybody who a man was' (*CW* 28:351). This premise underpins both *The Napoleon of Notting Hill* and *The Man Who Was Thursday*, in which schematic dress is made to operate as an externalised expression of both individual character and affinitive allegiance, extending from the social—the occupants of the various London districts adopt heraldic battle garb—to the existential—the participants in Sunday's carnival each embody a distinct element of creation.

As is so often the case, Chesterton's mature theorising was inspired by his youthful traumas. In his autobiography, he discusses both the anathematised Hankin and his younger self as thoroughgoing conformists in their adherence to bourgeois sartorial standards. Of Hankin, he writes that 'almost alone amid [the] ragged or ridiculous or affected artistic costumes' of the *fin de siècle*, 'he always wore evening-dress', a proof of his dubious ethical status as a 'man of the world' (146). Of his own youthful attire, Chesterton recalls that '[my] dress and appearance were just like everyone else's only worse. My madness, which was considerable, was wholly within' (137). Chesterton conceives his conventional, if slovenly, youthful appearance both as an attempted disguise and an objective corollary of his mental disarray, so that the construction of a personally meaningful, unconventional uniform within which to confront the world constituted a histrionic performance of mental ordering.

Chesterton's adoption of a schematic wardrobe therefore represented a further symbolic break with his unsettling past. By idealising and aestheticising his wife's role in constructing this edifice—the outfit was originally a 'work of art', not of 'the caricaturist', but of 'a lady artist' (*Autobiography*, 137)—Chesterton credits his exemplary icon of earnestness as a simultaneous ethical and sartorial *costumier*, literally reforming his pre-fame self. If this implies an attempt at going straight, it is a further irony that he accessorised the outfit with symbols of pantomimic criminality—the brigand's hat, cape, and swordstick—as an objectification oft his view that by rebelling against pessimism, he had placed himself beyond the bounds of contemporary cultural law: 'in becoming an optimist I had the feelings of an outlaw' (*Fancies*, 221). This adversarial relation to his culture helps to account for the apparent paradox that the accoutrements of Chesterton's outfit are near-identical to those supplied to Syme when he volunteers for the role of Thursday in the anarchist council and discovers 'a swordstick [and] a heavy-looking cape or cloak' (*CW* 6:493) waiting on a table for him to assume. Insofar as Syme is a double-agent who adopts this costume to cloak his subversive intention of moralising the society he has entered, it might be reasoned that Chesterton viewed his everyday life in Edwardian literary society as a similarly treacherous double-mission and dressed accordingly.

In a further juggling of the *comique significatif* and *comique absolu*, Chesterton's outfit not only exhibits an idiosyncratic rejection of the ascendant literary culture, but also a more radical form of self-othering. In a letter sent to Frances at the turn of the century, he rejects the laws of sartorial fashion with an equivalent vehemence to those of contemporary literature, while training an amused outsider's gaze upon the conventions of civilised existence itself. Discussing the act of dressing, he objects to society's demand that he 'shall get inside a house of clothing' and 'put on this foolish armour solemnly [...] For this is the Law' (Ward, *Gilbert*, 29 Sept. 1899; 103). By refusing to take the conventions of cultural fashion seriously, Chesterton situates himself beyond human 'Law' in a radically disruptive sense that mirrors the ambiguously detached status of the buffoon—he becomes an uncanny stranger, implicitly party to a separate temporal order.

The impression that this otherworldly performance produced upon the spectator is evoked in a lyrical account composed by Chesterton's editor at the *Daily News*, Alfred George Gardiner ('A Character Study', 18 July 1908). Written with the purpose of offering the reader a behind-the-scenes insight into his star columnist, Gardiner's tone is situated somewhere between canny publicist and breathless fan:

> A cloak that might be a legacy of Porthos floats about his colossal frame. [...] He is like a visitor out of some fairy tale, a legend in the flesh, a survival of the childhood of the world [whereas] most of us are creatures of our time, thinking its thoughts, wearing its clothes, rejoicing in its chains. [...] Time and place are accidents; he is elemental and primitive. He is not of one time, but of all times. One imagines him [...] exchanging jests with Falstaff at the Boar's head in Eastcheap, or joining in the intellectual revels at the Mermaid Tavern, or meeting Johnson foot to foot and dealing blow for mighty blow. With Rabelais he rioted and Don Quixote and Sancho were his "vera brithers".
>
> (*CDN* 5:100–101)

This tumbling panoply of literary archetypes recalls Chesterton's account of the textual disruptions that take place in dreams, in which the great comic figures of literary history consort together in a single wild extravaganza, presenting 'a picture of literary chaos as might be produced if the characters of every book from *Paradise Lost* to *Pickwick* broke from their covers and mingled in one mad romance' ('Dreams', *Speaker*, 24 Aug. 1901; collected in *Coloured*, 81–82). Chesterton's physical frame becomes an extension of the uncanny dream-text; he is a between-time figure, 'elemental and primitive', 'not of one time, but of all times', unbound by the myopia of fashion and place, and dextrously conflating true figures of history with fictive personalities in a disorientating display of trans-temporal shape-shifting. Just as Shaw had perceived his adversary to be cloned from the same mould that had produced Rabelais, Gardiner strains to present Chesterton as something considerably more substantial than a jobbing journalist: the embodiment of an entire strain of seriocomic literary culture.

Nonetheless, Gardiner's additional reference to Chesterton as 'the most conspicuous figure in the landscape of literary London' (*CDN* 5:100) also subtly attests to the utility of the conceit as a more prosaic means of self-publicising: this edifice, which succeeds in transcending the laws of time and space, remains a hostage to the laws of commerce. As Felstiner argues, the Edwardian era's emphasis upon literary celebrity was directly connected to the rise of the mass-circulation newspaper: 'London's papers took day-to-day notice of cultural phenomena, and the artist was more visible than before. In this atmosphere, it was important to make oneself recognizable' (23). Consequently, the physical self-display complements the textual self-positioning that Chesterton had articulated in his reassurances to Frances of his journalistic savvy. Once more, he strived to establish a pedagogic impetus to redeem the financial expedience of this enterprise, setting out to become more than a mere advert for himself. As with his textual compound role of self-defendant and defence counsel, his sartorial guise objectifies the allegiance to popular literature that he had announced in 'A Defence of Penny Dreadfuls'. Having composed the essay, he went on to practice in daily life what he preached in print, dressing himself *as* a penny dreadful and wandering the streets of London as a highly conspicuous sandwich board, promoting the literary pursuits of the masses.

Just as *The Defendant* had couched sincere encomia in parodic form, its author's outfitting grafted playful performance to earnest intent. The collection's insistence upon the trans-temporal equivalence of cultural modes that contemporary fashion decrees to be 'high' or 'low' is echoed in the similes arrived at by another of Chesterton's contemporary spectators, Holbrook Jackson: 'the traffic of Ludgate Circus [was] held up for him, as he strolled by in cloak and combrero [sic] like a brigand of Adelphi drama or a Spanish hidalgo by Velasquez' (qtd. in Clemens, 44). By invoking the comparative models of Victorian melodrama and Baroque art, Jackson not only juxtaposes discrete historical periods, but also signifiers of popular and 'high' culture. As this suggests, the interpretive ambiguity encoded within Chesterton's outfit works to relativise convention, reminding the viewer that the disreputable *habitué* of the modern penny dreadful is objectively indistinguishable from the Mediterranean gentleman captured in a sublime cultural artefact of the past.

Jackson would later find renown for his pioneering study of the Decadent movement, *The Eighteen Nineties: A Review of Art and Ideas at the Close of the Nineteenth Century* (1914). This intellectual hinterland perhaps explains his attentiveness to Chesterton's costuming, since the dualism of the outfit also correlates to *The Defendant*'s juggling of the textual clothes of more immediate predecessors in the culture wars of Decadence. Whitman's adornment of the frontispiece of *Leaves of Grass* (1855) with a photograph of himself had been foundational in inducting the concept of the authorial image as a stamp upon the textual body of work. While Whitman's visual performance provided a metaphor for the individualistic credo of the text—'I celebrate myself' (63)—the poet's adoption of the clothing of the anonymous working man also rendered his image an emblematic standard for the democratic sentiments of the text. In this way, the body of the poet becomes a corollary of the communal ethos of the verse, and Whitman achieves a curious balance of self-aggrandisement and self-effacement, employing his image as a publicity device for a philosophy that figures the author both as a remarkable individual and a universal type.

In 'The Mummers', Chesterton discusses emblematic costume in a manner that helps to account for the apparent tension in this mode of diffident self-projection. For Chesterton, mummery springs from 'the noble conception of making Man something other and more than himself when he stands at the limit of human things' (*CDN* 7:274). It is a 'ritual' based upon 'a profound paradox: the concealment of the personality combined with the exaggeration of the person', parading a 'pomp of obliteration and anonymity' within 'a rite [that] seeks to be at once invisible and conspicuous' (*CDN* 7:273). While Chesterton's costuming evokes a similar dynamic, it also represents a subtle departure. Even as his theatrical self-presentation as an every-brigand sets out to embody the literary enjoyments of the masses, it also radically differentiates his mode of dress from that of the vast majority of the populace. As with his rhetorical role as buffoonish demagogue, Chesterton is both of the mob and, as its standard-bearer, subtly apart.

In the battle of Notting Hill, Auberon Quin styles his regiment 'the 1st Decadents Green' (*CW* 6:328), a gesture that obliquely acknowledges the influence of Decadent culture upon Chesterton's sartorial vision. In the 1890s, Wilde had both imitated and opposed Whitman's approach to physical self-promotion, co-opting the latter's individualistic ethos and manufacturing of an emblematic 'type' for which he was to stand as the exemplar, but reassigning both attributes to a 'high' cultural level in a kind of sartorial reverse-travesty, by dressing in ostentatious Hellenic costume for publicity photographs. As with Chesterton's projection of a binary distinction between 'the democracy of the "Leaves of Grass" [and] the oligarchy of "The Green Carnation"' ('On My Anti-Americanism', *ILN* 21 Apr. 1928; *CW* 34:511), Wilde used his publicity shots to extol an alternative cultural lineage of esotericism, refinement, and artifice, rendering himself a paradoxical totem: an embodiment of the abstract principle of individualism.

In turn, Beerbohm established his parodic relation to Wilde by dressing with an ostentatious *absence* of flamboyance, while militating against any air of stolid conventionality by pushing the urbane performance to a theatrical extreme. As Chesterton put it, Beerbohm 'played in the masquerade of his time [...] and he dressed or overdressed for the part' (*Autobiography*, 98). For his part, Shaw reverted to a converse extreme of parodic conventionality in his everyday outfitting, offsetting his rhetorical pyrotechnics with a dour sartorial utilitarianism. As with Chesterton's use of costuming as an implied extension of his philosophy, Shaw pinned his ideological colours to his chest through the promotion of Jaeger outfits conceived to be hygienic, a corollary of his self-projection as a clean-living rationalist. By setting himself up in parodic relation to all four immediate precursors, Chesterton achieved a singular composite of the popular identification of Whitman, the dramatic ostentation of Wilde, the poker-faced irreverence of Beerbohm, and the ideological literalism of Shaw.

If this composite of influence contributed to the idiosyncratic *textual* version of buffoonery that Chesterton refined during the Edwardian era, his costume can be read as a further accoutrement of this performance, not only evoking the garb of the brigand, but also the baggy, amorphous outfit of the clown. In considering Chesterton's use of his body as a rogue text, it is instructive to consider Stewart's comparison of the 'formlessness [of] the costume of the clown or fool' to the tendency of 'texts [to] become increasingly "formless" or antiformal as they move away from a given system of order, for *form* is defined only in terms of congruence with the existing system of order' (61). Chesterton's amorphous cape accentuates the formlessness of his body—a transferal to the physical plane of the literary formlessness that he was continually accused of—as his many self-caricatures in costume illustrate. Take, for example, a later image of his 'disreputable' figure being shunned by a respectable member of Victorian society, a conceit that again places him outside an existing system of cultural order, while also confusing his place within the temporal order (Figure 2.3, overleaf).

Figure 2.3 A true Victorian cuts a disreputable author, G.K. Chesterton, 1932.

Nonetheless, the literal *uniform*ity of the costume also implies a danger of becoming unswervingly *true to form* and, with it, the spectre of unconscious self-parody. Churchill's observation that the comic facades of 'GKC' and 'GBS' threatened ultimately to swallow their creators is a risk that Chesterton implicitly draws attention to in a discussion of Shaw's rigid dress-code: his

> costume [has] become a part of his personality; one has come to think of the reddish-brown Jaeger suit as if it were a sort of reddish-brown fur [...] the man is so much of a piece, and must always have dressed appropriately.
>
> (CW 6:406)

In apprehending this further constrictive facet of modern public life, Chesterton seems to have come to consider the unchanging edifice of the brigand-clown as much an occasional burden as the rhetorical dress of the buffoon. If the cloak and swordstick dramatised his sense of literary society as a site of fraught ideological combat comparable to the central section of *Thursday*, a loosening of the constraints of his schematic public persona was occasionally required, rather as Carter imagined Shaw donning the disguise of 'Chesterton' whenever he needed a break from his own dogmas.

This scenario is suggestive of Bakhtin's account of carnival as a safety valve that releases the pressures of a proscriptive culture on a societal scale—a temporary 'escape into a world where things are not fixed horribly in eternal appropriateness' (*Defendant*, 65), as Chesterton writes of the disruptive value of nonsense. Throughout his adult life, Chesterton pursued a similar escape route through his participation in a carnivalesque compendium of public and private fancy-dress events. In a variation on Gardiner's vision of Chesterton as a one-man literary pageant, he used his body as the parodic frame upon which to drape a range of mythical, historical, and fictional figures—including Bacchus, Old King Cole, Samuel Johnson, and Sam Weller—each of whom embodied attributes with which he identified. As with the conjoining of 'pure' nonsense with satire in Chesterton's occasional verse, the reins are only loosened so far: an implicit ethical framework for these activities is retained by their affinitive structure, which once more posits a popular, seriocomic ancestral line to which the reveller is affiliated.

These dressing-up games ultimately brought Chesterton into the courtroom as a participant in the comic mock-trials held as charitable public events in Edwardian and Georgian society. Perhaps most famously, he took on the role of judge in the trial of John Jasper for the murder of Edwin Drood, which took place on 7 January 1914 in King's Hall, Covent Garden, with the stated aim of solving the mystery of Dickens's unfinished final novel. Chesterton invariably sought to inject a satirical bite into these burlesque scenarios, justifying his enjoyment of the dressing-up game by substituting meaningful rhetoric for the empty formulas that he perceived to dominate the conventional courtroom. As a result, fellow participants occasionally considered him to have violated the tone appropriate to such events. At a mock-trial in which he was called upon to prosecute leading headmasters of public schools for the crime of 'Destroying Freedom of Thought', Douglas Woodruff recalled that the defendants

> were volubly nettled at the drastic and serious case he had made inside the stage setting of burlesque, and seemed to think he had not been playing the game when he wrapped up so much meaning in his speech and examinations.
>
> (qtd. in Ward, *Gilbert*, 473)

One thinks of Katherine Blake's discussion of forms of 'tribal ritual', in which 'there exists the double knowledge that what is being enacted is not "real" and that it is not "not-real"' (15). This toying with conceptual thresholds was a still-more prominent feature of the pageants in which Chesterton took part, the most famous of which was his appearance as Samuel Johnson at the English Church Pageant held at Fulham Palace on 10–16 June 1909. Deborah Sugg Ryan argues that such spectacles produced a heightened sense of 'interaction between performers and audience' (44), causing boundaries to become 'blurred between the spectators and the spectated' (43) as the crowd's sense of quasi-participation engendered a collective self-consciousness similar to that promoted by Chesterton's carnivalesque journalistic strategies. As Bakhtin observes, carnival operates as a 'ritualistic' form of 'syncretic pageantry [...] a pageant without footlights' (*Problems*, 122), since 'the basic carnival nucleus' represents 'life itself, but shaped according to a certain pattern of play. [...] carnival does not know footlights, in the sense that it does not acknowledge any distinction between actors and spectators' (*Rabelais*, 7).

On 2 April 1910, as the Edwardian era drew to a close, Chesterton paused within his weekly article in the *Daily News* to dwell briefly on the carnivalesque dimensions of medieval Christian culture: 'When England believed in Christianity there were jokes in the church door—and in the church—Boy Bishops and Lords of Misrule' ('The Comic Constable', *CDN* 6:226). Two months later, his own fictional Abbot of Unreason, Father Brown, made his first appearance in print in 'The Blue Cross', a tale that turns upon the priest's execution of a series of riotous practical jokes—throwing a bowl of soup at a wall, upending a fruit stall, and smashing a pub window—committed in the cause of educating a self-avowed moral relativist, the trickster-thief, Flambeau, in the freewheeling possibilities of earthly and metaphysical law and order. While the story's madcap urban chase corresponds to Bakhtin's account of carnival as a 'hiatus between two moments of biographical time [...] a pure digression from the normal course of life' (qtd. in Clark and Holquist, 281), the protagonists' climactic showdown on a darkening Hampstead Heath gestures towards the motifs of the mystery play, presenting a theologically-grounded confrontation held within a pseudo-metaphysical limbo space. As Bakhtin explains, the mystery play conventionally formed the aesthetic centrepiece of the medieval carnival: a 'carnival atmosphere reigned on days when mysteries and soties [broad satires] were produced' (*Rabelais*, 5).

Chesterton's discussion of the merits of the medieval mystery play in 'The Humour of King Herod' (collected in *Uses*) draws these threads together, comparing the form to 'a detective story' (96), while praising its 'daring mixture [...of] extremes of tragedy and comedy' (97), which produces a model of 'democratic satire [...] far bolder in its burlesque [...and] buffoonery' (98/96) than subsequent modes of dramatic performance. The ultimate function of this ritual is to effect social reharmonisation. Bakhtin argues that '[p]eople who in life are separated by impenetrable hierarchical barriers enter into free familiar contact on the carnival square' (*Problems*, 123), a vision instilled literally in 'The Blue Cross' via the series of 'streets and squares' (*CFB* 5) anarchically traversed by the protagonists on their way to a reconciliatory conclusion.

The subversive potential of this premise is most ambitiously realised in the third of the *Father Brown* stories published in 1910, 'The Queer Feet' (*Storyteller*, Nov. 1910), in which the preoccupations that had permeated Chesterton's first decade in the public eye—the ethical buffoonery, the reconception of everyday life as dramatic play, and the utopian transmutation of nonsense into friendship—find their most comprehensive and sophisticated fictional realisation.

A Crisis of Tedium

'The Queer Feet' finds Father Brown entangled in the annual dinner celebrations of the private gentleman's club 'The Twelve True Fishermen' because one of its waiters, a Roman Catholic, has inconveniently died on the eve of the event. As Brown notes down the details of the waiter's confession in an ante-room, he is disturbed by a series of unusual footsteps in the hall, which turn out to be those of Flambeau, who has been adapting his gait halfway along the corridor from the leisurely step of a club member to the hurried step of a waiter. In this way, Flambeau successfully steals the club's cutlery merely by altering his demeanour as he moves between the table and the kitchen, physically parodying the gentlemen with silver spoons in their mouths in order to pocket the same silver. Upon guessing this explanation, Brown confronts Flambeau in the cloakroom, persuades him to hand back the cutlery, and then lets him go, before explaining to the guests what has taken place.

Such are the action-level events of the story. However, this *précis* does little justice to the bulk of the narrative, which is substantially composed of extended authorial digressions concerning the inhabitants of the club—digressions that bear little relevance to the mystery at hand, beyond conveying the conditions of mental torpor that make the crime possible, a requirement incommensurate with their vehemence and frequency. The detection narrative is subordinate to the satirical message: just as the club's extreme exclusivity enables Chesterton to establish the conditions of a Poe-inspired locked-room mystery, every detail of the plot is selected primarily for its capacity to bolster the social critique. The nature of Chesterton's message might be summarised by a rhetorical query posed in 'The Flat Freak', a journalistic article of the same year, in which Chesterton's simultaneously comradely and collusive rhetorical strategies are brought to bear in an account of the banality of the upper-class party: 'Why is it that *you and I* feel that *we* would (on the whole) rather spend the evening with two or three stable boys in a pothouse than take part in that pallid and Arctic joke?' (*CDN* 6:177; my emphases).

'The Queer Feet' makes extensive use of this intimate, insinuating narrative tone, staging a challenge to the reader's empowerment to contemplate the 'golden gallery' (*CFB* 38) of the club from behind the two-way

The Ethics of Travesty 87

mirror of the text. The story is obsessed with thresholds and the means by which they might be breached, transgressing the threshold between text and reader on the narrative level, and between popular and 'official' culture on the action level. From the opening line, the narrator points his finger from the page in a direct address, in which the second-person pronoun recurs nine times:

> If you meet a member of that select club, 'The Twelve True Fishermen,' entering the Vernon Hotel for the annual club dinner, you will observe, as he takes off his overcoat, that his evening coat is green and not black. If (supposing that you have the star-defying audacity to address such a being) you ask him why, he will probably answer that he does it to avoid being mistaken for a waiter. You will then retire crushed. [...] But since it is immeasurably unlikely that you will ever rise high enough in the social world to find 'The Twelve True Fishermen,' or that you will ever sink low enough among slums and criminals to find Father Brown, I fear that you will never hear the story at all unless you hear it from me.
>
> (*CFB* 36)

Here, Chesterton manipulates the famously heightened interactivity of the detection genre with its audience, in which, as George N. Dove notes, the role of 'the reader [is] an involved observer' (32), to suggest that the reader has become implicated in the world described through the act of reading, yet remains subtly disempowered by her/his adoption of a passive role in the reception process. This introductory address is followed by an extended passage of scene-setting, before an abrupt return to the jarring parenthetical tactic: 'When you enter (as you never will) the Vernon Hotel' (*CFB* 38). This prohibition, immediately counteracting the apparent liberties extended to the reader by the phrase '*when* you enter', dismantles the fourth wall only to brutally reinstate it within a single clause.

There follows a second-person tour of the interior of the hotel, supplying the reader with directions, or a tip-off, so that the 'you never will' might be conceived more conspiratorially as the wink that the informant tips to the burglar: 'you pass down a short passage [...] which opens on your right into passages leading to the public rooms, and on your left to a similar passage pointing to the kitchens and offices' (*CFB* 38). Although this suggests an invitation into the narrative world along the passage of the text, the introductory preamble has already stated that as things stand, the middle-class reader is the only member of society currently lacking agency to snoop around the golden gallery in reality. Whereas the clubmen gain access from above, Father Brown transgresses the boundary from below through his association with 'slums and criminals'. Meanwhile, Chesterton's speculative reader is trapped in the liminal space between the two, due to an implied lack of the necessary 'star-defying audacity' to challenge the specious air of fixity that surrounds the exclusivity of the upper classes, accompanied by an equally discreditable disregard for social justice: the narrator notes, again in parenthesis, that it is a 'vein of improbable conjecture' (*CFB* 36) that the reader might have met Father Brown, since the priest's principal work is conducted amongst the lower-classes.

Both satirical literature and detective fiction depend upon the reader bringing to the text various preconceptions informed by societal conventions, which are then overturned. In the present instance, the satirical efficacy of the story is predicated upon the likelihood that the reader will be in 'the habit of respecting a gentleman', a propensity that Chesterton considered 'a great national sin' ('Some Policemen and a Moral', *DN* 16 Apr. 1904; *CDN* 2:218). In frankly presupposing the reader's subscription to a bias that the author considers shameful, Chesterton's introductory enactment of the reader's social humiliation tests the absolute limits of his thesis that the reader of detective stories is 'only happy if he feels a fool' ('The Ideal Detective Story', *ILN* 25 Oct. 1930; *CW* 35:400). As with the slang meaning of 'queer'—to 'spoil, ruin […] trick, swindle, cheat' (Barnhart, 874)—Chesterton's textual swindle sets him up in the paradoxical role of ethical mountebank, queering the pitch of the conventional detective story by cheating the reader out of the expected literary transaction, in the cause of provoking a deeper querying of her/his cultural presuppositions.

The narrator's parenthetic asides convey the air of an oral reading in which the storyteller, exasperated at the circumstances he is being compelled to recount, intermittently adds his own sardonic, improvisatory gloss. Simultaneously, the reader is encouraged to emulate Brown's status as an attentive listener, the jarring notes in the narration forming a corollary of the sudden alterations in Flambeau's step, here serving to jolt the reader's projected passivity. Chesterton's disruptive methods conform to Maebh Long's account of the dramatic origins of parabasis, which derives 'from the Greek verb *parabainein*—"to step forward"—and describes a dramatic device used in Greek Attic comedies whereby the flow of the play's primary action was interrupted when the chorus stepped out to speak directly to the audience' (73). At such moments, the chorus 'steps away from its role as spectator and becomes a central spectacle', while 'chorus members may literally or metaphorically unmask themselves, and speak as "real" people' (75). The sophistication of Chesterton's conjoining of narratorial parabasis to the action-level events of 'The Queer Feet' is implied by Long's further observation that parabasis 'provides a path, a point of entry […] It is a certain gait, a particular way of walking, a rhythm or style' (76). In this sense, the 'progression/digression dichotomy' (330) that Dennis Porter identifies as a narrative staple of detective fiction becomes exaggerated in a manner suggestive of the perambulations of the criminal—dallying for a time before suddenly shooting forward along the passage—so as to hint archly at a complicity between the narrator and the criminal in the construction of the plot.

The confrontational narrative tone also echoes the 'impudence' ascribed to the transgressive heroes on the action level: while Flambeau penetrates the club's threshold in the guise of an '"archangel of impudence"' (*CFB* 49), as Brown terms him, the priest enters the club with a hybridised binary of 'meek impudence' (*CFB* 38). Later, the narrator's breaching of textual boundaries is mirrored by Flambeau's vaulting of the liminal footlight boundary of the cloakroom into Brown's off-stage area to remonstrate with his observer. Brown subsequently mimics Flambeau's transgression by hopping 'over the barrier' (*CFB* 48) in turn to explain what has taken place to a baffled clubman. This repeated vaulting of the barrier between audience and stage becomes suggestive of a prompt to the reader to become a disruptive actor in turn. In his obituary of Chesterton, Eliot emphasises this subversive streak, highlighting his 'abilities as a public performer' ('Obituary', 532) while comparing him to Samuel Johnson, in another palimpsestic vision of the back-scene glowing through the façade: 'Behind the Johnsonian fancy-dress, so reassuring to the British public, he concealed the most serious and revolutionary designs' ('Obituary', 531).

Chesterton's everyday outfit not only included a 'cloak' that 'disguised me' (*Autobiography*, 164), but also 'a walking stick which concealed a sword' (Chesterton, *Annotated*, 52n8), an accessory that connotes violent intent masked by a projection of harmless infirmity. Eliot's observations shed an interesting light on the recollections of the model for Father Brown, Chesterton's friend, Father John O'Connor: 'Let me point out his terrible power of invective, not generally understood, because he seldom used it. And let us be thankful for the fine charity which kept that weapon sheathed' (13). In the story at hand, the very impropriety of the narrator's interpositions forms a kind of textual sheath, a mediating comic effect through which the speaker is figured as an amusingly opinionated eccentric who is 'laughed at, as well as [...] laughing' (*Spice*, 22), as the 'Humour' essay has it, thus costuming the argument in a manner that charms the reader into receptivity towards otherwise unpalatable sentiments. Just as the various fancy-dress travesties that accompany Flambeau's criminal activities render him an object hidden in plain sight—an ambulatory rendition of Poe's purloined letter crossed with the simultaneously 'invisible and conspicuous' mummer—Chesterton's communication of his social principles entails 'concealing them by exposure' ('Obituary', 531), as Eliot puts it.

The sense of interactivity that this narrative methodology engenders proceeds organically from Chesterton's preference for dictating his literary output, fictional and journalistic alike, to his secretaries, an improvisational performance that foregrounds verbal intimacy and encourages colloquial asides, and helps to explain why his short stories and articles often bear such marked stylistic similarities. Ker records that when dictating his detective stories to one secretary, Chesterton 'enjoyed teasing her by pretending to stop "at the exciting moment"' (539). He verbally improvised almost all of the *Father Brown* stories from brief notes made on the backs of envelopes and other ephemera, a methodology occasionally adduced by commentators as proof of their literary paltriness.[6] Quite the contrary, this is the very locus of their value. As Chesterton writes elsewhere of George Macdonald, he was 'not a born writer; he was a born maker of spontaneous texts' ('George MacDonald', *DN* 23 Sept. 1905; *CDN* 3:197). In establishing this distinction, Chesterton alludes to a tradition of oral storytelling that stands in unofficial relation to the norms of 'high' literary production encoded within modernity. Chesterton's expositional methods establish a distinction between the 'storyteller' and the 'literary person' comparable to that identified by Bakhtin in his account of 'skaz' as a verbal disguise adopted by the author to subtly advance a social message:

> in most cases skaz is introduced precisely for the sake of someone else's voice, a voice socially distinct, carrying with it precisely those points of view and evaluations necessary to the author. What is introduced here, in fact, is a storyteller [...] not a literary person; he belongs in most cases to the lower social strata, to the common people (precisely this is important to the author)—and he brings with him oral speech.
>
> (*Problems*, 192)

Appropriately enough, in 'The Queer Feet' Chesterton focuses his critique upon the oral functions of the figures depicted, in the forms of verbal production and digestive consumption. The narrator's attempts to ginger up the narrative are consistently offset by the paucity of material offered by the inane chatter of the clubmen. While the story borrows its spectatorship-vexing techniques from the structures of the folk carnival, the banquet of the Twelve True Fishermen is the quintessential official feast, a world away from the 'grotesque symposium' (*Rabelais*, 285) that Bakhtin identifies as the verbal component of the popular carnival. The themes of carnivalesque 'table talk are always "sublime", filled with "profound wisdom", but these themes are uncrowned and renewed on the material bodily level [...] freely blend[ing] the profane and the sacred, the lower and the higher, the spiritual and the material' (*Rabelais*, 285–86). One thinks of the 'rollicking sagacity' ('Dr. Johnson', collected in Chesterton, *G.K.C.*, 65) that Chesterton ascribed to Johnson's table talk. The absence of either profound wisdom or boisterous repartee in the conversation of the Fishermen demonstrates their dislocation from the principles of popular

The Ethics of Travesty 91

festivity, the emptiness of their conversation echoing the vacuity of the event: 'The talk was that strange, slight talk which governs the British Empire, which governs it in secret, and yet would scarcely enlighten an ordinary Englishman even if he could overhear it' (*CFB* 42–43).

The company's verbal inadequacy is complemented by the unsatisfactory contents of the banquet, as outlined in another heavily accentuated, intemperate narratorial intervention, tonally indistinguishable from Chesterton's journalism:

> I do not possess a copy of the menu; and if I did it would not convey anything to anybody [... The *hors d'oeuvres*] were taken seriously because they were avowedly useless extras, like the whole dinner and the whole club.
>
> (*CFB* 42)

Here the collapsed repetition of 'any'—'anything to anybody'—evokes an air of negative presence located in the extreme codification of the fare on offer, as an allegory of the exclusivity *ad absurdum* of the club itself.

All forms of heavily coded discourse are critiqued as epistemologically vacuous in 'The Queer Feet', from the menu's description of what the Fishermen consume to the vapid secret-talk of empire—'"Splendid work young Moocher's doing in Burma"' (*CFB* 45)—that they emit. Accordingly, Chesterton's account, in 'A Defence of Slang', of the language of the 'man of fashion' as 'a mere string of set phrases, as lifeless as a string of dead fish' (*Defendant*, 144), finds a corporeal counterpart in the 'sacred fish course' that forms the centrepiece of the Fishermen's banquet, and consists '(to the eyes of the vulgar) in a sort of monstrous pudding' (*CFB* 44). Here the ostentation of the food tips over from the sublime to the ridiculous in a material rendition of bathos, while the further parenthetic interjection anticipates Chesterton's irreverent account of Wilde's verse, in which the laughable is disclosed by the spectator's capacity to view the sacred object through the sceptical eyes of the *vulgaris*.

A certain potential ambivalence might be thought to pertain to the narrator's remark concerning the *hors d'oeuvres*, since the abundance of 'avowedly useless extras' is the intrinsic point of a carnival feast, which should be a celebration of excess with 'no utilitarian connotation' (Bakhtin, *Rabelais*, 276). However, it is essential that this quality should contrast with the company itself. There should be a joyous dichotomy between the practicality of the company and their festive excess, whereas here every guest at the table is a comparably 'useless extra' or, indeed, *parasitos*—'beside food'—neither contributing to the event in the guise of conversationalist or producer of goods, nor, in Chesterton's view, to society in general. As Brown finally remarks to the colonel, in the plot that has unfolded, 'as in Hamlet, there are the rococo excrescences—yourselves, let us say' (*CFB* 49). This mischievous imputation of equivalence between Chesterton's popular fiction and perhaps the most venerated literary text in the English language forms an aesthetic counterpart to Flambeau's disruption of social conventions of low and high via his dual-role as waiter and guest. By acting 'two parts at once' (*CFB* 48), as Brown puts it, Flambeau splits himself into a hybridised binary of the two poles of the club, relativising sartorial convention in a manner similar to Chesterton's donning of the Velasquez/Adelphi cape.

In his autobiography, Chesterton discusses his distaste at the fine-dining of his day: 'those who really prefer eating good cutlets and omelets to living on gilt plaster and pantomime footmen had already found their way to delightful little dens off Leicester Square' (116). The reference to 'pantomime footmen' is instructive in relation to the roles of Flambeau and Father Brown in the story at hand. As John O'Brien explains, in the traditional pantomime the casting of the '"grotesque" characters like Harlequin and the Clown [...] as servants [...] flipped the usual format of mainpiece comedy, bringing what was typically a sub-plot involving servants to the foreground' (11). While Chesterton went on to explicitly reconceive Flambeau as 'the harlequin' (*CFB* 59) in 'The Flying Stars' (*Cassell's Magazine*, June 1911), the parallel is already implicit in his role of mischievously insubordinate servant in 'The Queer Feet'. Chesterton's deployment of Father Brown is also informed by the festive-comic schema of the Harlequinade—in structural terms, the priest represents the clown to Flambeau's Harlequin, his 'meek impudence' recalling the combination of shameless impudence and shameless humility that Chesterton identified in Beerbohm's buffoonery. When the pair infiltrate the club in the guises of wise fool and elemental trickster, the unofficial carnival becomes implanted within the official construct, sowing a disruption that serves to destabilise the 'eternal' truth of this 'phantasmal and yet fixed society' (*CFB* 43), as the narrator refers to the club, and, beyond it, the class system of his day.

The overriding purpose of this disruption is to dismantle the barriers of exclusivity. In 'The Beauty of Noise' (*DN* 18 Aug. 1906), Chesterton argues that a 'wicked refinement [...] has in our time separated the social classes more completely, perhaps, than they were ever separated before' (*CDN* 4:39). Dentith corroborates this account in a discussion of the social conditions that particularly invite parodic literary intervention:

> Strongly stratified societies [...] where separate classes live in relative social isolation, are very likely to produce mutual parodic characterisations of the social layers, whose manners of speech and writing are very strongly marked by class. This is very strikingly the case [...] in English society, between, roughly, the 1880s and the 1950s. This society was highly socially zoned, and its different groups lived in remarkable ignorance of each other.
>
> (30–31)

In 'The Queer Feet', the club's exclusivity prevents the community marriage that festive comedy seeks to effect, thus situating the diners in the blocking role conventionally allotted to the villain in the related genres of fairy-tale and detective fiction. In Chesterton's singularly vehement take on the comedy of manners, the club is described at the outset as 'an institution such as can only exist in an oligarchical society which has almost gone mad on good manners' (*CFB* 36). Again, this dysfunctional restrictiveness is accentuated by the contrastive presence of the narrator, whose difficulty in controlling his manners liberates him from the conventions of literary etiquette even as it contributes to a highly sophisticated narratorial manner.

The revelation of the theft initially reinforces the air of schism by exposing the guests' ignorance of the men constantly surrounding them: '"Know the waiter?" answered Mr. Audley indignantly. "Certainly not!"' (*CFB* 45). In his autobiography, Chesterton elaborates upon the alienation fostered by the class divide of the age, noting that the upwardly mobile late-Victorian household

> knew far too little of its own servants [...] in the class as a whole there was neither the coarse familiarity in work, which belongs to democracies [...] nor the remains of a feudal friendliness such as lingers in the real aristocracy. There was a sort of silence and embarrassment.
>
> (13)

The negative presences of silence and embarrassment also suffuse 'The Queer Feet'. Silence, in the sense of meaningful discourse, is the dominant theme prior to the theft—in a typically economical pun, the main course is eaten in 'devouring silence' (*CFB* 44)—while embarrassment reigns in its aftermath. The awkward revelation of the waiters' humanity is resolved via an immediate imaginative reification of the mechanistic waiting machine: 'these modern plutocrats could not bear a poor man near to them, either as a slave or as a friend. That something had gone wrong with the servants was merely a dull, hot embarrassment' (*CFB* 45).

In *What's Wrong with the World*, Chesterton contrasts the perilous insecurity of the homes of the poor with the position of the 'rich man [who] knows that his own house moves on vast and soundless wheels of wealth' (*CW* 4:72). When the theft occurs in 'The Queer Feet', the confused behaviour of one of the waiters compounds the guests' sense of disorientation along comparable lines:

> all those vague and kindly gentlemen were so used to the smoothness of the unseen machinery which surrounded and supported their lives, that a waiter doing anything unexpected was a start and a jar.

They felt as you and I would feel if the inanimate world disobeyed—
if a chair ran away from us.

(*CFB* 44)

While pausing to note the further conspiratorial 'you or I', the final image recalls us to Bergson's account of the 'unseen machinery' of human repetition, here in the context of servants being debased to the inanimate level of furniture. Of course, the contingent absence of a chair where one is expected—a service conventionally rendered by the waiter—is also the archetypal practical joke at the expense of inelasticity.

In Bergsonian theory, the revelation of unreflective habit as 'a mechanism superimposed upon life' (Bergson, 45) is directly related to the workings of the highly-codified ceremony:

> the stiff and starched formality of any ceremonial suggests to us an image of this kind. For, as we forget the serious object of a solemnity or a ceremony, those taking part in it give us the impression of puppets in motion. Their mobility seems to adopt as a model the immobility of the formula. It becomes automatism.
>
> (45–46)

In this sense, the Fishermen provoke Flambeau's arch parody not only through their socially schismatic exclusivity and anonymous interchangeability, but also their inelasticity: as Habib glosses Bergson's message, 'we are imitable [...] when we act mechanically' (67). Syme exploits a similar automatism in *Thursday*, ironically in the context of a society that considers itself the last word in anarchic rebellion: '"This is really not quite dignified"' protests the chairman during the formal ceremony that leads to Syme's election, as he explains the rules 'with mechanical rapidity [...] like a piece of clock-work suddenly started again' (*CW* 6:502–503).

Nonetheless, Chesterton departs from Bergson in the more trenchant, historicised nature of the satire that he pursues. As Habib demurs,

> Bergson's critique [...] is debilitated by its ahistorical foundation: what are actually tendencies of a specific era of bourgeois predominance—such as mechanisation, exhaustion of individual by group identity, transformation of human into thing—are ascribed by Bergson indiscriminately to "society".
>
> (69)

While Chesterton infuses his action-level account with universal comic archetypes such as the formalised ceremony and the disruptive trickster, his narrative-level exposition explicitly states that it is the conditions of this particular culture that engender the situation depicted: it is 'wholly the product of our time' (*CFB* 44–45). Shortly after a glancing reference

The Ethics of Travesty 95

to Bergson in *Where All Roads Lead* (1922), Chesterton implicitly juxtaposes the themes of *Thursday* and 'The Queer Feet' in a retrospective account of his responses to the dominant tendencies of the age: if there was an 'intellectual passion running parallel to my revulsion from fashionable pessimism, it was a revulsion from fashionable plutocracy' (*CW* 3:47–48).[7]

For Bakhtin, the official feast falsely proclaims itself to operate beyond the parameters of temporal fashion: it commemorates the specious 'triumph of a truth already established, the predominant truth that was put forward as eternal and indisputable' (*Rabelais*, 9). These terms are closely echoed in 'The Queer Feet': the

> society had a vast number of ceremonies and observances, but it had no history and no object; that was where it was so very aristocratic. You did not have to be anything in order to be one of the Twelve Fishers.
>
> (*CFB* 37)

This curious phrasing—'[y]ou did not have to be any*thing*', rather than 'anyone'—not only suggests a divorce of social function from status, but also a more uncanny divorce from material existence. As the narrator notes in a further parenthetical aside, 'nobody in this place ever appeared in person if he could help it' (*CFB* 38). While this account offers a further hint that the apparently ineluctable edifice is a phantasm that would disperse with the merest close observation, it also promotes a more disturbing atmosphere that again calls forth the deranging nonsense-voids of the Romantic grotesque.

In 'The Uncanny' (1919), Freud quotes Jentsch's assertion that an unsettling atmosphere will arise whenever there is '"doubt as to whether an apparently animate object really is alive and, conversely, whether a lifeless object might not perhaps be animate"' (*Uncanny*, 135). This uncertainty is consistently raised in 'The Queer Feet'. Images of reification not only attend to the waiters, but also the clubmen, who are conceived as lifeless marionettes when the revelation of the missing cutlery dawns upon them: 'none of the company could say anything except the man of wood—Colonel Pound—who seemed galvanised into an unnatural life' (*CFB* 45). The reification in wood, followed by the uncanny galvanisation, combines with the unusual phraseology—'could say anything' as opposed to 'could think of anything to say'—to convey a sense of petrifaction caused by extreme mental and physical torpor.

In this way, Chesterton once more invests a disorientating nonsense theme with a grounding satirical purpose. In 'The Flat Freak', he discusses the schismatic absence of humour that occurs when the upper classes attempt to stage a comic event, here the 'Freak Dinner', a high-society fancy-dress party on a grand scale: what is to be deplored 'is the abyss of inanity in such feasts—it may be literally called a yawning abyss' (*CDN* 6:179). In an echo of his intertwined critique of the detached refinement of Decadence and the derangement inducted by the 'starry abyss of nonsense', the 'yawning [...] abyss of inanity' in the official feast is combined with the 'horrible modern abyss between the souls of the rich and the poor' (*CFB* 45), as the story's narrator puts it, to produce an intertwined social and ontological breach of the Covenant of Things.

Having elaborated the club's atmosphere of alienation, Chesterton uses the revelation of the theft as the pretext for a re-integrative movement, enabled by the combined intervention of moral satire and the folk grotesque. Nonetheless, before the regeneration comes the reckoning. When Brown delivers his final summary of events, the fact that Flambeau has long since handed back the stolen cutlery liberates the priest to discuss the thief with a sympathy absent from the withering disdain that he shows for the institution itself: '"Odd, isn't it," he said, "that a thief and a vagabond should repent, when so many who are rich and secure remain hard and frivolous, and *without fruit* for God or man?"' (*CFB* 47–48; my emphasis). This un-regenerative imagery finds a later echo in the lays of *The Flying Inn*. Dalroy's song of 'Mr Mandragon the Millionaire' indicts this fantastical figure for his enervation—he relies upon a machine to haul him out of bed and wash him—before mocking his infertile isolation, which pertains even in death, thus contravening Chesterton's ethics of material immersion: 'he lies there fluffy and soft and grey, and certainly quite refined, / When he might have rotted with the flowers and fruit with Adam and all mankind' (161).

In explaining Flambeau's *modus operandi*, Father Brown notes irreverently that it '"was no new thing to [the waiters] that a swell from the dinner party should pace all parts of the house like an animal at the zoo"' (*CFB* 50). The slang-term 'swell' not only suggests Brown's verbal identification with the 'waiting' class, along with a tacit mockery of the diners' grotesquely bloated stomachs, but also introduces a cadaverous note. The same term arises in 'The Monstrosity' (*DN* 11 Mar. 1911), published five months after 'The Queer Feet', in a gruesomely burlesque metaphor for the imperial body politic: 'When a dead body is rotting, it does not diminish; it swells. [...] Our own country is really in this state of swollen decay' (*CDN* 7:88). In this light, Chesterton's choice of 'Moocher' as the title of the Fishermen's colonial associate conveys a subtle satire of imperial politics, since the word connotes, in British slang, aimless loitering and, in American slang, thievery.

The nomenclatural levelling effect of 'Moocher' echoes Brown's recourse to unrefined colloquialisms, forcibly conferring upon the upper-class figure a term usually associated with the lower class, while the colonial activities of Moocher are parodied by Flambeau, who loiters in the clubmen's indigenous environment with apparently unproductive aimlessness, while surreptitiously appropriating any valuables in the immediate vicinity. Whereas Chesterton's contemporaneous social treatise, *What's Wrong With the World*, notes that '[t]he English statesman [...] is born with a silver spoon in his mouth, so that he may never afterwards be found with the silver spoons in his pocket' (*CW* 4:61), Father Brown later observes, in 'The Red Moon of Meru', that '"the West also has its own way of covering theft with sophistry"' (*CFB* 630).

Flambeau's appearance at the feast constitutes a parodic return of the repressed, which causes the silver accumulated by colonial appropriation to mysteriously dematerialise. His mischief serves to highlight an unspoken crime of the society itself, in line with Freud's argument that the unmasking impetus of travesty 'comes into play when someone has seized dignity and authority by a deception and these have to be taken from him in reality' (*Jokes*, 262). Elsewhere, Freud explains that one definition of 'heimlich' is '"to steal secretly away"' (*Uncanny*, 129–30), so that 'the term "uncanny" (unheimlich) applies to everything that was intended to remain secret, hidden away, and has come into the open' (*Uncanny*, 132). In the case at hand, this principle applies to the story's exposure of the exclusive club itself, hidden in plain sight in central London, as well as the final revelation of Flambeau's intrusion and crime, which uncovers, in turn, the acts of domestic and colonial annexation that secure the club's existence. As Chesterton notes in 'The Very Decayed Gentleman' (*DN* 6 Nov. 1909), the wealthy man 'will not (as a rule) steal spoons; but he will steal common land' (*CDN* 6:124).

In view of Chesterton's vision of the imperial body as a decaying corpse, it is perhaps unsurprising that when the Fishermen discover that the presence of death has accounted for the malfunction of the waiting machine, their sense of discomfiture becomes particularly acute: 'For a few weird seconds they had really felt as if the fifteenth waiter might be the ghost of the dead man upstairs. They had been dumb under that oppression, for ghosts to them were an embarrassment, like beggars' (*CFB* 46). As Bakhtin notes, proverbially '[d]uring banquets ghosts appear only to usurpers or to the representatives of the old dying world' (*Rabelais*, 296). As an intermediary with the dead, the priest is an equally unwelcome presence, hidden away from the guests by the proprietor, Mr Lever, because 'a mere glimpse of him afar off might precipitate a crisis in the club' (*CFB* 38). The theological context of Brown's arrival as a father-confessor is lent a further irony by the fact that the feast of the 'Twelve True Fishermen' is a parody of The Last Supper—'they could occupy the terrace in the most luxurious style of all, being ranged along the inner side of the table, with no one opposite' (*CFB* 43)—in which the only religious figure present has been locked in a cloakroom.

Nonetheless, When Brown and Flambeau finally succeed in disrupting the 'crisis of tedium' (*CFB* 21) that grips the institution, their intervention engenders a more productive crisis, in the term's sense of a 'point in the progress of a disease when [... a] change takes place which is decisive of recovery or death' (*PTSE* 1:391).⁸ Chesterton sends the pair into the club not to serve terminal notice upon it, but, in accordance with the origins of festive comedy, to perform a regenerative fertility rite. In the eighteenth-century English Harlequinade, John Rich (alias Lun) portrayed Harlequin as a character whose 'necromantic powers [provided] an excuse for novel transformation scenes' (Welsford, 301–302), while more contemporaneously to Chesterton, Charles Adrien Wettach (alias Grock) had invested the Clown with an ethos that was 'vitalizing. When he passes by, unwound clocks begin to tick' (Welsford, 314).

Nonetheless, Brown and Flambeau not only embody the joyful vision of pantomimic regeneration articulated by Chesterton in 'A Defence of Farce', but also the more sobering symbol of egalitarianism set forth in 'A Defence of Skeletons'. As the narrator of 'The Queer Feet' explains to the apparently oblivious reader,

> [t]here is in this world a very aged rioter and demagogue who breaks into the most refined retreats with the dreadful information that all men are brothers, and wherever this leveller went on his pale horse it was Father Brown's trade to follow.
>
> (*CFB* 38)

Here Death is depicted as the archetypal carnivalesque boundary-crosser, breaking into closed societies with the 'dreadful information' of the brotherhood of Man, while Flambeau is conflated with Christ in the form of the Harlequinesque 'rioter and demagogue'.

Meanwhile, Chesterton's image elsewhere of death as an insatiable feaster 'devour[ing] all without distinction' is offset by the desiccated nature of the feast into which Brown and Flambeau ride their pale horse. The revelation of the presence of death causes the narrator to speculate that it

> may be (so supernatural is the word death) that each of these idle men looked for a second at his soul, and saw it as a small dried pea. One of them—the duke, I think—even said with the idiotic kindness of wealth: "Is there anything we can do?".
>
> (*CFB* 46)

Kindness is combined with uselessness here to devastatingly terse effect. At this late stage in the narrative, the duke's question strikes the reader more as a plaintive entreaty—as would be implied if one were to once more emphasise the 'anything'—than a disinterested offer of help, while the dried pea metaphor ties the account ironically to the feast-travesty itself, through the provision of a fittingly unappetising link between the diners and their dinner.

This moment of negative epiphany coincides with the appearance of Brown in the role of mystery disperser, explaining the theft that motivated Flambeau's '"dance of death"' (*CFB* 48), as Brown describes it. In the later story 'The Mirror of the Magistrate' (*Cassell's Magazine*, Apr. 1925), Brown is himself described as looking like '"some old black woodcut at the end of a Dance of Death"' (*CFB* 528), the late-Medieval allegory of the skeleton leading men to the grave, which Esti Sheinberg considers perhaps 'the most characteristic instance of the grotesque' due to its combination of 'the skeleton's fearsome traits with an incongruously amused dance', which produces a 'blurring of the boundaries between life and death, the animate and inanimate' (219). The introduction of the *Danse Macabre* into 'The Queer Feet' brings a further skilful balancing of the poles of satire and the grotesque. Much as Chesterton redeems the unnerving grotesquery of the skeleton by extrapolating a pedagogic lesson from its structure, in 'Morality and the Clown' (*DN* 28 Dec. 1907) he discusses the *Danse Macabre* in terms that correspond to the regenerative purpose of Flambeau's capering:

> It was the dance of death; but it was a dance. Not taking the body seriously it flung the body into fifty frantic attitudes. It had force, and the dance of death led the way to the dance of life.
> (*CDN* 4:388)

The same vitalising quality is present in Flambeau's pseudonymous embodiment of fire. As Bakhtin explains, 'the image of fire in carnival' is '[d]eeply ambivalent [...] It is a fire that simultaneously destroys and renews the world' (*Problems*, 126). In 'The Two Fires' (*DN* 1 July 1911), Chesterton elaborates upon the literal meaning of 'Bonfire'—'the Good Fire', which burns only the 'bad things' of a culture while preserving the 'good things' (*CDN* 7:162). From this premise, he develops an analogy of distinct modes of revolution, noting that while he would like to see 'the sneer [...] struck from the face of the well-fed', he nonetheless wishes to preserve 'all that wealth of wood that might have made dolls and chairs and tables' (*CDN* 7:162). In 'The Queer Feet', the positive regeneration of 'the man of wood', Colonel Pound, is demonstrative of this principle—a reanimation of the dead that Brown and Flambeau essay through their respective employment of mental agility and physical vitality.

At the story's conclusion, Father Brown mimics the colonel's reanimation, delivering his account of the theft while sitting on the cloakroom partition—'kicking his short legs like a little boy on a gate' (*CFB* 48)—rather in the manner of a wooden doll rescued from the fire. The image brings to mind the folk-devil, Petrushka, in the Russian puppet theatre, who conventionally 'launches [...] into a wordy monologue, often with his legs dangling from the booth in a gesture of familiarity with the crowd' (Leatherbarrow, 128). As William J. Leatherbarrow explains,

> [t]he primary function of Petrushka was to make people laugh, but the kind of laughter it sought to evoke was [...] disruptive laughter, challenging all social and moral conventions [...] the disruptive carnival mood invited collusion: It passed beyond the puppet booth and infected the audience.
>
> (127–28)

In a complementary action, Flambeau's *Danse Macabre* operates as a mime, a comic form that Kiremidjian identifies as a progenitor of the *Commedia dell'Arte*: in classical tradition 'the mimes [...] parodied the life of the lower and upper class alike, were sympathetic with the cause or grievance of the common people and represented a form of mediation between lowest peasant and highest aristocrat' (*Study*, 99).

In 'England and Caricature' (*DN* 28 Mar. 1908), Chesterton defends satirical scurrility on the grounds that conventionally '[m]en reminded a man maliciously of his bodily weakness [...] if it was set-off against his worldly power' (*CDN* 5:44). However, he also acknowledges the drawbacks of excessively caustic satire: 'We do not reconcile by pointing out the balance and distribution of glass eyes and wooden legs in all classes of the community. It produces equality, but hardly fraternity' (*CDN* 5:45). He finds the answer to this difficulty in the emollient strategies of caricature:

> this English literary style, coarse and yet kind, has done more than anything else to create the possibility of a genial grotesque [...] The wooden leg is insisted on, but not with contempt, and yet, again, not with commiseration. It is insisted on with gusto, as if the Admiral had grown his wooden leg by the sheer energy of his character.
>
> (*CDN* 5:45–46)

Recall the 'genial gusto' that Woolf attributed to Chesterton's fiction. As both would likely have been aware, geniality not only connotes friendliness or hospitable conduct, but also that which is 'nuptial, generative', from the Latin *genialis*—'festive (literally, pertaining to marriage rites)' (Barnhart, 427). In this spirit, the narrator of 'The Queer Feet' metes out a carnivalesque balance of 'praise and curses' (Kristeva, *Kristeva*, 49) to the 'vague and kindly gentlemen' of the club—phrasing that emphasises the members' evanescence while granting a concession to their essential decency.

The period of carnival not only empowers those normally unwelcome to enter into the exclusive event, it also liberates the members of the official feast to behave for once like real people. The narrator never denies the efficacy of the club as a socially disenabling space, exclusive in the literal sense: 'it was a thing which paid, not by attracting people, but actually by turning people away' (*CFB* 36). However, it is also made clear that the doors of exclusivity close in as well as out—absurdly the hotel's 'very inconveniences were considered as walls protecting a particular class' (*CFB* 37), so that the members' obsession with class discrimination leads to their privation, as illustrated by Brown's irreverent image of the guests as animals 'at the zoo'. While the narrator attempts to goad the reader into action, Brown's mockery scolds the clubmen to break free of their imaginative confines. The resulting revitalisation of the military 'man of wood' prefigures the central nonsense-motif of *The Flying Inn*, in which the titular pub sign represents 'the idea of dead wood walking about' (188). Much as Brown and Flambeau reinstate bygone popular-cultural traditions within modern society in order to acquaint Colonel Pound with his benevolent heritage, the sculpted tree of the pub sign is a metaphor of England, returned to a consciousness of its traditions, which 'until a little while ago the tree did not know that it knew' (*Flying*, 268).

By inscribing this moral at the conclusion of 'The Queer Feet', Chesterton achieves the high-water mark of his ambition to fuse satirical instruction with grotesque vitality. Bakhtin argues that 'Carnival is the place for working out, in a concretely sensuous, half-real and half-play-acted form, a new mode of interrelationship between individuals' (*Problems*, 123). A similar atmosphere of festive brotherhood pertains at the conclusion of 'The Queer Feet': Brown tells 'the story as easily as if he were telling it to an old friend by a Christmas fire', while the colonel, by now swept up in the ingenious mystery, notes admiringly that Flambeau '"must have been a clever fellow"' (*CFB* 48). Brown's disruptive laughter has produced a social conversion narrative that ends in benign collusion: the colonel reassures him, '"I don't want to get the fellow jailed; make yourself easy about that"' (*CFB* 48). If Flambeau represents a fictional rendition of Chesterton's pantomimic innocent criminal, his exoneration achieves a modest exposition of 'the redemption of the world by comradeship' that Chesterton had conceived in his ardent youth. At the very least, as he argues in *Charles Dickens*, 'fear of the waiter is the beginning of dining' (134).

Notes

1 With characteristic even-handedness, Chesterton acknowledges elsewhere that 'Maeterlinck is a very great man' (*Varied*, 209).
2 The quote is from Wilde's 'Sonnet to Liberty' (1881). The final phrase of the original is 'in some things'.
3 See Coates, *Chesterton*, 66–71, for an incisive analysis of Chesterton's Edwardian journalism and its relation to his audience.
4 See my book chapter 'A Playground for Adults: Urban Recreation in Chesterton's Detective Fiction' (in Beamont and Ingleby, *G.K. Chesterton, London and Modernity*, London: Bloomsbury, 2013) for a more detailed account of Chesterton's identification with the 'criminal class'.

5 Blatchford was the author of *Merrie England* (1893) and a hero of Chesterton's youth, but subsequently became his antagonist in the religious controversy that inspired *Orthodoxy*.
6 Christopher Hitchens advances this interpretation in 'The Reactionary'.
7 Since Bergson's *Laughter* (*Le Rire*, 1900) was not translated into English until 1911, the correspondence between the philosopher's theory and Chesterton's fictional practice would seem to have been coincidental, though no less striking for that.
8 The phrase, 'a crisis of tedium', derives from the preceding *Father Brown* story, 'The Secret Garden' (*Storyteller*, Oct. 1910).

3 A Hundred Visions and Revisions
Chesterton Refracted through the Avant-Garde of 1910

> It is incomprehensible to me that any thinker can calmly call himself a modernist; he might as well call himself a Thursdayite.
> —Chesterton, 'The Case for the Ephemeral' (*All Things*, 3)
>
> [W]e all three [...] are comedians, and have the secret of very perfect disguises. We can make up [...] so perfectly that practically we become different persons at once.
> —Evan Royal, in Lewis's *Mrs. Dukes' Million* (282)

In 'A Defence of Detective Stories' (*Speaker*, 22 June 1901), Chesterton proclaims the potential of detective fiction to aesthetically validate popular culture: a 'rude, popular literature of the romantic possibilities of the modern city' has recently 'arisen in the popular detective stories, as rough and refreshing as the ballads of Robin Hood' (*Defendant*, 161).[1] While Chesterton fulfilled his own prophecy at the close of the decade with the early *Father Brown* stories, Bentley also got in on the act—his 'parodic challenge' (Baldick, 275) to Sherlock Holmes, *Trent's Last Case*, was conceived in 1910 and finally published in 1913 with a dedication to Chesterton, on the grounds that 'I owe you a book in return for "The Man Who Was Thursday"' (1).[2] The detection genre had established an extraordinary cultural predominance in the intervening years, a rise attributable at least in part to Chesterton's success in achieving the aim ascribed to him by Bentley in 1900—that of 'educat[ing] the public up' to sharing his aesthetic values. Nonetheless, this infraction of 'rude, popular literature' upon the cultural marketplace soon provoked a countermovement within the intelligentsia. As Chris Baldick notes, highbrow commentators increasingly deplored 'the infection of intellectuals through the detective craze by the values and tastes of the common mob' (274), phrasing that suggests a class-based anxiety over the genre's capacity to transgress cultural boundary lines.[3]

Bentley's charmingly fallible sleuth, Philip Trent, not only commanded Chesterton's esteem—he later termed *Trent's Last Case* 'the best detective story of modern times' (*Autobiography*, 61)—but perhaps more surprisingly, that of Virginia Woolf, who wrote to David Garnett of her 'passion for Trent's Last Case', at the same moment in which she was 'trying to finish' *Mrs Dalloway* (Woolf, *Change,* 4 Jan 1925, 153). That this approval was only attested in private correspondence is suggestive of the cultural angst that surrounded the genre, which led to engagements sufficiently furtive to imply a fear of literary lawbreaking. Although T.S. Eliot was renowned amongst intimates for his 'party trick' of 'quot[ing] long passages of Sherlock Holmes from memory' (Ackroyd, 167), when he later emulated Chesterton with a series of articles in praise of detective fiction for the *Criterion* in 1927, he did so anonymously. Marianne Moore suspected Eliot of also *writing* detective fiction under a pseudonym (Kenner, *Invisible,* x), a clandestine activity that Wyndham Lewis actually did undertake in 1910, attempting to publish a mystery novel under a pen-name conceived 'to disguise its origin' (Lewis, *Letters,* 44).

When Chesterton's detective/thief double act injects the 'rude, popular' spirit of the public square into the sequestered confines of the Vernon Hotel, their elaborate practical joke at the expense of class exclusivity is conceived not only to bring various forms of cover-up to light, but also to counteract the cultural anxieties that engender them. That this incursion is infused with uproarious imagery of death and renewal is lent an irony by the status of 1910 as a wider threshold moment in modern literature, in which a younger generation of avowedly 'inverted Edwardians' (Heady, 25) threatened to render Chesterton aesthetically redundant at the very moment of his creative apotheosis. The proto-modernists of 1910 not only came to view Chesterton as an influence as interdicted as detective fiction, but also set about reconstructing the very walls of exclusivity that he had sought to demolish. Nonetheless, within the work and play of the new avant-garde, we not only discover deviations from, but also parallels with Chesterton's imaginative landscape, whether in the buffooneries of Bloomsbury, the practical jokes of Italian Futurism, or the range of textual comedians conceived by the young Eliot and Lewis, whose early avatars offered their creators the opportunity to become different persons at once: both modernists *and* Thursdayites.

The Latest Artistic Insanities

'The Queer Feet' was published in November 1910. A month later, Virginia Woolf also noticed that something had gone wrong with the servants. Famously, Woolf considered that 'on or about December 1910, human character changed' (Woolf, *Virginia,* 96), an everyday proof of which could be found in the sudden, disorientating mobility of domestic staff:

> one can see the change [...] in the character of one's cook. The Victorian cook lived like a leviathan in the lower depths, formidable, silent, obscure, inscrutable; the Georgian cook is a creature of sunshine and fresh air; in and out of the drawing-room, now to borrow the Daily Herald, now to ask advice about a hat.
>
> (Woolf, *Virginia,* 96–97)

In taking an interest in current affairs and fashion, Woolf's cook has begun to parody her leisured employer, much as the adaptive deportment of Flambeau transgresses the figurative boundary separating waiters and gentlemen, rendering the domains equivalent in the process.

In February 1910, Woolf had engaged in a little parodic boundary transgression of her own, participating in the 'Dreadnought Hoax', in which a group of Bloomsburyites, including Duncan Grant and Woolf's brother, Adrian Steven, disguised themselves as Abyssinian ambassadors, 'blacking-up' and donning false beards, so as to trick the Royal Navy into offering them a tour of its flagship vessel (see Downer, 94–137). The ringleader of this prank was Horace de Vere Cole, an Anglo-Irish aristocrat who went on to become a shadowy buffoon figure in the court of modernism, a kind of ersatz Flambeau who travestied many of the subversive aesthetic dictums of the avant-garde in an increasingly tawdry series of practical jokes and other acts of public parody. Although Woolf sought to distance herself from Cole's later antics, she enthusiastically recounted her part in the Dreadnought hoax at intervals throughout her subsequent career (see Stansky, 42–43).

As these examples from the domestic and public realms suggest, the earliest *Father Brown* stories' insistent confusion of cultural boundaries through acts of disruptive parody retained significance as subtle divergences arose in the manner in which a new generation of writers handled similar concepts. Perhaps the most telling of these alterations is the reversal of social viewpoint discernible in the comparable conceits of Chesterton and Woolf. Father Brown is assigned physical and verbal mannerisms—public disorder in 'The Blue Cross', slang in 'The Queer Feet'—that the intelligentsia associated with the lower classes, a conceit in which the priest is positioned at the bottom looking up, rather than the top looking down. Similarly, while Chesterton uses reifying and anthropomorphic nonsense-imagery in 'The Queer Feet' to characterise the plutocratic aristocracy as an uncanny 'other', Woolf's essay employs comparable tropes from the reverse social perspective, adopting a tone of amused, proprietorial indulgence in her description of the Victorian cook as a fathomless sea monster and the Georgian cook as a variant genus, the 'creature of sunshine'.

Woolf's tone betrays an estrangement from the domestic staff that runs counter to Chesterton's continual emphasis upon the importance of humour as a bridge between ostensibly disparate social and cultural groups. Whereas Woolf seemingly hands over the *Daily Herald* with a 'Whatever next?' shrug of the shoulders, Chesterton's pantomimic reanimation of the aristocratic 'man of wood' in 'The Queer Feet' draws Father Brown into sympathetic dialogue with a figure previously characterised as bafflingly alien. Similarly, Chesterton's early verse satire of Decadence, 'On the Disastrous Spread of Aestheticism in All Classes', pre-empts Woolf's vision of confusion between domestic staff and leisured aesthetes: 'Cooks recorded frames of mind / In sad and subtle chops' (*CW* 10.2:378). While Chesterton's nonsense poem is analogous to Woolf's account in its conveyance of a violation of norms of order, he again explores this incongruity from a reverse perspective, viewing the production of introspective literature, rather than platefuls of chops, as the ontologically dubious endeavour. If domestic boundaries are to be crossed, Chesterton recommends that the aesthete should join the cook in the kitchen, rather than vice versa—an example of his consistent questioning of the arbitrary valorisation of one area of creative expression over another. As he notes in an article on 'The Millionaires' Freak Dinner' (*ILN*, 24 Mar. 1906), '[t]o cook a cutlet in a really new way would be an act of the imagination' (*CW* 27:149).

Chesterton's view that the *littérateur's* unreflective assumption of superiority reflects a solipsistic mindset is supported by Peter Kaye's discussion of Woolf's belief in the central importance of 'an interior self that may in its freest expression be uncontaminated by other people' (67). Although Woolf gently satirises Clarissa Dalloway's self-absorption—'she could feel nothing for the Albanians, or was it the Armenians? but she loved her roses (didn't that help the Armenians?)' (*Mrs Dalloway*, 88)—and recurs insistently to the question of whether her heroine is 'at heart a snob' (*Mrs Dalloway*, 138), she implicitly approves Dalloway's urge for 'solitude; even between husband and wife a gulf' (*Mrs Dalloway*, 88). This privileging of a 'meditative isolation' situated 'beyond the reach of shared, public language' (Kaye, 90) accrued a real-life social corollary in Woolf's preference for inhabiting a milieu detached from the social other and 'dominated by the restraint and social homogeneity of upper-middle-class England' (Kaye, 67).

Accordingly, a further divergence from Chesterton's cultural politics is discernible in Woolf's public boundary crossing. Although the urban practical jokes of Father Brown and Flambeau bear a superficial resemblance to the hoaxing of Woolf and her friends, the antics of Chesterton's protagonists operate as a communication device, promoting a liberating estrangement from convention that enables establishment and anti-establishment figures to arrive at a productive mutual understanding. Conversely, Woolf's principal motivation for participating in the Dreadnought hoax lay in a desire to embarrass her disliked cousin, Willy Fisher, who was the flag commander to Admiral May on the ship (see Downer, 95). After the event, Cole and Fisher indulged in the penance of a mutual whipping—Cole for his infraction and Fisher for his credulity—thus carrying over the rituals of public school into public life. This again demonstrates the amenability of parodic nonsense to both open and closed, or popular and academic, applications. When Stansky identifies the Dreadnought episode as standing in the 'tradition of undergraduate hoaxes' (45), we discern Chesterton's carnivalesque exposition of similarity across borders supplanted by the internal monologue of a social elite subtly reaffirming its own values.

Similarly, although the hoaxers' physical parodying of African stereotypes ostensibly satirised the Navy's ignorance of foreign cultures and unreflective genuflection before dignitaries, there is a strong tincture of assumed comic abjection in the conceit—in a less than Swiftian development, much public amusement was derived from the nonsensical murmuring of 'bunga, bunga' (Stansky, 30) by the pseudo-Abyssinian contingent. The significance of this conflation of nonsense and abjection becomes clear when the prank is viewed in conjunction with the opulent fancy dress parties that found popularity amongst Woolf's set at this time, which closely resemble the aristocratic 'freak dinners' that Chesterton had implicitly drawn into the satirical range of 'The Queer Feet'. As he argues in 'The Flat Freak', there is nothing 'more abject than the union of elaborate and recherché arrangements with an old and obvious point' (*CDN* 6:179).

In 'The Millionaires' Freak Dinner', Chesterton elaborates the grounds of his irritation, discussing a 'South African Freak dinner', apparently held in England, in which 'pieces of bread [were] cut in the shape of diamonds' and 'rich men enjoyed pretending to be savages' (*CW* 27:150). While the immediate context of a crass celebration of the economic rewards of the Boer War, a conflict that he had bitterly opposed, was sure to raise Chesterton's hackles, his analysis also draws attention to the complacency of the racial binarism posited by such parodic events. He sees this as deriving from a blithe assumption of uncomplicated difference, rather than an enactment of the 'almost torturing truth of a thing being like oneself and yet not like oneself', which he considered to be the instructively analogic lesson to be derived from 'laughing at foreigners' ('Cockneys and Their Jokes', collected in *All Things*, 13). The 'superficial contrast covering a substantial congruity' that Chesterton identified as the essence of parody thus becomes a model for approaching the human race itself.

In the later *Father Brown* story 'The Mistake of the Machine' (*Pall Mall Magazine*, Oct. 1913), Chesterton employs an American 'freak dinner' as the satirical premise for a case involving the disappearance of an heiress. A journalistic report implanted within the text discusses the prior attendance of the town's 'exclusive citizens' at events such as the 'Cannibal Crush Lunch, at which the confections handed round were sarcastically moulded in the forms of human arms and legs, and during which more than one of our gayest mental gymnasts was heard offering to eat his partner' (*CFB* 231). The next event on the social calendar is a 'Slum Dinner' (*CFB* 241), conceived as a 'parody of the simple manners and customs at the other end of Society's scale' (*CFB* 231). Here, Chesterton extends the self-exempting laughter of the freak dinner to signify class-based, rather than racially-grounded, othering, in a parallel with Woolf's implied separation from both the servants and the Abyssinians. 'The Millionaire's Freak Dinner' puckishly confounds this assumption of binary difference by comparing the urge for 'solitude' evinced by the English aristocracy—and by Woolfian heroines such as Clarissa Dalloway—to that of the ostensibly uncivilised 'Ojibway' (*CW* 27:151). This insistent projection of equivalence recurs throughout Chesterton's journalism. Elsewhere, he notes that 'there is nothing which I so sincerely respect in savages as their widespread and generally ascertained disposition to wear top-hats' ('Summer Festivals and Ceremonies', *ILN*, 19 May 1906; *CW* 27:191).

In *The Return of Don Quixote*, Chesterton has Douglas Murrel speculate that '"it wouldn't take much to make the Smart Set black their faces as they used to whiten their hair"' (*CW* 8:53).[4] The acuity of this remark is illustrated by Woolf's attendance of a '"post-impressionist" fancy-dress ball' in December 1910, in which, as Martyn Downer records, she, Steven, and Grant 'donned native costumes and applied black make-up to attend the ball as savages from a Gauguin painting' (140). While this event shares the motif of dressing up as 'savages' with the South African freak dinner and Chesterton's satirical 'Cannibal Crush Lunch', the guests' physical appropriation of the contents of the exhibition literally parades the participants' identification with the avant-garde art even as it caricatures the subject matter. Again, this sets the guests at one remove from the implicitly abject figures imitated, with the metaphorical frame of the painting serving to hang quotation marks around the image. In a similar action, Stansky has noted the equivocal nature of the disguises adopted in the Dreadnought Hoax, in which the participants chose 'to impersonate a group of the "other," but in a rather elegant way and at an exalted rank' (18).

The deliberate category mistake of the ball's reification of people as paintings also highlights the nonsense foundation of the event. In 'The Millionaire's Freak Dinner', Chesterton's political critique is accompanied by an aesthetically grounded analysis in a passage that evokes his enduring anxiety over the correspondence between nonsense and Decadence:

> Nonsense of this sort is not imaginative for the very reason that it is infinite. [...] In good nonsense, as much as in any other kind of art, there are nine hundred and ninety-nine things that are wrong and only one thing that is right.
>
> (*CW* 27:149)

Much as he conceives the lack of an 'object' in 'The Flat Freak' to disclose a 'yawning abyss' of nonsense, he considers such events to lack the one 'right' component—a satirical and/or allegorical message of some kind—that would engender an ethical grounding to justify the conceit. Failing to find any such message, he compares these events, in emotive terms, to a 'horrible negative [...] unmeaning [...] nightmare' (*CW* 27:150).

The exclusivity of these events also presents a sharp contrast with the vision of meaningful, democratic public performance that Chesterton found embodied in the pageant and the mystery play, instead summoning up 'the oppressive pomp [of] a conservatory or a masquerade ball' that Borges detects in the popular view of Wilde's 'notion of art as a select or secret game' (79). This re-emergence of the high-society nonsense games of Decadence is also a feature of the avant-garde spectacle that inspired the Post-Impressionist fancy-dress ball. As the name suggests, the party was conceived as a jocular response—perhaps a burlesque pun on *impression*ism—to Roger Fry's Post-Impressionist exhibition, which opened at the Grafton Galleries on 5 November 1910. Fry's contentious show is commonly cited as a further cultural context informing Woolf's assertion that December 1910 formed a threshold moment in the history of human character. The motifs of nonsense and hoaxing that punctuated Woolf's life and writing come together in the public controversy that accompanied the event, which focused almost entirely upon the apparent impossibility of establishing any coherent interpretative framework through which to comprehend the works on display, and the consequent supposition of the bourgeoisie that it was the collective victim of an elaborate hoax (see O'Keefe, 101–2).

In view of the broader imaginative confusion of life and art that characterised the era, Flambeau's contemporaneous emergence as a popular fictional character coincides fittingly with Philip Burne-Jones's suspicion, voiced on 17 November 1910, that the exhibition was 'a huge practical joke organised in Paris at the expense of our countrymen' (qtd. in Stansky, 220). If this was so, there was no Father Brown on hand to extrapolate a moral. For Chesterton, these aesthetic developments again demonstrated the intimate correlation of art-for-art's sake with nonsense-for-nonsense's sake—an ostentatious private joke in which no avenue of communication was left open to the observer, and no instructive or dialogic element could be detected to ground the work within any form of collective understanding. As these intimations of detachment and derangement suggest, the psychological challenge at stake evokes Chesterton's apprehensive reading of *Alice*, specifically Lecercle's account of the threats that Carroll's heroine confronts in her dealings with the aggressively inscrutable looking-glass characters who construct 'the framework for a [...] nightmare. Tweedledum and Tweedledee are trying to make Alice as mad as they are' (84).

Rhetoric of mental imbalance suffused the reception of the new avant-garde. A year after the Post-Impressionist exhibition, a correspondent to the *New Age* (14 Dec. 1911) joked that Wyndham Lewis's contributions to the second exhibition of the Camden Town Group 'might have a soothing effect as decorations for the walls of a lunatic asylum, as they are, one would suppose, so exactly akin to the mental vision reigning there' (Evans, F., 166). Five days before the publication of this review, Chesterton had railed against 'the latest artistic insanities' ('The Mystagogue', *DN* 9 Dec. 1911) in response to a reproduction of Picasso's Cubist still life, *La Mandoline et la Pernod* (1911), in the *New Age*, while commiserating with the artist over having evidently 'had the misfortune to upset the ink and tried to dry it with his boots' (*CDN* 7:261). Here we perceive the public buffoon in full motley, affecting to explain away the destabilising high-concept philosophy of the artist as a pitiable expression of an abject frailty—clumsiness—in which brute physicality overwhelms intellectual agency.

This account can be read as another of Chesterton's attempts to repel imagery that too closely resembles his own experiences of mental disturbance. In *Thursday*, Syme's alarm over Sunday's nightmarish visage might be mistaken for an incredulous review of Picasso's later Cubist portraiture: 'The eye was so far away from the nose that it wasn't an eye'. Nonetheless, Chesterton again translates psychological unease into cogent cultural critique, arguing that the artist's supporters 'seek to terrify democracy by the good old anti-democratic muddlements: that "the public" does not understand these things' (*CDN* 7:261). Chesterton's mockery serves, once more, to situate him as the figurehead of the excluded public at large. The organisation of the private Post-Impressionist ball as a parodic response to Fry's public exhibition reflects Chesterton's view that the conceptual exclusivity of this art was directly linked to the literal exclusivity of the leisure activities of the cultural elite from which it arose.

Chesterton's display of scepticism over Picasso was also explicitly conceived to offset the suspiciously acritical 'eulogies' (*CDN* 7:261) with which the intelligentsia often responded to such innovations. A week earlier in the *New Age* (30 Nov. 1911), John Middleton Murry had confessed somewhat absurdly that

> ultra-modernist, as I am in my artistic sympathies, I frankly disclaim any pretension to an understanding or even an appreciation of Picasso. I am awed by him. [...] That his later work is unsaleable confirms my conviction that Picasso is one of those spirits who have progressed beyond their age.
>
> ('Art', 115)

In an earlier article on a similar theme ('Aristocrats as Mystagogues', *ILN*, 25 Jan. 1908), Chesterton had argued the reverse of Murry's final point, discussing the counterintuitive commercial efficacy of setting up barriers to comprehension that deliberately estrange the audience. Characterising the late-Edwardian era as 'the age of mystagogues', he explains that rather than cultural products being

> praised because they are popular [...] this is the first time, perhaps, in the whole history of the world in which things can be praised because they are unpopular. The demagogue succeeds because he

makes himself understood [...] the mystagogue succeeds because he gets himself misunderstood.

(CW 28:31–32)

In such a climate, aesthetic mystagogues will 'declare themselves great artists because they [are] unsuccessful: that is the peculiarity of our own time, which has a positive bias against the populace' (CW 28:32). In an anticipation of the symbiotic link between the high-minded Post-Impressionist exhibition and the burlesque Post-Impressionist ball, Chesterton goes on to note that

we have seen the process of secrecy and aristocracy introduced even into jokes. [... A] small school of aesthetes [...] have introduced an almost insane individualism into that one form of intercourse which is specially and uproariously communal. They have made even levities into secrets.

(CW 28:32)

Lisa Ede observes of Alice's frustration in Wonderland that '[i]t is hard to play when everyone knows the rules of the game but you' (47). Chesterton's vision of culture is one in which everyone should be invited to play, and he responds with Alice-like disdain when he feels left out. Typically, he also responds with parody. As Kathleen Blake argues, mimicry operates partially as an 'assertion of control [...] a way of mastering reality' (62). The act of parody offers a means both of reaffirming one's epistemological mastery and of teaching the parodied figure a lesson in the principle of democratic immersion, serving proof that one has not only understood the joke, but capped it, drawing the would-be isolated artist into an enforced dialogue in the process. Accordingly, in 'Aristocrats as Mystagogues', Chesterton joins in with the production of deliberate category mistakes in order to highlight the absurdities of heavily codified fashion, imagining the mystagogue enquiring, '"[y]ou don't see anything wrong in drinking a Benedictine on Thursday?... No, of course *you* wouldn't"' (CW 28:35).

This battling of nonsense with nonsense, which Chesterton had first undertaken in his sallies against Decadence in *Greybeards*, again reflects his urge to manipulate Carroll's 'pure' nonsense to the purpose of moral satire. As Alfred Noyes has argued, '[y]ou might as well say—the phrase so familiar to readers of Alice in Wonderland—clinches Chesterton's arguments again and again with some aptly absurd illustration of a logical fallacy' (127). He soon had cause to mobilise this faculty in relation to a movement that came to embody all that he found most politically, philosophically, and psychologically characteristic—and antipathetic—in the culture of the modern era: Futurism.

Chesterton versus the Future

Two further cultural events of late 1910 particularly help to pinpoint the terms of the emergent schism between Chesterton and his new antagonists in the vanguard of modernism—Filippo Marinetti's first public lecture in Britain, held at the Lyceum Club in December 1910, and Lawrence Irving's adaptation of Fyodor Dostoevsky's *Crime and Punishment* (1866) at the Garrick Theatre in November 1910, an event that engendered a sudden increase in awareness of Dostoevsky's work amongst the English cognoscenti. Chesterton was at the forefront of critics attentive to the significance of both figures, evincing a strong identification with Dostoevsky, whom he later described as 'one of the two or three greatest novelists of the nineteenth century' (BL Add MS 73283 fol.30), and an equally marked deprecation of Marinetti.[5]

With the emergence of Marinetti's Futurist movement, the diverse cultural developments that Chesterton had been critiquing over the previous decade became crystallised within a single wide-ranging and programmatic doctrine. In the broadest possible cultural terms, Futurism was frankly predicated upon annihilation of the past: 'We intend to destroy museums, libraries, academies of every sort' (Marinetti, 'Founding', 51). In aesthetic terms, the movement espoused a doctrine of extreme subjectivism that was equally primed to provoke Chesterton's ire. In the visual arts, Marinetti's artistic companions demanded the abandonment of 'traditional Form and Color' (Boccioni, et al., 'Futurist Painting', 64) while declaring that 'a portrait, in order to be a work of art, must not resemble the sitter' (65). In literature, Marinetti claimed that poetry must progress beyond even the loose strictures of *vers libre* to what he termed 'words-in-freedom' ('Destruction', 146). As Marinetti explained, it had now become 'imperative to destroy syntax and scatter one's nouns at random' in order to do away with 'the ridiculous inanity of the old syntax' ('Technical Manifesto', 119). These echoes of, and developments beyond, the extreme of sceptical fragmentation that Chesterton had deplored in Decadent aesthetics are allied to an overtly nonsensical doctrine in Carlo Carrà's demand that Futurist art should be founded upon 'the painting of sounds, noises and smells' (156), a conceit that achieves its novelty through a deliberate category mistake that literally confounds sense. As Chesterton later contended, 'the Futurists of to-day [...] despise the separate senses' ('The Asceticism of the Futurists', *T.P.'s Weekly*, 4 July 1914; 6).

Chesterton articulates his philosophical opposition to Futurism in 'The Turk and the Futurists', a chapter from *The Flying Inn* that centres upon a 'Post-Futurist exhibition' (222) attended by various more or less baffled socialites. The critique is framed by Chesterton's consistent distinction between the ethical grounding of satire and pure nonsense's derangement of referents. As he explains in 'A Defence of Nonsense', in terms that differentiate between the urge to heighten and to confound discrete identity, the satirist, 'seeing in the Kaiser's moustaches something typical of him, draws them continually larger and larger', whereas the nonsense practitioner, 'for no good reason whatever, imagines what those moustaches would look like on the present Archbishop of Canterbury if he grew them in a fit of absence of mind' (*Defendant*, 64–65). In *The Flying Inn*, the Futurist enthusiast, Lord Ivywood, confuses this distinction—'"[e]verything lives by turning into something else. Exaggeration is growth"'—only to receive the impatient reply,

> "I cannot find a hint of what it is they want to exaggerate. You can't exaggerate the feathers of a cow or the legs of a whale [...] you can distort [physical form] up to a certain point: after that you lose identity [...] Don't you see this prime fact of identity is the limit set on all living things?"
>
> (226–27)

In another use of cattle to clinch a point, 'The Asceticism of the Futurists' identifies an Idealist strain in the Futurist's apparent contempt for the concrete, which runs counter to Chesterton's continual emphasis upon embodying the essence in the physical exterior, or 'the forms of things' (6). He argues that, in conventional historical portraiture, 'there is a soul in the portrait because there was a soul in the man', whereas 'these artists would profess to find a kind of essence of ox; a sort of transcendental Bovril' (6) by producing images that bear no relation to the actual form of a cow. In another article of 1910, Chesterton develops the principle of the 'cosmic stew-pot' to express his distrust of the view 'that there is something high and spiritual about things being blended and absorbed into each other' ('The Cosmic Stew-Pot', *T.P.'s Weekly*, Dec. 1910; Chesterton, *Man Who*, 108). A cosmic stew is a dish into which transcendental Bovril might appropriately be added: each image literally renders down Idealist rhetoric through a hybridisation of the sublime and the corporeal.

Once more, beneath the burlesque buffoonery, Chesterton's analysis is acute. Marinetti's claim that the Futurist perceives the self to be involved 'indefinitely in perpetual becoming' ('We Abjure', 95) is closely allied both to Bergson's then-fashionable concept of *durée*, in which the flux of 'becoming' is figured as a higher reality, and to neo-Hegelian philosophy's appeal to evolutionary improvement, in which, as Coates puts it, 'the dialectic would work on endlessly resolving all contradictions' (*G.K. Chesterton*, 12). Chesterton's distaste for such rhetoric set him at odds with the most conservative and the most radical cultural voices of the time. While Marinetti might be expected to share little common ground with the Dean of St. Paul's, Chesterton was replaying the same controversy that had helped catalyse his Edwardian persona as a materialist buffoon: William Inge's railing against capering mountebanks had been prompted by Chesterton's criticism of the Dean's apparent 'disgust at the idea of spiritual things having a body and a solid form' (qtd. in Ker, 601).

In its more ebullient moods, Futurism was wont to explore corporeal themes that accord with Chesterton's Edwardian preoccupations, albeit with further telling variations. Although his sartorial precepts are echoed in Giacomo Balla's avowal that '[w]e want to give men beautiful festive clothes', the Futurist version features nonsensical innovations such as 'assymetrical' sleeves (194–95). Similarly, Chesterton's conflation of culinary conceits with the aesthetics and philosophy of Futurism proved prescient when the Futurists' advocacy of referential derangement eventually extended to freak dinners—'Polyrhythmic salad' (Marinetti, *Futurist*, 125) and 'Veal Fuselage' (Marinetti, *Futurist*, 160) are just two of the tempting dishes to be found in Marinetti's *La Cucina Futurista* (1932). In 'The Blue Cross', Father Brown's buffoonish innovations in dining—coffee with salt and soup *a la* wallpaper—carry significance as non-verbal communicative devices, while Flambeau's removal of the diners' cutlery in 'The Queer Feet' provides Father Brown with the opportunity to convey a satirical moral. Conversely, although Marinetti's cookbook is full of similar 'practical jokes' (Chamberlain, 20), they are not conceived to communicate a message, but, rather like the menu in 'The Queer Feet', 'would not convey anything to anybody' because there is no coherent social satire at play—the conceits operate as pure nonsense.

A class distinction again attends to this conceptual disparity. While Futurist dining is somewhat Chestertonian in the sense that it is 'almost slapstick in its attacks on bourgeois habits [and] stuffy professors' (18), as Lesley Chamberlain puts it, Marinetti attacks the bourgeoisie from above rather than below: '[f]or an anti-bourgeois he is addicted to pomp and official titles' (Chamberlain, 20). While it would not be surprising to find 'sad and subtle chops' amongst Marinetti's culinary innovations, this is not an example of the pastimes of the idle rich being contrasted unfavourably with the traditions of the poor, as with Chesterton's satirical nonsense-verse. Instead, Marinetti expressly denounced traditional Italian peasant food—most notably, pasta—while designing expensive novelty dishes to temporarily buoy up the jaded appetites of the rich. Consequently, Marinetti's account of the ideal Futurist dinner party in his 'Manifesto of Futurist Cooking' (*Gazetta del Popolo*, 28 Dec. 1930) bears a curious resemblance to the enervated feast of Chesterton's Twelve True Fishermen, with suggested attributes including the 'abolition of speech-making and politics at the table' (Marinetti, *Futurist,* 40) and the 'abolition of the knife and fork for eating food sculptures' (Marinetti, *Futurist*, 39). In this correspondence with the progress of Chesterton's plutocratic banquet, we again discover the exclusivity of nonsense becoming allied to that of class. The apparent necessity of possessing access to motorised transport in order to become a *bona fide* Futurist led Chesterton to view the movement as an exemplar of the aesthetics of oligarchy: 'It is quite clear [...] that you cannot be a Futurist at all unless you are frightfully rich' (*CDN* 6:139).

Chesterton makes this observation in 'The Futurists' (*DN*, 13 Nov. 1909), an article that responds to the recent delivery of a copy of Marinetti's doctrinal polemic, 'The Founding and Manifesto of Futurism' (*Le Figaro*, 20 Feb. 1909), to his home. Chesterton's admiration of Dostoevsky and antipathy towards Marinetti come together here in a satirical volley that draws upon the former to attack the latter, adapting the portentous religious imagery of Dostoevsky's counterrevolutionary novel, *Devils* (1872), to a burlesque register as a means of mocking the vaunted radicalism of Marinetti's text. Chesterton begins by invoking the same biblical metaphor that Dostoevsky inscribes as the allegorical foundation of *Devils*—that of the Gadarene swine, in which Christ cures a man of madness by extracting the devils that possess him and transferring them into a herd of swine: 'Then went the devils out of the man, and entered into the swine: and the herd ran violently down a steep place into the lake, and were choked' (*Devils*, 2). In Dostoevsky's novel, the 'man' represents Russia, while the 'swine' represent the Russian nihilists of the 1860s. In Chesterton's rendition, these roles are occupied allegorically by Western civilisation and the Italian Futurists, while being occupied literally by Chesterton's postman and a litter of pigs: 'It was a warm golden evening, fit for October, and I was watching (with regret) a lot of little black pigs being turned out of my garden, when the postman handed to me, with a perfunctory haste which doubtless masked his emotion, the Declaration of Futurism' (*CDN* 6:138).

In an account that mirrors the purgative ethos of Dostoevsky's text, Chesterton goes on to muse that

> [t]here is a certain solid use in fools. It is not so much that they rush in where angels fear to tread, but rather that they let out what devils intend to do. Some perversion of folly will float about nameless and pervade a whole society; then some lunatic gives it a name, and henceforth it is harmless.
>
> (*CDN* 6:140)

The anarchists in Dostoevsky's novel exemplify Chesterton's critique of the revolutionary who sets 'out to break down without having, or even thinking he [has], the rudiments of rebuilding in him', enjoying destruction for its own sake, rather than pursuing the Chestertonian principle of drawing upon the past to constructively renovate the present. Chesterton's perception of a comparable tendency in Futurism finds expression in his mockery of Marinetti's enthusiasm for destroying museums: he notes witheringly that while 'the Futurist stands outside a museum in a warlike attitude, and defiantly tells the official at the turnstile that he will never, never come in [... the] old Radical ghosts go by, more real than the living men' (*CDN* 6:140).

Chesterton's view of Marinetti and Co. as a pallid travesty of the radicals of the past is demonstrated further when he moves on from sympathetic pastiche of Dostoevsky to satirical parody of Marinetti, with a direct appropriation of the terms of the manifesto. Although he discusses Marinetti's poetry elsewhere with a characteristically judicious balance of praise and curses—'there is a definite amount of good poetry scattered through his crazy pages [...] I give the devil his due' (*CW* 28:445)—in this instance Chesterton derides Marinetti's assertion that the Futurists will 'sing' the praises of the effects of technology upon man's relationship to the material world, by exposing the clumsily unpoetic language in which the claim is couched. To this end, he employs the most basic form of parody—the exact repetition of another's words with an implied change of register:

> A notion came into my head as new as it was bright
> That poems might be written on the subject of a fight;
> No praise was given to Lancelot, Achilles, Nap or Corbett,
> But we will sing the praises of man holding the flywheel of
> which the steering-post traverses the earth impelled
> itself around the circuit of its own orbit.
>
> (*CDN* 6:139)

Chesterton's skit exposes the bathetic consequences of Marinetti's contention that the pioneering Futurist writer could not 'care less about punctuation or finding the right adjective' ('Destruction', 145), while also drawing the metrical disruption of *vers libre* into the range of his critique. Although the sing-song simplicity of his own contribution might be thought to edge towards unconscious self-parody in turn, inadvertently corroborating Marinetti's vision of 'the ridiculous inanity of the old syntax', Chesterton's adherence to regularity of metre and rhyme should again be understood in terms of his democratic opposition to exclusivity. He conceives metrically conventional verse to produce 'a chorus so familiar and obvious that all men can join in it', while *vers libre* enacts 'the separation of art from the people' by self-adjudged 'outlaws [who] are more exclusive than aristocrats' ('The Romance of Rhyme', collected in *Fancies*, 18). As Patrick Dalroy, Chesterton's rendition of an authentic outlaw, declaims ebulliently in *The Flying Inn*, 'the song of the happy Futurist is a song that can't be sung' (61).

In addition to highlighting Marinetti's mystifying phraseology, Chesterton particularly deprecates the implied failure to 'praise' the achievements of one's precursors in the headlong forward march to the future. Consequently, the sketch enacts a schematic 'fight' between appreciation for the past and mania for the future, bifurcating the two factions with a pivotal 'But'. With this pointed segregation, Chesterton reverses the conventional dynamic of parody, in which a text considered to be representative of the past might be modified to produce a comment on cultural progress. Here the parodied text is, as it were, a dispatch from the future—Marinetti's introductory 'we will' even postpones his praise of technology until an unspecified future time. Consequently, Chesterton's parodic deviation lies in his inscription of the past within a text that seeks to dispense with it entirely: he forces historicism upon Futurism while making the very withholding of praise the context for its instantaneous tacit reinstatement: '*No* praise was given to Lancelot, Achilles, Nap or Corbett' (my emphasis).[6] With a screeching of the brakes followed by a hundred-and-eighty degree turn, the parodist wrests the flywheel from the 'Futurist aeropoet' (Marinetti, Puma, Masnata, 298) and forces him to gaze upon a dizzyingly condensed pageant of past firebrands, much as the holy fool, Michael, takes control of the flying ship from Professor Lucifer in the prologue to *The Ball and the Cross*, as the vessel careers towards the cultural monument of St. Paul's.

To return to the terms of the 'Humour' essay, Chesterton's speculation over Marinetti's ignorance of Achilles might be read as a metaphor of the absence of a self-reflexive 'confession of human weakness' in the Futurist's braggadocio—a blustering exhibition of strength that ironically constitutes the Achilles heel that leaves him vulnerable to satirical attack. In *The Flying Inn*, Lord Ivywood is arraigned on the same grounds—he possesses 'no humour' (227) and no sense of weakness: 'Unlike Nelson and most of the great heroes, he knew not fear' (254). In 'Worship of the Future' (*ILN*, 18 Dec. 1909) and 'Modern Moral Creeds' (*ILN*, 29 Jan. 1910), two further essays on Futurism from the same period, Chesterton expands upon the ethical danger of these failings when combined with a drive 'to exalt the future and trample on the past' (*CW* 28:442). As these broad-brush, binary terms suggest, Chesterton considered the absence of any cogent, specific moral critique to reveal Marinetti's credo as little more than a nonsensical expression of blind aggression, a view perhaps informed by the latter's Nietzschean declaration in the Manifesto that he is 'against moralism' *per se* and believes that 'Art, in fact, can be nothing but violence, cruelty, and injustice' ('Founding', 51/53).

Marinetti's motiveless aggression again recalls the antagonistic antics of the inhabitants of Wonderland; in another battling of nonsense with nonsense, Chesterton inserts a Carrollian category mistake into his song of the Futurist, via a further rhyme with 'orbit': 'petrol is the perfect wine, I lick it and absorb it' (*CDN* 6:139). However, Marinetti invested the creatively sublimated violence of Carroll's nonsense world with a very literal brutalism, which eventually found expression in his fascist propagandising. With the benefit of hindsight, a sinister undertone is consistently discernible beneath the buffoonery—even the apparently innocuous nonsense of Futurist cookery was framed by Marinetti as a (rather unlikely) means of readying the Italian male for the physical demands of war.

Nonetheless, Chesterton considered the probable personal reality to jar with the tenor of the propagandising. Despite Lord Ivywood's Nietzschean bombast, the fictional Futurist aristocrat's ultimate ambition is to withdraw into the 'lonely [...] adventures' of 'the ever advancing brain' (*Flying*, 228). Chesterton surmises that far from reflecting a bustling alpha-male vitality, worship of the future actually represents a convenient escape from alarming implication within the ethical complexities of the present: 'when I turn my face to the future, then everybody bows down to me; then everybody prostrates himself; because there is nobody there but myself' (*CW* 28:444). The moral that Chesterton draws from this timorous flight from engagement with the high wire of day-to-day reality is that 'decadence, in its fullest sense of failure and impotence, is now to be found among those who live in the future' (*CW* 28:445), because '[h]e who lives in the future lives in a featureless blank; he lives in impersonality' (*CW* 28:43). While Chesterton directs these admonitions towards Marinetti, the allusion to a return of Decadence, the intimations of solipsistic withdrawal, and the critique of living 'in impersonality' also offer a foretaste of Chesterton's later jousts with a figure who was, at this time, yet to accede to the public stage: T.S. Eliot.

At Times, the Fool: Eliot in 1910

In January 1910, while still a student, Eliot published 'Humouresque' in the relatively modest environs of the *Harvard Advocate*. This poem bears the first fruit of Eliot's recent discovery of Jules Laforgue, through Arthur Symons's pioneering study of the late nineteenth-century continental avant-garde, *The Symbolist Movement in Literature* (1899). Eliot later affirmed that 'I owe more [to Laforgue] than to any one poet in any language' (*Inventions*, 409). Not the least of these debts was to Laforgue's inscrutably ironic approach to poetic discourse, which Eliot went on to refine from 'The Love Song of J. Alfred Prufrock', which he began in 1910 and had completed by July 1911 (see Ricks, 'Preface', xxxix), to 'The Hollow Men' in 1925. The 'deliberate disguises' that the authorial voice of Part II of 'The Hollow Men' accumulates as a means of avoiding an unwanted 'meeting' (*PTSE* 1:82) are first tried on for size in 'Humouresque', which appropriates Laforgue's vision of the artist as a detached puppet master projecting forth poetic avatars, whose capering before the reader operates as a textual 'mask *bizarre*!' (*PTSE* 1:237) raised to the face of the elusive poet.

The narrator of 'Humouresque' expresses regret over the recent demise of one such puppet, a flawed model, 'weak in body as in head', who later makes contact from a new home in 'Limbo' (*PTSE* 1:237). As this imagery suggests, Eliot's early work shares Chesterton's fascination with masks and marionettes, but again rehearses these themes with telling variations. As we have seen, *The Man Who Was Thursday* forcibly reverses the historical drift of the mask motif, restoring the pre-Enlightenment symbol of 'change and reincarnation', in Bakhtin's words, so as to overturn the Romantic conception of a façade overlying a 'terrible vacuum' of identity. Bakhtin argues that the 'theme of the marionette' (*Rabelais*, 40) possesses a comparable cultural dual identity. Although the puppet plays an important role in 'Romanticism [and] folk culture' alike, in the former 'the accent is placed on the puppet as the victim of alien inhuman force, which rules over men by turning them into marionettes' (*Rabelais*, 40). Whereas 'The Queer Feet' sets out to overturn this Schopenhauerian vision, galvanising the doll-like inhabitants of the gentleman's club into a genial materiality through the performance of a carnivalesque *Danse Macabre*, the evanescent authorial masks and uncertainly animated marionettes of Eliot's 'Humouresque' remain entrenched in the alienating realm of the Romantic grotesque, lost amid a hubbub of '[h]aranguing spectres' (*PTSE* 1:237).

If Eliot's sombre vision recalls the correlation that Chesterton drew between pure nonsense, ontological scepticism, and the precepts of Schopenhauerian pessimism, the poet later identified Laforgue to be 'the nearest verse equivalent to the philosoph[y] of Schopenhauer', while explaining the latter's central tenet to be that of 'annihilation' (qtd. in Habib, 64). As Habib explains, Eliot's early philosophical position emphasises the 'potential of irony as infinite, as transcending all closure' (143), thus placing him at the most disorientating outer reaches of the Romantic grotesque. His early verse presents an aesthetic illustration of this philosophical thesis, via a continually shape-shifting impersonation of other identities, carried out in the value-neutral, subjectivity-undermining mode of pastiche—the sub-heading of 'Humouresque', 'After J. Laforgue' (*PTSE* 1:237), advertises the poem's uncritical gesture of identification, divested of the moral satirist's urge to harness irony to the purpose of discriminative evaluation.

Eliot's vexing of identity contracts a further debt to Laforgue, since the latter's stress upon the ironic 'playing [of] voices against one another' (Gordon, *Eliot's*, 29) represented an attempt to complicate the reader's understanding of the author's position in relation to the sentiments of the text. This deliberately alienating action militates against an uncomplicated 'meeting' between poet and reader in a manner comparable to that of which Chesterton had complained in his account of the rise of the cultural 'mystagogue'. Eliot compounds this alienating effect with a deflation of anything that resembles an unmediated expression of emotional conviction, achieved through forms of purposefully engendered bathos and burlesque. Accordingly, the over-straining of the marionette in 'Humouresque' to assert its stylistic originality—it boasts of possessing '"[t]he newest style, on Earth, I swear"' (*PTSE* 1:237)—can be read as a Baudelairean act of authorial self-policing, a ventriloquistic warning-to-self of the absurd consequences of affecting pristine novelty, which also serves to tip off the critical reader that the poet is alive to this pitfall.

The result is a curious conjunction of vertiginous disruption of identity and exorbitant heightening of self-consciousness. As Eliot famously went on to argue, with an admixture of bravado and self-criminalisation, '[i]mmature poets imitate, mature poets steal' (*Sacred*, 125). While imitation might imply an unconscious appropriation that would leave the artist open to satirical exposure, stealing entails premeditation. This urge to retain an iron grip on his materials helps to explain why Eliot invokes the inadvertently self-parodic inventions of Carroll's White Knight in the title of the notebook of his early poems, *Inventions of the March Hare*. As with Chesterton's arch gloss on the 'Sonnet to a Stilton Cheese', the absurdity of the White Knight's parody of Wordsworth, 'Haddock's Eyes', in *Through the Looking Glass*, arises from the details of the original having 'trickled through my head / Like water through a sieve' (Carroll, *Annotated*, 311), while Alice achieves an inverse sense of mastery by correctly identifying the tune that the White Knight has unconsciously borrowed. Eliot's title advertises the unlikeliness that he would make an error comparable to that of Carroll's incompetent *pasticheur,* while also conflating his character with the insane dinner guest, the March Hare, whose pronouncements are so inscrutable that it becomes impossible to judge whether he is a natural, or an artificial, fool.

Eliot's youthful exploration of Carroll's Wonderland had corroborated his innate view of the dialogic interlocutor as a critical consciousness to be consistently outwitted, and of cultural exchange as a fraught contest for mastery. In hypothesising unmediated encounters with other minds as antagonistic scenarios—a battle of wills, in the Schopenhauerian sense—Eliot remained cautious to always carry a 'ghostly flavor of irony [...] about his manner as though he were preparing a parody' (qtd. in Chinitz, 178), as I.A. Richards put it. Richards's terms call to mind Chesterton's portrayal of the 'pure satirist' (*CW* 6:379), the jester-king of *Napoleon*, Auberon Quin, a figure recognised 'by the entire reviewing world as Max Beerbohm' (Ward, *Gilbert*, 153). Quin's absolute absence of earnestness finds expression in an urge to turn the world into a giant burlesque, composed of meaningless private jokes. A forerunner of Chesterton's cultural mystagogue, Quin declares, after an exuberant monologue of nonsense-riddling, '[h]itherto it was the ruin of a joke that people did not see it. Now it is the sublime victory of a joke that people do not see it' (*CW* 6:243).

Eliot's resemblance to Quin is an irony in itself, since his attempts to confound stable identification were essayed partially as a means of outwitting critical detectives such as Beerbohm. He later confided to Woolf that 'humiliation' (qtd. in Ackroyd, 84) was his greatest fear. As John Soldo argues, his early work is that of 'an intellectually astute, but emotionally insecure person, intent upon using humor as a protective shield to ward off invasions of his inner sanctum' (144). In approaching the public stage, he appropriated Beerbohm's essayistic manner, in which Woolf discerned a doubt over 'whether there is any relation between Max the essayist and Mr. Beerbohm the man' (*Selections*, 130), as the model for a poetic practice that would render him invulnerable to the very figure whose persona he had purloined. As 'The Hollow Men' avers, 'Between the emotion / And the response / Falls the Shadow' (*PTSE* 1:84); despite the note of lamentation introduced here, in Eliot's earlier work there is a sense that he prefers it this way.

Another of Eliot's early marionettes takes a more aggressive approach to navigating the audience-performer dynamic. 'Suite Clownesque', composed in October 1910, introduces 'the comedian', an entity whose exuberant physical grotesquery contrasts sharply with the enervation of the 'weak' puppet of 'Humouresque':

> [...] through the painted colonnades
> There falls a shadow dense, immense
>
> It's the comedian again
> Explodes in laughter, spreads his toes
> (the most expressive, real of men)
> Concentred into vest and nose.
>
> (PTSE 1:252)

This premonition of the shadow that will later fall between the emotion and the response interpolates the 'comedian' into the space between Eliot and his projected audience as a comic mediator. Here, Baudelaire's vision of the imperturbable comic master of *dédoublement* is filtered through Eliot's experience of haunting the music halls during his time in Paris in 1910, again with Laforgue as the overriding influential presence. Laforgue's verse recurs repeatedly to the world of the *Commedia Dell'Arte*, and Symons conceived him as the court jester of continental Decadence, pursuing 'a kind of travesty' of conventional poetry delivered with an unconventional 'familiarity of manner' (*Symbolist*, 106/107). Nonetheless, his was not the immersive buffoonery advocated by Chesterton; instead, Laforgue followed Schopenhauer and Baudelaire in his urge to split the subjective consciousness into an arch double act of 'mocking commentator and droll sufferer' (Habib, 31). As Eliot later explained in a letter to Conrad Aiken, the trick 'is to be able to look at one's life as if it were somebody else's' (*Letters*, 30 Sept. 1914, 1:58).

'Suite Clownesque' also owes a more surreptitious debt to the prologue of Symons's own Decadent verse collection, *London Nights* (1895), in which the music hall stage is used to symbolise a sense of simultaneous alienation from, and identification with, the spectacle of the self as a maladroit puppet-figure under public scrutiny: a startled repetition attends to the revelation that it is 'I, I, this thing that turns and trips!' (Symons, *Selected*, 38). However, 'Suite Clownesque' overturns Symons's view of physicality as a painfully compromising factor. The power of Eliot's 'comedian' derives from the discrepancy in vitality between his brazen 'belly sparkling and immense' and the enervated gentility of the 'potted palms' and 'terra cotta fawns' (*PTSE* 1:249) around which he performs. Whereas Eliot's marionette in 'Humouresque' is an ineffectual Pierrot, '[f]eebly contemptuous of nose' (*PTSE* 1:237), the 'comedian' is an invulnerable Clown, possessed of an '[i]mpressive, sceptic, scarlet nose' that 'interrogates the audience' (*PTSE* 1:249).

The two extremes collide in the third, and most fully realised, of the marionettes that Eliot conceived in 1910: J. Alfred Prufrock. Prufrock's confluence of intellectual sensitivity and burlesque physicality results in a monologue that marries the isolation of the Romantic grotesque with the immersion of the folk grotesque, and consequently rehearses an uncertain rebounding between Laforgean detachment and Chestertonian implication. If Prufrock is the Baudelairean self-parodist *par excellence*, he is also a half-conscious eccentric, equivocating over his status as '*almost* ridiculous [...] *at times*, the Fool' (*PTSE* 1:9; my emphases). In a sense, the dramatic tension of Prufrock's 'crisis' (*PTSE* 1:7) centres upon whether he will finally prove capable of fully embracing this carnivalesque condition.

As Maud Ellmann notes, Eliot's protagonist consistently 'acts as his own voyeur, pinned and wriggling under his own pitiless eye' (69). Excruciatingly conscious of potential criticism, he becomes a compulsive self-satirist, while evincing an equally strong urge to parody others in turn. This duality is exemplified by the 'hundred visions and revisions' (*PTSE* 1:6) for which Prufrock finds time. The phrase correlates to the dynamic of parody, in which the visions of the artist are followed by the revisions of the parodist, while internalising this relationship to refer equally to the protagonist's bathetic self-revisions. Take, for example, the time it takes for Prufrock to wonder '"Do I dare?" and, "Do I dare?"' (*PTSE* 1:6), the two occasions for which involve an emendation of the 'overwhelming question' (*PTSE* 1:5), 'Do I dare / Disturb the universe?' (*PTSE* 1:6) to the farcical conundrum, 'Do I dare to eat a peach?' (*PTSE* 1:9), thus rendering a sublime vision ridiculous through parodic revision.

When Prufrock's portentous speculation that there will be time 'to murder and create' (*TPSE* 1:6) resolves itself in his prevarication before the peach, the revision transmutes the cerebral into the corporeal, reframing the disturbance of the universe as the act of digestion, in a scatological rendition of murder and creation. The first of the two questions also happens to be an unattributed quotation from Laforgue's correspondence (see Kenner, *Invisible*, 21)—the peach adaptation produces a burlesque rendition of a phrase of the forebear even as it draws the protagonist's own inconsequentiality into the sphere of criticism, in a particularly economical exposition of Bakhtin's 'carnival participant' who 'is both actor and spectator [... split] into a subject of the spectacle and an object of the game' (Kristeva, *Kristeva*, 49). This dynamic brings Prufrock into proximity with the ludicrous self that Chesterton had adopted in the Edwardian era as a means of negotiating his public persona. To borrow the terms of Eliot's prose poem, 'Hysteria' (1915), 'Prufrock' is an uneasy treatise on being 'involved in [...] laughter and being part of it' (*PTSE* 1:26).

Prufrock's famous invocation of the prototypical melancholy puppet, Prince Hamlet, disclaims the right to emulate the stately artificial fool, gravitating instead towards the more abject figure of the court buffoon. This represents a further equivocal pastiche of Laforgue, whose mock-heroic rewrite of Shakespeare's text, in his ironically titled parody collection, *Moral Tales* (1887), reconceives Yorick as Hamlet's father. Chesterton also produced 'burlesque' renditions of Shakespeare 'in modern dress' (Ward, *Gilbert*, 30) in his youth, and of course, Father Brown claims archly that 'The Queer Feet' might be understood as a modern update of *Hamlet*. Chesterton's story was published in the same period in which Eliot was composing the earliest drafts of 'Prufrock', and both texts turn upon nonsensical renderings of paltry banquets, conceived to convey the vacuity of the high-society dinner party. The corporeal motifs that permeate Chesterton's narrative also pepper the burlesque world of 'Prufrock' in which, as Sewell notes, the protagonist's Sisyphean ordeal is to attend an 'endless tea party, interminable as the Hatter's' (qtd. in Eliot, *Inventions*, 8). Much as Chesterton's tale turns upon an oppressive 'silence and embarrassment', the agonised self-consciousness of Eliot's protagonist is heightened by the extreme formality of the gatherings that he attends. Each text achieves an air of farcical comedy through the juxtaposition of stiff social codification and ungovernable energies, whether in the form of Flambeau's physical exuberance or Prufrock's superabundance of mental discomfort.

However, these surface similarities also cast a light upon the deeper divergence of the visions of Chesterton and Eliot at this time. For example, the re-integrative impetus of the baffling cross-city chase scenes of *Thursday* and 'The Blue Cross' is given a pessimistic overhaul in Prufrock's anxious urban perambulations, which lead only to ever-greater abysms of alienation. The theme of isolation in 'Prufrock' also results in a conflation of nonsense and Futurism comparable to that articulated by Chesterton in the same period, but inscribed with a greater degree of ambivalence, and even identification, on Eliot's part. In a letter of 1913,

Aiken wonders what Eliot has lately 'been writing—Futurist poems?' (*PTSE* 1:364), before asking him to send on a copy of 'Prufrock'. John T. Mayer argues that 'the comedian' in 'Suite Clownesque' is Eliot as he would like to be: 'the final turn is clearly his own fantasy, with himself as star' (83), a claim that carries an echo of Chesterton's account of the solipsistic Futurist's daydream dictatorship-of-one. The rhetoric of 'Suite Clownesque' also suggests a link to Marinetti. While Eliot's clown possesses a '[n]ose that interrogates the stars' (*PTSE* 1:249), Marinetti's manifesto of 1909 also dares to disturb the universe: 'we fling our challenge to the stars!' ('Founding', 53). Eliot would almost certainly have been familiar with the Futurist manifesto and may have attended Marinetti's Parisian lecture in January 1911 while studying at the Sorbonne. Marinetti was often compared to a music hall performer in early British press notices, and the Italian's famously browbeating style of public performance and self-professed 'contempt for the audience' (Marinetti, 'Pleasure', 96) has much in common with the aggressive buffoonery of Eliot's 'comedian'.

It is probable that the ever-prudent Eliot was wary of Marinetti's extremism from an early stage—recall the absurdity of his marionette (one might say, Marionetti) hawking '"[t]he newest style, on Earth, I swear" [...] Mouth twisted to the latest tune' (*PTSE* 1:237). Giovanni Cianci pinpoints Eliot's later 'open hostility towards Futurism [...] during and after the First World War' (123-24), rightly observing that the poet's deprecation of the 'search for novelty' (Eliot, *Sacred*, 57) stands in direct opposition to Marinetti's blithe contempt for tradition. However, the younger Eliot might well have been intrigued by the combative means through which Marinetti conveyed his message. Certain linguistic correspondences that arise between Prufrock's monologue and Marinetti's prose suggest that Eliot's antihero might be read as a self-monitory reflection on the invidious attractions of the Futurist project. The most striking of these is Prufrock's incessant use of 'will' in a predictive context. As Sam Rohdie notes of this curious semantic quirk of Marinetti's manifestoes, 'the Marinettian sense is a conditional future, both assertive and unsure' (Rohdie). This is equally true of Prufrock's obsessive refrain, 'there will be time' (*PTSE* 1:6), a phrase that constitutes a Carrollian philosophy of 'jam to-morrow' (Carroll, *Annotated*, 247)—or marmalade tomorrow in Prufrock's case—which recalls Chesterton's account of Futurism as a world of perpetual postponement, expressive of an urge to escape the nerve-racking immanence of the present.

If Prufrock's part self-reassuring, part apprehensive use of 'will' suggests the tacit timorousness of the Futurist, the other notable context in which the verb appears in the poem evokes the more overt projection of aggression common to Futurism and nonsense. While the alarming tendency of Prufrock's fellow diners to 'drop a question on your plate'

(*PTSE* 1:6) prefigures the disorientating, dining-related category mistakes of Marinetti's cookbook, his parenthetical speculations over what the guests might exclaim behind his back suggest a fear of attack from high-society Futurists, affronted by his lack of vitality: 'They will say: "How his hair is growing thin!"'; 'They will say: "But how his arms and legs are growing thin"' (*PTSE* 1:6). This passive application of the suggestively Schopenhauerian 'will' reorients the threatening promises of the Futurist manifesto from the collective pronoun—'we will'—to the third-person plural, while presenting an equally sharp contrast with Chesterton's confrontationally assertive introduction to 'The Queer Feet', in which the second-person predictive 'you will' is fired off five times in quick succession.

The inexplicable brutality of Lear's limerick world also haunts Eliot's lines—in Lear, the appearance of an amorphous 'they' frequently presages the threatened, or actual, infliction of physical violence upon the protagonist:

> There was an Old Man of Ibreem,
> Who suddenly threaten'd to scream;
> But *they* said, "If you do,
> *We will* thump you quite blue,
> You disgusting old man of Ibreem!"
>
> (Lear, 130; my emphases)

Although Eliot's protagonist possesses too much self-restraint to suddenly threaten to scream, the abjection of Lear's 'disgusting old man' finds a close echo in Prufrock's depersonalised apprehension of his own corporeal degeneration. Prufrock's doubts over his capacity to enact inconsequential feats of daring also suggest a self-assessment informed by the grandstanding rhetoric of 'strength, daring, and "a scorn of woman"' (*CW* 28:469) that Chesterton found so tiresomely exorbitant, and finally ridiculous, in Futurist prose. A similar scorn of woman is traceable in Prufrock's jibes at the women who 'come and go / Talking of Michelangelo' (*PTSE* 1:5/6), a spritely couplet that conveys the sing-song contempt of the stage fool—a further echo of the carnivalesque 'comedian', stepping forward to provide the audience with an arch gloss on the drama from a position once removed. In directing his critical laughter towards inane dinner party conversation, Prufrock echoes the parabasic narrator of 'The Queer Feet'. However, in orientating his contempt towards the women's admiration of Italian Renaissance art, Prufrock vaunts his radical, Marinettian credentials, rather than mirroring Chesterton's appeal to the centric traditions of historical humanity.

The contrast that Chesterton develops between the enervated denizens of the club and his vibrant pantomime duo also coincides with the imagery that accumulates around Eliot's 'comedian', a lithe, arch figure who 'gets away with it', turning the tables on his fellow performers, while training his gaze back upon the complacent audience in turn: 'A jellyfish impertinent [...] Leaning across the orchestra' (*PTSE* 1:249). However, this correspondence again serves to illustrate a more fundamental discrepancy. In 'Suite Clownesque', we are given no indication of the purpose of the comedian's parabasis—his haranguing is an end in itself, a form of blind aggression that mirrors Chesterton's view of Futurism as purely destructive in intent. Similarly, Prufrock is just as coercive as Chesterton's narrator in his attempts to draw the reader into a compact against the vacuity of high society, employing 'you and I' from the first line in the aggressively familiar manner of Chesterton's journalism, while proffering a double dare to '[l]et us go' (*PTSE* 1:5) into these exclusive soirées in his company. However, Eliot's audience-implicating methodology ultimately engenders 'equality, but hardly fraternity', in Chesterton's phrase, because the disillusion that he proceeds to sow in the reader is not followed up with any counter-impetus towards regeneration.

This deviation can be attributed partially to a further instance of social distinction. If the anticipated mockery of Prufrock's shrinking arms, legs, and hair finds him disintegrating before the spectators' astonished gaze, this evanescence also implicates him within the ontological vacancy that Chesterton had identified in the official high-society feast, in a manner that the pantomime servants, Father Brown and Flambeau, are not. This leads to a reversal of social perspective in the construct of the *Danse Macabre*: 'I have seen the eternal Footman hold my coat, and snicker' (*PTSE* 1:8). Prufrock's acute sense of personal abjection finally vitiates his capacity to 'force the moment to its crisis' (*PTSE* 1:7) in the manner that produces a liminal leap of faith into reconciliation in Chesterton's tale of social crisis. Rather than meeting the eternal footman with an open laugh, Prufrock merely mimics the smirk, reflecting that he ought to have 'bitten off the matter with a smile' (*PTSE* 1:8), an anti-material pun in which the elimination of physical and intellectual matter is conjoined with the ironist's enigmatic grin, via an image of discreet consumption that mirrors the 'devouring silence' of Chesterton's banquet.

Eliot's remorseless build-up of imagery of alienation and withdrawal colludes in the Hankin-like social world of pure nonsense that he depicts, divesting his vision of the elements of pedagogic moral satire and 'genial' folk grotesque through which Chesterton finally leavens alienation with a movement towards reconciliation and regeneration. Whereas Father Brown possesses the human voice that wakes Colonel Pound from the nonsense world in which he dwells, the imaginative drift of 'Prufrock' is closer to Woolf's apprehension of the invasive other encroaching upon the private self: the awakening from voluntary solitary confinement is figured as the moment at which 'we drown' (*PTSE* 1:9). Although this valedictory 'we' ostensibly recovers a belated sense of commonality, the demoralising context subverts its own gesture of identification, evoking a collective death by water.

At this point, let us turn to the third figure who will play a leading role in the second half of this narrative. While the masks that Eliot was toying with in 1910 were textual and explored in privacy, in the same period Wyndham Lewis was experimenting ebulliently with public masks, in a complex conflation of sartorial and textual costuming. Ford Madox Ford later recalled Lewis's attitude in this period as one of brash generational supersession: 'Your generation has gone. [...] What people want is me, not you. They want to see me. [...] You and Conrad had the idea of concealing yourself when you wrote. I display myself all over the page' (*Bodley*, 244). Although Prufrock also displays himself all over the page, his simultaneous, paradoxical self-effacement might seem the reverse of Lewis's bustling self-aggrandisement. Nonetheless, Lewis's revelatory disguises draw upon a strikingly comparable range of influences to those of Eliot, again flirting with the themes of the Chestertonian folk carnival before withdrawing into the trapdoor ironies of the Romantic grotesque.

The Materialisation of Wyndham Lewis

The biographies of Chesterton and Lewis seem to accumulate images of uncanny self-galvanisation: Garry Wills notes that in 1900 'Chesterton seemed [...] to have appeared from nowhere' (*Chesterton*, 80), while Kenner reports that according to self-perpetuated legend, Lewis 'materialized one day in 1909' (*Wyndham*, 1). The similarity of this imagery is not coincidental. In a quotidian sense, it reflects the pair's relative outsider status in relation to the London literary establishment; in a more performative sense, it reflects the playfully self-mythologising methods that they employed to storm the citadel. In Lewis's case, it also indicates the formative influence of Chesterton. Kenner argues that prior to the official date of Lewis's materialisation, it was within 'the world of Dorian Gray and The Man Who Was Thursday' that he 'slowly came into possession of his powers' ('Mrs.', 85). This background influence is manifested in Lewis's urge to infuse everyday life with a spirit of play. While Father O'Connor recalled that Chesterton 'was bitten with costume drama and would without provocation "lurk" by the jamb of a doorway with cloak-and-sword' (qtd. in Clemens, 137), Lewis was known to play the 'game of turning up in cafés in what he imagined to be disguise, having first defied acquaintances to recognize him' ('Mrs.', 90). As Kenner surmises, '[w]hat he was playing at [...] was being a character in [...] a tale by Stevenson or Chesterton, of intrigue, romance and jolly disguise' ('Mrs.', 90).

If the young Lewis took a ludic pleasure in casting himself as the real-life protagonist of a Chestertonian mystery story, he gradually became equally conscious of the psychological and promotional value of this performative approach to literary self-creation. In a later essay on 'The Dress-Body-Mind Aggregate' (*New Statesman*, 24 May 1924), he discusses the significance of personal appearance to the creative artist as an objective corollary of the intellect, a scenario in which 'the personality is expressed deliberately on the outside [...] the dress-body is a co-ordinate, the expression of the mind of the person' (*Creatures*, 100–01). This use of the physical body as a means of grounding identity and externalising one's allegiances returns us to the psychological benefits that Chesterton sought to derive from sartorial travesty. When Lewis goes on to explain the commercial applications of this principle, we are reminded equally of Chesterton's earlier tailoring of his public image in the Edwardian marketplace: 'the window ought to be the finest thing about the shop. For all said and done very few people ever come into the shop, whereas a great many people pass it' (*Creatures*, 100). In 'The Code of a Herdsman' (*Little Review*, July 1917), Lewis lends this principle a galvanic air, arguing that '[y]ou will [...] acquire the potentiality of six men [if you leave] your front door one day as B. the next march down the street as E.', while accumulating a 'variety of clothes' to enhance 'this wider dramatisation of yourself' (Lewis, 'Imaginary', 4). At the outset of his career, Lewis put this guidance into practice, employing dramatic self-display as a means of accumulating the potentiality of six seemingly eclectic literary men: Carroll, Chesterton, Dostoevsky, Marinetti, Schopenhauer, and Wilde.

In his second volume of autobiography, *Rude Assignment* (1951), Lewis lifts the veil on the prehistory of his materialisation, discussing the years in Paris that he spent reading widely in nineteenth-century Russian literature, and particularly emphasising the catalytic impact of Dostoevsky's *Devils* in provoking a generative 'crisis' (144) in his thought. Such was his immersion in this imaginative world that by the time of his return to London in December 1908, Lewis considered himself 'spiritually a Russian—a character in some Russian novel' (*Rude*, 148). In view of this self-identification, it is striking that the exact circumstances of his first mythic manifestation read as a real-life pastiche of two famous incidents from Dostoevsky's fiction—Raskolnikov's mounting of the pawnbroker's stairs with the fateful axe in *Crime and Punishment*, and Rogozhin's knife-wielding stairwell ambush of Prince Myshkin in *The Idiot* (1868). According to Ford's later account, Lewis was first discovered lurking on the staircase of the *English Review* in the 'costume' of an 'immense steeple-crowned hat' and 'ample black cape' (*Bodley*,

233/232). Ford's secretary reported 'rather agitatedly that there was an extraordinary-looking man on the stairs. [...] He seemed to be a Russian' (*Bodley*, 233). To the secretary's alarm, Lewis 'established himself immovably against the banisters and began fumbling in the pockets of his cape' (*Bodley*, 232). Rather than producing a weapon, the sinister stranger began to yield up literature, brandishing a copy of his short story 'The Pole', which he thrust upon the venerable editor. In Ford's account, the body becomes a façade of the text:

> [Lewis] produced crumpled papers in rolls. He produced them from all over his person—from inside his waistcoat, from against his skin beneath his brown jersey. He had no collar or I am sure he would have taken that off too and presented it to me and it would have been covered with hieroglyphs.
>
> (*Bodley*, 232–33)

Although the conclusion that Ford reaches—'[h]e must be Guy Fawkes' (*Bodley*, 233)—serves to reify Lewis as a harmless effigy, the reference to the archetypal English conspirator also draws the revolutionary figures of *Devils* into the implicit frame of reference. Ford never directly refers to Dostoevsky's text in the account, but his recollection of being harried by Lewis and Pound closely recalls the intimidating means through which Verkhovensky and Stavrogin terrorise the naïve provincials of Dostoevsky's novel: 'Those walks were slightly tormenting. Ezra talked incessantly on one side of me in his incomprehensible Philadelphian', while Lewis appeared 'more and more like a conspirator [and] went on and on in a vitriolic murmur' (*Bodley*, 244).

Lewis and Pound had become acquainted in 1909, shortly after Lewis's return to London from the continent (see O'Keefe, 143), and by 1910 they were already beginning to plan their takeover of the British avant-garde, having identified Ford as the requisite mythologising patron-figure. When Ford began to circulate the story of his first meeting with Lewis, his decision to tacitly frame the anecdote in the context of Dostoevsky's texts—esteemed literary artefacts with which Lewis identified and which Ford published in the *English Review*—validated Lewis's self-image and gave him a promotional fillip.[7] As A. David Moody observes of Ford's similar anecdotes about Pound, they were designed to provide 'shining additions to the myth and legend' (113).[8] Impressed by 'The Pole', Ford passed it on to Lytton Strachey, another admirer of Dostoevsky (see Kaye, 68), who dutifully bolstered the burgeoning Lewis legend, drawing the histrionic inference from the story's 'fiendish' energy that '[l]iving in the company of such a person would certainly have a deleterious influence on one's moral being' (qtd. in Meyers, 28). Again, this account implicitly conflates the individual with the art object, evoking the demoralising effect of Holbein's atheistic rendition of Christ upon Rogozhin, and the daemonic impact of Joris-Karl Huysmans' Decadent novel, *A Rebours* (1884), upon Dorian Gray.

In another of Ford's accounts, this theme is given a burlesque twist when the memoirist is attacked by one of Lewis's paintings (see Meyers, 52), a farcical reanimation that conjures the spirit of Bloomsbury's Post-Impressionist fancy-dress ball. Again, *Devils* lurks in the background of this absurdist proto-modernism: the calamitous fete that forms the novel's centrepiece 'includes a literary quadrille, danced in masks and costumes, in which participants pretend to be literary journals' (Leatherbarrow, 130), a nonsense motif later co-opted by the *Folies-Bergère* in its 'Presse-Ballet' of 1888, 'featuring a cast of dancing newspapers and magazines' (Kindley, 33). This festive conceit proliferated far and wide within *fin de siècle* literary culture. Despite Chesterton's publicly advertised preference for more populist forms of costume play, he attended a fancy-dress 'Book Party' in 1900, in which the guests were invited to disguise themselves as a favourite text (see Ward, *Gilbert*, 125–26). With this broader motif of textual embodiment in mind, it is instructive to consider Strachey's overwrought speculations in the light of a passage from *The Man Who Was Thursday*. In the opening pages, the narrator discusses the self-publicising of the 'anarchic poet' (*CW* 6:478) Lucian Gregory in terms that may strike a chord with those familiar with Lewis's later publicity shots (Figure 3.1):

He was helped in some degree by the arresting oddity of his appearance, which he worked, as the phrase goes, for all it was worth. [... His] hair parted in the middle was literally like a woman's, and curved into the slow curls of a virgin in a pre-Raphaelite picture. From within this almost saintly oval, however, his face projected suddenly broad and brutal, the chin carried forward with a look of cockney contempt. This combination at once tickled and terrified the nerves of a neurotic population.

(*CW* 6:476–77)

Figure 3.1 Wyndham Lewis photographed by George Charles Beresford, 1913.

Lewis's success in tickling and terrifying the nerves of Bloomsbury is evidenced not only by Strachey's remarks, but also by Woolf's private speculations that he might be a 'master of horrid secrets' (*Question*, 26 Mar. 1916, 85) and Duncan Grant's puzzled observation that being in Lewis's presence caused him to 'go into [...] hysterics' (qtd. in O'Keefe, 80). If Lewis was compelling life to imitate art, it is notable that Wilde's essayistic dialogue on 'The Decay of Lying' not only influenced Chesterton's novel with its image of 'silly boys who [...] alarm old gentlemen [...] with black masks and unloaded revolvers [...] after reading the adventures of Jack Sheppard', but also inaugurated the theme of confusing Dostoevskian texts with real-life figures. Vivian observes that the '[n]ihilist, that strange martyr who has no faith [...] is a purely literary product. He was invented by Tourgenieff, and completed by Dostoieffski' (Wilde, *Intentions*, 32).

Lewis's extraordinary manoeuvre in 1910 was to graft the two seams together. As with Holbrook Jackson's account of Chesterton as part Velasquez painting, part Adelphi villain, Ford's descriptions of Lewis range from the high art of the Dostoevskian revolutionary to a rather more Chestertonian pantomime villain: his cloak was 'the type that villains in transpontine melodrama throw over their shoulders when they say "Ha-ha!"' (*Bodley*, 232). Ford's self-consciously farcical accounts and Strachey's over-cooked verbal clichés should be understood as appropriate responses to a figure assembled as much from the tropes of the penny dreadful as those of refined literary culture. This cross-pollination of 'high' and 'low' imagery extended from Lewis's physical personae to the eclectic range of textual guises with which he was experimenting in this period. At the moment of his materialisation, he was not only composing arch vignettes such as 'The Pole', and beginning his formally radical künstlerroman, *Tarr*, but was also putting the finishing touches to *Mrs. Dukes' Million*, a pseudonymous pastiche of the Chestertonian mystery novel, aimed at the commercial market.[9]

The hero of *Mrs. Dukes' Million*, Evan Royal, works for a criminal 'Actor-Gang' (183) assembled by a mysterious Asian aristocrat named Raza Khan. A master of disguise and gifted mimic, Royal is called upon to assist in the kidnapping of the titular landlady and thereafter to imitate the real Mrs. Dukes in order to steal her inheritance. The bulk of the narrative relates how the 'genial actor Evan Royal, in his famous part "Mrs. Dukes" of Marbury Street' (187) succeeds in evading exposure before finally double-crossing Khan's gang and diverting 'the residue of his fortune' (361) back to the original Mrs. Dukes, while apportioning the lion's share to himself and two of his actor accomplices. Royal is consistently portrayed as an embodiment of the dynamics of parody. Before usurping Dukes, he begins by training himself in verbal parody—'aping her way of speaking'—a habit that causes the landlady to view him as 'a sort of man-parrot' (19). As Anne Quema observes, Royal 'is never singular but always the sum of two images' (47). Accordingly, he combines the agency of Baudelaire's dextrous comedian with Lewis's guidance on accruing vitality through sartorial mimicry, explaining to his accomplice, Hercules Fane, that as '"comedians"' the gang '"have the secret of very perfect disguises. We can make up [...] so perfectly that practically we become different persons at once"'.

Kenner has argued that Chesterton's work is 'the sort of fiction *Mrs. Dukes' Million* derives from' ('Mrs.', 90); certainly, Lewis's central premise is closely reminiscent of two stories from Chesterton's first mystery collection, *The Club of Queer Trades* (1905). In 'The Tremendous Adventures of Major Brown', the titular figure finds his mundane life turned upside down by the intervention of the 'Adventure and Romance Agency' (CW 6:77), a troupe of actors who transform his house into a real-life theatre set and contrive baffling practical jokes against him. Meanwhile, 'The Awful Reason of the Vicar's Visit' (*Harper's Weekly*, 28 May 1904) tells the shaggy dog story of a vicar, who later turns out to be a con man, being 'dressed up [...] and made to take part in a crime in the character of an old woman' (CW 6:109). Other areas of similarity suggest anticipation rather than indebtedness. Chesterton's satirical treatment of the gentlemen's club of 'The Queer Feet' is presaged by Lewis's account of the embassy in which Khan resides, which is 'ominously silent and uninhabited, as though it were not decent that one should know that such extremely illustrious people do such a thing as inhabit at all' (189). This image of negative presence implies an accretion of status translating into an occlusion of the body, which leads in turn to a quasi-nonsensical conflation of wealth with infirmity: the embassy contains 'large and small men and women in various advanced stages of prosperity' (189).

Lewis's narrator also engages in Chestertonian parabasis. At one stage, he begins by aping the language of mystery cliché only to impatiently debunk it in the next breath:

> The clerk was rooted to the spot. We should say that his hair stood stiffly on end, but we do not believe that people's hair ever does stand on end, having frequently been extremely terrified ourselves, but never having remarked any commotion on the scalp.
>
> (212–13)

Here the urbane detachment of 'we' and 'ourselves' is also subtly immersive—Lewis seems to chide the reader, 'this language is demeaning to us both, could we not drop it?' Meanwhile, Royal's carnivalesque cross-dressing draws upon the pantomimic lineage to which Flambeau belongs; as Augustus John observed, Lewis's 'view of life was based largely on the Commedia Dell'Arte' (qtd. in Munton, 'Wyndham Lewis', 141).

At one stage, Royal presents 'the grotesque sight of a bent old woman, standing in a man's shirt, pants and socks, and flying round the room with the rapidity of a monkey' (146); later, he hides his presence within a marching band, while taking the opportunity to commit 'a thousand indiscretions and impertinences with his trombone [...] in the midst of some of the most touching pianissimos of the German's repertoire' (358). This imposition of the absurd upon the sublime engenders a carnival atmosphere amongst the players: 'The bandsmen felt it was in a sense a day off. [...] They gave reign to their fancy. The French horn no longer waited for the cornet, it began when it pleased and left off as unaccountably' (359).

If this playful exposition suggests the kind of review that Chesterton might have given to a concert by Antheil or Stravinsky, Lewis's narrator also essays more blatant pastiches of Chestertonian hobbyhorses, at one point inveighing against the absurdities of fashionable vegetarianism (42)—a phenomenon that does not otherwise seem to have greatly exercised Lewis. As the narrator notes of Royal's research into Mrs. Dukes' character, '[h]e had lately used several expressions that were her personal property. [...] His voice was changing, and it was becoming like hers!' (11). There is an equally unscrupulous form of pastiche at play in Lewis's authorial *modus operandi*, which vitiates the tentative steps towards moral satire suggested by his pathologising of prosperity. At this stage in his career, he was content for his real-life sartorial play to function primarily as a means of self-promotion, feeling no urge to invest it with the sense of pedagogic purpose that Chesterton had anxiously pursued; similarly, although he is in textual cahoots with his Harlequinesque criminal to just as thorough an extent as Chesterton, this is with commercial rather than moral purpose. If Royal finally triumphs in Lewis's imaginative landscape by dressing up as the unfortunate individual whom he robs, his creator attempts to pull off a similar feat—to procure money through a theft of Chesterton's pantomimic mystery formula, conducted under a false name.

These deviations indicate the harnesses being pulled away from Chesterton's ethical framework of buffoonery. Lewis was as well acquainted as Chesterton with the premises of festive culture, having enthused over the 'incredible' (qtd. in Munton, Wyndham Lewis', 142) carnivals that he attended during his youthful travels in Germany. However, *Mrs. Dukes' Million* essays a telling departure from the founding principle of carnival as a temporary state of being. By rewarding Royal for his misdeeds, Lewis emulates the spirit of Eliot's comedian—'here's one who gets away with it' (*PTSE* 1:249)—a resolution that stands in direct opposition to Flambeau's consistent reining in at the hands of Father Brown, who catches the trickster on an 'unseen hook and an invisible line' (*CFB* 48) of theological ethics in 'The Queer Feet'. In contrast, Lewis is proposing perpetual carnival; not so much the worshipper's half-holiday as the worshipper's permanent vacation. This breaching of boundaries is complemented by a wider disruption of the conciliatory conventions of festive comedy.

In this sense, it is to *The Man Who Was Thursday* that we should ultimately turn for the germ of the novel's imaginative conceit and, with it, a rather more subversive form of parodic appropriation. Specifically, the usurpation of Dukes's personality revisits the scene in which Chesterton had rehearsed his ambivalence towards Bentley by revealing the pessimistic Professor de Worms to be a jolly policeman in disguise. Having broken character, the policeman explains that the real philosopher is now trapped in a nightmarish scenario in which he is perpetually assumed to be the copyist: merely 'an impertinent fellow [who] had dressed himself up as a preposterous parody of myself' and 'is [now] received everywhere in Europe as a delightful imposter' whose 'apparent earnestness and anger [...] make him all the more entertaining' (CW 6:550–51). The psychological cruelty of this curiously horrifying revenge upon the philosopher goes blithely unremarked by the narrator, implying a brutal satire of Schopenhauer's insistence upon the vexed relationship between appearance (ephemeral objective representation) and reality (abstract competitive will), in which de Worms merely reaps the material consequences of his deranging Idealist philosophy.

There is no such combative moral at hand in *Mrs. Dukes' Million*; rather, in true parodic fashion, Lewis retains the letter while subverting the spirit, making a virtue of the same vertiginous ontology that Chesterton's text had been conceived to combat: the theft of Mrs. Dukes's identity is depicted with just as unnerving a sanguinity as that of de Worms, but the landlady has done absolutely nothing to morally justify her fate. Similarly, although Royal's parodic status as 'the sum of two images' superficially recalls Syme's anarchistic disguise, Lewis's comedian is the reverse of the 'poet of law' (CW 6:478)—he is a metaphysical anarchist in old lady's clothing, conducting his deceit not for satirical purposes but purely for commercial gain.

When the novel ends with an exposition of Royal's aeronautical feats, the uproarious derangement of the Chestertonian mystery story is capped not with a communal utopian allegory in the vein of *Thursday*, but with a capitalistic exposition of the hero as a solitary Marinettian entrepreneur. As Daniel Schenker observes, 'the narrator makes a point of remarking that Royal has not approached the building of airplanes with altruistic motives, but "entirely as a business speculation" that promises to yield an immense personal fortune' (27). The technophile tenor of Lewis's *denouement* is almost certainly informed by the first Futurist manifesto, which was published shortly before he completed the novel, in an edition of the *Tramp* (August 1909) that also featured Lewis's early short story, 'A Breton Innkeeper'. Whereas Chesterton's article on 'The Futurists' pastiches Dostoevsky in order to satirise Marinetti's radicalism, Lewis's novel ends by pastiching Marinetti in order to satirise Chesterton's sentimentalism.

Notwithstanding Lewis's half-hearted attempt to morally rehabilitate Royal at the conclusion by having him return a portion of the money, the ontological drift of his absurdist nonsense world more closely resembles Carroll than Rabelais. Prior to his final success, Royal conceives the challenges that he faces as a series of nonsense-games, suggestive of Bentley's account of the abstract 'wit contest' of chess: 'He had routed Hillington. This was the first move in this game, and he had won it. But there were many moves on both sides yet to come' (*Mrs.*, 320). Augustus John reported that the youthful Lewis approached the social world in a similar spirit: he 'played the part of an incarnate Loki [...] He conceived the world as an arena, where various insurrectionary forces struggled to outwit each other in the game of artistic power politics' (qtd. in Meyers, 18). Royal is also a descendent of Loki, the archetypal trickster figure, and a female impersonator so skilful that his disguise is impossible to penetrate. Like Loki, Royal stands at the limit of the human: he '"seems to be looking at you from behind a mask. [...] when he's not playing the boisterous bohemian quite so much, his real voice seems to appear and it is quite expressionless, like his eyes. [...] He seems an inhuman sort of person"' (*Mrs.*, 14–15). Once more, we are in the realm of the Romantic grotesque, in which the mask is not a symbol of regeneration and change, but a façade overlying a vacuum, as Royal's *evan*escent forename suggests: the term derives from *vanus*, or 'empty' (Barnhart, 347).

This build-up of imagery begins to evoke another empty vessel whom Lewis conceived as an avatar in this period: Frederick Tarr, who considers '*deadness*' to be 'the first condition of art' (*Tarr*, 299).[10] Tarr is, in effect, Royal transferred to a different generic plane: he constructs 'a grinning, tumultuous mask for the face he had to cover. = The clown was the only role that was ample enough' (*Tarr*, 29), and he has a similar passion for financial gain: he 'would have driven his entire circle of acquaintances into commerce if he could' (36). In a pivotal and much quoted passage, Tarr's personality is explained as

> a Chinese puzzle of boxes within boxes [...] the husk he held was a painted mummy case. He was a mummy case, too. Only he contained nothing but innumerable other painted cases inside, smaller and smaller ones. The smallest was not [... a] live core, but a painting like the rest. = His kernel was a painting. That was as it should be!
> (58–59)

If this celebratory vision of a panoply of psychological false bottoms seems to subversively skew Chesterton's apprehension in *Thursday* of 'that final scepticism which can find no floor to the universe', it is telling that Tarr, the self-proclaimed '"panurgic-pessimist, drunken with the laughing-gas of the Abyss"' (26), is 'remembering Schopenhauer' (58) when the Chinese box analogy occurs to him. It is little wonder that

Chesterton came to view the landscape of the emergent avant-garde as the site of a disturbing re-enactment of his youthful battles. The 'comic, dull grimace' of Eliot's 'deceaséd marionette' (*PTSE* 1:237) in 'Humouresque' is mirrored in Lewis's unnervingly hollow rendering of Royal and Tarr: both writers borrow from Chesterton's imaginative landscape only to reinstate the very condition that he had been striving to slough off.

When *Tarr* was eventually published in 1917, Rebecca West delighted Lewis with a review in which she speculated that the novel might be taken for a 'pastiche of Dostoevsky' (qtd. in O'Keefe, 206). This appraisal formed the apotheosis of Lewis's *entrée* to literary London as a Dostoevsky character made flesh. Much as his body had yielded text in Ford's account, Lewis had successfully translated his parodic embodiment of the Dostoevskian antihero into the composition of a quasi-Dostoevskian text. Nonetheless, this conflation with the novelist's characters exposes an irony embedded within Lewis's early reception: *Tarr* is not so much a pastiche of Dostoevsky himself, as a text that might have been written by a character from a Dostoevsky novel, much as *Mrs. Dukes' Million* might have been contrived in a moment of levity by Chesterton's 'anarchic poet', Lucian Gregory.

Although West discerned a psychological resemblance between Lewis's abject buffoon, Otto Kreisler, and Dostoevsky's Stavrogin (see Meyers, 16), Tarr is ultimately the more Stavroginian figure, insofar as Dostoevsky's antihero is also presented as possessing an uncanny, impenetrable façade: 'His face was said to resemble a mask' (Dostoevsky, *Devils*, 44). As with the contra-Chestertonian rendering of Royal's amoral tricksterism, *Tarr* subverts Dostoevsky's attempt to convey the ontological perils of nihilism, arguing instead that this disturbing vacuity is 'as it should be'. Equally, Evan Royal is a pantomime Raskolnikov, echoing the latter's intellectual self-justifications—'"Crime! What is crime? [...] It is only the sordid intention that makes the really despicable criminal"' (*Mrs.*, 67)—while ending the novel as a genuine 'Napoleon' (365), in contrast to Dostoevsky's monitory antihero, who learns too late that he is not an exception to the moral rule of law.

If *Devils* and *Thursday* are anti-anarchist texts from which Lewis extrapolates an anarchic anti-moral, there is a subversive quality to this misreading that transcends mere misidentification with the writers' intent to suggest a more wilfully parodic unveiling—think of Lewis's later account of Proudhon's view of anarchism as '*the negation of* author*ity*' (qtd. in Munton, 'Lewis', 106; inverted emphasis mine). Knight argues that 'the main purpose of [Chesterton's] dedication' in *Thursday* is to 'guide our reading' (91) of a text that the author recognises to possess an interpretive instability. Nonetheless, there arises an echo of William Godwin's famous reading of *Paradise Lost* (1667) as a text in which, as Peter Schock puts it, a tension arises between the 'actual impression made on the reader over the consciously intended moral' (83). Knight considers the vividness of the 'nightmare' section of *Thursday* to potentially undermine the force of the counter-impression created by the carnivalesque resolution: 'the appearance of the grotesque threatens to reveal nothing rather than the external world that Chesterton values so greatly' (25).

As Robert L. Caserio explains, *Thursday* is built upon a form of 'double-writing' that sets out to balance equivocality and certainty—the conclusion attempts 'to consolidate definiteness, after provocatively wandering away from the latter', with the result that its final 'unequivocal certainty' remains contingent 'upon a process or medium of multiple and uncertain meanings' (66). If Lewis's methods in *Mrs. Dukes' Million* mobilise the lacunae latent within Chesterton's conscious intent, a more explicit inversion was later essayed by a Soviet theatre group, whose topsy-turvy adaptation of the novel provoked Chesterton's chagrin: 'they tried to turn [my] Anti-Anarchist romance into an Anarchist play [...] making it mean the opposite of everything it meant' (*G.K.C.*, 202). Lucas H. Harriman explains that although the purpose of this adaptation was to 'betray [Chesterton's] statement of intention in order to see what it might prohibit in the work's reception [...] this textual "other"' merely accentuates the 'undecidability' encoded within the original: 'It is a reading the book's ambiguity facilitates' (109/118).

This vulnerability to misreading is a trait that Chesterton shares with Dostoevsky, whose prefiguration of Chesterton's use of dialogic methods to challenge the dominant thought of his age famously raises the complication that the reader may find sympathy with characters conceived in a monitory spirit. Kaye argues that this scenario was particularly common amongst Dostoevsky's early twentieth-century avant-garde audience: the 'persistently non-literary assessments of Dostoevsky' conducted by leading modernists frequently 'collapsed distinctions between author and characters' (25), while 'some readers, such as Middleton Murry, even insisted that Dostoevsky endorsed the views of his most criminal and perverse creations' (18). Chesterton's successful decoding of Dostoevsky's message in *Devils*—as implied by his sympathetic pastiche in 'The Futurists'—represented a rare exception to this misreading from a figure whom few would think to connect to the Russian, but whose greater affinity with the 'comic nightmare' (Leatherbarrow, 92) of Dostoevsky's text enabled him to correctly interpret the author's intent.

This affinity was not only ideological, but also aesthetic. Dostoevsky's novels career from 'grotesque farces to religious parables' (Kaye, 26), relentlessly juxtaposing 'the sublime with the grotesque' (*Problems*, 103), as Bakhtin puts it. In view of this carnivalesque correspondence, the cross-pollination of Chesterton and Dostoevsky in Lewis's literary imagination is not as counterintuitive as it might initially seem. West's comparison of Stavrogin to Kreisler was presumably inspired partially by the rather unorthodox duels in which each becomes involved. Syme's duel in *Thursday* also arises from the protagonist's gratuitously provocative behaviour, and each of the three confrontations ends in farce: Stavrogin fires off a wilfully incompetent shot, Kriesler attempts to sexually assault his opponent, and the Marquis demands that Syme should tug off his nose. Nonetheless, as with the structural progress of 'Prufrock', as distinct from that of *Thursday* or 'The Queer Feet', these burlesque thematic resemblances end in morphological departure: Syme's duel is a further staging post towards his ultimate recovery of a more benign vision of existence; Kriesler and Stavrogin finally commit suicide.[11]

If Royal's entrepreneurial success as a parodist represented a wish-fulfilment fantasy on Lewis's part, this did not yield a real-life corollary—*Mrs. Dukes' Million* was rejected by the literary agent, J.B. Pinker, whose response persuaded Lewis that the novel was 'not marketable' (Lewis, *Letters*, 44). Lewis's exploratory message to Pinker had been frank about the expedients of the enterprise, pondering whether this 'miserable pot-boiler has [...] any money value' and seeking to assure Pinker that 'the only thing of which there is question as far as this book is concerned is money-making' (*Letters*, 43). To this end, Lewis offers a number of potential concessions that neatly echo the fiscal amorality of his protagonist. Various edits are posited, including, most strikingly, 'disagreeable remarks about newspaper reporters to be removed, and replaced by agreeable ones' (*Letters*, 43) if the manuscript should be offered to a newspaper for serialisation.

Lewis's failure to place the novel arises from a lack of credit in a deeper sense: the Latin *credere* means to 'believe, trust' (Barnhart, 233), and the ethical untrustworthiness of Lewis's narrative voice is complemented by the author's failure to invest sufficient belief in his projected audience. As 'The Queer Feet' makes abundantly clear, Chesterton had made his mystery writing marketable precisely by refusing to moderate his opinions, while also striving to implant highly sophisticated aesthetic techniques within the popular format. Conversely, Lewis's chronic underestimation of the intelligence of his imagined readership often leads to passages of unintentionally ludicrous exposition, lacking the arch manoeuvre into critical parabasis found elsewhere in the text. At one stage, Royal is 'kidnapped just like an old woman, like Mrs. Dukes!' As Lewis goes on to helpfully explain, '[i]t was, in this sense, an ironical happening' (188). Elsewhere, he inserts infantilising vernacular surplus words into the exposition: 'Royal waited all day *long* in expectation of some new development in the *brand* new situation' (168; my emphases). At other times, the extraneous language takes the form of rhetorical cliché: 'He was not surprised to find the butler's head very close to his own, and this time almost unbelievably inscrutable and impassible—with the impassibility of death!' (306).

Lewis's inscriptions of linguistic redundancy stand in sharp contrast to his contemporaneous methodology in *Tarr*. As he later explained, this 'was approached with austerity. I clipped the text to the bone of all fleshy verbiage [...] I abstained from the use of clichés [... and] eschewed sentimental archaisms' (*Rude*, 129). These accretions were dispatched to

Mrs. Dukes' Million, precisely in the hope of appealing to a commercial market that might enable him to 'get [...] a little money so that I could complete comme il faut my other novel' (Lewis, *Letters*, 43). In this sense, the severity of *Tarr*'s formal innovation is parasitic upon the spectral counter-presence of the unpublished novel. *Mrs. Dukes' Million* becomes a burlesque shadow text to the high-modernist totem; an abject repository for Lewis's verbal waste products.

This covert symbiosis is essential to a proper understanding of Lewis's later immoderation on the subject of popular culture. Despite his protestations to Pinker, there are a great many ways to make money beyond the production of popular mystery fiction—Eliot famously took the stolid option of working nine to five for Lloyds Bank from 1917 to 1925. Lewis chose this specific route because the activity satisfied a side of his personality that could not find expression through literary forms considered legitimate by his contemporaries. One thinks of Chesterton's later imputation that modernist aesthetics formed a perverse straightjacket: 'the modern poet must always be on his best behaviour; I mean, of course, that he must always be on his worst behaviour' ('On the Prison of Jazz', collected in *Avowals*, 105). Chesterton's equivocal phrasing not only echoes 'The Blue Cross', in which we receive a potted history of Flambeau's 'best days (I mean, of course, his worst)' (*CFB* 3), but also the crocodile tears shed by the narrator of *Mrs. Dukes' Million* over 'the poor old woman so shamefully, so wonderfully despoiled' (360). In this light, Lewis's occasionally uncritical use of cliché might be read as winningly ingenuous rather than cynically commercial: the author getting caught up in the wonder of the plot, momentarily forgetting his shame over composing it.

Rather than reflecting that his pitch to Pinker might have been poorly calculated to inspire enthusiasm, Lewis took the rejection to be 'a lesson showing the futility of pot-boiling for me' (*Letters*, 44) and set the book permanently aside. The humiliation of this episode had a largely unrecognised impact upon Lewis's later career. If he had initially evaded modernist culture's wider misreading of Chesterton and Dostoevsky, he now realised that his more subtle blurring of cultural boundary lines would be commercially impolitic to pursue. When Pound took the opportunity to promote *Tarr* in the *Little Review*, he set about re-establishing a clear divide, arguing that while Lewis was 'the only English writer who [could] be compared with Dostoievsky' ('*Tarr*', 424), his novel would 'not be praised by [...] Mr Chesterton' (429). Thus, the philosophy of disguise developed in *Mrs. Dukes' Million* began to enjoy a superannuated life outside the text. Kenner argues that the moral implied by Evan Royal's triumph is that '[v]ery simply, the way to affluence and power is to make yourself be thought to be somebody else' ('Satirist', 267); Lewis had 'no thought of salvaging Mrs. Dukes' Million ever. He had always, he would have us believe, been serious' (Kenner, 'Mrs.', 90). As Frederick Tarr notes, in an instructive aside, '"Half of myself I have to hide"' (22).

Eliot exercised more caution than Pound in his assessment of the Dostoevskian dimensions of *Tarr*. Reviewing the novel for the *Egoist* (Sept. 1918), he observed that the 'analogy [has been] fostered by Mr. Lewis's explicit admiration for Dostoevsky', nonetheless '[h]is mind is different, his method is different, his aims are different [...] he must be allowed the hypothesis of a dual creative personality' ('Tarr', 105). As the saying goes, it takes one to know one. Although James Rother tentatively suggests that the 'Do I dare?' passage of 'Prufrock' might be read as a merger of the 'jocular anxieties of Lear' with 'a concatenation of events' such as one might find 'in a detective story by, say, G. K. Chesterton' (190), Chesterton has long remained buried in the shadows of Eliot's reception, an influence assumed to be eccentric to the poet's own stated canon. Like Lewis, Eliot instead advertised his youthful reading of Dostoevsky during a formative period in Paris, and Lewis's real-life rendition of *Crime and Punishment* at the offices of the *English Review* finds a textual complement in Prufrock's more timid negotiation of a staircase, in which there remains '[t]ime to turn back and descend the stair' (*PTSE* 1:6).

Upon learning of John C. Pope's contention that the imagery of 'Prufrock' owed a debt to Dostoevsky's novel, Eliot responded, with poker-faced legalese, 'you have established very conclusively the essentials of your case' (Pope, 319). Eliot went on to volunteer further, unsolicited confessions to Pope, noting that the poem's 'Prince Hamlet' section 'show[s] the influence of Laforgue' (Pope, 319). As with the apparently self-deprecatory gesture of the subheading, 'After J. Laforgue', in 'Humouresque', this breadcrumb-trail serves to subtly police the terms of his reception. Disarmed by the poet's apparent modesty, the reader is less likely to carry out further investigations. Although Kenner considers Eliot to be 'a habitual [...] tacit imitator' (*Pound*, 438), he is also a singularly indiscreet thief, hiding his purloined letters in plain sight in order to fess up to a venial crime in advance, much as Prufrock's sense of being pursued relentlessly by private eyes leads him to hand himself in to the reader with a confession riddled with coercive literary allusions. One thinks of Father Brown's response to a similar case of voluntary self-criminalisation: '"I've heard a good many confessions, and there never was a genuine one like that. It was romantic; it was all out of books"' (*CFB* 512).[12] As Evan Royal explains to an accomplice who becomes alarmed by his attention-seeking antics, this is all part of the plan:

> "one can't overdo it. To draw people's attention [...] to get talked about and be much in evidence, all this takes people further away from finding out the *real* person I am, and the fraud that is being practised on them."

(269)

Appropriately enough, given Lewis's exposure of the effaced potentialities of *The Man Who Was Thursday*, the next move in this insipient game of textual dialogue between Chesterton and the new modernist avant-garde was an attempt on Chesterton's part to expose this fraud, in a story that presents a new, darker twist on the trickster figure, replacing Flambeau's genial *Heimlich* manoeuvres with a more Marinettian *modus operandi*.

Notes

1. First published as 'The Truth about Popular Literature: II—The Value of Detective Stories'.
2. See Bentley, *Those*, for an account of the novel's lengthy gestation process (249).
3. Baldick is writing specifically of Q.D. Leavis.
4. As well as denoting a patina of moneyed sophistication in a general sense, *The Smart Set* (1900–30) was an American literary magazine that published work by Conrad, Ford, Joyce, and Lawrence and employed Pound as a talent scout. Father Brown refers to the Twelve True Fishermen as 'the Smart Set' (*CFB* 50) in 'The Queer Feet'.
5. See Mark Knight's article 'Chesterton, Dostoevsky, and Freedom' (*English Literature in Transition, 1880–1920*, 43:1, 2000, pp. 37–50) for an account of Chesterton's engagement with Dostoevsky. As Knight explains, Chesterton's interest was most probably fostered earlier in the Edwardian era by his close friendship with the Russophile, Maurice Baring.
6. 'Nap or Corbett' most probably refers to Napoleon and Robert Corbett.
7. The edition that features 'The Pole' (May 1909) also includes Dostoevsky's 'An Honest Thief'.
8. Ford also turned Lewis back into fiction. In *The Marsden Case* (1923), George Heimann is a sympathetic portrait of Lewis: a 'mystery man without a past', dressed in a '"high-crowned hat [and] coat, black and buttoned-up round his neck, like a uniform"' (qtd. in Meyers, 30).
9. The novel was never published in Lewis's lifetime, and the title is not Lewis's own—his preference was for 'Khan and Company' (Lewis, *Letters*, 44).
10. Unless otherwise stated, all references to *Tarr* are from the 1918 edition.
11. The curious entanglement of the three authors is illustrated by one further subtle correspondence: *The Ball and the Cross* features a chapter titled 'The Idiot', in which a holy fool is incarcerated in an asylum, thus echoing Prince Myshkin's fate in Dostoevsky's novel. Finding himself in an adjacent cell, Turnbull develops 'a hatred' for an 'objectless iron peg in the wall' *CW* 7:221), thus uncannily prefiguring the emotions of Mrs. Dukes when she finds herself in a hospital possessed of similarly under-refined furnishings: she 'gradually became conscious of an insane desire to get up and touch this nail with her finger—to pull it out' (50).
12. Eliot perhaps hints at this chicanery in the epigraph to 'Portrait of a Lady' (1915), from Christopher Marlowe's *The Jew of Malta* (1592), in which a more grave accusation is artfully parried:

Thou hast committed—
Fornication: but that was in another country (*PTSE* 10)

4 We Discharge Ourselves on Both Sides
The Parodic Commerce of Chesterton and the Men of 1914

> [P]rogress should be something else besides a continual parricide[.]
> —Chesterton, introduction to *The Defendant* (16)

> You cannot carry your father's corpse around everywhere you go (*On ne peut pas transporter partout avec soi le cadavre de son père*)
> —Guillaume Apollinaire, *The Cubist Painters* (7)

In January 1913, Chesterton resigned his position at the *Daily News* in spectacular fashion, publishing a thinly veiled, astonishingly intemperate verse satire of the paper's plutocratic proprietor, Lord Cadbury, in the *New Witness*:

> Cocoa is a cad and coward
> Cocoa is a vulgar beast
> Cocoa is a dull, disloyal
> Lying, crawling cad and clown.
>   ('A Song of Strange Drinks', 23 Jan. 1913; collected in
>   *Flying*, 199–200)

Although Gardiner sought to pour water on the resulting fire, Chesterton chose to force the issue in a curiously passive-aggressive manner that rendered his continued employment impossible, before announcing his resignation in an open letter to the *Daily Herald*, the syndicalist paper that had so intrigued Virginia Woolf's cook.[1] This terminated a relationship that had been deteriorating gradually from around the turn of the decade, as Chesterton's increasing impatience with the Liberal government and his ever-more strident anti-capitalist pronouncements began to alienate the paper's readership and ownership alike. As Julia Stapleton notes, gone was the 'affable manner' (*Christianity*, 36) that had characterised Chesterton's earlier journalistic jousts. The mask of the Johnsonian humourist was beginning to slip, disclosing the unmediated revolutionary.

Chesterton's overture to the *Herald* led to an offer of work from the radical newspaper, thus providing him with a marginally more ideologically sympathetic employer in the period leading up to the outbreak of war.[2] The *New Age* also came down squarely on his side in the *Daily News* controversy:

> Mr. G. K. Chesterton has [lately] been proving his moral and political honesty by resigning from the 'Daily News' [...] it is gratifying to know that there is still one honest man in Fleet Street. [...] We cannot see that the 'Daily News' has now any reason for existing.
> (Orage, 'Notes of the Week', 20 Feb. 1913; 370)

On the face of it, this was a counterintuitive ally for Chesterton to have acquired at this time. In the pre-war years, the *New Age* had become a thriving hub of proto-modernist thought, publishing Lewis's 'Our Wild Body' essay (5 May 1910) and 'Brobdingnag' short story (5 Jan. 1911), employing Pound to produce cultural dispatches intermittently from 1911 onwards, and regularly publishing work by T.E. Hulme, Katherine Mansfield, and a range of other figures who would come to be closely identified with the modernist movement. However, Orage was a singularly independent minded, non-partisan figure, as supportive of the ideological unconventionality of Chesterton as the aesthetic unconventionality of Lewis and Pound, and his periodical formed a rare space of textual mediation between literary factions that were beginning to harden into an entrenched hostile binary.

Chesterton's reciprocal interest in the *New Age* would almost certainly have caused him to come across Pound's writing in this period, and it seems equally likely that their paths would have crossed in another, more materially communal space: The Square Club. This was a literary society co-founded by Chesterton in the late-Edwardian era 'to do honour to Fielding' (Jepson, 134), which formed a briefly fashionable *rendezvous* for such apparently disparate cultural figures as Bentley and Ford (see Jepson, 138).[3] The tirelessly networking Pound frequented the club in 1910, and his self-promoting antics were gossiped about by his fellow patrons. Edgar Jepson, a writer of detective fiction and fellow *habitué*, later recalled the histrionic figure of Pound 'feeling his way' (142) into literary society at the club, with 'velvet jacket' and 'abundant hair' which made him look 'very much [...] a poet' (142). This performative ethos accords with Douglas Goldring's account of the impression created by Lewis and Pound in the period: 'I have never seen anybody so obviously a "genius" as Wyndham Lewis [...] in clothes, hairdressing and manner [Pound and Lewis] made no secret of their calling' (qtd. in Meyers, 32). Dennis Brown argues that this likeness was imitative on Pound's part—in the years immediately following their first introduction, 'Pound's chief "persona"' became 'himself as Lewisian poet' (*Intertextual*, 39).

Against this backdrop of professional and social commerce, Chesterton published a new *Father Brown* story—'The Paradise of Thieves'—in

August 1913 (*Pall Mall Magazine*), in which his increasing preoccupation with commercial unscrupulousness in business merged with a sceptical interrogation of the public image-mongering of the pre-war avant-garde. The story formed the opening salvo in a protracted confrontation between Chesterton and the Men of 1914 in the years that followed—a cultural stand-off in which the protagonists' anxieties over the traffic of public finance and personal identity found expression in commerce of a more parodic, textual nature.

A Bundle of Masks

'The Paradise of Thieves' tells the story of a crooked English banker, Mr. Harrogate, and Ezza Montano, an Italian Futurist impresario and 'modernist' (*CFB* 193) who is in his pay. The most obvious models for the latter character are, of course, Marinetti and the near identically forenamed Pound. Chesterton's Ezza is a double of the self-dramatising Square Club Pound, possessing a 'very vivacious [head], that rose abruptly out of the standing collar like cardboard and the comic pink tie' (*CFB* 183). If Montano is conceived as a composite of Marinetti and Pound, his friend Muscari bears a striking resemblance to the caricature of Lewis propounded by Ford, whose burlesque recollections of their first meeting would almost certainly have done the rounds of the Square Club. While Ford's Lewis wears a diaphanous cape that resembles 'the type that villains in transpontine melodrama throw over their shoulders when they say "Ha-ha!"', Chesterton's Muscari 'carried a black cloak, and might almost have carried a black mask, so much did he bear with him a sort of Venetian melodrama' (*CFB* 189).

Of course, this description not only evokes Ford's account of Lewis, but also Holbrook Jackson's vision of Chesterton roaming the streets 'in cloak and combrero like a brigand of Adelphi drama'. In sartorial terms, Muscari is a kind of Chesterlewis, and in consequence, he is handled with considerably more sympathy than Ezza, whose 'ironical' (*CFB* 196) countenance twice breaks into a 'sneer' (*CFB* 192; 200) in a telltale giveaway of Chestertonian disapproval. The narrator's observation that Ezza's 'costume was the most aggressively opposite to [Muscari's] own' (*CFB* 189) hints at the characters' status as another of Chesterton's polarised double acts, here exemplifying the positive and negative connotations that he attached to the younger generation: Muscari represents the avant-garde's playful, unworldly aspect, Ezza its cynical, manipulative side. Ezza's arch inscrutability forms a sharp contrast with the hot-headed ingenuousness of Muscari, whose 'intensity smelt of danger or even crime. Like fire or the sea, he was too simple to be trusted' (*CFB* 189), a melodramatic account that recalls the fevered apprehension of Lewis exhibited by Bloomsbury. In a further gesture of covert identification, Muscari's impetuosity not only hints at Lewis's habitual acts of self-sabotaging indiscretion—not least his contemporaneous highly damaging dispute with Roger Fry (see Meyers, 39–50)—but also Chesterton's recent travails in the 'Cocoa' controversy.

Meanwhile, the narrator's depiction of Ezza as a risibly unsuccessful renaissance man seems calculated to cut the hitherto uncelebrated Pound to the quick: 'when he appeared in the world he failed, first publicly as a dramatist and a demagogue, and then privately for years on end as an actor, a traveller, a commission agent or a journalist' (*CFB* 190). Ezza's new career as the 'King of Thieves' (*CFB* 192) offers an acting role that provides a romantic veneer of brigandage to obscure his more prosaic complicity in Harrogate's plan to embezzle funds from his company. Chesterton inserts a barbed parody of the Futurist manifesto into this premise via the 'public document' that Ezza releases, a '"proclamation, soon to be published to all Italy"' (*CFB* 197) that constitutes a list of ransom demands.

From here, a series of events unfold that consistently combine aesthetic play with fiscal underhandedness. When Muscari first encounters Ezza after several years' separation, he expresses surprise at finding him 'dressed up as an Englishman', to which Ezza responds that this is '"not the costume of an Englishman, but of the Italian of the future"' (*CFB* 190). In articulating his indiscriminate admiration of all things new, Ezza conflates the commercial and the sartorial—'"the newest factories, the newest motors, the newest finance—the newest clothes"' (*CFB* 190)—before juxtaposing the preeminent Italian businessman of the day and the preeminent Italian poet: '"to me Marconi, or d'Annunzio, is the star of Italy [...] That is why I have become a Futurist—and a courier"' (*CFB* 190). Both men were early influences upon Marinetti, and Pound later praised d'Annunzio, a figure famed for his unscrupulous methods of self-promotion.[4] As far back as 'A Defence of Penny Dreadfuls', Chesterton had argued that 'to be a many-faced and fickle traitor [...] is a simple summary of a good many modern systems from Mr. d'Annunzio's downwards' (*Defendant*, 27). By the time of 'The Paradise of Thieves', his view of the chameleonic trickster-aesthete as a figurative traitor had progressed to a more literal, political apprehension of pantomimic perfidy—recall that Cadbury is depicted as a 'disloyal [...] clown'.

It is no surprise, then, to find 'The Paradise of Thieves' advancing a more sceptical view of the regenerative moral efficacy of the Harlequin than had been presented in 'The Queer Feet'. Although Muscari's quixotic playacting bears traces of Flambeau's magpie-like thievery, Ezza's ironical sneer and entrepreneurial criminality situate him as a more malign, amoral trickster. When Muscari scorns the money that might be extracted from Harrogate—'"[t]o be clever enough to get all that money, one must be stupid enough to want it"—Ezza responds morosely that he is '"stupid enough for that"' (*CFB* 191). Similarly, whereas Flambeau is conceived as a quasi-mythological Harlequin, transported into the present and sartorially travestying a contemporary gentleman, Ezza represents the reverse—a contemporary spiv travestying the garb of an elemental trickster: 'This figure was clad in tweeds of a *piebald check* [... and] *contrived* [...] to look at once startling and commonplace' (*CFB* 190; my emphasis). As Ezza's plan unfolds, Chesterton conceives a sartorial twist on the palimpsestic transformation scene. The back scene begins to glow through the façade when a mundane commercialism begins to leak out onto Ezza's piratical carapace: 'he had assumed a flapped fantastic hat and swinging baldric and cutlass in his capacity of bandit king, but the bright prosaic tweed of the courier showed through in patches all over him' (*CFB* 199).

There is a certain prescience to this satirical exposure in view of the commercial rhetoric that Pound consistently turned to in his subsequent cultural manoeuvres, from the imagery of fiscal criminality that underpins his advice to Eliot—'let me throw the bricks through the front window. You go in at the back and take the swag' (qtd. in Carpenter, 264)—to the Marinettian marriage of unfocused aggression and capitalistic accumulation that he employs to express his enthusiasm for Lewis's artwork under the punning sign of the pound: 'every kind of whirlwind of force, ££££££' (Letter to John Quinn, 10 Mar. 1916; qtd. in Ellmann, M., *Poetics*, 167).[5] In a presumably unconscious echo of Lewis's portrayal of Evan Royal, Chesterton's depiction of Ezza conjoins a preoccupation with accruing capital to character traits suggestive of the Romantic grotesque.[6] When Muscari discovers the venal nature of his friend's true occupation and indignantly challenges him to a duel, Ezza responds with a vision of evanescent identity that evokes both the subjective plurality of Pound's 1909 volume, *Personae*, and Frederick Tarr's 'Chinese puzzle of boxes within boxes':

> "What's the good, old man?" he said in spirited Italian slang; "this damned farce will soon be over."
> "What do you mean, you shuffler?" panted the fire-eating poet. "Is your courage a sham as well as your honesty?"
> "Everything about me is a sham," responded the ex-courier in complete good-humour. "I am an actor; and if I ever had a private character, I have forgotten it. I am no more of a brigand than I am a genuine courier. I am only a bundle of masks, and you can't fight a duel with that".
>
> (*CFB* 200–201)

The sartorial swashbuckling of Ezza and Muscari also extends Chesterton's satirical exposé from the commercial to the aesthetic, positing Pound and Lewis as closet lowercase romantics. The performative accoutrements of the double act invest them with an air of superannuated Decadence—what Vincent Sherry has recently dubbed the 'elaborate artifice Pound ostensibly rejected but more than discernibly exhibited' (230) in this period—while the plot device of Ezza's fraudulent activities produces a more trenchant interrogation of authenticity, lampooning Pound and his co-conspirator as pseudo-Wildean performance artists on the make. Chesterton's story is a wilful provocation, initiating an argument about who is the true bearer of the anti-Decadent flame, implying that the new generation is composed of ill-intentioned false pretenders to his rightful status as the culture's preeminent agent of regeneration.

In Chesterton's verse parody of Marinetti in 'The Futurists', the effect of having the unmediated voice of the Futurist supersede that of Chesterton suggests a propagandising radio station being abruptly changed to an alternative signal, producing a pessimistic conclusion to the 'fight' at hand, in which Marinetti appears to push the parodist out of the way to steal the final word. In this respect, Chesterton gloomily enacts his own generational obsolescence, projecting himself as a victim of the wider cultural parricide of Futurism. Just five months after the publication of 'The Paradise of Thieves', Orage called forth this sense of transition in the *New Age* in a double-edged tribute to Chesterton's seeming embodiment of the values of the previous era: a 'study of Mr. Chesterton would dispense us from the necessity of considering any of his contemporaries'; nonetheless, 'his age has nearly passed' ('Readers and Writers', 25 Dec. 1913; 241).

'The Paradise of Thieves' also revisits 'The Futurists' in other ways. In fleshing out the implied argument of the article, the story not only borrows the 'theme of imposture' (Leatherbarrow, 130) that informs Dostoevsky's *Devils*, but also that novel's inter-generational decline narrative, in which cultural credos that previously possessed an ethical impetus, however self-deluding, become subverted and corrupted by less idealistic descendants. Notwithstanding the potential complacency of a scenario in which the father bemoans the sons' squandering of his imaginative legacy, Chesterton's depiction of Ezza as an amoral Harlequin also conveys a more subtle note of parental self-interrogation, much as Dostoevsky conceived the liberalism of his own generation to have opened the door to the nihilism of the 1860s.

This self-critical edge is discernible in Ezza's characterisation as the 'King of Thieves', a title that had been attributed to Flambeau in an earlier story (see *CFB* 106), and which alludes to the designation conventionally attributed to Autolycus, the son of Hermes in Greek mythology and of Mercury in Roman mythology. Both Chesterton and Pound were discussed by their contemporaries in terms that placed them at the limit of the human—much as Gardiner had extolled Chesterton as 'elemental and primitive' in 1908, Lewis later credited Pound with the 'Energy of a discriminating Element' (*BLAST* 2:82). The 'mischievous humour' (Guirand, 134) of Hermes leads Hutcheon to consider him an apt representative of the parodist's 'challenges to as well as re-inscriptions of authority' (xvii). Nonetheless, Hermes is also 'the god of commerce, the god of profit—lawful and unlawful' (Guirand, 133), a combination of pedagogic play and persiflage that accords with the Edwardian reception of Chesterton's buffoonery. Ovid informs us that Autolycus was 'talented in all trickery' and wont 'to make white black, and black white, not unworthy of his father's skill' (qtd. in Pavlock, 114), having inherited the ability to hide objects in plain sight, a talent that enables him 'to commit numerous thefts' (Guirand, 137).

With this background in mind, there develops a sense that the sons are not so much corrupting the benign legacy of the father as pursuing a premise that the father had inherited from the grandfather to its logical conclusion. In his review of *The Importance of Being Earnest*, William Archer had thrown up his hands at its Harlequinesque amorality: 'What can a poor critic do with a play which raises no principle, whether of art or morals [...] and is nothing but an absolutely wilful expression of an irrepressibly witty personality?' (190). Father Brown alludes to Wilde's play in 'The Blue Cross' in the course of ethically instructing Flambeau, explaining that he learned the trick of swapping parcels from a thief who used to do the same 'with handbags he stole at railway stations' before adding that this figure is 'in a monastery now' (*CFB* 17). With 'The Paradise of Thieves', Chesterton would seem to have belatedly recognised that the energies of the trickster ultimately confound such reassuring circumscription. The conceptual tension at hand might be compared to Lewis's later account of satire: 'In its origins it was not moralist. The Christian made it that'; instead, it was simply 'a combat between two opposite forces [...] the satirist must be the better man—whether we mean by "better" of a more edifying character, or [...] a more powerful intelligence, is a matter of taste' (*Mysterious*, 143). Proverbially, the trickster 'knows neither good nor evil' (Williams, 6), while Welsford notes that the only constant qualities of Harlequin 'through the centuries are agility, resilience and, as a rule, complete absence of the moral sense. Unlike the fool in cap and bells, he can tap no hidden source of mysterious knowledge or unworldly wisdom' (303).

Accordingly, 'The Paradise of Thieves' divests the trickster archetype of its veneer of anarchic glamour to reveal the sordid venality into which the principle is more likely to devolve if applied in the real world. In the process, the story comes to read as a malign parody of the earliest motifs of *Father Brown*. Muscari anticipates Lewis's non-moral account of the satirist as 'the better man' when he impatiently scoffs that Harrogate is '"I suppose, human"', though one cannot say '"that he's a cleverer man than I, or bolder than I, or even more energetic. He's not clever; he's got eyes like blue buttons; he's not energetic, he moves from chair to chair like a paralytic"' (*CFB* 191). While this imagery of decrepitude gestures back to Chesterton's reframing of Futurist bravado as the impotent reveries of a doddering physical dependant—'I feel full of energy while sitting in a car' (*CDN* 6:139)—it also recalls his satirical exposition of the slothful 'swells' of 'The Queer Feet'. However, when the narrator of 'The Paradise of Thieves' notes that Harrogate 'might have been a colonel' (*CFB* 191), the observation draws our attention to the discrepancy between the earlier desire of Father Brown and Flambeau to vitalise Colonel Pound and the present situation, in which neither the protagonists nor the narrator display any interest in regenerating the corrupted representative of the older generation.

In a corresponding inversion, when the police respond indulgently to Harrogate's nefarious deeds, the effect is to warp the idealistic *denouement* of 'The Queer Feet'. The Colonel's reassurance to Brown that he has no wish to get Flambeau arrested is invested with a disquieting moral relativism when Harrogate is finally revealed to be the true trickster of the piece:

> The anger of the Italian policeman [...] was largely mixed with admiration. "It was like him to escape us at last," he said. "He was a great brigand if you like [...] for years he's been doing things as good as that, quite as good as that"'.
>
> (*CFB* 202)

If the policemen's remarks echo the enjoyment of the narrator of 'The Blue Cross' in recounting Flambeau's 'best days (I mean, of course, his worst)', Harrogate's depiction as a 'colossus of finance' (*CFB* 197) directly echoes the earlier story's portrayal of Flambeau as a 'colossus of crime' (*CFB* 3). As with the imaginative correspondence between Chesterton's accounts of d'Annunzio and Cadbury, the artistic trickster has become confounded with the economic traitor.

In corrupting the tentative optimism that had underpinned the genial subversion of class exclusivity in 'The Queer Feet', 'The Paradise of Thieves' illustrates the increasing pessimism of Chesterton's cultural worldview, a development intimately bound up with a questioning of his wisdom in positing the energy of the Harlequin as a social panacea. In this sense, the title of the collection into which 'The Paradise of Thieves' was placed—*The Wisdom of Father Brown*—comments self-reflexively upon the naive 'Innocence' of the previous collection, hinting at the intervening process of disillusion undergone by the stories' creator. Chesterton's most stinging self-criticism is located in the pessimistic inversion of the earliest stories' benign invasion narrative, whereby the foreign trickster, Flambeau, had been introduced to British shores as a means of reanimating its society. When, at the conclusion of 'The Paradise of Thieves', Muscari asks Ezza what he plans to do next, the latter turns once more to Futurism as the nearest approximation to a credo of which he is capable, while proposing a rather different imaginative invasion to that undertaken by Flambeau:

> "Didn't I tell you I was a Futurist? I really do believe in those things if I believe in anything. Change, bustle, and new things every morning. I am going to Manchester, Liverpool, Leeds, Hull, Huddersfield, Glasgow, Chicago – in short, to enlightened, energetic, civilized society!"
> "In short," said Muscari, "to the real Paradise of Thieves".
> (CFB 202)

While Muscari's rueful rejoinder ends the story with a satirical flourish, his epigram conveys a mordant note of defeat: Ezza's nihilistic energies are directed towards an England ripe for exploitation. Within a year, Chesterton would be deploring the real-life emergence of the 'English Futurists' ('Asceticism', 5).

Primitive Mercenaries in the Modern World

In the summer of 1914, Marinetti was back in the news, following his placement of an article in the *Observer* ('Futurism and English Art', 7 June 1914), which sought to promote Futurism further in Britain. The piece included a contribution from the artist Christopher Nevinson, providing a list of contemporary 'Futurist painters' (Marinetti and Nevinson, 198), including Lewis. This attempt to appropriate Lewis within a wider Futurist collective backfired the following week when he signed a letter to the *Observer* (14 June 1914) disavowing any involvement with Futurism. This repudiation might reasonably have surprised Nevinson, given that Lewis had personally endorsed Marinetti just a fortnight earlier in a brief journalistic squib—'A Man of the Week: Marinetti' (*New Weekly*, 30 May 1914)—which praised the Italian, in somewhat Chestertonian language, as 'an individual crackling with good sense' (Lewis, *Creatures*, 29).

A week after this *volte-face*, Lewis published the first issue of *BLAST* (20 June 1914), the journal that he and Pound conceived as a promotional vehicle for their newly-conceptualised Vorticist movement, complete with a verbally coruscating manifesto and accompanying segregation of a retinue of cultural figures and phenomena into the categories of the blasted and the blessed. Although the text is studded with haughty anti-Futurist *aperçus*, two months earlier, Pound had referred to *BLAST* as a 'Futurist, Cubist, Imagiste Quarterly' (*Pound/Joyce*, 1 Apr. 1914; 26) in a letter to Joyce, and its adversarial 'blast' and 'bless' conceit purposefully aped Apollinaire's distinction, in *Antitradition futuriste* (1913), between '"[r]oses" (members of the Futurist movement)' and the 'shit' of various other artists and institutions (qtd. in Peterson, 47). The resulting tension between imitation and repudiation repeatedly infiltrates the text—Lewis dismisses Futurism as merely 'a sensational and sentimental mixture of the aesthete of 1890 and the realist of 1870' (*BLAST*, 1:8), while conceding that '[o]f all the tags going, "Futurist," for general application, serves as well as any for the active painters of to-day' (*BLAST*, 143). The reader might be forgiven for being a little confused.

Given the melee of claims and counter-claims that were circulating in this period, it is perhaps unsurprising that Chesterton selected his terms cautiously when returning to the attack a fortnight after the publication of *BLAST*, with his article on 'The Asceticism of the Futurists'. Here, he explains that his argument concerns 'Futurism, and similar aesthetic schools' (5) before moderating his earlier disapprobation of Marinetti in order to focus upon the greater perniciousness of 'English Futurists' (5), an umbrella term that implicitly encompasses Lewis's breakaway collective. Chesterton turns to literally carnivalesque language to explain his increasing leniency towards Marinetti: 'I rather like Mr. Marinetti; he, I think, is simply playing the fool. He wants to have a sort of carnival' (5). However, Chesterton ventures to suggest that there is nothing especially new about the conceits to which Marinetti is drawn—his insistent confounding of spectatorship has a place within the long tradition of disruptive mischief that finds expression in academic parody:

> When he suggests that the New Drama should consist of calamities happening to the audience [...] I quite agree that it would be devilish funny. But why the well-established institution called 'a students' rag' should have anything to do with new aesthetic canons I do not understand.
>
> (5)

Chesterton's chiding again sets out to remind Marinetti of the weight of historical precedent that the latter seeks to deny—here the long comic tradition, frequently exploited in the early *Father Brown* stories, of the 'good old Christian practical joke'—while asserting that 'Mr. Marinetti's only originality is in the dithyrambic and transcendental way in which he talks about it' (5). Chesterton then employs his own customary audience-implicating technique—the 'you or I' device—to draw the reader into a compact against the rhetoric of Futurism. As with his earlier verse parody in 'The Futurists', he again debunks Marinetti's language through a juxtaposition of distinct styles, here employing a reverse travesty, in which an elementary concept is conveyed through comically 'dithyrambic and transcendental' discourse:

you or I might say, in the casual course of our custom: 'Let's make a butter-slide for the bishop.' But Mr. Marinetti would say: 'The Priest, laden with the age-long fatness and slowness of a blind and swinish Past, shall suddenly change his plodding tread for one mad moment of the Glory of Speed. His legs shall aviate with an insane smoothness; he shall claw the air with hooked fingers; he shall find the impossible postures'.

(5)

While playfully mocking Marinetti's language, Chesterton goes on to speculate that the impresario is at least partially in on the joke: 'there is a certain Latin lightness of touch in the way he does it, that makes it very hard for me to believe that he takes such seriousness seriously' (5). Conversely, 'there is no light touch about the English Futurists, and one must deal with Mr. C.R.W. Nevinson as with a professor' (5) rather than a rowdy student.

In Chesterton's anti-academic cultural lexicon, professorship denotes both the physical atrophy that Syme apprehends in Professor de Worms in *The Man Who Was Thursday* and the maniacal solipsism displayed by Professor Lucifer in *The Ball and the Cross*. In view of the air of diabolism that suffuses the latter example, Chesterton's argument that Nevinson's art is expressive of a 'heresy of evil asceticism' (6) produces an ominous echo of his earlier assertion that the use of fools like Marinetti is to 'let out what devils intend to do'. The cultural evil is now projected beyond Marinetti to within England itself and manifested in Nevinson's apparent deprecation of the corporeal: if 'there is an idea behind all [the] acoustic statuary or algebraic literature' currently in vogue in English culture, '[i]t is the idea of *getting out of the body*; and a very bad idea it is' (Chesterton, 'Asceticism', 6). Again, Chesterton stresses that there is nothing particularly original in this ascetic disposition; it simply marks the return of age-old heresies: 'there has regularly arisen a philosopher who combined asceticism with anarchy; and who based both the asceticism and the anarchy on a kind of pessimism, but especially on a furious contempt for the body' (6).

Although Lewis is not mentioned in Chesterton's piece, he took it upon himself to respond with furious contempt a week later.[7] In 'Futurism and the Flesh' (*T.P.'s Weekly*, 11 July 1914), Lewis violently rejects Chesterton's interpretation of modern art in an attack that can be read both as commercially driven and curiously personal. Lewis begins the article by establishing his distinction in the aesthetic marketplace, with the complaint that 'Mr. Chesterton evidently includes in "Futurism" every new manifestation of art today' (*Creatures*, 35). This not only misrepresents what Chesterton actually said, but also contradicts his own remarks in *BLAST*, a muddle compounded by the sub-heading inserted by *T.P.'s Weekly*, no doubt to Lewis's chagrin, which explains that the article is a 'personal and lively reply from Mr. Wyndham Lewis, one of the foremost Futurists and the editor of "Blast"' (*Creatures*, 388). The euphemistically 'personal and lively' element of the text comes to the fore in Lewis's blistering response to Chesterton's depiction of Marinetti as a carnivalesque practical joker:

> [Chesterton] weak-mindedly succumbed to the romance of the practical joke many years ago, and has been its maudlin and dribbling swain ever since. The pages of his discourses are one long mechanical dribble of empty inversions and wearisome similes from the nursery.
>
> (*Creatures*, 35)

This assault artfully locates the constancy and ingenuousness of Chesterton's ardour for the practical joke as the particular source of his weakness. In Bergsonian fashion, unselfconscious mechanical repetition leaves the target open to attack, and it is a neat irony that Lewis cites Chesterton's unswerving adherence to the practical joke—the comic medium that particularly exploits inflexibility—as the very locus of his rigidity. Accordingly, Lewis concludes that Chesterton's journalism 'can be dismissed as the unavoidable drivelling of an imbecile clothing the first object met with the stuff of his particular folly' (*Creatures*, 35). This passage combines a thematic evocation of sartorial travesty with a formal rhetorical travesty. Chesterton's mania for 'clothing the first object met' with his obsessions conjures a burlesque image of the subject forcibly applying an incongruous motley to anyone unfortunate enough to cross his path, rather as the *Thursday* dedication foists the 'cap and bells' upon the would-be detached figure of Bentley. Meanwhile, the manner in which the point is made illustrates the extreme tonal impropriety that Lewis brings to the genteel art of essay writing, an indication to the reader that he is more juvenile delinquent than austere professor, in contrast to which Chesterton's dribbling connotes both early infancy and late senility.

As with Chesterton's praise of the exuberant 'metaphors [that] a coster puts into a curse' (*Defendant*, 145) over the pallid wit of the bohemian drawing room, Lewis purposefully invests his early controversial writing with the bad manners of the London street, exhibiting a pleasure in the ingenuity of the verbal attack that seems to exceed the level of genuine grievance. The result is a cross between the 'cursing matches' (Perrino, 14) characteristic of carnival and Auden's account of 'flyting', a bygone mode of literary discourse that now seems

> only to survive in the impromptu exchanges of truckdrivers and cabdrivers. The comic effect arises from the contradiction between

> the insulting nature of what is said which appears to indicate a passionate relation of hostility and aggression, and the calculated skill of verbal invention which indicates that the protagonists are not thinking about each other but about language and their pleasure in employing it inventively.
>
> (383)

Lewis's bellicosity also reflects the burgeoning gang mentality of the Men of 1914. Longenbach asserts that upon arriving in Britain, Pound 'quickly became involved in several of the "gangs" (as he called them) that made up London's literary society' (qtd. in Hofer, 486) before settling on Lewis's band as the most amenable to his tastes. Thereafter, Lewis and Pound portrayed themselves as atavistic throwbacks to a more vital time, in which artistic rivalries carried a boisterous energy lacking from the etiolated landscape of post-Edwardian British culture. As Lewis puts it in *BLAST*, he has assembled a collective of 'primitive mercenaries in the modern world' (30). Once Eliot joined the gang, he began to be promoted in similar terms. May Sinclair's review of *Prufrock and Other Observations* in the *Little Review* (Dec. 1917) cites Eliot's involvement in the second issue of *BLAST* as evidence that 'Mr. Eliot is dangerous. Mr. Eliot is associated with an unpopular movement and with unpopular people', his 'directness of method is startling and upsetting to comfortable, respectable people' (9–10). In their respective reviews of *Tarr*, Eliot and Pound sought to corroborate this group image. Pound deemed Lewis's prose 'uncouth [....] brimming with energy' ('*Tarr*', 425), while Eliot amazed at Lewis's 'superabundant vitality', famously defining the novel as a temporal hybrid text, possessing both 'the thought of the modern and the energy of the cave-man' ('Tarr', 106). As Lewis later noted, these plaudits had proved a helpful marketing strategy: 'I was launched as a "caveman"' (*Blasting*, 88).

The element of commercial expedience in these manoeuvres somewhat undermines the coherence of the trio's critique of the age. If Lewis's phrase, 'primitive mercenaries in the modern world', seems well suited to the image of Ezza in 'The Paradise of Thieves', it is safe to say that Chesterton would have applauded the primitive, while pausing at the mercenary, a term unavoidably suggestive of fiscal unscrupulousness. In one of Chesterton's earliest sallies against Futurism, he links his ridicule of the movement's projection of machismo to the shameless publicity-seeking of these 'absurd mountebanks' (*CW* 28:469), while modifying them from dangerous devils to model Christians. Although Marinetti and friends 'profess [...] eagerly, that they themselves are awfully ruthless and cold', they demonstrate an admirable 'creed of forgiveness' in responding to his textual blows by sending him ever-more Futurist literature in the post: 'The cheeks of the Futurists are formally smitten; and they only give me more of their cheek' (CW 28:469). Despite his long-standing mockery of the movement, in May 1914 Chesterton was invited to a dinner given in Marinetti's honour by Harold Monro, along with modernist figures such as Aldington, Ford, and Thomas Sturge Moore, presumably in the hope that he would subsequently broadcast his contempt for the events that unfolded. He turned down the invitation (see Whelpton, 83).

In a similar vein of indiscriminate self-promotion, Lewis later acknowledged of his pre-war machinations alongside Pound that the 'disorders and absurdities in our publicist experiments [... were] regarded as of no more consequence than hand-bills' (*Time*, 55). This admission is germane to 'Futurism and the Flesh'. In an earlier article on 'Satire in the Open' (*ILN* 5 Oct. 1907), Chesterton had identified an increasing scurrility in modern satire, while contending that those adopting this approach had missed the point: in the Augustan era of Johnson, Pope, and Swift, satire 'might have been slanderous and obscene past expression, but there would have been a solid moral substance to it' (CW 27:565). While Chesterton sympathises strongly with the urge to ginger up an enervated culture, Chesterton demurs at the absence of a coherent moral dimension to the critique, defining this new form of satire as 'the stinging-butterfly style, which combines all the disadvantages of a man obviously irritated with all the disadvantages of a man obviously insincere' (CW 27:565). Both disadvantages are detectable in 'Futurism and the Flesh'. Despite the superficial blows that Lewis lands against Chesterton's inadvertently self-parodic recursion to the practical joke, it is no coincidence that when he turns from *ad hominem* assault to a perfunctory engagement with Chesterton's analysis of the anti-corporeal turn in modern art, his argument not only loses its vivacity, but becomes shifty and unconvincing.

As we find so often, beneath the surface buffooneries of 'The Asceticism of the Futurists', Chesterton's underlying point is unerringly acute. In the same period, Lewis praised Cubism for its 'inhuman and pure' (*Letters*, 59) aesthetic in an open letter to the *New Age* (2 Apr. 1914). He later described 'the abstractionist' as possessing a 'puritan-eye' (*Blasting*, 100), while *BLAST* informs the reader that 'the actual human body becomes of less importance every day' (141). Accordingly, Bechhöfer's parody of *BLAST* in the *New Age* refers to Lewis as the 'ascetic of Great Ormond Street' (308). Despite the lavish earthiness of Lewis's essay title, his aesthetic sensibility in 1914 conforms closely to the merger of 'asceticism with anarchy' that Chesterton identified in 'English Futurism', in this instance combining physical asceticism with metaphysical anarchism—a programme doubly at odds with Chesterton's insistent recourse to the physical grotesque as a means of inculcating a deeper sense of metaphysical order.

The inconsistency in Lewis's public pronouncements at this time derives partly from his uncertainty over the most personally beneficial line to take in the cultural dispute between Chesterton and Futurism. One thinks of the economic terms through which he would later portray Tarr's character building: 'he impressed you as having inherited himself last week, and as under a great press of business to grasp the details and resources of the concern' (*Tarr*, 38). The solution that Lewis arrived at was to make good on another of his claims in *BLAST*: 'we discharge ourselves on both sides' (30). Despite the influence of Marinetti's automotive swashbuckling upon the narrative of *Mrs. Dukes Million*, the Lewis of *BLAST* declares, with an urbane yell, 'AUTOMOBILISM (Marinetteism) bores us' (8). The reader of Lewis's article on 'Futurism and the Flesh' might have been equally surprised to learn of the rather Chestertonian guidance offered to Hercules Fane in Lewis's unpublished detective novel: he should 'regard all this as a big practical joke' (153).

Lewis's discharging of simultaneous volleys against the forces of reaction and revolution in the summer of 1914 represented a canny strategy to maintain his avant-garde credentials by denouncing Chesterton, while distancing himself from the revolutionary figure whose ridiculous side Chesterton had consistently succeeded in drawing to the public's attention. Accordingly, rather than cogently rebutting Chesterton's argument, Lewis's primary concern is simply to convince the reader of his absolute dissimilarity to both of the figures under discussion. If this underlying objective helps to account for the insincerity of Lewis's article, the irritation that he manifests is perhaps traceable back to the reception of his exhibition with the Camden Town Group in 1911—specifically, the condescending tone of a critic from the *Times*, who mooted the possibility that his 'geometrical experiments' might be mistaken for 'bad practical jokes' (Anon, 'Picture', 12) just two days after Chesterton had ridiculed Picasso's 'artistic insanities' in the *Daily News*.

For both Lewis and Pound, the urge of critics to defuse the impact of radical artists through bluff mockery emblematised a persistent strain of anti-intellectualism in liberal British culture that militated against aesthetic innovation. In 'The English Sense of Humour' (*Spectator*, 15 June 1934), Lewis explains the infuriating behaviour of the English critical community as a form of snobbery, thus subverting the characteristic criticism levelled at modernist art:

> since his Sense of Humour has probably been aroused and mobilized by your displaying passion of some sort—anger, it may be, or some imaginative enthusiasm—the Englishman will certainly convey the impression that his possession of this 'sense' confers upon him a very conspicuous superiority to you.
>
> (*Creatures*, 204)

Lewis's lingering irritation over the *Times* review would surely have been reawakened by Chesterton's bathetic depiction of Marinetti as a harmless practical joker. Thereafter, Chesterton emerged as the unspoken figurehead of the form of British humour against which Lewis was battling. Throughout his career, Lewis referred to the inane grin of John Bull as a metonym of British cultural philistinism, announcing his intention to 'Kill John Bull with Art' (*Outlook*, 18 July 1914) and later comparing this mythic Briton to Chesterton in *The Art of Being Ruled* (1926; see Lewis, *Wyndham Lewis*, 157). One of the many terms of deprecation assigned to Chesterton in 'Futurism and the Flesh'—'maudlin'—re-emerges in *BLAST* 2, in an account of the 'English sense of humour [as] a perpetual, soft, self-indulgent, (often maudlin) hysteria' (11), while the contemporaneously composed preface to *Tarr* advises the reader to drop, once and for all, 'the maudlin and the self-defensive Grin' (14).

Lewis's allusive conjoining of Chesterton to a broader strain of philistinism is rendered overt in Pound's contemporaneous correspondence: Chesterton is a 'yahoo' (*Letters*, 5 Mar. 1916; 118), a 'pandar to public imbecilities' (*Pound/Joyce*, 29 May 1916; 278), who 'creates an atmosphere in which art is impossible'. The last remark arises in one of Pound's many letters to the influential patron of high modernism, John Quinn. As he explains, in an ironic inversion of Chesterton's approval of Dickens as 'a mob in revolt' (*CW* 15:455), 'Chesterton *is* so much the mob, so much the multitude [...] a symbol for all the mob's hatred of all art that aspires above mediocrity' (*Letters*, 21 Aug. 1917; 171). Pound's apprehension of Chesterton's support for 'the mob' was, of course, largely correct. Chesterton considered the new avant-garde to represent an escalation of the reactionary aesthetics of oligarchy that he had identified in the previous generation, a development that ran directly counter to his 'hope that the people themselves will make the politics of the future. Yes, and the art of the future' ('On Loveliness and Electric Trams', *DN* 8 Apr. 1905; *CDN* 3:75). Chesterton was not merely presuming to give voice to the mob's aesthetic insensibility; he was proposing that the mob should supplant the current practitioners.

Pound's public criticisms of Chesterton skirt around the anti-popular element of his disgruntlement, instead settling upon the more winning tack of a disinterested advocacy of excellence. In a near-contemporaneous brouhaha caused by an intemperate sally against Chesterton in the *New Age*, Pound sought to articulate his position to the paper's readers:

> [Chesterton] wrote some years ago: 'If a thing is worth doing, it is worth doing badly.' That is his declaration, his basis. In those

words he arrays himself on the side of chaos and camouflage and obscurantism, and against every true writer whose sole aim and hope is that he may some day 'do the thing really well.' The mental status quo of contemporary periodicals [...] has no more powerful, and therefore no more damnable supporter, than Mr. Gilbert K. Chesterton.

(*New Age*, 10 Jan. 1918; 'Letters', 219)

While pausing to note that Pound is deliberately obscuring the intended meaning of Chesterton's epigram—that a childlike enthusiasm for artistic expression, regardless of aptitude, affiliates the dabbler with 'the uproarious amateurishness of the universe' (*CW* 4:199)—here we find an attempted mirror-image reversal similar to Lewis's accusation that the English critic is the true snob, with Pound arguing that Chesterton is the true mystagogue, whose taste for 'chaos and camouflage' sounds remarkably similar to that of Ezza Montano.

Pound returned to the attack in 1920, devoting an article in his series 'The Revolt of Intelligence' (*New Age*, 1 Jan. 1920) to the 'Chestertonian system of journalism', which he considers to be 'uninterruptedly admired from one end of Fleet Street to the other', because '[h]e is the man who has taught them how to do it' (139). The first of Pound's broadsides of 1917 in the *New Age* articulates a similar point: Chesterton is a figure 'for whom there is, so far as I can see, no extenuation whatsoever' since he has 'definitely done considerable harm to contemporary letters'; nonetheless, 'I give him the credit for having been sufficiently effective to do harm' ('Studies in Contemporary Mentality', 27 Dec. 1917; 168). As this suggests, although Pound was willing to concede that Chesterton's critical writing might occasionally possess substance beneath the buffoonery, he considered it to exert an inexcusable mischief by setting a public tone imitated slavishly by lesser critics. In a typically evenhanded move, Orage interceded in the controversy to state his disagreement with Pound over Chesterton's relative merits, while conceding that

> [t]here is undoubtedly a fragment of truth in Mr. Pound's view of Mr. G. K. Chesterton's influence. It is this: that Mr. Chesterton is a most dangerous man to imitate. His imitators really become apes. But that is not to say that Mr. Chesterton is not himself a great writer.
>
> ('Readers and Writers', *New Age*, 17 Jan. 1918; 231)

In the same response, Orage gestures towards Pound's more commercial motivations for mounting the attack, expressing the point in a somewhat patronising tone that rather confirms Lewis's view of the

English snob: 'his pose [...] is still a little that of the *enfant terrible*: a pose, no doubt, impressive in America, but much less terrifying than irritating in this ancient world of England' (231). The twice-iterated accusation of posing returns us to the issue of insincerity, and the pragmatic impetus for Pound's gang to take on Chesterton's mob. In many ways, a happy symbiosis pertained between the avant-garde and the masses at this time, with the former content to encourage heckling as a proof of its radicalism, which might impress that invaluable contingent to whom Lewis sought to appeal: the 'small band of wealthy people, who are open to Ideas' (*BLAST* 2:11). As Rulo notes, Pound's broader rhetoric betrays 'a very definite hope that the public will "resent" the artistic class, as such resentment alone would prove its legitimacy' (265).

A month before the publication of 'The Paradise of Thieves', Stravinsky's ballet, *The Rite of Spring*, had received its London premiere (11 July 1913), just two months after the notoriously fractious Parisian premiere (29 May), around which a legend had quickly accrued of the composer defiantly facing down a mob. Henceforth, the image of the lone artistic visionary confronting a crowd of baying philistines would become a foundational myth of modernism and a central tenet of its aesthetic philosophy and commercial practice. Marinetti had already composed a pugnacious essay on 'the pleasure of being booed' ('Pleasure', 97) in his 1911 tract, *Le Futurisme*, while Pound informed his parents that he considered negative reviews to offer good '"adv[ertising]" value' (*Ezra Pound to His Parents*, Sept. 1909; 187). However, it was essential that this heckling should be inarticulate; Chesterton represented that most unnerving of paradoxes: a perspicacious mob.

Perhaps the most unwelcome aspect of Chesterton's debunking for a vanguard eager to project its radicalism was the theme to which 'The Paradise of Thieves' also draws attention: the oligarchic underpinning of modernist patronage. If Lewis and Pound had become aware of the story, as seems eminently plausible, they would have experienced Chesterton's burlesque satire as a commercially compromising threat of exposure, combining mockery of their artistry, criticism of their ethics, and a disorientating confusion of their identities with Chesterton's own. For Lewis, the last element would have been particularly galling. Having tried and failed to market a Chestertonian mystery of his own three years earlier, he was now on the receiving end of the genuine article—impugned by a figure who had influenced his own imaginative development and conceptually presided over his commercial failure as a producer of pot-boilers.

The themes of Chesterton's story also form an instructive background when considering Pound's singling out of Chesterton as a satirical target in 'The New Cake of Soap', a verse contribution to *BLAST*:

> Lo, how it gleams and glistens in the sun
> Like the cheek of a Chesterton
>
> (*BLAST* 1:49)

Although the most salient purpose of this stab at Imagist satire is to pillory Chesterton's allegedly sanitised wit—or the 'cheek' that he had shown to Marinetti—Luke Seaber observes that the indefinite article in the second line more subtly attempts to typify Chesterton as 'the symbol *par excellence* of a commercialized mass-production of "literature" [...] Chesterton, the commercializer, the sold-out, is himself transformed into a commodity' ('Meaning', 199). As with Lewis's Bergsonian reference to the 'mechanical dribble' of Chesterton's journalistic output in 'Futurism and the Flesh', Pound ingrains a rhetoric of incontinent over-production in his attack, figuring 'a Chesterton' as a factory-line item, implying a reification caused by financial dependence upon the press, which results in excessive, automatous literary production. Thus, in what looks like a choreographed dual assault in texts published within three weeks of one another, Lewis and Pound turn the criticism of unscrupulous commercial practice back upon the author of 'The Paradise of Thieves', while setting out to signal Chesterton's cultural obsolescence at the very moment at which he had reached the apex of his ubiquity.

Pound was rehearsing an argument already aired a year earlier by Shaw, who had taunted Chesterton over being 'the personal property of George Cadbury' (Wills, *Chesterton*, 227n11) at a public debate shortly before Chesterton announced his resignation from the *Daily News*. Nonetheless, the very context of the resignation lends Pound's critique a further note of insincerity—the imputation of anodyne commercialism is hardly an appropriate criticism of a figure who had recently forfeited one of his main sources of income through a public attack upon an employer with whom he ethically disagreed.[8] There is a further irony in Pound's attack on Chesterton as a sell-out in connection with soap at this time, since the latter's 'cheek' on this subject had recently left him threatened with a libel case, brought by Sir William Lever, when Chesterton likened Lever's soap manufacturing factory-line at Port Sunlight to 'a slave-compound' at a public lecture (see Ker, 323). In view of this correspondence, Pound's reference to the 'sun' seems more than adventitious, though it is curious, to say the least, that he should have chosen to attack Chesterton in the very place at which he seems least vulnerable. While Pound's connective 'like' strains to convey a sense of equivalence between the satirical barbs and their object, Chesterton advocated a more straightforward agent of sanitation to soap in a metaphor for engagement in high-risk controversy: 'I believe in getting into hot water. I think it keeps you clean' (*ILN* 10 Mar. 1906; *CW* 27:142).

In 'Bret Harte', Chesterton notes that 'those who hate authors fail to satirise them, for they always accuse them of the wrong faults'

(*Varied*, 185). As well as repeatedly placing his commercial viability at risk through the public expression of unwelcome sentiments, Chesterton famously evinced a complete absence of financial acumen in his private life. Ward observes that he was 'so poor a tradesman' as to 'lavishly give what he might have sold' (*Return*, 170) and reports that he was offered 'a large sum' by an American visitor for the manuscript of a series of parodies titled 'School English Composition: *Exercise CCXXII. B: The "Tomato" in Prose and Prosody*', but declined on the grounds that the text had been offered as a private gift to a friend.[9] In this light, Chesterton's public and private actions begin to appear somewhat more ethically coherent than Pound's highhanded aesthetic posturing. Prior to his later, quixotic espousal of social credit and inveighing against 'the infamies of usura' (*Cantos*, 482), Pound's putative anti-commercialism was itself something of a performance—a commercial for modernist values—which contrasted sharply with his private financial and promotional savvy. Bechhöfer satirises the resultant tension in his parody of *BLAST*, in which the journal's sales advertisement is reimagined as a Poundian Imagist poem:

> Copies may be obtained from
> Mr. Wyndham Lewis
> [...]
> 2s. 6d., published quarterly;
> 10s. 6d. yearly subscription.
> Am I not a highbrow poet?
> Sure thing.
>
> (308)

Although it seems likely that Lewis and Pound had privately agreed upon Chesterton as the figure in literary London who might most profitably exemplify all that their new movement ran counter to, the motives for this anathematisation also extend beyond marketing value to more atavistic intergenerational patterns of behaviour. Male friendship groups frequently conceive themselves as a righteous 'youth racket' (*Blasting*, 252), as Lewis later characterised his contemporaries and himself—a rebel band cementing its camaraderie through rejection of the value systems of the 'old gang' that had forged the milieu through which the 'new gang' emerges.[10] Indeed, this was precisely the way in which Chesterton had mounted his challenge to Decadent culture, in league with Edwardian allies such as Belloc and Maurice Baring. It is no coincidence that of all the 'Men of 1914', Joyce—the most geographically and temperamentally detached of Lewis's quad—exhibited no interest in publicly disparaging Chesterton, instead giving the impression that the latter barely troubled his consciousness. Conversely, the greater stake in London's cultural politics, as well as the greater intimacy of group interaction between Lewis and Pound, and later Eliot, led them to inscribe a pristine polarity between themselves and Chesterton in order to advertise a suspiciously clean break with the immediate past and to bolster a sense of group identity.

Eliot's arrival in London in August 1914 brought a further dimension to the adversarial group dynamic. He wasted little time in getting to know Lewis and Pound, having already absorbed the orthodoxy of their cultural likes and dislikes through a preparatory surveillance of their activities. He first met Pound in September 1914 (Eliot, *Letters*, 1:63 fn.1), who then introduced him to Lewis in early 1915 (see Meyers, 75). Arriving late to an already established group, Eliot displayed a palpable anxiety to fit in to a pre-established pattern of behaviour, employing forms of mimicry to convey sympathy with their aims. Shortly before his introduction to Pound, he sent a letter to Conrad Aiken from Germany in which he aped Lewis's use of the terms 'BLAST' and 'BLESS' (Eliot, *Letters*, 19 July 1914; 1:40). As Peter Ackroyd notes, once he began to correspond with Pound, Eliot increasingly modified his innate tone of cautious equivocation to present himself as one 'egregious Yankee addressing another' (235). Ackroyd alludes to the element of pastiche that suffuses these missives: Eliot demonstrated an 'extraordinary ability to mimic Pound's verbal mannerisms, as if he were willingly immersing himself in his personality. He even goes so far as to fabricate his signature in a way similar to Pound's' (236). As with Chesterton's early attempts to please Bentley by echoing his sentiments and modes of expression, for some time Eliot was keen to say the kind of things that Lewis and Pound would say.

Although his subsequent collaborative intimacy with Pound caused the pair to become the most closely associated of the 'Men of 1914' in the public mind, Eliot's philosophical and aesthetic leanings in that inductive year were more directly comparable to those of Lewis. As we have seen, the young Eliot sought to project a trapdoor personality comparable to the Chinese box construct of *Tarr*. This concordance derives from the pair's shared early leaning towards relativism—in August 1916, Eliot reported to Aiken that he was 'still a relativist' (*Letters*, 1:145)—and an associated espousal of what Lewis would later term 'non-moral' (*Men*, 103) satire. If this phrase recalls Bentley's discussion of the 'unhuman [...] unmoral' chess game, Lewis explicitly highlights the ontological (unhuman) and ethical (unmoral) complementarity of his brand of satire: 'non-moral' satire is concerned 'with man, and not with manners', since it diagnoses 'a *chronic* ailment' (*Men*, 124) rather than a local condition for which a satirical cure might be found. Lewis identifies this absolutist position as a 'non-human' form of '"the grotesque"', which he considers to be 'the same thing' (*Men*, 121) as the form of satire in which he deals.

In other words, as with Chesterton's assessment of Hankin, Lewis is 'a very fastidious judge', who posits the unsatisfactory nature of the human condition *per se*, while disputing the viability of any objective table of ethics against which it might be coherently assessed. This position encourages an empathy-free, solipsistic detachment, which authorises, in turn, an unscrupulous, gloves-off approach to cultural controversy. As with the inhuman trickster, the non-human satirist affects to stand beyond good and evil, feeling no empathy with her/his victims, but simply setting out to win the game at hand by all possible means. As Blissett observes, the '"Men of 1914" took the huge projected image of G.K.C. and shied missiles at it as an Aunt Sally' ('Chesterton and English', 130), rather than a genuine human being. As will be noticed, this behaviour also corresponds closely to the attitude of the nonsense practitioner. Much as Bentley's clerihews toy airily with the biographies of the public figures that fall within his purview, the early strategies of the London-based Men of 1914 accord with Sewell's account of the detachment that underpins the cruelty of Lear's limerick world:

> If people are things in the Nonsense game, they must, when they meet, treat one another as such, and this involves detachment from any form of affection or kindliness. Relationships between them will be matter-of-fact but not matter for feeling.
>
> (*Field*, 141)

As Sewell explains, 'a good deal of rough treatment is involved' in this denial of the target's subjectivity (*Field*, 138).

In pursuing this premise, these primitive mercenaries in the modern world took recourse to other forms of atavistic trans-temporality: 'we who are heirs of the witch-doctor and the voodoo [...] are about to take control' (qtd. in Rulo, 265), as Pound announced with characteristic bluster. In 1914, Lewis's understanding that satire has 'its roots in the goat-choruses of [...] the Greeks; half ritual, half savage bucolic backchat' (*Mysterious*, 142) became conjoined to the principle of the 'scapegoat or sacrificial victim' (Welsford, 69) of antiquity that he and Eliot had separately discovered in James Frazer's *The Golden Bough* (1890). The scapegoat is conventionally driven forth to enable a cultural renewal, collecting a community's 'diseases [...] and bind[ing] them upon some unfortunate animal or man' who would be 'kill[ed] or drive[n] off from the community' (Welsford, 68). As Fredric Jameson notes, satire also 'has its prehistoric origins in the magical curse and the ritual expulsion of the scapegoat', the purpose of which is the 'cleansing of the polis' (*Fables*, 137). Welsford argues that in past ages, 'the abusive buffoon and the ritual scapegoat became one and the same person' (69). If one were setting out to establish a modern update of this primitive practice, the society's most vocal 'festival-fool' (Welsford, 72) and self-ordained mocker-in-chief of the avant-garde would make a singularly fitting repository, not least since Pound considered Chesterton to have been 'so long an advocate of atavism in thought' (Pound, *Ezra Pound's*, 4: 94) himself.

That 'The Paradise of Thieves' had found Chesterton at the top of his satirical game only made the moment all the more propitious. When Lewis later discussed the scapegoat ritual in *The Lion and the Fox* (1927), he emphasised the composite of negative and positive functions attributed to the victim. As Perrino glosses Lewis's interpretation,

> the death of a surrogate god may be a purgation in which the [...] sins of the people are conferred onto him and borne away; or his death at the peak of his vitality may ensure continuation of a natural or supernatural power.
>
> (117)

As this balance of praise and curses implies, the spirit of carnival accompanies the Victorian nonsense sensibility and the atavistic ceremonial as a third background context for the sublimated persecution at hand. Alan Munton observes that for Bakhtin 'Carnival beatings are unserious' ('Wyndham Lewis', 150), since the carnival king 'is not actually killed [...] only ridiculed' (Perrino, 118). In this way, the 'King of the Carnival is uncrowned and torn apart, but his carnival "death" ensures life and vitality for the community' (Munton, 'Wyndham Lewis', 144).

In an article published under the pseudonym T.S. Apteryx in the May 1918 issue of the *Egoist*, Eliot places Chesterton at the centre of a portentous vision of cultural apocalypse, while alluding to his aesthetically conservative, and exceptionally popular, *Ballad of the White Horse* (1911):

> I have seen the forces of death with Mr. Chesterton at their head upon a white horse. Mr. Pound, Mr. Joyce, and Mr. Lewis write living English; one does not realize the awfulness of death until one meets with the living language.
>
> (Eliot, 'Observations', 69)

Of course, this premise directly inverts that of 'The Paradise of Thieves', in which it is the younger generation who are arraigned for their degenerative impact. For Bakhtin, societal regeneration is the ultimate mystical purpose of carnival, which 'celebrates the destruction of the old and the birth of the new world' (*Rabelais*, 410). In this sense, Eliot's panorama of deceased and living *litterateurs* can be viewed as a serious-minded attempt to police the vitality of form, via a carnivalesque representation of Chesterton as a cultural relic who refuses to die to enable the younger generation to 'purify the dialect of the tribe' (*PTSE* 1:205), as Eliot would later put it, after Mallarmé, in 'Little Gidding' (1942).

Interpreted another way, Eliot's partisan drawing up of distinct cultural battle-lines demonstrates a canny eye for his own commercial self-positioning within a radical vanguard superseding a passé older generation. The long-form literary debuts of Eliot and Lewis—*Prufrock* and *Tarr*—had been published the year before and, as we have seen, Pound had figured Chesterton as an inverted critical barometer when marketing *Tarr* in the *Little Review*, positing his assumed disapproval as an evidence of its merits. Eliot's blanket dismissal of Chesterton's corpus came just two years after he had recommended Chesterton's critical works to students attending his wartime extension lectures (see Schuchard, 35–36). This discrepancy between public condemnation and private commendation suggests a parallel with the expediency-driven relativism practised by Lewis and Pound. As Eliot explained ebulliently to his friend Eleanor Hinkley in November 1914, shortly after his first exposure to *BLAST*, '[o]ne must have theories, but one need not believe in them!' (*Letters*, 1:73).

A Vile Scum on the Pond

Eliot's revelation of 'the awfulness of death' in contemplating Chesterton's verse also hints at a more phobic apprehension of the antecedent, which discloses a further atavistic dimension to the cultural agon at hand: fear of the abject. In Revelation, the rider on a white horse is represented as a warlike figure, '*bent on conquest*' (Morris, 101), 'a demonic parody of Christ, evil masquerading as good' (Resseguie, 127). Meanwhile, the 'forces of Death' are embodied by the rider on a pale horse whom Chesterton had invoked in 'The Queer Feet', a figure who trails pestilence in his wake (see Morris, 105). The pale horse has also been translated as 'yellowish green', due to the ambiguity of the term '*chlōros*'—green or pale—in the original Koine Greek, which has led some interpreters to consider the horse to possess the 'colour of a corpse' (Morris, 104). This gruesome note suggests that the apocalyptic inflection of Eliot's jibe might be read as an act of bravado more subtly motivated by an irrational fear of the all-conquering predecessor, comparable to Chesterton's apprehension of the Decadents who 'ruled the culture of the age' in his youth. If we recall Chesterton's observation, in relation to the imperial body politic, that '[w]hen a dead body is rotting, it does not diminish; it swells', consider the tenor of the caricatures of Chesterton that were circulating in the press during this period.

166 *We Discharge Ourselves on Both Sides*

Figure 4.1 Caricature of G.K. Chesterton by Max Beerbohm, 1912.

Figure 4.2 Caricature of G.K. Chesterton by Edmund Kapp, 1919.

Beerbohm's grotesquely inflated Chesterton of 1912 (Figure 4.1) and Edmond Kapp's frame-threatening rendition (Figure 4.2, collected in *Personalities: Twenty-Four Drawings*, 1919), present an alarmingly elephantine spectacle, not only highlighting Chesterton's increasing physical bulk in the post-Edwardian era, but also suggesting a metaphor comparable to his own view of Wilde as a figure who took up more space than anyone else on the *fin-de-siècle* stage. As Andreas Huyssen observes, the 'conscious strategy of exclusion' that informed the marketing of modernism implies 'an anxiety of contamination by its other: an increasingly consuming and engulfing mass culture' (qtd. in Ferrall, 3-4). With this in mind, Eliot's conflation of Chesterton's cultural pre-eminence with a pestilential scourge is instructive in the context of Christopher Butler's account of Pound's sense of regenerative mission: he 'felt himself throughout 1914 to be performing for England a function like that of Marinetti and Apollinaire elsewhere', leading him to approvingly cite the latter's Futurist sentiment, 'you cannot carry your father's corpse along with you wherever you go' (231). It seems likely that Eliot would have been amongst the auditors of Pound's Apollinairean *aperçu* when the pair first met, and that this precept informed his own response to Chesterton when the latter stubbornly refused to play dead in the years that followed.

For Julia Kristeva, 'the corpse' is the quintessential signifier of the abject: 'a boundary that has encroached upon everything' (*Powers*, 3).

To be made to carry the corpse of the father would operate as a near-perfect metaphor of the discomforting status of abjection as a condition located simultaneously within, and external to, the self: 'a revolt of the person against an external menace', which 'one has the impression [...] may [also] menace us from inside', producing 'a desire for separation [...] and also the feeling of an impossibility of doing so' (Kristeva qtd. in Oliver, 55). As this suggests, the dynamic of abjection mirrors that of the antimodern and of parody—navigating an unresolvable tension between implication and extrication, proximity and distance—while also functioning as an inversion of carnival: a reflexive repulsion of the non-self, which counteracts the immersive impetus of Bakhtin's folk grotesque. Nonetheless, if the carnivalesque is fascinated with the breaching of thresholds, the abject is equally engrossed by what is '"in-between" [...] what is on the border, what doesn't respect borders' (Oliver, 56) and, therefore, becomes another productive context through which to navigate the boundaries both erected and traversed by the factions under discussion.

When Pound argues that 'Wilde was [...] the father of Chesterton' ('Revolt', 139), we begin to perceive a recursive irony to this phenomenon. Fear of infection from rejected representatives of the preceding generation is a consistent feature of Chesterton's accounts of Decadence, informing the suspiciously black and white battle lines that he attempts to establish between the Decadents on one side and himself and Bentley on the other in the *Thursday* dedication. As Kristeva notes, abjection is characterised by an 'apocalyptic inspiration' (*Powers*, 205). Accordingly, in 'Milton and Merry England', Chesterton mirrors Eliot's literally apocalyptic terms, describing his revolt against an abject Decadence as the very birth moment of his literary career: 'My first impulse to write' arose from 'a *revolt of disgust* with the Decadents', who seemed to augur 'the end of the world' (*Fancies*, 220; my emphasis).

In *The Victorian Age in Literature*, Chesterton's analysis of the 'toppling possibility of the absurd' that produces bathos in Wilde's poetry is accompanied by a disquieting association of the forebear with death and decay. The poet's graveside injunction, '"Plant lilies at my head" has something wrong about it; something silly' (*CW* 15:518), an astute aesthetic judgement that also serves to establish the critic's detachment from an image that invokes a disturbing merger of the vegetable and the human in the context of bodily corruption. Elsewhere in the same analysis, Chesterton discusses Wilde's literal handling of the world of objects in terms of an alarming confusion between the inert and the animate. In the process, his projection of objective critical distance suddenly lapses into subjective emotionalism, and the critique of effete aestheticism is conveyed in a manner that evokes a still-more hypersensitive disposition: '*I for one cannot endure* [...] his sensual way of speaking of dead substances, satin or marble or velvet, as if he were stroking a lot of dogs and cats' (*CW* 15:519; my emphasis).

Chesterton's sense of Wilde as a threat to the 'frames and limits' (*Autobiography*, 32) upon which he set such existential store is reflected in his wider anxiety over rhetoric of indeterminacy. In an article on Yeats—perhaps the most famous example of a writer successfully breaching the imaginative boundary between Decadence and modernism—Chesterton complains that he 'tends always to talk of twilight, that is, of the mixed and vague thing, of the thing that is almost something else' ('George MacDonald', *DN* 23 Sept. 1905; *CDN* 3:198). Elsewhere, he indignantly addresses certain amendments recently made by the poet to his early verses:

> Mr. Yeats has simply no right to alter a poem; it was not he that wrote it, but another man, the man of a moment, who will never live again. The moment a poem has really passed out of him, it no more belongs to him.
> ('Mr. Yeats Revisited', *DN* 19 Apr. 1901; *CDN* 1:76)

In criticising 'the destructive character of the poet's improvements' (*CDN* 1:76), Chesterton suggests that the older poet's misidentification with his own text has led him to corrupt the integrity of the original, producing an inadvertent self-parody. As with his identification of bathos in Wilde, the analysis of Yeats's artistic lapse is persuasive. However, when Chesterton goes on to explain the grounds of his irritation, another telling note of emotionalism slips into his rhetoric: 'To see a poem which already belongs to us altered is like seeing a friend's face horribly deformed in a nightmare' (*CDN* 1:77). Of course, the latter phenomenon also befalls Bentley in the role of Professor de Worms in *The Man Who Was Thursday*, a text subtitled *A Nightmare*.[11] In *George Bernard Shaw*, he returns to the imaginative landscape that had summoned up de Worms, arguing that in the 1890s, '[t]he decay of society was praised by artists as the decay of a corpse is praised by worms. The aesthete was all receptiveness, like the flea' (*CW* 11:401). This image of the Decadent artist as a parasite upon a dead cultural body returns us to Eliot's vision of Chesterton riding into battle with a pestilent corpse trailing in his wake, while the fear of contamination conveyed by Chesterton's reference to the flea—an archetypal symbol of infection—is also discernible in the bifurcating terms through which Eliot cordons off his allies from the representatives of death.

Canonical modernist productions have long been discussed in terms of abjection theory. Kristeva's foundational text, *Powers of Horror: An Essay on Abjection* (1980), cites Molly Bloom's closing monologue in *Ulysses*, in which 'far from preserving us from the abject, Joyce causes it to break out' (22). This willing accommodation of the abject helps to explain the increasing repulsion displayed by Lewis and Pound towards Joyce's work as his processes and predilections drifted inexorably towards the wholesale boundary liquidation of *Finnegans Wake*. Conversely, Maud Ellmann has argued that Eliot's early work, from 'Prufrock' to *The Waste Land*, is structured upon a compulsive retreat into intellectual detachment as a bulwark against a forbidding landscape swarming with repellent detritus (see *Poetics*, 93–94). Eliot is an extraordinarily apt model for Kristeva's account of the 'borderline' patient, seeking both to defend and overcome narcissistic neurosis through recourse to a language made up of a 'shell of ultra-protected signifier' that 'keeps breaking up' (*Powers*, 49). Meanwhile, Hal Foster interprets Lewis's early visual art as a projection of machismo conceived as a defence against the encroachment of disturbing existential threats: 'Lewis registers dread or shock, but often only to turn dread into aggression, shock into protection—as if to convert any breaching into an armouring that both shields and aggresses' (142).

Moving beyond the totemic works to the occasional journalism and correspondence, we find a veritable casebook of abjection set forth in the rhetoric used by Lewis and Pound to execrate Chesterton. Lewis's broadside in 'Futurism and the Flesh' is built upon a refrain that draws obsessive attention to Chesterton's 'dribbling' and 'drivelling': this 'maudlin and dribbling swain' produces 'one long mechanical dribble of empty inversions' suggestive of 'the unavoidable drivelling of an imbecile'. This feature of Lewis's rhetoric illuminates the subconscious stresses that underpin the tonal irritation and evasiveness of the article: we are dealing with a peculiarly literal rendition of what Harold Bloom terms the 'anguish of contamination' (xi) experienced by the literary practitioner in relation to her/his forebears. In an echo of the combined physical and conceptual disproportions that characterise Chesterton's discussions of Wilde, Lewis's imagery evokes an exorbitant apprehension of this incontinent 'giant' roused from his 'Bab-Ballad cave' and roaming the cultural landscape in pursuit of the 'impious blood [of] painter[s]' (*Creatures*, 36).

The status of this ogre as a 'jettisoned object' (*Powers*, 2) in Kristeva's terms—an erstwhile influence upon the younger writer's imaginative landscape, now expelled and anathematised—makes his sinister omnipresence all the more irritating to the nerves, not least since Chesterton had insisted upon emphasising his Lewisian dimensions in 'The Paradise of Thieves'. This apparently conciliatory gesture of identification takes on a curiously passive-aggressive dimension in view of Lewis's anxiety to efface any air of mutual resemblance. The effrontery of this insistence upon complicity is exacerbated by Chesterton's status as a burlesque humourist. Not only do practical jokers frequently force the victim into involuntary proximity and undignified collusion, the really ambitious practical joker will also strive to wrestle down a moving target—a dynamic suggested by Lewis's account, in *BLAST,* of English humour 'conventionalizing like gunshot, freezing supple REAL in ferocious chemistry of laughter' (17).

The last phrase concords linguistically with Lewis's later vision of Chesterton, in *Time and Western Man (1927),* as a '*ferocious* and foaming' Toby jug (387; my emphasis), a term also found in 'Kill John Bull with Art', in which the titular figure is conceived as a 'ferocious national animal [...] committed to the extermination of art' (*Creatures,* 40). As with his use of 'maudlin' to refer both to Chesterton and to the wider culture in separate texts, this recourse to the same term in a series of temporally and thematically distinct works indicates Lewis's enduring identification of Chesterton with the cultural forces ranged against him as an artist, this time framed in language connotative of both violence and incontinence—the antagonist is not only 'ferocious', but also 'foaming'. Rather incongruously, given Chesterton's famously mild disposition in his personal affairs, Lewis imagines him as a rabid dog, threatening an aggressive violation associated with the contraction of disease, much as the infirmity of the dribbling antagonist in 'Futurism and the Flesh' presents a threat of pollution, only to be forcibly repelled by Lewis's incantatory imprecations.

The Lewisian satirist comes to resemble Kristeva's sufferer from neurotic disorder, chronically fearful 'of being bitten' (*Powers,* 38). In the introductory preamble to 'Futurism and the Flesh', *T.P.'s Weekly* refers to the 'biting satire' (*Creatures,* 387) of Chesterton's initial article. As the *BLAST* manifesto thunders with aggressive self-defensiveness, 'CURSE those who will hang over this Manifesto with SILLY CANINES exposed' (17). Elsewhere, in another image of dental violation, Lewis argues that the conventionalising drive of English humour can only be countered effectively through a violent act of mirroring: 'We set humour at humour's throat' (*BLAST* 1:31). If these terms seem to imply imitation as much as opposition, it is instructive to dwell further on the 'SILLY CANINES'. 'Silly' is one of Lewis's favourite terms of disapprobation, perhaps surprisingly since it forms a peculiarly bluff term of disapproval, suggestive of the English philistine—recall that Chesterton discovers 'something silly' in Wilde's bathetic verses. However, the etymological root of 'silly' is 'blessed' (*selie*; see Barnart, 1006): in the act of blasting a rejected attribute of the cultural other, each writer ends up unconsciously blessing it.

This consistently Janus-faced aspect of Lewis's rhetoric corroborates his assertion that Vorticists are wont to 'discharge ourselves on both sides', a phrase that economically aggregates dutiful action, incontinence, potency, infection, invalidism, financial withdrawal, debt repayment, moral exemption, and military irresponsibility. Again, this dualistic premise causes Marinetti to be drawn into the sphere of criticism in equivalent proportion to Chesterton. Aware of Lewis's newly minted position on Futurism, Pound declares that 'Marinetti is a corpse' (154) in *BLAST*, thus expelling the figure with whom Chesterton had conflated him in 'The Paradise of Thieves'. Although *BLAST* reserves comparable opprobrium for the 'PRACTICAL JOKER' (15), Pound took on precisely this role in his efforts to prove himself an anti-Futurist. As Vivien Whelpton reports, in 1914 Pound and Aldington began to treat 'Marinetti chiefly as an object of derision, and [...] hatched a scheme to ridicule him publicly', turning up to a lecture on 'Futurist clothing' wearing 'green trousers, orange shirts and blue jackets' (83)—a stunt that would have struck the uninitiated spectator as difficult to distinguish from adherence to Futurist fashion.

In the *Pisan Cantos* (1948), Pound recalls that he and Lewis first met in the guise of one 'bull-dog' (*Cantos*, 507) attacking another. While this scene unconsciously echoes the inductive wrestling match of Chesterton and Bentley, it also offers an appropriate metaphor for the man who famously considered Western civilisation to be 'an old bitch gone in the teeth' (Pound, *New*, 117). This literal vision of decadence, propounded in his ambiguously self-implicating satire of aestheticism, *Hugh Selwyn Mauberley* (1920), is anticipated by 'The New Cake of Soap', in which Chesterton's toothless humour implicitly contributes to the civilisation's loss of cultural bite. Thus, Pound appropriates Chesterton's Edwardian self-projection as a subversive cultural outlaw, while disputing Chesterton's right to claim such a status. In the self-consciously anarchic context of *BLAST*, Pound's lampoon suggests that contact with Chesterton's morally-cleansed cheek might, paradoxically, act as a pollutant, sanitising the radicalism of the 'new gang' unless it is kept at a safe distance. The satirical act of repulsion is conceived as a measure to prevent the father-figure washing the Vorticists' mouths out with soap.

Pound's view of Chesterton as a perverse locus of abjection becomes still clearer when we look more closely at his correspondence in the period, not least the letter to Quinn discussed earlier, the underlying purpose of which was to lobby for the republication of 'The New Cake of Soap'. In setting out his argument in favour of this action, Pound asserts that his satirical method possesses a moral foundation—'one should name names in satire' (*Letters*, 170); this is not a question of 'cruelty to a weak man' (171)—before swapping the poem's ambivalent theme of sanitisation for a more straightforward rhetoric of pollution, branding Chesterton 'a vile scum on the pond' (171) of British culture.

As Noel Stock notes, throughout 1917 'Pound was unable to mention Chesterton without lapsing into abuse' and exhibited 'almost uncontrollable feelings' (199) towards him. As with Lewis's obsessive recapitulation of Chesterton's incontinence and Eliot's vision of him calling forth a pestilence, Pound's vituperation goes beyond a wily exercise in strategic cultural alignment, or a justified aesthetic *cri de coeur*, to become expressive of an intimate revulsion grounded in a neurotic fear of pollution. In a letter sent to his father on 6 April 1917, he compares Chesterton's output to the 'burble' of a '[d]unghill' (Pound, *Ezra*

Pound to His Parents, 393). A month later, he remarks to Jepson that the very 'mention of [...] Chesterton' brings upon him 'the sensation of being thrust head downward up to chin into the mire of an open privy' (*Letters*, 29 May 1917; 167).[12] Immediately after making this observation, Pound examines his response in pathological terms, wondering if it is caused by 'hyper-aesthesia' (167). Similarly, in the Quinn letter, he ponders whether a '[c]omplex of my own vanity' might be responsible for his visceral antagonism to Chesterton, before demurring, rather too late, that 'I don't want to be hysterical over two lines' (*Letters*, 171).

In attempting to justify his methods to Quinn, Pound argues that the 'multitude of [Chesterton's] mumblings cannot be killed by multitude but only by a sharp thrust' (*Letters*, 171). This image inadvertently evokes Chesterton's metaphor of the sword as a symbol of oppositional satire (see *Spice*, 23), while dispensing with the balancing, existentially grotesque confession of internal contradiction that Chesterton finds symbolised in the cross—a conceptual imbalance towards oversimplification that helps to explain why Pound's satire is so ineffective. In 'The Decline of Satire', Chesterton explains that moderating one's antipathies is essential to the production of successful satire:

> To write great satire, to attack a man so that he feels the attack and half acknowledges its justice, it is necessary to have a certain intellectual magnanimity which realises the merits of the opponent as well as his defects.
>
> (*Twelve*, 52)

Although Pound possessed sufficient critical acumen to draw the same conclusion—he concedes to Quinn that 'The New Cake of Soap' is 'contemptuous, and contempt may not be a very formidable weapon' (*Letters*, 171)—his inability to moderate his response to Chesterton renders him incapable of acting upon these precepts. In his suggestively titled series of articles for the *New Age*, 'The Revolt of Intelligence', Pound finally concedes Chesterton's essential benignity, only to conclude on a startling note of rhetorical disproportion, literally wishing his antagonist dead: 'He is also, I believe, without malice. He has his points, or, rather, his contours. I wish he had never been born; but the wish is idle' (139).

Pound's urge to deal 'a sharp thrust' to Chesterton brings to mind Lewis's portrayal of Kreisler's farcical duel in *Tarr*, with its bizarre slapstick homoeroticism: 'A cruel and fierce sensation of mixed origin rose hotly round his heart. He loved that man! But because he loved him he wished to plunge a sword into him, to plunge it in and out and up and down!' (270). In the correspondence with Quinn, Pound expresses dark misgivings that he 'should probably like G.K.C. personally if I ever met him' and that this suspicion had actually 'heightened' (*Letters*, 171) his reaction against him.[13] The plot thickens: why should Pound have so strenuously execrated a figure with whom he felt a latent sympathy, going so far as to self-analyse this response as involuntary and quasi-pathological?

Yeats's argument that Pound possessed an urge to achieve 'complete undisturbed self-possession' (qtd. in Ellmann, R., *Identity*, 239) supplies one starting point. Humphrey Carpenter notes that Pound's early poem, 'Ballad of the Goodly Fere' (1909), is 'a pastiche of the Chesterton [...] manner' (118), composed 'in the popular idiom' (117). Though the poem was published by Ford in the *English Review* (Oct. 1909), therefore meeting with a more positive reception than Lewis's attempted cribbing of the Chestertonian mystery formula, Pound's subsequent urge to emulate his friend's radicalism rendered this verse an incriminating presence in his back catalogue, hinting at a shameful history of identification with the anathematised figure. As Seaber notes of the 'almost universally negative' (3) references to Chesterton that would later permeate George Orwell's prose, '[e]ndeavouring not to resemble G.K. Chesterton' (*G.K. Chesterton's*, 1) represents an inverted expression of relation that may be just as critically suggestive as homage.

A further, interrelated explanation for Pound's 'hysterical' response lies in Chesterton's critical acuity. While his combination of discernment and populism disrupted the clear-cut distinctions that Pound sought to draw between his perceived sites of cultural cleanliness and filth, 'The Paradise of Thieves' had already illustrated the threat that Chesterton's unsympathetic critical gaze presented to him as a medium of public exposure. Beyond the story's theme of fiscal unmasking, its motifs of upper- and lowercase R/romanticism were perhaps even more disquieting to the figures under attack. In order to understand why, it is necessary to take full stock of the influence exerted upon Eliot, Lewis, and Pound at this time by the aesthetic philosophy of T.E. Hulme. Blissett argues that Pound 'saw in [Hulme] everything the Imagist poet should be' ('Chesterton and English', 134), while Eliot acknowledged that he had been 'enormously influenced' (qtd. in Habib, 66) by Hulme, and Lewis—not a man renowned for his readiness to lavish praise—termed Hulme a 'remarkable man' (*Blasting*, 99).

Two specific critical interventions on Hulme's part had a decisive impact on the aesthetic progress of all three men—his essay on 'Romanticism and Classicism', published in *Speculations* (1911), and his lecture on 'Modern Art and Its Philosophy', delivered in London on 22 January 1914, with Lewis and Pound in attendance. In 'Romanticism and Classicism', Hulme posits a pristine division between the two titular modes, proposing that the allegedly uniform romanticism of the nineteenth century should be superseded by an equally uniform classicism, while rejecting 'the infamous attitude of the person with catholic tastes who says he likes both' (Hulme, *Collected*, 60). Hulme argues that 'the bad romantic aesthetic' of Victorian verse is characterised by an incontinence that will soon be superseded by 'a period of dry, hard, classical verse [...] from which the infinite [will be] excluded' (Hulme, *Collected*, 69). As Hynes aptly remarks, Hulme is best understood as 'a sort of intellectual policeman [...] one of the great simplifiers' (124/123).

Hulme's vision of culture is also radically anti-populist. Despite being an early advocate of Bergson, he turned against the philosopher when Bergson's theories began to grow in popularity, drawing heaving crowds to his lectures in a manner that Hulme found unnerving. As Henry Mead notes, henceforth '[f]or Hulme, Bergson's ideas had been debased into a kind of populist wonder-cure' (Mead). Nonetheless, Hulme 'nourished in his own life a cult of personality' and was not above investing philosophical discourse with showmanship—rather like Chesterton brandishing his outsized knife at a public debate, Hulme was known for 'flourish[ing] knuckle-dusters in philosophical discussions' (Hynes, 123). Hulme's lecture of 1914 replaced the influence of Bergson with that of Wilhelm Worringer, adapting Worringer's historical thesis that two opposed responses to existence recur throughout history: 'the tendency [...] towards empathy' and 'towards abstraction' (Hulme, *Speculations*, 108).[14] As Mead explains, 'Worringer had provided terms that matched romanticism and classicism in aesthetic terms' (Mead).

Lewis later argued that he and Hulme had been 'made for each other, as critic and "creator". What he said should be done, I *did*. Or it would be more exact to say that I did it, and he said it' (*Blasting*, 100). Despite Lewis's belated attempt to complicate the direction of influence, at the time, Hulme's status as a critic enabled him to assume the role of judge over Lewis's relative adherence to his precepts. In an article in the *New Age* on 26 March 1914, Hulme quibbles that Lewis's 'sense of form seems to me to be sequent rather than integral', while deeming the work of the Camden Town Group with which Lewis was then involved 'a kind of romantic heresy' ('Modern Art—III. The London Group', 661). The 'sequent' compositional style of Lewis's specific artworks finds a macroscopic corollary in his progressive aesthetic drift towards abstraction. He had begun experimenting with increasingly avant-garde methods in the aftermath of Fry's post-Impressionist exhibition and gradually moved beyond the qualified mimesis of post-Impressionism to the radically expressionist works of pure geometric abstraction that characterise his output of 1914.

Hulme found particular praise for Lewis's transcendence of the 'transience of the organic' (qtd. in Butler, 227), a phrase that further illustrates the justice of Chesterton's claim that contemporary art had withdrawn into an extreme asceticism. In 'Futurism and the Flesh', Lewis attempts to sidestep the validity of Chesterton's argument through aggressive physical self-promotion. With a commercial acumen characteristic of his machinations in this period (though singularly lacking from his cultural endeavours thereafter), Lewis employs his own body as an advert for his aesthetic, accompanying the article with a publicity photograph taken from the same session that had yielded his Lucian Gregory-like headshot. This image was presumably included at Lewis's request, since Chesterton's article had not featured a photograph. By presenting the author at his most rakishly dandified, Lewis introduces his refined image to the public as an *embodiment* of the 'severely classical' (Lewis qtd. in Meyers, 64) art and prose that he practised at the time: recall his account of *Tarr* having been 'clipped [...] *to the bone* of all *fleshy* verbiage' (my emphases). In contrast, Chesterton is portrayed in physically grotesque terms in 'Futurism and the Flesh', and his 'foaming' is later dubbed 'romantic' (387) in *Time and Western Man*.

Lewis's attempt to control his reception through the dissemination of branded imagery manipulates the evidential cache of photography to counteract the interpretations of contemporary caricaturists. The collection of caricatures in which Edmond Kapp offers his gargantuan rendition of Chesterton also includes a likeness of Lewis, first drawn in 1914. Whereas the caricature of Chesterton is captioned '[a]s he would have us think him' (Kapp, 6), in reference to the exaggeratedly grotesque self-image that he projected in his journalistic buffoonery, Lewis is presented as he would not have us think him (Figure 4.3).

Figure 4.3 Caricature of Wyndham Lewis by Edmund Kapp, 1914.

While 'The Paradise of Thieves' had portrayed the Lewisian Muscari as a throwback to the 1890s, this had at least been in the form of a vigorously playful aesthete; Kapp's rendering is more suggestive of a washed-out, morose Decadent. Far from resembling a dynamic descendant of Loki, Kapp's Lewis carries an enervated air, with an emptied Martini glass before him and a cloak more suggestive of an invalid's shawl than the cape of a Dostoevskian villain. As Kapp's hinting at unpurged romanticism suggests, Lewis's acceptance of Hulme's case for abstract classicism left him in a distinctly uneasy position in relation to the aestheticised personae that he and Pound had paraded in the preceding years. Reviewing *BLAST* for the *Egoist*, Richard Aldington mocks Pound's unsanitariness in the course of questioning his aptitude for satire, while drawing attention to the poet's affinity with Decadence:

> the uncleanness of his language increases to an almost laughable point [...] It is not that one wants Mr. Pound to repeat his Provençal feats, to echo the 'nineties'—he has done that too much already—it is simply the fact that Mr. Pound cannot write satire.
>
> ('Blast', 273)

In correspondence with Felix E. Schelling, Pound offers a further assessment of the state of contemporary letters, arguing that it 'isn't enough to give the Rabelaisian guffaw' (in other words, an open laugh) in response to the malaise—what is necessary is the 'work of purgation of minds, meritorious as the physical products of Beecham' (*Letters*, 249). This reference to internal purging directly echoes the rhetoric of the letter to Quinn, in which Pound argues that satirical opposition to Chesterton's 'slop [...] purges one's soul' (*Letters*, 171). As will be noticed, this phrasing relocates the field of battle from the wider culture to the self. Hulme's lecture was delivered just five months after the publication of 'The Paradise of Thieves' and five months before the publication of *BLAST*, and his bifurcating rhetoric separates the two texts just as decisively. Henceforth, a troupe of creative artists of innately R/romantic temperament were persuaded that they, and the culture from which they had emerged, needed to be 'disciplined by order' (Hulme, *Collected*, 61) as a means of sloughing off, rather than succumbing to, the last vestiges of Decadence. Kristeva discusses the dynamic at hand in terms of a sharp thrust directed inward: 'The one by whom the abject exists [... casts] within himself the scalpel that carries out his separations' (*Powers*, 8).

In this light, the satirical scapegoating of Chesterton carried out by Eliot, Lewis, and Pound can be understood to occupy a point of intersection between private neurosis and public ritual. To again quote Kristeva, the cultural 'defilement rite' constitutes 'a social elaboration of the borderline patient': in 'primitive societies religious rites are purification rites whose function is to separate this or that social, sexual, or age group from another one, by means of prohibiting a filthy, defiling element' (*Powers*, 65). This cleansing process applies not only to the cultural exterior, but also to the psychological interior. Foster argues that the hybridised binary of Lewis's phrase, 'effeminate lout within' (11) in *BLAST*, causes 'nation and subject [to] mirror one another in a bodily image [...] In the nation, this "lout" seems to be the masses; in the subject, it seems to be the unconscious' (Foster, 130–31). The much-vaunted urge of the Men of 1914 to impose an austere classicism upon a polis that they considered riddled with decadent romanticism finds a subjective correlative in the unruly internal mob, resistant to being drilled into neat classical formation. As Paul Edwards notes, Lewis 'attributed to the Romantic [a] chaotic subjectivity' (*Apes'*, 91). This mob must be subdued by a rigorous jettisoning of discordant voices, to be replaced by an orderly singularity, however artificial and, ultimately, unsustainable.

While the rhetoric of the London-based Men of 1914 is consistently characterised by an urge to remain unpolluted by various cultural projections of the non-self, it is also invested with a deeper impetus to remain detached from, and undisturbed by, life itself, in the form of the tumultuous 'fuss' (*BLAST* 1:149) execrated throughout *BLAST*. As Lewis later explained, following their exposure to Hulme's ideas, the group project of the Men of 1914 had become founded upon an urge 'to get away from romantic art into classical art [...] back into the *detachment* of true literature' (*Blasting*, 250; my emphasis). The Schopenhauerian basis of this aesthetic project is suggested by Lewis's later parsing of the philosopher's message. In *Time and Western Man*, he explains that Schopenhauer's guidance was 'to remove yourself as far as possible from' the 'mechanical buffooneries' of a 'quite aimless, [...] nonsensical, Will', which demands 'enforced participation in [the] quite imbecile impulsiveness and fuss' (*Time*, 332–33) of life.

Although the Lewis of *BLAST* proclaims that '[o]ur vortex rushes out like an angry dog at your Impressionistic fuss' (*BLAST* 1:149), when he finds praise for English humour it is because it might form a 'hysterical WALL built round the EGO', structured upon the 'separating [...] solitude of LAUGHTER' (*BLAST 1:26*). As with Chesterton's argument that the Futurists were not so much fearsome fighting machines as frightened little boys, the jostling aggression of Lewis's typography contrasts jarringly with the timorous rhetoric that it conveys. Eliot displayed an empathetic understanding of his associate when he assessed Lewis to be a 'highly-strung, nervous man' (qtd. in Meyers, 56). For all his outbursts of aggressive clowning and approval of the armoured 'scarab' over the amorphous 'jelly-fish' (*Blasting*, 104), Lewis's imagery leans more towards Prufrock's fantasy of transforming into 'a pair of ragged claws / Scuttling across the floors of silent seas' (*PTSE* 1:7).

When Lewis chooses a 'painted mummy case' as the uncanny image through which to portray Tarr's trapdoor personality, there is a further subtle echo of Prufrock's abject self-image and timid urge for withdrawal: Tarr's interior becomes the site of a preserved corpse, located within a sarcophagus that reassuringly swaddles the self against the incursion of the material world, much as the vortex that swirls around Lewis in Kapp's caricature seems to cocoon a convalescent. Bakhtin argues that 'images of the Romantic grotesque usually express fear of the world' (*Rabelais*, 39), a principle summarised succinctly by Prufrock: 'in short, I was afraid' (*PTSE* 1:8). Equally, Lewis's coveting of 'solitude' mirrors the reclusive temperament that Woolf ascribes to Clarissa Dalloway, and Chesterton to the 'Ojibway'. In 'The Red Angel', Chesterton argues that the 'timidity of the child or the savage is entirely reasonable; they are alarmed at this world, because this world is a very alarming place' (collected in *Tremendous*, 102). As Foster notes, Worringer's thesis is that 'naturalism and abstraction [...] express two opposite relations to the world, an empathetic engagement and a shocked withdrawal' (135). In pursuing the latter course, the primitive mercenary strives to achieve the state of *ataraxia* that Bentley had also sought: 'The primitive turned to abstraction, according to Worringer, because he was "dominated by an immense need for tranquillity"' (Foster, 135).

Chesterton's self-assigned role as materialist buffoon therefore provides a further context through which to understand his execration by adversaries striving to outmanoeuvre the 'transience of the organic'. When Lewis argues in *BLAST* that the modern artist should not 'suck up to life' (1:148), one thinks once more of Beerbohm's image of 'Mr G.K. Chesterton giving the world a kiss'. Beyond the cultural contamination of his populism, Chesterton's ethics of buffoonery entails an insistence upon a more visceral contamination of the proud individual by the abject world, via the image of the existential practical joke: 'now I come to think of it, we are mud pies ourselves' ('Ashes', *DN* 11 Feb. 1911; *CDN* 7:73). Here, the world dines upon the material matter of the individual—a distinctly unwelcome *memento mori* for the neurotic abstractionist. In Chesterton's earlier dispute with William Inge, it was his accusation that the Dean possessed a 'horror of matter' (qtd. in Ker, 602) that roused the latter to intemperately abuse this 'obese [...] mountebank'. Likewise, Lewis complains that Chesterton 'gives you a butter-slide (which you are meant to enjoy)' (*Creatures*, 35), while fulminating against 'VEGETABLE HUMANITY' (*BLAST* 1:15) and cursing English humour as the 'FIXED GRIN Death's Head symbol of Anti-Life' (*BLAST* 1:17).

Similarly, Pound's attack on Chesterton's taste for 'chaos and camouflage' evokes Stewart's argument that the '[l]umpishness' of the clown's outfit 'suggests chaos', thus confronting the unnerved 'audience [...] with something relatively shapeless, yet material' (61). The element of neurotic alarm underpinning Pound's self-defeating aggression is brought out by

Jepson's observation that 'were it not quite so full-throated', Pound's 'satire would have a sharper bite' (153), phraseology that suggests a terrified shriek as much as a berserker's battle-cry. Beatrice Hastings satirises Pound's roistering self-image in the 'Pastiche' column of the *New Age* on 2 September 1915, parodying his emblematic Imagist poem, 'In a Station of the Metro' (1913), while portraying him as an effete, paranoiac attendee of a pallid high-society banquet:

> The apparition of Ezra at the Party
> To his right the curling sandwiches
> And the fruits that are somehow watching him
> The apparition of Ezra
> Under the tree branches triangularly waving
> A strawberry ice on his knee
> [...]
> Ezra at the Party, half friz, half nibble
> Ezra talking Art.
>
> ('Higgledy-Piggledies', 435)

Hastings's skit conceives Pound as a Prufrockian party-goer, perhaps talking of d'Annunzio while manoeuvring his way through the hyper-refined world that the Men of 1914 affected to despise. The central hidden contradiction of Pound's public and private selves was the network of auspicious contacts that he was cultivating throughout this period, which enabled him to exercise a pervasive influence over the *Egoist* and the *Little Review* (see Benstock, 363–65) during the war years. Following the installation of Harriet Shaw Weaver as editor of the *Egoist* in July 1914, Pound 'virtually controlled' (Benstock, 23) the journal's output, effectively rendering it the house magazine of the Men of 1914. The increasing abundance of satirical exposures of Pound's commercial machinations, as set in motion by 'The Paradise of Thieves', drove him towards the increasing intemperance of his post-war persona, in which the mask of anti-commercialism began to meld to the poet's true face, with rather more seriously damaging consequences for his public reputation and personal sanity.

Pound's self-righteous versifying in *BLAST 2* offers a prefiguration of things to come, beginning one piece with a revision of 'Prufrock' that advertises his clear distinction from Eliot's protagonist on the question of courage:

> Cowardly editors threaten: 'If I dare'
> Say this or that, or speak my open mind,
> Say that I hate my hates,
> Say that I love my friends,
> [...]

> They will cut down my wage, force me to sing their cant,
> Uphold the press, and be before all a model of literary decorum.
> Merde!
>
> (22)

While the paradoxical discretion of the francophone obscenity succinctly rehearses Pound's inner contradictions, it will be noticed that his wider rhetoric presents a very adequate pastiche of Chesterton's position during the *Daily News* controversy. Lewis and Pound were expending their energies on denouncing a phantom Chesterton: the carnivalesque Edwardian buffoon had already withdrawn from the public stage, to be replaced by a figure more closely resembling their own intemperate extremism.

The first editor of the *Egoist*, Dora Marsden, alludes to this transition in Chesterton's temperament in the edition of November 1915. Marsden had remained contributing editor following the 1914 putsch, much to Pound's irritation, and her favourable notice of Chesterton might have cut the poet to the quick, since she enthuses over his continuing 'most ingenious' use of the 'transformation scene' (168) as a metaphor for the discrepancy between reality and press propagandising. However, Marsden goes on to regret Chesterton's increasingly strident partitioning of friends from enemies: 'the sole reason' for his use of the transformation scene in a recent instance was 'to assist him to divide the world into two parts: the Goblins he preferred—all his own friends; and the Widows he couldn't abide: those whom he and his friends were inclined to dislike' (168). The pantomimic metaphor that had once stood for a sense of imaginative double vision in Chesterton's writing—recall the stereoscopic 'ordinary man' of *Orthodoxy*, who can accept 'contradiction' because 'he sees two different pictures at once and yet sees all the better for that'—was now being manipulated to the service of a binary segregation, more reminiscent of the schematising urge of the monomaniacal rationalist.

Perhaps in a veiled allusion to the dogmatists who had recently gatecrashed her periodical, Marsden ends by observing that these 'ruminations are set forth as a caution: for the guidance mainly of—the "Egoist"' (168). As this implies, the two factions were beginning to mirror one another in the very act of protesting their dissimilarity. Chesterton's departure from the *Daily News* was the first warning sign of an increasingly Poundian urge to project stable cultural fault lines, engendered precisely by anxiety over the fiscal compromises within which he was implicated: 'the skeleton begins to shine through the cupboard' (qtd. in Marsden, 168), as he notes in an inadvertently self-revelatory passage of the article cited by Marsden. Chesterton now found himself in as uneasy a relation to his recent past as Lewis and Pound—a formerly sanguine advocate of the popular press, his disillusion with the mechanisms of the commercial marketplace was drawing him into dangerously self-schismatic territory.

Something High and Shrill That Might Crack

On being asked his opinion of Chesterton, Lytton Strachey spoke for many of his contemporaries when he replied, 'I like him very much except when he's pretending to be Belloc' (qtd. in Ward, *Return*, 59). In his caricature series, *The Old and the Young Self* (1924), Beerbohm dramatises this imitative dynamic, imagining an encounter between the younger and older Chestertons, in which the former scoffs at the notion of 'the determination of the Jews to enslave us', to which the latter replies, '[w]ell, you haven't met Belloc' (qtd. in Blissett, 'G.K. Chesterton', 122). This sketch crystallises a view that gained increasing traction in literary circles from the pre-war period onwards—that the outbursts of anti-Semitism that increasingly began to disfigure Chesterton's fictional and polemical work derived largely from subservience to the will of his domineering friend. Much as Shaw conceived the Chesterbelloc as a species of grotesquely entwined Hobby Horse, Beerbohm considers Chesterton to have lashed himself to the obsessions of his friend in a manner that makes him ridiculous, because it places him at odds with himself. Chesterton's uncritical desire to emulate his idealised friend becomes the cause of a fundamental breach in his integrity: post-Belloc, he is no longer his own man.

Donald Barr argues that in later years, Chesterton's anti-Semitism was perpetuated by the reverse problem to a schismatic temporal breach, an inflexible adherence to an *idée fixe*: his 'anti-Semitism had become a tic' (*CW* 8:41). In a proof of Auden's view that '[a]fter the rogue, the commonest object of satire is the monomaniac' (384), Chesterton's obsessional discourse attracted the satirical attention of Reginald Arkell, who produced a skit on Chesterton's 'Song of the Dog Named Quoodle' (first published in the *New Witness*, 27 November 1913), a poem that famously conjures an image of the 'noselessness of man' as a symbol of humanity's tendency to backslide into unreflective complacency, while making a fleeting, superfluous reference to 'the park a Jew encloses' (*Flying*, 164). Arkell's parodic variation on Chesterton's air identifies, in the latter remark, the beam in Chesterton's own eye—a comparably unwitting lapse into unreflective thinking, which the detective-parodist boasts of having rooted out:

> Gilbert oft discloses
> As only Gilbert can,
> His curious hate for noses
> Worn by the sons of Moses,

He'd like them, one supposes,
Built on a different plan.

(qtd. in Ward, *Return*, 116)

In Arkell's account, Chesterton's inability to sniff out the ridiculous in his own contradictory rhetoric leaves him vulnerable to satirical attack.[15] Nonetheless, Chesterton's capacity to activate inwardly-directed critical laughter often enabled him to anticipate, and to attempt to neutralise, such parodic demurral. For example, *in The Flying Inn*, into which the 'Song of the Dog Named Quoodle' was incorporated, a vicarious confession of eccentricity seems to lie behind the interpretation of the narrative put forward by a foolish correspondent to the 'Pebbleswick Globe', 'who called it all a plot of frenzied foreigners against Britain's shore' (91). A further example of implicit self-criticism is discernible in a contemporaneous *Father Brown* story, 'The Duel of Dr. Hirsch' (*Pall Mall Magazine* Aug. 1914), in which the action centres upon 'another Dreyfus case' (*CFB* 204). The story can be read as a conflicted attempt on Chesterton's part to accommodate Belloc's long-standing, and manifestly anti-Semitic, anti-Dreyfusard stance with his own half-conscious sense of its irrationality. When Father Brown and Flambeau begin to discuss the original case, Chesterton's characters enter into implicit critical dialogue with their creator. In positing an explanation with which Chesterton had presumably toyed—that Dreyfus might somehow have committed the treachery half-consciously while convincing himself that he was not doing so—Father Brown merely succeeds in tying himself in knots, before lapsing into frustrated, *aporic* inarticulacy:

"I can't describe these things; I know what I mean."
"I wish I did," said his friend.

(*CFB* 209)

When Brown finally acknowledges the inadequacy of the theory, the narrative effect is suggestive of the characters pausing to gaze askance from the page at their creator:

"I've told you the only theory I can think of that could satisfy anybody. It doesn't satisfy me."
"Nor me either," replied Flambeau frowning, while the other went on eating fish with an air of entire resignation. "If all you can suggest is that notion of a message conveyed by contraries, I call it uncommonly clever, but... well, what would you call it?"
"I should call it thin," said the priest promptly. "I should call it uncommonly thin."

(*CFB* 210–11)

The solution that Chesterton arrives at in the story at hand—that of hybridising the traitor and the patriot within the persona of a single glory-hunting Machiavellian—is thinner still. The logical drift would seem to be that Dreyfus's relative innocence or guilt is somehow irrelevant, since all statesmen are mere composites of masks, interchangeable one from another, and all engaged in prosecuting shadowy confidence tricks upon the public. The validity of this conclusion has already been destabilised earlier in the narrative by the interjection of another buffoonish character, this time a hot-headed French patriot: '"I believe it's some plot!" snapped Valognes—"some plot of the Jews and Freemasons"' (*CFB* 211). The effect is to implant a ventriloquistic self-parody within the text, ridiculing the paranoid undercurrent of Chesterton's own narrative by parsing its implications in the voice of a fool.[16]

In puzzling out the apparently paradoxical nature of this act of self-sabotage, it is instructive to consider that the 'para' prefix, discussed in my introduction in relation to parody, is also present in 'paranoia', the literal meaning of which is 'beside mind' (*nous*) (see Barnhart, 756). Barr's analysis of Chesterton points towards a similar condition of self-alienation, in which he is

> both protagonist and antagonist. [...] Chesterton was of two minds, both minds made up, each with its own selection of facts and its own habitual phrases—a culture of its own, in short—and each [...] covertly uneasy with the other.
>
> (*CW* 8:42)

In her 1913 article, 'Mr Chesterton in Hysterics: A Study in Prejudice' (*Clarion*, 14 Nov. 1913), Rebecca West mounts an assault upon Chesterton's pre-war social pronouncements, while mediating her anger with a perspicacious refrain of mental imbalance: having had 'the greatest possible admiration for "Tremendous Trifles"', West is dismayed to find in Chesterton's more recent work a 'revival of [the] insane cowardice' of anti-Semitism, accompanied by 'howlings against aliens' from a writer 'writhing in the paroxysm of anti-Semitic or anti-Feminist hysterics' (5).[17]

Chesterton's textual self-contradictions derive from the fact that he was thoroughly beside himself in this period; his nerves strained to breaking point by anxieties over the prospect of war, the breach with the *Daily News*, the threat of litigation from Lever, and his brother's prosecution for libellous reporting of the Marconi scandal in the *New Witness*. The *Father Brown* stories that flank Cecil Chesterton's trial are concerned, respectively, with an ethically dubious newspaper editor whose proprietor is a soap manufacturer ('The Purple Wig', *Pall Mall Magazine*, May 1913), and a miserly scion of the British military establishment who wears a repellent false nose, thus adopting the fancy-dress outfit of a caricatural Jew ('The Head of Caesar', *Pall Mall Magazine*, June 1913). The grotesque nasal appendage is viewed as '"a living nightmare"' by the female protagonist of the story, who nonetheless puzzles over '"why a touch on the nose should affect my imagination so much"' (*CFB* 249). As Chesterton attempts to resolve his racial anxieties through physical burlesque—the nose seems 'a separate and comic thing [...] "[turning] from left to right like an elephant's proboscis"' (*CFB* 254/52)—the weary auditor of his pre-war prose reflects that the answer to the heroine's query is all too on the nose.

Nonetheless, this conceit is not merely grounded in cartoon anti-Semitism—the imagery points towards deeper anxieties for which this context can be understood as a local corollary. In 'Futurism and the Flesh', Lewis mirrors Chesterton's disquiet over the wielding of false noses, expressing discomfort over the latter's would-be magnanimous gesture towards Marinetti: 'I would wear a false nose at his carnival with pleasure' ('Asceticism', 5). Lewis responds gloomily, 'I should not want Mr Chesterton in a carnival myself', before speculating that it is 'the opportunity of promenading his nose' that draws Chesterton into publicly parading 'the exigencies of his unfortunate madness' (*Creatures*, 35–36). During the proto-Kreislerian duel in *The Man Who Was Thursday*, one of the seconds protests that 'one can hardly call one's nose a weapon', only for the Marquis's 'pasteboard proboscis' (*CW* 6:576) to come away in Syme's hand. The example of Eliot's comedian—his virility '[c]oncentred into vest and nose'—illustrates that one most certainly can call one's nose a weapon: a symbol of an intimidating, grotesquely physical vitality.

When combined with an uncanny detachability, this quasi-phallic symbol of the folk grotesque becomes alarmingly confused with the false bottoms of the Romantic grotesque, a domain that frequently threatens to muscle in on Chesterton's most benign visions. In *Thursday*, the 'supernatural terrors' (*CW* 6:574) of the duel scene are finally resolved in benign burlesque, while being presided over by Syme's second, Dr. Bull, who has recently been divested of a pair of impenetrably 'black spectacles' (*CW* 6:571) that had previously terrified the protagonist. As Knight observes, in Chesterton's most well-balanced fiction, 'spectacles often mask the fact that there is nothing behind the terror that has been felt so intensely' (102). Conversely, in 'The Head of Caesar', the blackmailer's 'eyes marked with dark spectacles' (*CFB* 248) and uncertainly corporeal nasal appendage merely compound the sense of terror before the void of identity.

In November 1914, just two months after filing the last of the stories that make up the *Wisdom* collection, Chesterton suffered a complete mental and physical breakdown.[18] A.L. Maycock argues that throughout his pre-war journalism, later collected in *The Utopia of Usurers*

(1917), one finds 'a wildness of expression, a note sometimes rising almost to a scream, that makes one realize how near he was coming to breaking-point in those immediately pre-war years' (28–29). While pausing to observe that the title of this essay collection is, in Chesterton's worldview, a near-exact synonym of 'The Paradise of Thieves', we might also note the relationship of Maycock's term 'breaking-point' to the verb 'snapped' that Chesterton uses to describe Valognes's outburst in 'The Duel of Dr. Hirsch'. In an aside in *William Blake* (1910), Chesterton invests the term's connotations of lost self-control and hysterical irritability with an alarming ontological dimension, remarking that 'the horizon line is not only hard but *tight*, like a fiddle string' before confessing that 'I have always a nervous fear that the sea-line will *snap* suddenly' (47; the second emphasis is mine).

Chesterton had begun the inaugural *Father Brown* story, 'The Blue Cross', '[b]etween the silver ribbon of morning and the green glittering ribbon of sea' (*CFB* 3), an image of existential binding that heralds the series' philosophical purpose of defending the modern world against disarray through the mediation of his exemplar of religious reason. Since Chesterton's priest is particularly preoccupied with debunking groundless conspiracy theories that alienate individuals from one another, it is a canary in the mine of the author's deeper psychological unrest to find his pre-war detective fiction becoming infected with the very paranoia that he had conceived the format to inoculate against. This inversion is again expressed via imagery of metaphysical rupture: a geographic boundary line comparable to that of 'The Blue Cross' emerges in 'The Head of Caesar', only for the binding motif to be immediately subverted, as the quasi-Jewish villain 'silently burst[s] the barrier between land and water' (*CFB* 249) in pursuit of a missing coin.

In her thoughtful study of Chesterton's politics, Margaret Canovan pauses to express puzzlement over his uncharacteristic lapse into prejudice: 'By the standards of the time his anti-Semitism was very mild—but why was it there at all?' (139). Once more, Kristeva's work on abjection offers a helpful theoretical framework through which to puzzle out this aberration. The figure of 'the Jew' is an enduring focus of abject rhetoric because as a symbol of the

> phantasmatic and ambivalent [...] he holds elusive power. His ubiquity is not limited to space, he is [...] on our land and under our skin, the very closest neighbor, the nearly same, the one we do not differentiate, the dizziness of identity.
>
> (Kristeva, *Powers*, 182)

In an early article on 'Jews Old and New' (*Speaker*, 2 Mar. 1901), Chesterton attempts to grapple humanely with the vexed issue of Jewish identity, while nonetheless recurring to images of invasion and contagion to frame the 'problem': 'the real lesson of the Jewish plutocratic problem [is] the utter futility of attempting to crush a fine race [...] We forbade to the Jews all natural callings except commerce', and the result is the *'internal disease* [of] Jewish *commerce*' (BL MS Add.73381 fol.22; my emphases).

Chesterton's view that the Boer War had been conducted largely for the benefit of transnational Jewish finance helps to account for the conflicted nature of his account. The venue of the article, the *Speaker*, was the preeminent pro-Boer organ of the *fin de siècle*, and Chesterton's first journalistic home, alongside Belloc and Bentley.[19] His sense of affinity with Belloc had first been forged in the crucible of the conflict, and found instructive expression in an incident in which the pair baited a 'jingo mob' that had assembled outside the Queen's Hall in Westminster. Chesterton later recalled how this act of 'patriotic parody' had involved a pedagogic filtration of friends from enemies, drawing the crowd's attention to the status of figures such as Alfred Beit—the German-Jewish financier whose wealth was accumulated in South Africa—as moral, if not literal, 'enem[ies] of England' ('The Rich Man', *DN* 21 July 1906; *CDN* 4:12):

> I remember waiting with a Pro-Boer friend in the midst of a Jingo mob outside the celebrated Queen's Hall Meeting which ended in a free fight. My friend and I adopted a method of patriotic parody or *reductio ad absurdum*. We first proposed three cheers for Chamberlain, then three cheers for Rhodes, and then by degrees for more and more dubious and demi-naturalised patriots. We actually did get an innocent cheer for Beit [...] But when it came to our impulsive appeal to the universal popularity of Albu, the irony of our intention was discovered; and the fight began.
>
> (*Autobiography*, 110–11)[20]

This premise inverts the benign counting game upon which *Thursday* is structured. Rather than sequentially disclosing perceived enemies of the state to be friends, here public figures misapprehended as friends are revealed to be enemies, a gesture of apocalyptic satirical discrimination that contrasts sharply with the novel's reconciliatory ethos of grotesque accumulation. Consider, in this light, Bentley's clerihew on Beit, which was illustrated by Chesterton in a manner that imposes a meaning not necessarily implied by the verse itself. Bentley's rhyme characteristically combines a loss of bodily volition with inscrutability over the cause:

Mr. Alfred Beit
Screamed suddenly in the night.
When they asked him why
He made no reply.

(*Complete*, 8)

These lines inscribe a fundamental ambiguity over the cause of Beit's nightmare, implying an obscure, existential form of terror, while borrowing from Lear's limericks in the invocation of an oppressive 'they' clamouring to demand an explanation. The effect is comparable not only to Father Brown's more restrained inarticulacy over Dreyfus, but also to a moment of aporia that Carroll implants within *The Hunting of the Snark* (1874):

To the horror of all those who were present that day,
He uprose in full evening dress,
And with senseless grimaces endeavoured to say
What his tongue could no longer express.

(*Works*, 752)

In contrast to Bentley's ambiguous verse, Chesterton's accompanying illustration of Beit in bed surrounded by bags of money and German insignias encourages the specific inference that his underhand activities in South Africa are disturbing his conscience (Figure 4.4):

Figure 4.4 Caricature of Alfred Beit by G.K. Chesterton, 1905.

Here, Chesterton marshals Belloc's worldview to counteract Bentley's: oppositional moral satire becomes a bulwark against the vertiginous precipices of the Romantic grotesque. Similarly, while 'The Head of Caesar' is suffused with imagery drawn from the Romantic grotesque—in addition to the black spectacles and false nose, the villain possesses a cadaverous 'waxen bloom [...] that belongs to a barber's dummy' (*CFB* 251)—the action concludes in 'Mafeking Avenue, Putney' (*CFB* 250), a geographic symbol of the Boer ignominy implanted satirically within the home nation, and the miser is found dead amongst bags of money that recall Beit's bedside-scene: 'the man in the brown dressing-gown lay amid his burst and gaping brown-paper parcels' (*CFB* 254). In the case of the caricature, Chesterton's reluctance to detach himself from moral judgement leads him to reply to Beit's interrogators on his behalf, so as to police the reader's reception of the verse. As he argues elsewhere, '[p]rint is at best a temptation; a picture is an assault' ('Truth and Lies in Popular Histories', *ILN* 9 Nov. 1907; *CW* 27:587). In a conceit that correlates to Lewis's obsessive recourse to images of dental aggression, Beit's screaming mouth offers Chesterton the opportunity to link the name to the personality, with the massed ranks of teeth in the trap-like mouth suggesting the financier's association with material rapacity: the bite of Beit.

Recall Auden's account of the motivation for producing 'caricatures of our enemies' in which they are petrified in a characteristic attitude—this precludes 'the possibility of their having a change of heart so that we would have to forgive them'. Chesterton's drive to establish a firm fixity of ethical standpoint is linked to his view that modern relativistic philosophy, or 'that final scepticism which can find no floor to the universe', threatens to enact a simultaneous breakdown of personal and moral coherence. A month before his expression of irritation at Yeats's interference with the poetry of his past self, Chesterton composed 'A Defence of Rash Vows' (*Speaker*, 9 Mar. 1901), in which he notes approvingly that the 'man who makes a vow makes an appointment with himself at some distant time or place' (*Defendant*, 33). He goes on to identify a modern lack of faith in the possibility of keeping vows, which he considers to derive from a 'fear that by that time [one] will be, in the common but hideously significant phrase, *another man*' (*Defendant*, 33).

This anxiety finds an echo in the 'Scylla and Charybdis' episode of *Ulysses*, in which Joyce initiates an internal dialogue in order to split Stephen Dedalus's self in two, one side of which reminds him of a debt, while the other attempts to mobilise contemporary scientific authority to justify an act of fiscal unscrupulousness: 'You owe it. Wait. Five months. Molecules all change. I am other I now. Other I got pound' (242). Dedalus goes on to achieve a combined recovery of ethical and subjective coherence through the intuition that 'I, entelechy, form of forms, am I by memory' (242). In 'A Plea for Popular Philosophy' (*DN* 22 June 1907), Chesterton engages in a similar thought process, in confronting the challenges set to the conventional understanding of subjectivity by recent scientific and philosophical advances. He outlines what he considers to be 'the three or four sanities and certainties of human free thought', each of which centres upon a discrepancy between the way '[a]ll sane men' intuitively behave, and what is nonetheless 'unproved and unproveable' (*CDN* 4:242) about the world in which they find themselves. The third of these dicta states that although 'it is definitely disputed by many metaphysicians' that 'there is such a [thing as a] paramount "I"', nonetheless '[a]ll sane men believe that there is such a thing as self or ego, which is continuous. There is no inch of my brain matter the same as it was ten years ago. But if I have saved a man in battle ten years ago I am proud, if I have run away I am ashamed' (*CDN* 4:242).

In other words, despite compelling scientific evidence to the contrary, one must make a leap of faith in the existence of an integral 'I' in order to extrapolate any ethical dimension to one's actions. Consequently, while Carroll has Alice reason that 'it's no use going back to yesterday, because I was a different person then' (*Annotated*, 138), Chesterton turns to a different nonsense practitioner in his autobiography, when framing his enduring opposition to the Boer War as a product of the ethical grounding of memory: 'As no less an authority than Mr. Discobolus says in Lear's Nonsense Rhymes, I thought so then and I think so still' (*Autobiography*, 130). The persuasiveness of Chesterton's point is only slightly undermined by the fact that he has misremembered both the speaker—the Pelican chorus—and the precise phrase—'[w]e think so then and we thought so still' (Lear, 168).

Although Chesterton's urge to establish a temporally stable 'I' invests his best satirical work with ethical coherence, it becomes counterproductive when applied with excessive stringency, at the expense of double-mindedness. This imbalance increasingly permeates Chesterton's polemical and fictional writing in the months leading up to the First World War, as his underlying fears over metaphysical integrity become localised in paranoid visions of an inability to safeguard national selfhood against shadowy forces invested with the capacity to breach various figurative and literal boundaries. In language again denotive of snapping, he later characterised the period immediately preceding the conflict as possessing an 'unearthly unreality [...] like something high and shrill that might crack; and it did crack' (*Autobiography*, 234). Maycock's pen portrait of Chesterton internalises this account, arguing that a '*shrillness* [and] lack of restraint' makes his pre-war articles 'at times, almost terrifying to read, so obviously are they the work of a man overwrought to a dangerous degree' (28; my emphasis).

As with Pound's neuroses, Chesterton's imbalance often expresses itself in an urge to over-simplify. When Father Brown observes in 'The Head of Caesar' that '"[w]hat we all dread most [...] is a maze with no centre"' (*CFB* 246), he speaks of a fear shared by his creator, which occasionally manifests itself in an urge to deny the existence of the maze. As Wills observes of *The Flying Inn*, it 'lacks the dialectic of separate but positive principles' that enlivens Chesterton's earlier fiction with a spirit of productive ambivalence, instead pursuing a baldly adversarial framework that 'tends rather to over-simplification than to the complication and extension of life' (*Chesterton*, 152). Chesterton's anti-Semitism was exacerbated by an increasing refusal to engage with the complicating factors of empathetic connection, accompanied by a withdrawal into the reassuring certitudes of abstract theory. As Mead summarises Worringer's thesis, the 'abstract is produced by a state of mind that desires certainties in an uncertain world' (Mead). This scenario places Chesterton in the company of Hulme, whose distaste for 'emotions that are grouped round the word infinite' (Hulme, *Collected*, 66) implies a Chestertonian disquiet over the implications of the Romantic grotesque—a fear that '[b]eneath our orderly rationalised human structures lies a world of flux and disorder' (Mead), which leads to an urge to seek refuge in the reassuring frames and limits of the classical.[21]

It is perhaps no coincidence that Hulme was the most sympathetic of his contemporaries to Catholicism. Nicolas Bentley reported that his father offered two possible explanations for Chesterton's conversion: the first, 'subservience […] to Hilaire Belloc's will' (42); the second, that he 'felt the burden of existence too heavy to support without [a] spiritual opiate' (42–43). As this suggests, Chesterton's desire to appease his idealised friend is an insufficient means of accounting for his more problematic pronouncements. Belloc's reassuring certainties, whether theological or conspiratorial, merely catalysed the same neurosis over the 'dizziness of identity', in Kristeva's phrase, which led Borges to discern 'something in the makeup of [Chesterton's] personality [that] leaned toward the nightmarish' which he forcibly 'restrained' (84).[22] Unfortunately, in the pre-war years Belloc's seemingly stabilising inoculation against the Romantic grotesque proved more ethically and psychologically imperilling than the disease.

As with the suspicion of the Men of 1914 that the menace of R/romanticism was located as much within themselves as within the culture that they sought to purge, Barr reports that Belloc was 'so dedicated to sniffing out disguised Jews that a rumor began to spread among psychological initiates that he really came from a cosmopolitan family named Bloch' (41). If we consider that at the outset of his journalistic career, Chesterton was initially denied the financially important opportunity to contribute to the *Speaker* on the rather absurd grounds that the literary editor thought his handwriting looked Jewish (see Ward, *Gilbert*, 113), we seem to be dealing once more with a dark suspicion that the rejected site of abjection is somehow bound up with an equally anathematised self. However, the discontents produced by the attempt to purge abjection again manifest themselves in an imitation of the very condition battled against: the shriek attributed to Beit begins to leak into Chesterton's own discourses in the 'note sometimes rising almost to a scream' identified by Maycock.

Inadvertent mirroring is a characteristic feature of abjection, as is 'the shame of compromise' and a sense of 'being in the middle of treachery' (Kristeva, *Powers*, 2)—think of Chesterton's disloyal accusation of disloyalty in his uncompromising attack on Cadbury. Kristeva notes that the abject also finds expression in apparent paradoxes such as 'the criminal with a good conscience' (*Powers*, 4). This echo of Chesterton's 'Innocence of the Criminal' not only evokes the ingenuous amorality of Flambeau, but also the more sinister easy conscience of Ezza Montano, thus returning us to Chesterton's tacit self-criticism for having naïvely engendered an invasion narrative that had drawn ungovernable energies into the culture. If the aesthetic invasion of 'The Paradise of Thieves' takes on politico-economic overtones in the 'Head of Caesar', the accusation of fiscal impurity that Chesterton directs towards Ezza is another critique into which he appears to half-consciously implant himself. The return of Father Brown in 1913 after two years' silence was inspired partly by a need to ameliorate the financial uncertainty caused by his self-sabotaging resignation from *Daily News*: the purity of his ideological scruples had led him into the mechanistic production of popular literature for a marketplace that he increasingly distrusted.

Hesketh Pearson asserted that, in later years, whenever Chesterton's secretary 'told him that money was needed he would say: "Very well. Let us write a 'Father Brown' story"' (214), while V.S. Pritchett claimed that he eventually 'affected to despise' the stories (325). In this sense, when Ezza notes that '"this damned farce will soon be over"', there is a subtle hint that Chesterton's modernist villain might be voicing his creator's own impatience. This self-reflexive gesture carries an unconscious echo of Lewis's meta-textual manipulation of Evan Royal, who expresses irritation over the development of the plot of *Mrs. Dukes' Million*, while implicitly bemoaning his creator's woebegone financial position:

> "instead of living interest, always this same cold, mechanical scheme of robbery—always this blight of sordidness! I believe my employer to be a remarkable man, he has somewhat the same feelings as myself. But like many artists he is unfortunately poor, and is compelled always to do only the things that pay, and alas! also, only in the way that pays. What we are doing now need not be a pot-boiler, but it is. What a terrible thing poverty is!"
>
> (117)

After his breakdown, Chesterton abandoned *Father Brown* for a further decade, before finally reanimating the priest in the mid-1920s as a means of funding a newly inaugurated journal that he hoped to mould ethically in his own image: *G.K.'s Weekly*.[23] The same period saw the re-emergence of Lewis after a period of relative creative quiescence, caused largely by a protracted struggle to recover emotionally from the experience of war. On 4 August 1914, a month after the publication of *BLAST*, and in the same month as the publication of 'The Duel of Dr. Hirsch', Britain had declared war on Germany. In the years that followed, any fugitive sense of psychological affinity that had pertained between Chesterton and the Men of 1914 seemed swept away by a conflict that opened up a further, apparently decisive, cultural fault line. Chesterton now found himself in the pro-war camp, and his former role as sceptical interrogator of the motives for modern war was appropriated by the younger generation of the avant-garde, not least Lewis. Chesterton later recalled that his breakdown had been immediately precipitated by an attempt to 'write a reply to Bernard Shaw', and that his eventual recovery was signalled by a renewed urge 'to answer Mr. Bernard Shaw' (*Autobiography*, 249/52); similarly, when Lewis finally re-emerged in the mid-1920s, it was to Chesterton that he turned once more as a philosophical and aesthetic foil.

Notes

1 See Ker, 325–26, for further details. Chesterton claimed, rather unconvincingly, that the verse was merely a misunderstood expression of contempt for the hot drink, and argued in his autobiography that the association was merely 'a comic coincidence' (*Autobiography*, 274). The chiming repetition of 'cad' suggests otherwise.
2 Chesterton's other regular employer, the *Illustrated London News*, kept his weekly 'Our Note Book' column running through thick and thin from 1905 to 1936.
3 Mr. Square is a character in Henry Fielding's *Tom Jones* (1749). Jepson recalls the club opening 'about 1908' (134) and that while Bentley 'attended most meetings' (138), Chesterton 'did not come often' (135) because he found the atmosphere uncongenial.
4 Marinetti consistently praised Marconi (see *Futurist*, 62) and was influenced by d'Annunzio before later denouncing him (see Marinetti, 'We Abjure', 94). Marconi later became the focal point of Cecil Chesterton's libel case (see Ward, *Gilbert*, 283–309).
5 The pound signs were most probably used as an improvised means of deleting text—a suggestively unorthodox method of doing so under the circumstances.
6 Although it initially seems unlikely that Chesterton could have heard of Lewis's unpublished mystery novel, one begins to wonder during an exchange between Dorian and Ivywood in *The Flying Inn*, during the 'Post-Futurist exhibition', in which Dorian argues that if Ivywood 'wake[s] up to-morrow and you simply are Mrs Dope, an old woman who lets out lodgings at Broadstairs' (227) he will not have progressed to a new stage of evolution, but simply changed neutrally into an entirely different identity. Of course,

there is every possibility that Lewis's unsuccessful literary activities might have reached Chesterton's ears through the gossip of the Square Club.
7 This confrontation seems to have been engineered deliberately by Holbrook Jackson, whose editorship of *T.P.'s Weekly* began in the week in which Chesterton's article was published. See Kane, 14.
8 Stapleton persuasively links Shaw's attack to Chesterton's resignation, arguing that it caused him to suffer 'a rare sense of humor failure' *Christianity*, (112). Shaw's remark was made in the period between Gardiner's letter to Chesterton, in which he hoped that the matter could be resolved, and Chesterton's reply, in which he made it clear that it could not.
9 The recipient was Joan Nicholl (see Ward, *Return*, 170). Although the precise date of composition is unknown, it must have been written after the summer of 1928, when the Chestertons first met the Nicholls (see Ffinch, 319). Ward demonstrates that Chesterton was prodigious in producing parodic texts that he passed on as gifts to friends of the family (see *Return*, 89, 120, 139–41, 145, 182).
10 These terms derive from Lewis's later polemic, *The Old Gang and the New Gang* (1933), which applies his mature sense of the arbitrary antagonism of the generational divide to the political sphere.
11 When later discussing the novel, Chesterton alluded to a suggestive linguistic nearmiss: in nightmares 'even the faces of friends may appear as the facesof fiends' (*G.K.C.* 204)
12 See Hofer for an illuminating discussion of 'The New Cake of Soap', which highlights the implicit connection to Chesterton's buttocks—the couplet 'superimposes on the reader's consciousness the multiple "cheeks" of its subject's face, buttocks, and style' (473).
13 Stock reports that Pound declined a potential introduction when both men were in Granville's in 1917; around the same time, Pound spotted Chesterton in the street and almost introduced himself, but decided against it at the last moment (199).
14 Found in his doctoral thesis, *Abstraktion und Einfühlung* (1907).
15 Humbert Wolfe also satirises Chesterton's anti-Semitism in *Shylock Reasons with Mr. Chesterton and Other Poems* (1920) and *Lampoons* (1925).
16 Chesterton believed uncomplicatedly in Dreyfus's innocence before he met Belloc (see Ward, *Gilbert*, 117); He explained his increasing scepticism to have arisen from the behaviour of Dreyfus's supporters in the British press, whom he considered to have effaced certain complicating factors in the case. See Stapleton, *Christianity*, 45–46, 141, for an account of Chesterton's enduring puzzlement and incoherence over the Dreyfus case.
17 Many years later, Chesterton praised 'the remarkable talent of Miss Rebecca West' (*CW* 21:609).
18 Ker reports that he was most probably seriously ill from September onwards (see 355).
19 Bentley displays anti-Semitism in the diary, noting on 21 January 1905: 'Don't like Outlook sympathisers. Compatriots altogether too smart and splendid—too many Jews' (MS.Eng.misc.e.870). Nonetheless, in an earlier entry from his time at Oxford, he demurs at Belloc's position on Dreyfus, as articulated in a university debate: 'Belloc vehemently anti-D[reyfus]. Had no case at all I think' (3 Dec. 1898; MS.Eng.misc.e.869).
20 The 'friend' is tentatively identified as Belloc by Stapleton (*CDN* 8:6). Chesterton discusses the same incident in 'The Fountain of Honour' (*DN* 13 Jan. 1912), noting that he incurred a black eye from the eventual fight (*CDN* 8:5). George Albu was a German-born magnate, whose fortune was made in the diamond and gold mines of South Africa.

21 Hulme had occasion to quote Chesterton with implicit approval in his early writing, before gradually displaying greater disdain for him over time (see Blissett, 'Chesterton and English', 134).
22 Beerbohm corroborates this view with an evocative metaphor: 'Chesterton and Belloc were men whose minds were vast and hospitable houses, with little dark closets in the attic into which—there were so many other rooms, gay and sunny—you didn't have to go' (*Conversations*, 231).
23 One new story had appeared in December 1923 and another two in February and May 1924 before a sudden glut from April 1925 onwards, a month after the first edition of *G.K.'s Weekly*.

5 *Le Mob c'est Moi*
1920s Modernism as Monstrous Carnival

> [W]e are all in the melting pot. I resist the process of melting so have a very lively time of it. I know if I let myself melt I should get mixed up with all sorts of people I would sooner be dead than mixed into.
> —Lewis, *Blasting and Bombardiering* (15)

> It was like some frightful fancy-dress ball to which the two mortal enemies were to go dressed up as each other. Only the fancy-dress ball was to be a dance of death[.]
> —Chesterton, 'The Dagger with Wings'
> (*Nash's Magazine* Feb. 1924; CFB 473)

In November 1914, the War Propaganda Bureau published *The Barbarism of Berlin*, a political tract assembled from articles that Chesterton had recently written for the *Daily Mail*, in which he sets out his case for supporting Britain's involvement in the war.[1] Again, anxiety over the breaking of bonds is central to his argument. For Chesterton, the 'Prussian' invasion of Belgium threatened the precept of reciprocity upon which he considered civilisation to rest, a point that he makes in the text via a gaming analogy:

> It is said that the Prussian officers play at a game called *Kriegsspiel*, or the War Game. But in truth they could not play at any game; for the essence of every game is that the rules are the same on both sides.
> (45)

Characteristically, he centres his argument upon the dangers of solipsism, arguing that Germany's gesture of geopolitical exceptionalism derives from an 'egomania that is honestly blind to the fact that the other party is an ego', exacerbated by a 'quite unproved [theory of] racial supremacy [which] is the last and worst of the refusals of reciprocity' (60). In these circumstances, Chesterton considered withdrawal from support for the aggressed nation to represent an irresponsible advertisement of ethical and martial weakness.[2]

As this *précis* suggests, notwithstanding Chesterton's surprising willingness to collaborate with the periodical he had once derided as the 'Daily Jingo' ('Empire Day and England', *ILN*, 13 June 1908; *CW* 28:120), *The Barbarism of Berlin* presents a comparatively restrained and cogent argument in defence of the international rule of law, largely free of the shrill notes found elsewhere in his contemporaneous writing. Although his support of Britain's involvement remained unswerving, it was far from gratuitously belligerent in comparison to many of his journalistic contemporaries, and he privately applauded Bentley's journalism on precisely this point: 'I think you have done something to save this country; for the *Telegraph* continues to be almost the only paper that the crisis has sobered and not tipsified' (20 July 1915; BL MS Add. 73191 fol.227). The degree of anxiety that Chesterton felt over the conflict is reflected in the breakdown that he suffered in the same month in which *The Barbarism of Berlin* was published. His autobiography implies an intimate correlation between the public and private crises: on the night of his collapse he had gone 'to Oxford [to] speak to a huge packed mass of undergraduates in defence of the English Declaration of War. That night is a nightmare to me; and I remember nothing except that I spoke on the right side' (248–49). He subsequently fell into a coma, was confined to bed until the following Easter, and only began to return to public life in the summer of 1915, just as Lewis was preparing to publish the second and final edition of *BLAST*: the 'War Number' (20 July 1915).

In the editorial of *BLAST 2*, Lewis derides the Chestertonian position on the conflict, scoffing at 'articles by our leading journalists proving that "the Hun" could only see his side of the question, that this was the peculiarity of "the Hun," whereas other races always saw with their neighbours' eyes' (6).[3] Nonetheless, he goes on to concede that the Germans 'dismissed Treaties as "scraps of paper"' (15), while mimicking Chesterton's gaming metaphor: 'They are inclined to gouge out people's eyes preparatory to bowling, to prevent them making a run' (9). An equally confused dynamic of concord and dissent emerges on the question of culture. While making the Chestertonian complaint that Germany is 'saturated with the mechanical obsession of history' (5), Lewis finds this flaw to be manifested most notably in 'official' German culture's preoccupation with the perpetuation of 'the Romantic Spirit' (5), which has recently resulted in the 'vulgarity and democratization' (10) of its culture.

In contrast, he conceives 'unofficial' (5) German culture to be a terrain populated by a species of Teutonic Vorticist: 'a tribe of detached individuals [...] Genial and Realistic Barbarians' (6). He explains that 'the Kaiser, long before he entered into war with Great Britain, had declared merciless war on Cubism and Expressionism' because he despises these movements' 'puritanism' (9); it is '[u]nder these circumstances, apart from national partizanship, [that] it appears to us humanly desirable that Germany should win no war against France or England' (5). If each writer backs intervention and desires a British victory, Chesterton's appeal is to the preservation of a common democracy; Lewis's to that of an aesthetic elite. Elsewhere in *BLAST 2*, the reader is advised that the next edition will feature 'Notes from the Front by Wyndham Lewis' (7). However, a third issue never emerged. Lewis spent much of the following year in protracted negotiations over the role that he might play in the conflict while finishing work on *Tarr*. He was finally mobilised on 24 May 1917 and went on to serve as a bombardier on the battlefields of Ypres and Passchendaele during some of the bloodiest stages of the conflict. In his absence, Pound ensured the continuing publication of his work, helping to arrange the serialisation of *Tarr* in the *Egoist* in 1916–17 and running a series of Lewis's 'Imaginary Letters' in the *Little Review* in 1917.

The third instalment in this series is 'The Code of a Herdsman', a text that encapsulates Lewis and Pound's hyper-elitist vision of high modernism, as well as the paradoxically 'low' language through which this vision was conveyed. In a parody of the instructive tone of an army information booklet, Lewis's imaginary correspondent conjures a ribald conflation of military horrors with the emissions of the herd, while evoking both protective and pantomimic forms of mask: '[s]tagnant gasses from these Yahooesque and rotten herds are more dangerous often than the wandering cylinders that emit them. See you are not caught in them without your mask' (Lewis, 'Imaginary', 7). Though not published until 1917, 'The Code of a Herdsman' was originally composed in 1915 as a projected component of 'The Crowd Master', a narrative fragment set during the mobilisation, which Lewis used to close *BLAST 2*.[4] The texts' common origin is reflected in their shared preoccupation with the troubling relationship between the isolated individual and the infective, deathlike masses, with the abject imagery of 'rotten herds' emitting 'stagnant gasses' complementing the view expressed in 'The Crowd Master' that with mobilisation the popular 'NEWSPAPERS [...] smell carrion' (*BLAST* 2:94).

Two years later, and just four days after Lewis arrived at the front, Chesterton made an uncharacteristically rash public intervention in the conflict that would have confirmed Lewis in his view of the press. On 10 June 1917, Chesterton lent his name to a newspaper campaign to conscript the avant-garde sculptor, Jacob Epstein—a figure lauded by Lewis and Pound in *BLAST 2*—following his successful application to be exempted from the call-up on the grounds that he was an 'irreplaceable artist' (Downer, 191; Rose, J., *Demons*, 106). The exemption was subsequently overturned, and although Epstein never saw action (having suffered a nervous breakdown while still in England), his modernist peers were outraged by this intervention (see Downer, 192). The sculptor and

198   Le Mob c'est Moi

Vorticist fellow traveller Henri Gaudier-Brzeska had already been killed in action, and Hulme followed on 28 September 1917. Pound was increasingly incensed that important artists and thinkers were being killed in a war that he considered groundless, and it is perhaps no coincidence that he furnishes Quinn with a report of Lewis's military activities in the same letter in which he mounts his most sustained attack upon Chesterton (see Pound, *Letters*, 170–71).[5] Although Pound's vituperations predate the Epstein affair, the incident helps to further contextualise the intemperate and apprehensive tenor of the remarks made later in 1917 and into 1918 by Pound and Eliot, with their refrains of horrified disgust and invocations of warlike imagery. For the Men of 1914, Chesterton had progressed from mere cultural irritant to existential threat.

It is difficult to defend Chesterton's actions in the Epstein affair, not least because he had allowed himself to be duped into participating in a malevolent prank: the campaign against Epstein was instigated by Horace de Vere Cole, the architect of the Dreadnought Hoax, who had a personal grudge against the artist (see Downer, 185–86). Though it is highly unlikely that Chesterton would have been conscious of this unedifying background context, it is hard to avoid the suspicion that his critical faculties were dimmed by the presumption of Epstein's Jewish heredity. In mitigation, one might note that Chesterton's beloved brother was now at the front—he had taken over Cecil's editorial duties at the *New Witness* in 1916—and was dead the following year. In a pre-war response to a letter from Wells attacking his brother, Chesterton had conceded archly that the journalists of the *New Witness* were more conspicuous for their 'courage and honesty than acquaintance with the hierarchy of art'.[6] He framed his intervention in the Epstein case in similar terms, while again drawing on the precept of reciprocity: 'It seems to me a dangerous principle to say that because a man is a great artist he should not share the ordinary responsibilities of citizenship' ('Art and War – Noted Sculptor's Exemption', *Illustrated Sunday Herald* 10 June 1917; qtd. in Rose, J., *Demons*, 106).

Lewis makes a comparable point in his memoir, *Blasting and Bombardiering*, in a bitterly ironical account of the manoeuvrings of his more well-connected literary contemporaries:

> The 'Bloomsburies' were all doing war-work of 'national importance', down in some downy English county, under the wings of powerful pacifist friends; pruning trees, planting gooseberry bushes, and haymaking, doubtless in large sunbonnets. One at least of them, I will not name him, was disgustingly robust. All were of military age. All would have looked well in uniform.[7]

(184)

However, the key difference is that Lewis was on the frontline in 1917 and Chesterton was not; he was intervening in another man's fate from the safety of his bureau. A decade later, the historic offence re-emerged in Lewis's writing in oblique form, merging with his increasingly fevered sense of victimhood at the hands of interwar aesthetes and populists alike, to produce a surrealistic nightmare presided over by a distinctly Chestertonian ogre.

A Sanguine Grin Fiercely Painted On

Recalling his pre-war artistic skirmishes in *Blasting and Bombardiering*, Lewis depicts the conflict as a biographical threshold moment; a progress from innocent play-fighting to brutal reality: 'Life was one big bloodless brawl, prior to the Great Bloodletting' (35). His account of a public spat with Marinetti in June 1914 seems poised upon the cusp of this transition, parodying a journalistic dispatch from the front line to evoke a mock-militaristic spirit of play:

> Marinetti brought off a Futurist *Putsch* about this time. [...] I counter-putsched. I assembled in Greek Street a determined band of anti-futurists. [...] After a hearty meal we shuffled bellicosely round to the Doré Gallery. Marinetti had entrenched himself upon a high platform, and he put down a tremendous barrage in French as we entered. Gaudier went into action at once. [...] He was sniping at him without intermission [...] The Italian intruder was worsted.
>
> (*Blasting*, 33)

Elsewhere in the memoir, Lewis describes his view of the war as that of a 'group of people crossing a bridge. The bridge is red, the people are red, the sky is red. [...] And the principal figure among those crossing the bridge—that is me—does not know that he is *crossing* anything, from one world into another' (2). Lewis saw this Blakean passage from innocence to experience not only as a schismatic moment of mass cultural disillusion, but also as the catalyst for the construction of a more sober personal bearing. As Michael Hallam has recently noted, Naomi Mitchison considered Lewis's development of his 'enemy' persona after the war to be 'a constructive pose, a satirical mode meant to enable genuine social reflection and change. Lewis, the enemy of infantilism, wanted all society to grow up' (74). Thus, the obstreperous delinquency that he had first developed as a playful method of commercial self-identification became reconceived as a pedagogic weapon. Complementarily, the swaggering sartorial games that he had played with Dostoevsky's texts in the pre-war years were superseded by a darker mimicry, as he added the embittered 'underground man' to his retinue of Dostoevsky characters—in

Blasting and Bombardiering, he refers to the early 1920s as his 'underground' (212) period.[8]

When Lewis resurfaced in 1925, it was with a substantially expanded literary portfolio, incorporating an enormous multiform text bearing the title *The Man of The World*. When it became evident that this project was not commercially viable, the contents were broken up into a series of separate texts, including *The Art of Being Ruled* and *Time and Western Man*. Each of these tracts includes a disparaging reference to Chesterton. While *Time and Western Man* features the fleeting 'ferocious and foaming [...] dogmatic toby-jug' jibe, *The Art of Being Ruled* fleshes this image out at length, elaborating a nightmarish vision of 'the cackling and grimacing humorousness [...] of this strange individual' (Lewis, *Wyndham Lewis*, 158), whose 'cartoon-like John Bull physique' is topped off with 'a sanguine grin fiercely painted on' (157). The whole 'compose[s] a sinister figure such as you would find, perhaps—exploiting its fatness, its shrewdness, its animal violence, its blustering patriotism all at once—in the centre of some nightmare Bank Holiday fair' (Lewis, *Wyndham Lewis*, 157). This imagery substantially ramps up the rhetoric of 'Futurism and the Flesh', building to a near-hysterical conception of Chesterton as a physically threatening presence. It also reads as an uncannily accurate gloss on the figure of the Bailiff in *The Childermass*, a satirical fantasia begun in 1925 as a fictional complement to *The Man of the World* and finally published as a stand-alone text in 1928.[9]

The Childermass follows the posthumous journey of Satterthwaite and Pullman, two fallen soldiers, through the 'city of the dead' (38) to an appointment with the Bailiff, a sinister demagogue who holds the salvation or damnation of his deceased petitioners in his power. The second half of the novel records their spectatorship of a confrontation between the Bailiff and his 'legendary enemy' (153), the 'classical' (55) figure and ostensible authorial surrogate, Hyperides. Lewis's otherworldly landscape operates, in part, as a fantastical rendering of the battlefields of the war, with Pullman compelled to maintain constant vigilance over a hostile terrain in which individuals and objects discorporate at a moment's notice, and inexplicable shifts in the landscape cause continual disorientation. Pullman embodies the stoic, longsuffering serviceman, the 'staunch attendant' (19) of Satterthwaite, who represents, in turn, the capitulation of the adult to a state of infantilism, inhabiting a 'baby-world' (112), in which he clings needily to Pullman, 'a shell-shock waggle' (19) to his walk.

Satterthwaite is explained to be a 'victim of the devils of Humour, of war pestilence and famine' (59), a conflation of the horsemen of the apocalypse with a superintending Satanic comedian that merges Eliot's vision of Chesterton at the head of 'the forces of death' with Lewis's rendering of his 'cackling and grimacing humorousness'.

Hyperides later launches a tirade against the Bailiff's '"cackle"' while lamenting his influence over '"this helpless mass of bottle-sucking cannon-fodder"' (158). If Lewis wanted all society to grow up, it was Chesterton whom he blamed for placing it in this state of arrested development. Accordingly, the 'death-gas' (59) in Satterthwaite's throat becomes conflated with laughing gas when Pullman describes the effect of watching the Bailiff perform: '"You'll simply die with laughing [...] you'll absolutely choke yourself with cheeky fun"' (123–24). Once more, the cheek of a Chesterton is advanced as the locus of wider societal malaise.

The Bailiff is an incessant parodist—when an interlocutor scratches his head, he mimics him 'in comic time' (203)—and a highly self-conscious practitioner of sartorial travesty: '"I am compelled occasionally to modify my appearance, of course"' (181); '"[n]ature I can promise you had no part in my appearance. It was entirely my own idea"' (267). His many pseudonyms include 'Trimalchio' (72), the gluttonous, drunken feaster in *The Satyricon*, and 'Bailiff-Bacchus' (184), both prototypes for Chesterton's carnivalesque persona, while a moment of hilarity causes him to 'roll about majestically, like Dr Johnson upon the seashore' (294).[10] Elsewhere, the Bailiff is rendered as a buffoon-figure: 'a thick light of servile buffoonery illuminates his face' (138); later he boasts, '"I always behave 'beneath my dignity', it is my most settled policy"' (287). Like Chesterton, he propagandises for the physical grotesque in opposition to '"the snobbery of the old deep-seated dualism which attached disgrace to physical nature"' (150), and explains that '"we oppose the flesh of Demos [to] the idea of the Greek 'gentleman'"' (264). In other words, the Bailiff is a caricatural composite of all of Chesterton's most publicly recognisable attributes and attitudes.

The riotous courthouse arena within which the Bailiff performs not only recalls the scenes of the theatrical mock-trials in which Chesterton participated throughout the period, but also his putative location at the centre of 'some nightmare Bank Holiday fair' in *The Art of Being Ruled*.[11] In the novel, this inversion of festivity into a 'gay carnival of fear' (*Blasting*, 68), as Lewis later described the build-up to war, is elaborated upon in lurid detail: the Bailiff resembles 'Uncle Punch amongst his jolly children [...] all grinning vulpine teeth, puckered eyes [... and] rubicund cheeks', with a 'great red bud of [a] head to adumbrate the bludgeon-skull of the Britannic Bulldog, all of a portly piece [...] with Mr Bull's bluff eye' (151/189). His 'pseudo-infant-minions' (159) listen rapt as he expounds his anti-intellectual dogmas '[f]loridly fiercely and irresponsibly' (309)—recall Chesterton's 'sanguine grin *fiercely* painted on' (my emphasis). Of course, sanguine not only means optimistic or (John) bullish, but also 'bloody, bloodthirsty' (Barnhart, 956), from the Latin *sanguineus*.

The Bailiff's patronage of his 'jolly children' carries a linguistic echo of Lewis's claim in *The Art of Being Ruled* that Chesterton thrilled at the idea of 'a jolly old war (with all the usual accompaniments of poison gas and bombs)' (Lewis, *Wyndham Lewis*, 158). Although this is, to say the least, a distorted and reductive interpretation of Chesterton's response to the conflict, Lewis's attentiveness to the implications of language remains acute. As Michael Wood has noted, Chesterton 'love[s] words like "fierce" and "furious", and he delights in images of irrevocable violence' (8). His epic war poem, *The Ballad of the White Horse*, was said to have been carried by servicemen in the trenches, and Lewis's imagery implies the potential irresponsibility of such sanguinary literary enthusiasms in a figure who enjoyed such substantial public influence.

When the Bailiff explains to his audience, '"[y]our rights, gentlemen, can be summarized in one word, Petition. You are petitioners, for better or worse"' (209), the imputations of irresponsibility and bloodthirstiness seem to go further, since Lewis would surely have been aware of Chesterton's response to Epstein's petition to be excused from service. In an apt revenge upon a figure who had delighted in exposing the hidden narratives of modernism, Lewis offers a mordant take on Chesterton's frequent recourse to the pantomime transformation scene: when the Bailiff occasionally interrupts his inane capering to authorise executions, the back scene of the military tribunal of Jacob Epstein seems fleetingly to glow through the merry mock-trial of John Jasper.

If we consider Chesterton to be the unspoken presiding genius of *The Childermass*, the novel's title—a reference to the Feast of the Holy Innocents—once more places Chesterton and Lewis in intergenerational conflict. Pullman reveals that another of the Bailiff's pseudonyms is 'Herod' (72), a detail that would seem to situate Chesterton as a modern-day rendering of the quintessential malign father figure, demanding the massacre of all the young males of a generation. By placing Chesterton in the role of an 'autocratic and seemingly omnipotent' (Chapman, 169) arbiter of salvation or damnation, whose principal name invokes the landlord's agents who harassed the penurious Lewis throughout the early 1920s, his resentment of Chesterton's enduring cultural influence becomes compounded with the tincture of fiscal threat and then filtered through Chesterton's support for a war through which he had suffered, to produce a multi-dimensional air of existential injury.[12]

Perhaps Lewis's most damning imputation is that Chesterton is not even an authentic populist. As Hena Maes-Jelinek notes, the Bailiff 'appears to glorify the masses while he actually despises them' (189). When the Bailiff exclaims '"*Le mob c'est moi!*"' (268), the phrase offers a francophone facsimile of Pound's definition of Chesterton as 'so much the mob'. By compelling the Chestertonian figure to reframe Pound's attack in the ironically elevated form of untranslated French, Lewis implies that the Bailiff is, in truth, a highly refined individual—when he first speaks it is with 'a pleasant strong voice of great cultivation' (137)—whose rabble-rousing is a disingenuous and cynical manipulation of the mob, undertaken for dubious personal motives. In another apparent swipe at Chesterton in *BLAST 2*, Lewis had conjured a vision of a disreputable cultural figure whose backing of the war is commercially driven: 'thinking of his rapidly depreciating "shop," [he] says triumphantly. "This War with all its mediaeval emotions" (for it gives him mediaeval emotions) "will result in a huge revival of Romanticism"' (13). A decade later, Lewis portrays this revival as having come to pass, with the Bailiff as its arch-representative. Although the war had been won, the 'Romantic Spirit' of 'vulgarity and democratization' that he had attributed to Teutonic culture had, in his view, triumphed nonetheless, and the underground activities of the German avant-garde under the oppression of the Kaiser must continue in the guise of the Hyperidean '"heretical faction"' (*Childermass*, 257).

The imagery of binary contrast could not, apparently, be more baldly conceived—as the narrator notes, the Bailiff and Hyperides are the 'oldest opposites in the universe' (153). Accordingly, symbols of abjection proliferate once more, as Lewis's urge to ward off any suspicion of resemblance between the idealised self and the anathematised other manifests itself in imagery that merges anti-Semitism with anti-populism.[13] The Bailiff's hook-nose associates him simultaneously with the caricatural Jew and the quintessential popular-cultural figure, Punch: 'a dark-robed polichinelle' (*Childermass*, 131) with 'a hump and paunch' (130), he performs in 'a lofty tapering Punch-and-Judy theatre' (129) embossed with a Star of David. Of course, throughout the era, Punch also lent his name to a popular magazine famous for its irreverent, and frequently philistine, parodies of high art. While the magazine rarely reflected on the ethics of its endeavours, in an article on 'Punch and Judy' (*DN*, 26 Oct. 1907), Chesterton scrutinises the principle of Punch more searchingly, in terms that correspond to Father Brown's Petrushkan rendering in 'The Queer Feet': the character's unlikely victories are 'a genuine historical survival of the old Christian farce, in which the clown or fool had always the best of everybody' (*CDN* 4:332).

If Father Brown triumphs over a topsy-turvy culture that confers abjection upon the priesthood, Chesterton elaborates Punch's similarly despised status in lurid terms: 'The victories of Punch are, indeed, the victories of a violent person, but they are the victories of a hunchback. That is, they are the victories of a grotesque cripple. [...] The whole point of the drama is that one highly ridiculous person with a hump is a match for all the organized forces of society' (*CDN* 4:331). This situation sounds familiar. When Lewis's Hyperidean partisan, Alectryon, argues that 'the Western World [...] is busy erecting a barbedwire-entanglement about a super-caste of Untouchables' *Childermass*, (302), we find Lewis's self-image rendered in strikingly comparable terms of topsy-turvydom: Brown's sequestering in the cloakroom of the gentleman's club is translated into a vision of the 'highbrow' as the lowest caste, a disgraceful cultural presence to be annexed and hidden from view. As with Lewis's parodic warping of *The Man Who Was Thursday* into a condition of perpetual, lawless carnival in *Mrs. Dukes' Million*, he again borrows from Chesterton's fictional landscape only to subvert it, here appropriating Chesterton's use of festive culture as a model for regenerative moral satire, while turning the same principle against his forebear in an act of imaginative scapegoating.

The same edition of the *New Age* that features Bechhöfer's parody of *BLAST* includes a letter to the editor mocking Lewis's article on 'Futurism and the Flesh': 'unless Mr. Lewis can put an end to Mr. Chesterton's powers of speech in some such way, I do not see how in the world he is to avoid being blasted' (Arnold, 311). The correspondent wonders if perhaps Lewis's best option might be to don 'a false nose and a dunce's cap' and counteract Chesterton's capering with practical jokes of his own. If we consider the continuities between the historical Childermass festival and the events of the novel, it becomes clear that this is precisely the strategy that Lewis later adopted. Traditionally, the Childermass is a festival of practical joking involving boy bishops, occurring around Christmas—a context that turns Chesterton's well-known fixation with seasonal revelry to his disadvantage, while also playing upon Lewis's conception of the war as a 'saturnalian [...] serio-comedy' (*Blasting*, 192/207).[14]

Chesterton had highlighted the role of Herod in such festivals himself in the same article in which he praises the mystery play: 'He has made a massacre of children, and been made a figure of fun in a Christmas pantomime for the pleasure of other children. Precisely because his crime is tragic, his punishment is comic' (*Uses*, 100). In Latin cultures, the pranksters of the Childermass are conventionally figured as the *inocentes*, a designation that debars their victims from expressing anger towards them. Amongst the most enduring of these events is the two-hundred-year-old '*Els Enfarinats*' festival, held in Ibi in Alicante, in which a mock *coup d'état* is staged in the form of a flour-fight conducted by figures dressed in military costume (see Taylor). In Lewis's novel, the Bailiff is the victim of a comparable practical joke in which '[t]he powder from [a] snuff box, batted upwards, explodes into [his] face', while a Hyperidean boy bishop 'tugs [his] nose violently this way and that' (235).

The Bailiff responds to such humiliations with rhetoric that implies indulgent sham-indignation towards naughty children—'"You are a damned impertinent young puppy and if I have much more of this nonsense you young ruffian I will have you horse-whipped"' (307)—much as the narrator of *Mrs. Dukes' Million* coddles his criminal gang as an 'army of scamps' (352). In other words, Lewis's fictional demolition of infantilism is powered by the dynamics of a festival that mirrors the 'big bloodless brawl' of his pre-war juvenility, constructed as a revenge upon the 'monstrous carnival of [...] thwarted desires and ambitions' (*BLAST* 2:6) that he perceived the war to represent. His activation of the carnival licence and role-reversals traditional to European festive culture suggests an attempt to get away with attacking the man whose activities he blamed for encouraging the 'great bloodletting' while escaping any risk of retaliation. Because it is conventionally held around midwinter, Childermass Day is traditionally understood to signify the old world giving way to the new. Likewise, the projected triumph of Hyperides over the Bailiff operates as a fictional enactment of the bloodless cultural coup that Lewis hoped to achieve over Chesterton on behalf of the younger generation who had survived the war.

However, in pursuing this self-aggrandising regenerative premise, Lewis would have done well to reflect on a further correspondence between the ritual and the text: in Britain, Childermass has historically been held to be an 'unlucky day [...] for the commencement of any work or task' (Carew Hazlitt, 111). The timing was not propitious for Lewis's interrelated fictional and critical enterprises of the mid-1920s, with their execration not only of Chestertonian populism, but also of the perceived romanticism of avant-garde luminaries such as Joyce and Gertrude Stein. He considered all of these figures to be complicit in the pernicious fashions of the age—Pullman is commonly interpreted to be a satirical portrait of Joyce, since his uncritical approval of the Bailiff accords with Lewis's discussion of his great rival in *Time and Western Man* as possessing an 'unorganized susceptibility to influences' (91). If this phrasing recalls Chesterton's account of the aesthete who is 'all receptiveness, like the flea', Lewis's determination to evade such parasitic receptivity suggests that he may have internalised another criticism that he had received in the pages of the *New Age* in 1914. In the edition of 26 November, Orage surveys the contemporary literary scene and praises Chesterton over Lewis for his capacity to maintain a sceptical distance from contemporary fads: 'I know only a few living authors who have touched the new world of ideas without defiling themselves from a literary point of view [...] Mr. Wyndham Lewis [...] became blood-shot and turgid in the new world of astral experience. [... Amongst] the more fortunate have been Mr. G.K. Chesterton [who] escaped by laughter' ('Readers and Writers', 97–98).

As Charles Sumner notes, *The Art of Being Ruled* inveighs against the 'hypnotic spell of mass culture' (29). Hyperides accuses the Bailiff of practicing the same trick in a manner that serves to confound Chesterton with Marinetti: '"illusionist hypnotist or technical trick-performer [... taking] all the objects of sense [and] softening and confusing them in your 'futurist' [...] alchemy"' (153). One thinks of Frank Kuppner's parody of *The Waste Land,* 'West Åland, or Five Tombeaux for Mr Testoil' (2004), in which William Wootten discerns 'the sound of someone shouting abuse to stop themselves falling back under the mesmerist's trance' ('Fame and Fleabites', *Guardian*, 26 Feb. 2005). Having been accused of credulous modernism in his youth, Lewis was now vaunting an equally full-blooded antimodernism. However, in essaying his own escape by laughter, he attained a state of repudiation too all-consuming either to be philosophically or commercially tenable. Once more, Lewis was discharging himself on both sides, but rather than staking out a distinct space in the cultural landscape, he succeeded merely in isolating himself from virtually all potential venues of support.

Lewis's multi-directional fire helps to explain certain apparent anomalies in the Bailiff's rendering, such as his adherence to Bergsonian *durée*, a philosophical vogue for which Chesterton would have had as little time as Lewis. As Robert Chapman explains, the Bailiff is conceived as 'an incarnation of the *Zeitgeist*' and can consequently 'transform himself into any one of its facets' (173). This composite characterisation has the effect of entangling Chesterton with a crowd of interwar aesthetes in whose literary company he would have been rather surprised to find himself. In a particularly remarkable passage, the Bailiff is gripped by a sudden 'fit' (272), which causes him to channel various voices of romanticism in the cultural air. This results in a complex parodic set-piece in which Leopold Bloom's protestation in *Ulysses*, 'I am a man misunderstood. I am being made a scapegoat of. I am a respectable married man' (583), is given a thematically Chestertonian and formally Steinian makeover: '"I am a respectable jolly Punch-like person who is sadly misjudged [...] I am jolly I am misjudged I am a Punch-like person (jolly and misjudged)' *Childermass,* (273).

As Munton observes of Lewis's linking of Charlie Chaplin to Gertrude Stein in *Time and Western Man*, he treats 'popular discourse [...] as equivalent to contemporaneous "high" culture, because the same underlying forces are' conceived to be 'at work in both' ('From Charlie', 168). In *The Childermass*, Satterthwaite's baby talk results in extended parodies of the Steinian stream of consciousness (see 44), thus locating Stein's work as an expression of the same 'Child-cult' (*Time*, 70) within which Lewis considered Chesterton to have taken a presiding role. Meanwhile, Joyce's polyvocal prose is blamed for breaking down coherent categorisation in a manner that recalls Chesterton's approval of 'the man in the mob [who] has been melted in a monstrous furnace', a disintegration of discrete personality that finds a corollary in the Bailiff's chaotic consciousness. By conjoining Chesterton and Joyce within the Bailiff's fit, Lewis implies that their common promotion of a humanist version of the physical grotesque illustrates a philosophical concordance that is generally overlooked due to their surface stylistic disparity. Recall Chesterton's view of the operation of parody: 'a superficial contrast covering a substantial congruity'. Lewis goes on to impugn the popular-cultural applications of parody, even as he obsessively recurs to it as a critical technique: in a first-person parody of Joyce, the Bailiff boasts of the '"cross-word polyglottony in the which I indulges misself for recreation bighorror"', after which his acolytes delight in guessing which famous author he has been '"doing"' (178).

In an echo of Chesterton's performance of quasi-possession by Marinetti in 'The Futurists', the purpose of the Bailiff's fits of ventriloquism is to highlight the unquestionable distinction of Lewis's style from the mode under attack. However, this parodic urge rebounds upon the satirist in a manner that complicates clear-cut propagandising. Despite his recourse to the prophylactic anti-mask of the Bailiff, we remain ever-conscious that Lewis is responsible for conjuring these voices himself, and seems to take a great deal more enjoyment in the performance than he does in setting forth the dreary diktats of Hyperides, a two-dimensional cipher made to behave with such irksome pomposity that it is hard to avoid the conclusion that Lewis is inexplicably spiking his own guns.

If the narrator seems to be of the Bailiff's party without knowing it, this suggests a disruptive beside-mindedness comparable to Chesterton's half-conscious act of self-sabotage in 'The Duel of Dr. Hirsch. The discontents of Lewis's paranoia over his cultural isolation result in a case of 'surreptitiously backing a rival horse' (*Wyndham*, 43), as Kenner writes of his earlier handling of Kreisler. As with *Mrs. Dukes' Million*, there is also a sense that Lewis has gradually lost consciousness of his original theoretical purpose for constructing the narrative and become immersed ingenuously in the action, an impression heightened by the technique of automatic writing that engenders the Bailiff's fits. As he acknowledges elsewhere, although the 'satirist sets out to destroy what he considers bad [...] the satirist is an artist [... and] may even forget, at times, the end, in his enjoyment of the means' (*Mysterious*, 144).

As these details suggest, the parodic strategies of *The Childermass* ultimately undermine its foundational apocalyptic premise, building to a proliferation of mirror-image resemblances. When the Bailiff claims that his role in parodying Joyce is ultimately that of "rival clown cutting counter capers"' (173), one thinks of Adeline Glasheen's account of the 'mutual [...] flyting of Joyce and Lewis' (167) in the 1920s, as they set about establishing a symbiotic sparring partnership not so far removed from the publicly projected polarity of the Chesterton-Shaw dyad. At one stage, the Bailiff is tasked with voicing Lewis's sense of grievance that Joyce is not sufficiently frank about this buffoonish dynamic, projecting instead a '"genteel canine pathos—he's as bourgeois as a goldmedalled spaniel and he gets as offended when you kick a few tears out of him as though the jest were not on the other leg as often as not"' (178).

There is some justice in this complaint—Dennis Brown notes that Joyce mobilised his cultural allies to initiate a coordinated 'scapegoating' ('James', 36) of Lewis following the publication of *Time and Western Man*—though Lewis's projection of injury is somewhat undermined by his own role as ringleader in the scapegoating of Chesterton a decade earlier. Lewis sets out to expose the fathomless violence that he perceives to lie beneath the niceties of cultural discourse by having the Bailiff perform a nonverbal parody of Joyce's genteel canines immediately after he callously consigns an avant-garde artist to damnation. In a gruesome physical mime of Stephen Dedalus's vision of the godlike, disinterested artist 'paring his fingernails' (Joyce, *Portrait*, 166), 'The Bailiff examines his nails, one contemplative eye foremost, gnaws and prises at their quicks with his flanking teeth' (208). This sanguinary image once more links Joyce to Chesterton—recall that in 'Futurism and the Flesh' Chesterton is pictured demanding the 'impious blood' of a 'painter'. When the Bailiff exclaims, '"I prefer hot-blood to your beastly intellects"' (309), Marinetti is added to the malign melting pot, via an echo of Lewis's earlier speculation over the Futurist's likely response to the war: '[t]here is one man in Europe who must be in the seventh heaven: that is Marinetti. [...] He must be torn in mind, as to which point of the compass to rush to and drink up the booming and banging, lap up the blood' (*BLAST* 2:25).

Nonetheless, Lewis's mockery of Marinetti's childish enthusiasm for 'booming and banging' is mirrored in a parody of *BLAST* implanted by Chesterton within an article on 'The Meaning of Metre': modern 'writers have broken writing to bits to make it explosive [... they] make an explosion, or at least a noise, by some line like, "Burst. Blast. Burst-BLAST back-blasted. Bang!"' (collected in *Common*, 215). Likewise, Lewis's accusation that Chesterton and Marinetti are guilty of irresponsible bombast is a little rich in view of Lewis's speculation in *BLAST* that '[k]illing somebody must be the greatest pleasure in existence' (1:133).[15] If the Chestertonian Bailiff is a 'Britannic Bulldog' and Joyce a deceptively feral 'goldmedalled spaniel', the novel's canine conceit also pre-empts Pound's image of himself and Lewis as a pair of attack dogs. One is reminded of Sewell's observation that Chesterton's criticisms of Wilde appear to be directed at all 'the points at which they seem most to resemble one another' ('G.K. Chesterton', 571). Lewis's account of the 'nightmare bank holiday fair' in *The Art of Being Ruled* situates Chesterton as the focal centre of a whorl of malign activity—a kind of festive Vorticist, whose 'cartoon-like [...] sanguine grin fiercely painted on' is lifted wholesale from Lewis's sinister self-portrait, *Mr Wyndham Lewis as a Tyro* (Figure 5.1, overleaf).[16]

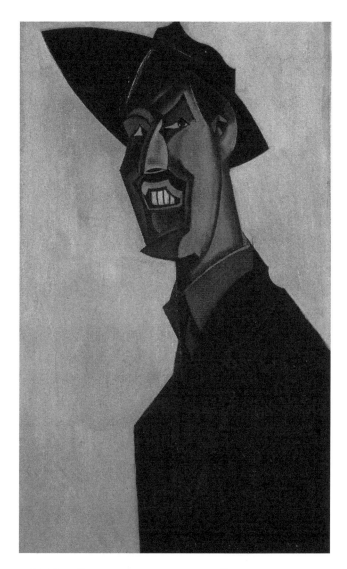

Figure 5.1 Mr Wyndham Lewis as a Tyro, Wyndham Lewis, 1921.

Lewis's explanatory 'Note on Tyros' describes this new genus of 'puppet' in terms that combine the 'flanking teeth' of the Bailiff with the cheerful amorality of Evan Royal: Tyros 'brandish their appetites in their faces [and] lay bare their teeth' as they bask 'in the sunshine of their own abominable nature' (*Tyro*, 2). In this light, Lewis's self-parody as a Tyro, with its rat-like, portcullis mouth, speaks of the process of self-questioning in which he had recently begun to engage—a happier consequence of his exorbitantly self-monitory urge to avoid the slightest lapse of critical detachment.

In addition to Herod and Trimalchio, we learn that the Bailiff occasionally goes by the name of 'Loki' (72), the elusive trickster who had presided over Lewis's early self-image. When Alectryon complains to the Bailiff, '"[y]ou are never the real thing. All your imitations ring false in some particular"' (307), the accusation of ontological slipperiness sets up an antagonistic confrontation between the trapdoor ethos of Lewis's younger self and the alarm at all forms of ethical and existential 'false bottom' (Lewis, *Revenge*, 256) to which his later fiction obsessively recurs. As with Chesterton's tacit auditing of past irresponsibility with his satire of the Harlequinesque Ezza Montano—a trickster-spiv who would not look out of place amongst Lewis's Tyros—the Bailiff is a simultaneous critique of the other and the self, exemplifying Kenner's argument that 'what [Lewis] had learned in 1914 [was] not that the illusionist, the virtuoso of semiotics, commanded the time's imagination—he knew that already; rather that this being's activities were dangerous' ('Mrs.', 87).

In one sense, the 'novice' status of the Tyro—from the Latin *tiro*, meaning 'young soldier' (Barnhart, 1180)—suggests a sympathy with the traumatised *inocentes* of the conflict. Like the manipulated serviceman, the Tyro is 'a puppet worked with deft fingers, with a screaming voice underneath' (*Tyro*, 2). However, these brutish figures are as much villains as victims. As with Pound's 'full-throated' satire, their screams are poised uncertainly between terrified repulsion and violent self-assertion. When Hyperides refers to the Bailiff as a 'showman-puppet' (158), he echoes the parenthetical designation attributed to the Tyro portrait, *Tyros (Showmen) Breakfasting* (1921), as well as Lewis's near-contemporaneous discussion of his authorial surrogate, Kerr-Orr, as a 'showman', in the foreword to the collected *Wild Body* stories. As Kerr-Orr explains to the reader, 'I know more about myself than people generally do. For instance I am aware that I am a barbarian [...] when I laugh I gnash my teeth' (5). When Kerr-Orr articulates the ethical formula that he has established as a means of 'working off my alarm at myself' (6), he chooses a term that Lewis had applied both to Chesterton and the Bailiff: 'I am a large blond clown', in whom 'all the *fierce*ness has become transformed into *laughter*' (*Wild*, 5; the first emphasis is mine). Lewis recommends a comparable process of domestication in *Men Without Art* (1934), via another canine metaphor: 'I approve of a barking man myself—I find that I have less occasion, with his likes, to anticipate a really serious bite' (114).

Lewis's view of himself and Joyce as rivalrous clowns reflects his urge to transform the modern public stage and, beyond it, modern life itself into a vast carnivalesque arena, in which a sublimation of literal violence through satire is conceived as the ethical complement to a grotesque democratic universality: '[e]veryone should be laughed at, or else *no one* should be laughed at' (Lewis, *Men*, 109). Lewis's tentative testing of this immersive precept upon himself in *The Childermass* proceeds organically from the novel's conceptual grounding in carnival. If the festive licence established by the Childermass conceit privileges the author to scapegoat cultural antagonists without censure, it also establishes a liminal space in which cultural allegiances can be turned topsy-turvy, thus sanctioning a more disruptive form of temporary amnesty.

As Len Gutkin observes, a certain air of 'self-parody attends the depiction of Hyperides's cult, a preposterous wannabe Hellenic militia' (Gutkin). Not only is the villainous Bailiff part-Lewis, the Lewisian Hyperides is part-fool. Nonetheless, while Hyperides' suspiciously immoderate protestations of anti-romanticism suggest a tacit self-reflexive commentary upon Lewis's contemporaneous critical enterprises, the fictional rendering finally leans closer to the humourless dogmatism of Hulme and the bumptious histrionics of Pound. Pullman's dismissive view of Hyperides' faction as a '"highbrow circus"' (145) not only mirrors Lewis's account of the Bailiff's entourage, but also anticipates his later irreverent portrayal of the 'Pound circus' (264) in *Blasting and Bombardiering*, an ensemble in which Hulme was the 'philosophic turn' (99), occupying the role of 'clownish sophist' (107). A comparable mirroring attends to Lewis's remark that 'Ezra is a crowd' (86) in *Time and Western Man*, a near-exact replication of the Bailiff's assessment of Hyperides: 'you are a crowd, not a person' (289). Elsewhere, the Bailiff labels the followers of Hyperides a '"mob"' (267), to which the insurgent responds, as one pinching his brow to stave off a migraine, '"[t]ry not to refer to them as mob and as herd"' (268).

Blasting and Bombardiering takes pains to infantilise Pound's role as coordinator-in-chief of the avant-garde:

> [He] was never satisfied until everything was organized. He had a streak of Baden Powell in him [...] we were not the most promising material for Ezra's boyscoutery. But he did succeed in giving a handful of disparate and unassimilable people the appearance of a *Bewegung*. (252)

Time and Western Man explodes this projection of unanimity, reserving its most blistering critique for Pound: 'a sort of revolutionary simpleton' (54). If this phrase overturns the conventional satirical rendering of Pound as an artificial fool, conceiving him still-more insultingly as a 'natural' (*Time*, 90) one, this characterisation is subtly prefigured in *The Childermass*, when the novel's simpleton figure, Satterthwaite, begins fleetingly to channel Pound. In view of the latter's epistolary attacks on Chesterton, Satterthwaite's stream of consciousness explanation of his abhorrence of the Bailiff suggests that Lewis could be recapitulating a private conversation from memory: '"With me it's a sensation under the skin to be near him fills me [with] loathing, I fear him but much more still I have that toad-reaction, for me he's a toad oh everything that's disgusting"' (72).

Lewis and Pound had quarrelled during the early stages of the novel's composition when Pound attempted to broker a 'W.L. art supplement' (*Pound/Lewis*, 6 June 1925, 149) in the Parisian modernist periodical, *This Quarter*, while tactlessly dismissing the likely commercial interest to be aroused by the non-fictional components of *The Man of the World*. In the exchange that followed, Pound suggested that the only valid reason for producing works of 'controversy or criticism' was to assist in 'advertising one's friends, or their supposedly vendible products' (Pound, *Pound/Lewis*, 12 May 1925, 148). This is precisely the reverse of the policy that Lewis had now begun to pursue, and he scorned Pound's professed position in his reply, while noting that simply because 'in the glorious days of Marinetti [...] we were associated to some extent in publicity campaigns, that does not give you a mandate to interfere [...] in my career' (Pound, *Pound/Lewis*, 11 June 1925, 150). Pound then weighed in with the blunt assessment that Lewis should stop behaving like 'a God Damn fool' (Pound, *Pound/Lewis*, 152), a pay-off for which Lewis would later extract compensation by inserting Pound into the role of the revolutionary simpleton, as represented fictionally by the blustering Hyperides and the imbecilic Satterthwaite.[17]

If Pound's ongoing professions of commercial cynicism now jarred with Lewis's self-perceived ethical sobriety, it is also probable that, as the only member of the Men of 1914 to have seen active service, he had grown to resent Pound's piratical aesthetic posturing. *Time and Western Man* melts Pound into Marinetti, articulating Lewis's suspicion that 'from the start, the histrionics of the milanese prefascist were secretly much to [Pound's] sensation-loving taste' (58). Appropriately enough, this conjunction finds expression in imagery appropriated wholesale from 'The Paradise of Thieves', as Lewis attempts to transform Pound into a composite of the cynical Futurist, Ezza Montano, and the play-acting poet, Muscari, thus redacting himself from Chesterton's satire entirely. While Ezza's commercially motivated duplicity finds expression in Lewis's reference to the 'discrepancy between what Pound said [...] and what he did' (*Time*, 55), Chesterton's account of Muscari's 'fire-eating' (*CFB* 200) flavour of the 'troubadour' (*CFB* 189) is translated into Lewis's view of Pound as a 'half-impresario, half-poet' (*Time*, 54) with 'fire-eating [...] trouvere airs' (*Time*, 55). By offloading these echoes of Chesterton's satire onto Pound, Lewis pursues a self-acknowledged bid to 'dispel [the] associations in people's minds' between himself and his erstwhile colleague, in order to secure the 'success of my new enterprise' (*Time*, 54), a candid revelation that ironically recalls nothing so much as the irrepressible ingenuousness of Muscari.

Lewis's repudiation of the high-modernist enterprise in the mid-1920s was inextricably bound up with his sense, from 1922 onwards, that he was the least commercially successful of the Men of 1914, as *The Waste Land* and *Ulysses* made Eliot and Joyce world-renowned and Pound's advisory role in the texts' construction and publication lent him the air of a literary oracle. Rather than Hyperides, the character who most closely resembles the Lewis of the 1920s is the obdurate avant-garde painter, Joseph Potter, a member of neither faction, whose aesthetic precepts are mockingly indulged by the Bailiff: '"he's a pure creature of the surface [...] Never to see anything except the outside—what an admirable trait"' (207). In the same passage, the Bailiff hints at Lewis's effaced identification with popular culture—he considers Potter to be 'as pleased as Punch' (207) with himself—while the financial motivation for *Mrs. Dukes' Million* lurks behind the brickbats of the Bailiff's acolytes: 'dirty pot-boiler!' (205). When the Bailiff explains to Potter that his occupation in the present society has been poorly chosen, since '"[w]e much prefer bank-clerks to painters"' (201), one wonders to whom Lewis could possibly be referring. Despite Eliot's continuing, loyal propagandising for Lewis's work, his ascendency rankled. As we will see, this pre-eminence was initially fostered by a projection of opposition to Chesterton quite as stringent as that essayed by Lewis, but also by more subtle attempts to distinguish himself from Lewis and Pound as the era progressed.

Performing Professionalism

In the period between the publication of *Prufrock and Other Observations* (June 1917) and the end of the war (November 1918), Eliot set about establishing the unmistakable dissimilarity of himself and Chesterton in the pages of the *Egoist*. These sallies include the stylistic rebuttal in which Chesterton appears at the head of the forces of death, only to be repelled by the linguistic vitality of the Men of 1914. A month earlier in April 1918, again under the pseudonym Apteryx, Eliot had disparaged Chesterton's critical, rather than creative, efforts in a coquettishly titled article, 'Professional, or...', which places Chesterton alongside Alice Meynell as a duo of 'non-professionals in criticism', who pursue 'a kind of style fleshed and boned in irrelevance' (61).[18]

While this critique takes its cue from Pound's contemporaneous condemnation of Chesterton's advocacy of amateurism, Eliot's line of attack should also be understood in the context of conservative reviewers' criticisms of *Prufrock* for introducing apparently irrelevant burlesque matter into the serious business of poetry. In embattled response, Eliot began to perform the role of unimpeachably severe judge of relevance, possessing a critical sensibility that resembled, in Gross's words, 'a kind of sieve: the finer it is, the more it rejects' (250). In constructing this persona, Eliot found a convenient foil in Chesterton's purposefully scattershot digressions upon cultural ephemera, against which he sharpened his reputation for scrupulous professionalism and, in so doing, created the contrary taste by which he was to be relished. As 'Professional, or...' stresses, 'we must learn to take literature *seriously*' (61), a schoolmasterly admonition that might be taken as a rebuttal of Chesterton's introduction to the indiscriminately titled *All Things Considered* (1908), in which he had confessed that 'I cannot understand the people who take literature seriously', advising such individuals 'to keep clear of this book. It is a collection of crude and shapeless papers' (1).

If the last phrase calls to mind the implicit conceptual link between the formlessness of Chesterton's physical and textual bodies, Eliot's peculiarly corporeal turn of phrase, '*fleshed and boned* in irrelevance', hints at the comparable, if contrary intertwining of Eliot's sartorial and rhetorical stratagems in this period. His famously severe dress served as a rebuke to the flamboyance favoured by Chesterton, deliberately rejecting the role of rumbustious romantic poet. An early reviewer, perhaps alluding to Chesterton's performative façade, had accused him of possessing 'an irrelevant moustache' (Anon, Unsigned, 296); Eliot made it his business to leave no such traces of irrelevance about his own flesh and bone. As Auden later attested, Eliot taught by example that 'it was unbecoming to dress or behave in public like the romantic conception of a poet' (Eliot, *Letters*, 4:385n1). Instead, Eliot actively *disguised* his poetic calling by dressing as a city gent, first in the role of dutiful banker and later as venerable publisher. This performance externalised a rejection of bohemianism that mirrored his associates' eschewal of Bloomsbury's effete aestheticism: Lewis had advised his fellow Vorticists to avoid '[v]elvet jackets and floppy ties' (Kate Lechmere qtd. in Meyers, 52) at all costs. However, it also constituted a rejection of the rakish swagger of the early publicity photographs of Lewis and Pound. Instead, Eliot's outfitting projected a pared-down sobriety—an *embodiment* of the professionalisation of literary criticism that he advocated.

As this performative gesture implies, despite the ostensible asceticism of Eliot's post-war *mien*, the exaggerative extreme to which he took the sartorial conceit also conveyed a subtle spirit of play, comparable to that of Beerbohm 'overdress[ing] for the part' that he chose to play, or Ezza Montano contriving to appear both 'startling and commonplace'. In an echo of the comedy double act of contrasting types rehearsed by Chesterton and Shaw, and Wilde and Beerbohm before them, if Lewis and Pound were the impudent, imprudent swashbucklers, then Eliot was the urbane utilitarian, parading a paradoxically histrionic understatement. One thinks of Chesterton's description of the magistrate in *The Ball and the Cross*, who 'looked like a gentleman, and yet, somehow, like a stage gentleman' (*CW* 7:58). For David Chinitz, Eliot 'certainly overplayed [his] character; crucially, though, he overplayed it with tongue in cheek [...] He was almost, one might say, a caricature from the music-hall stage' (176). In this respect, the famous photograph of Eliot posing outside the offices of Faber and Gwyer is best read as a self-parodic manipulation of his public image. As Ackroyd notes, his attendance to every last cliché of the dress code of the upright English man of the world is 'almost too perfect to be entirely serious—as if he were posing in fancy dress' (153) (Figure 5.2, overleaf).

Figure 5.2 T.S. Eliot photographed by Henry Ware Eliot, 1926.

If this produces an uncanny resemblance to a mannequin, the Chaplin-esque bowler hat and cane also suggest a plainclothes clown, exhibiting the 'ostentatious secrecy' that Chesterton considered 'the soul of Mumming'. In this sense, the outfit can also be read as an arch modern update of the pre-Enlightenment sartorial principles espoused by Chesterton. As with the ethos that underpins mummery and pageantry, Eliot's extravagant performance of conformity renders him 'something other and more than himself': the emblematic type of the modern publisher. Eliot alludes to Chesterton's passion for pageantry in another of his 1918 broadsides in the *Egoist*, his famous essay 'In Memory of Henry

James' (Jan. 1918): 'What matters least of all is [James's] place in such a Lord Mayor's show as Mr. Chesterton's procession of Victorian Literature' (1). In suggesting that Chesterton's critical study, *The Victorian Age in Literature*, displays an outmoded, stolidly linear conception of literary history, Eliot impugns a text that he had privately recommended to his extension lecture students (see Schuchard, 35), in order to publicly advertise his contrary advocacy of a writer renowned for his perplexing textual circumlocutions.

Eliot's remark also encourages the reader to infer Chesterton's disapprobation of James. In fact, *The Victorian Age in Literature* finds praise for the 'real originality [of] artistic design' in James's 'very finest literature', even as Chesterton has fun burlesquing his prose convolutions as the 'Obstacle Race Style, in which one continually trips over commas and relative clauses' (*CW* 15:521). In a fitting counterblow to such high-spirited raillery, Eliot goes on to execute a rhetorical parody of Chesterton, manipulating the latter's taste for paradox to his own ends. Having coined the famous witticism that James possessed 'a mind so fine that no idea could violate it' In Memory', (2), Eliot follows this counterintuitive compliment with a criticism of Chesterton by comparison, again expressed in terms of ostensible paradox: 'Mr. Chesterton's brain swarms with ideas; I see no evidence that it thinks' (2). As Philip Furbank has noted, this was 'a most unfair, and rather Chestertonian, remark' (20). In an exemplary parodic gesture, Eliot invokes Chesterton's rhetorical voice in order to criticise it.[19]

This barb also discloses a comingling of nonsense and parody in Eliot's responses to Chesterton. The allusion to the *Alice* books in the title of Eliot's early notebook, *Inventions of the March Hare*, not only associates the author with an insane inhabitant of Wonderland, but also with a symbol of regenerative vitality, much as Pound liked to compare himself to the wily trickster, Br'er Rabbit. In *Through the Looking Glass*, Alice closely prefigures Eliot's terms in the 'Henry James' essay, remarking of 'Jabberwocky' '"it seems to fill my head with ideas—only I don't exactly know what they are!"' (*Annotated*, 197). Immediately after this episode, she encounters the disdainful Rose: '"It's *my* opinion that you never think *at all*," the Rose said, in a rather severe tone' (*Annotated*, 203). Trading on the resemblance of Chesterton's more bluff pronouncements to Anthony Burgess's later description of Alice as a 'very pert "Fiddlesticks!" Victorian miss who will stand no nonsense' ('Nonsense', 20), the Henry James essay figures Eliot as a fantastical Carrollian creature, bamboozling his victim with disorientating wordplay, while conveying a paradoxical sense that Chesterton is too mentally disordered to rationalise the radical aesthetic gymnastics of the artists occupying the Wonderland of literary modernism.

However, a further textual correspondence to his phrase, 'I see no evidence that it thinks', suggests that Eliot's attack may also carry the seed of a more subtle urge to surmount antagonism. If we consider that four years later, Eliot's accusation of mental intractability would be echoed by the female interlocutor in *The Waste Land*, conventionally understood to represent Vivien Eliot addressing her husband, a sense of Eliot's subconscious identification with Chesterton, as well as the edge of hysteria underlying his apparently urbane criticism, comes to the fore:

> What are you thinking of? What thinking? What?
> I never know what you are thinking. Think.
>
> (*PTSE* 1:59)

Coates has argued that, in the James essay, 'Eliot meant think ideologically, pulling no punches, accepting no qualifications, checks or balances and no humour, in the statement of an intellectual position' (*Chesterton*, 243). However, in the context of the wider argument of the essay, it seems much more plausible that the opposite is true—he is regretting the alleged absence of a Jamesian capacity for psychological subtlety, or nuanced private life, in Chesterton, as opposed to the factory-like churning out of public 'ideas' like so many new cakes of soap. As he argues elsewhere in the essay, in a nonsense exposition that makes its point through a deliberate category mistake, '[i]n England, ideas run wild and pasture on the emotions; instead of thinking with feelings (a very different thing) we corrupt our feelings with ideas' ('In Memory', 2). When paired with its echo in *The Waste Land*, Eliot's witticism, delivered in a ventriloquistic rendition of Chesterton's rhetorical voice, comes to read as a frustrated call for personal sympathy from a writer stifled by the artificially polarised terms of the game of public controversy that he had belatedly joined. Throughout his early critical responses to Chesterton, Eliot subtly draws himself into the critique in turn: it is *we* who 'corrupt our feelings with ideas', *we* who 'must learn to take literature *seriously*'.

Much as Eliot's marionette in 'Humouresque' possesses a '[h]alf bullying, half imploring air' (*PTSE* 1:237), the twin textual correspondences to *Alice* and *The Waste Land* in the Henry James essay reveal an apparently contradictory bipolarity of subconscious motivation—the first inscribing an urge for detachment, the second for sympathy. This vacillation presents a further concordance with the ambivalent dynamic of parody, which Sewell finds to rely 'on close emotional kinship (a kinship that itself involves a compelling pull toward sameness and a death of subjectivity) before ultimate self-assertion (a pull toward difference)' (*Field*, 276–77). Ackroyd observes of Eliot's broader rhetoric that 'the instinct to conform and the instinct to stand apart' frequently 'merged in a subtle, almost ironic, imitation of those around him' (88–89). In the present instance, Eliot selects terms that project an explicit opposition that meets the need to display public allegiance with his friends, while implicitly retaining a loophole that satisfies a personal need to retain an equivocal ambiguity.[20]

Although Lewis later deprecated this trait as a proof of Eliot's '*pseudo* everything' (*Men*, 77) temperament, the dynamic at hand is not dissimilar to his own placarded segregation of the Bailiff and Hyperides, which is offset by a simultaneous inscription of more subtle correspondences and cross-currents. In both cases, the quicksilver effect is not so much connotative of the nihilistic false bottoms of the Romantic grotesque, as a more constructive urge to dynamically traverse the poles of adherence and departure, informed by a tacit understanding that 'truth is tricky', in Chesterton's phrase. Even Eliot's apparently clear-cut, polarising image of Chesterton at the head of the forces of death is embedded with a subtle get-out clause, since the rider on a white horse is the only horseman not uncomplicatedly associated with destruction, being variously interpreted either as wicked or righteous, and even as a Christ-like figure (see Morris, 101). Likewise, in *The Childermass*, Pullman explains that although 'Satan' is another of the Bailiff's pseudonyms, '"even some madman said Jesus' (72), a conflation of antagonist and saviour that mirrors the more overt metamorphosis of the Wildean Sunday in *The Man Who Was Thursday*.[21]

The nuances of this double-voicing were not always clearly audible to early critical adherents of high modernism. By 1925 Eliot had increasing cause to regret the success of his performance of professionalism as a self-constructed trap, a dawning comprehension that was accompanied by a shift in his private and public allegiances. In an article on Browning published towards the end of his tenure at the *Daily News* ('Robert Browning', *DN* 7 May 1912), Chesterton discusses the poet's reception in terms that closely prefigure Chinitz's account of the violence done to Eliot's corpus by the embalming procedures of his scholarly adherents, who 'needed' the 'portentous, the elitist, the mandarin Eliot [...] and so produced him' (189). For Chesterton, the Browningites do their damage 'by turning a poem into a puzzle', with the result that 'Browning's legacy is not even Browningesque; it is not a dilution of his wine; it is a sort of deadly antidote' (*CDN* 8:72). As Chesterton explains, the 'whole fate of Browning in letters depends upon the battle which is still going on between Browning and the Browningites. If he conquers he will live; if his admirers conquer he will certainly die' (*CDN* 8:72). Eliot's increasing awareness of the applicability of this dilemma to his own cultural position finds complex poetic expression in 'The Hollow Men'.

Here's the Comedian Again

If, as Kristeva argues, a symbol of the abject is 'a friend who stabs you' (*Powers*, 4), abjection would seem to have been the prevailing characteristic of Eliot's friendship group in 1925. In January, he suddenly contracted the animus of Lewis, following his failure, due to illness, to provide a prompt reference on Lewis's behalf to a house agent. The offence coincided with Eliot's publication in the *Criterion* of a piece of art criticism by Clive Bell, one of Lewis's numerous Bloomsbury enemies, a concatenation of events that drove Lewis to the extravagant conclusion that Eliot was engaging in acts of personal 'treachery' (Lewis, *Letters*, 149) against him.

In the same month, a more public accusation of treachery was levelled against Eliot by Pound with the publication of *A Draft of XVI Cantos*. At the conclusion of 'Canto XIV', the first of Pound's scurrilous, carnivalesque travesties of Dante—the 'Hell Cantos'—he launches a stinging attack upon Eliot, situating him amongst the 'unamiable liars' (*Cantos*, 63), a phrase that conflates a withholding of camaraderie with an act of deception.[22] Eliot's direct appearance in the text is prefaced by an extremely unamiable parody of the lines from *The Waste Land* that run 'If there were rock / And also water / And water' (*PTSE* 1:68):

> Bog of stupidities,
> malevolent stupidities, and stupidities,
> the soil living pus, full of vermin,
> dead maggots begetting live maggots,
> [...]
> the air without refuge of silence,
> the drift of lice, teething,
> and above it the mouthing of orators,
> the arse-belching of preachers.
>
> (*Cantos*, 63)

As with the Bailiff's parodies of the Joycean stream of consciousness, the free-associative quality of Pound's lines, which lends them a certain protean force, mimics Eliot's own method of automatic writing when composing 'What the Thunder Said', while the echoes of Eliot's 'dead mountain mouth of carious teeth' and 'not even silence in the mountains' (*PTSE* 1:68) situate Pound's satiric survey of Hell as a parasitical revision of Eliot's own visions. There seems a certain irony in Pound traducing a text that he helped bring to birth, particularly by furnishing lurid amendments to a textual body that he had originally pared down. The ambivalence of this dynamic is rendered explicable by the emergence of Eliot at the head of the preachers, as '.....m Episcopus, waving a condom full of black-beetles' (*Cantos*, 63).[23]

The allusion to Eliot as '[Possu]m Episcopus' suggests that his burgeoning religious conviction, first confessed to an incredulous Pound in 1923 (see Gordon, *T.S. Eliot*, 210) in terms of a fear of *going to Hell*, was viewed by the latter as an act of infidelity, betraying the premises upon which their friendship was initially founded in a manner that drew Eliot ideologically closer to the interdicted figure of Chesterton. The invocation of Eliot in the 'Hell Cantos' follows directly on from that of Chesterton, who is also portrayed as a treacherous figure—one of the 'betrayers of language', 'the press gang [...] who had lied for hire' (*Cantos*, 61). It is tempting to read into this line an allusion to the Epstein affair: the phrase 'press gang' imaginatively conjoining jolly Fleet Street journalism with a method of coercing reluctant individuals into military service.

In a letter sent to Pound between the publication of the 'Hell Cantos' and 'The Hollow Men', Eliot hints at his tentative alignment with Chesterton, advising Pound to omit 'The New Cake of Soap' from a projected collected edition of his verse—a suggestion that Pound ignored (see Eliot, *Letters*, 28 Oct. 1925, 2:767).[24] Eliot was delicately probing the boundaries of the friendship. Referring to *The Waste Land*, Gordon observes the peculiarly self-effacing nature of 'Eliot's submissiveness to Pound's idea of the poem' (*Eliot's*, 116). His diffident dedication of the poem to Pound—'*il miglior fabbro*' ('the better craftsman'; *PTSE* 1:53)—is suggestive, since 'dedication' is a key factor in the formation of friendship groups, connoting as it does the state of being 'devoted to an aim or vocation; having single-minded loyalty or integrity' (Thompson, 351). These qualities, emphasised by the allegiance rituals of undergraduate societies, are literalised in the dedications affixed to the works of Eliot and Chesterton: *The Waste Land* to Pound, *The Napoleon of Notting Hill* to Belloc, and *Greybeards at Play* and *The Man Who Was Thursday* to Bentley. Nonetheless, as we have seen, the public avowal of loyalty often masks considerably more ambivalent private feelings.

Eliot's shifting allegiances help to explain Hofer's observation that while 'Chesterton was Pound's first public enemy in the field of cultural production [... his] eventual replacement in that role [was] Eliot' (464). Much as Joyce's increasing embrace of abject materiality constituted, in Pound's view, an aesthetic offence that left him messily implicated as the author's sometime advocate, Eliot's first intimations of religious conversion placed Pound in ambivalent ideological relation to his most successful protégé. Accordingly, the 'Hell Cantos' revisit Eliot's association of Chesterton with the 'forces of death' in order to suggest that the poet has latterly swapped sides, assembling an array of images of pestilence and sterility to situate Eliot as the source of the malaise that he deprecates. While the juxtaposition of the physical 'teething' of lice with the verbal 'mouthing of orators' mirrors Lewis's orally-focused anxieties, Pound's imagery of incontinence and contagion closely recalls that which he and Lewis had previously employed when stigmatising Chesterton as dribbling and scum-like. Likewise, the preachers' 'arse-belching' suggests a conflation of mouth and bowels comparable to Pound's punning execration of Chesterton's 'cheek', as well as Pound's own verbal emission of 'Merde!' in the splenetic, culturally partitioning verses of *BLAST 2*.

One thinks again of Mason's attempt to crystallise the self-evident distinction of Chesterton and Eliot: the 'popular bowels and clerkly head' of British culture. As Marnie Parsons explains, Bakhtin considers these ostensibly polarised regions to correlate as sites of admittance that undermine detached subjectivity: 'the genital regions are not the only regions that interact with, and affect, the world. The senses [...] may also be construed as points of intersection' (94). By invoking this intersection of corporeal gates in a text that brings Chesterton and Eliot into affiliative proximity, Pound laments the breaking down of the cultural barriers that he had so diligently set about erecting to replace the 'walls of Jericho' at which Brodzky had imagined the Men of 1914 blasting away. In a letter sent to Simon Guggenheim in 1925, Pound recalled counselling the young Eliot that because he was not 'as explosive as Lewis [...] he'd better try a more oceanic and fluid way of sapping the foundations' (31 Mar.; qtd. in Chace, 220). With his petulantly insistent revision of 'water' to 'stupidities', Pound seems to belatedly repent this guidance, perhaps reflecting upon a similar lesson to that which tacitly informs 'The Paradise of Thieves': the ultimate incapacity of cultural satirists to circumscribe the activities of the agents of disruption that they unleash.

Given the strength of Pound's attack in 'Canto XIV', it is particularly ironic that by 1925 the air of synergistic 'ventriloquism' that he and Eliot had 'mutually cultivated' (Stillman, 244) in the preceding decade had led them to become associated in the public consciousness as a double act, 'seeming to join two persons, elusively, as one' (241), as Anne Stillman puts it. If this image calls to mind Shaw's 'pantomime elephant', the Chesterbelloc, the comparably politic foundation of the Eliot-Pound hybrid rendered it just as unwieldy a public contrivance. Eliot was becoming increasingly alarmed by Pound's intemperance, which mirrored the 'partisan viciousness' (Wells, 131), that Wells deprecated in Belloc. In contrast, Eliot's prudent *politesse* in dialogue with other factions, from Chestertonian conservatives to socialite aesthetes, became a source of irritation to his increasingly embattled colleagues. Whereas Lewis and Pound had discharged themselves on both sides, a sense arises that the pair considered Eliot to be paid on both sides: a double agent in the Vorticist camp.

In view of Pound's consignment of Eliot to Hell, one wonders if Lewis is tauntingly referring to their friend's public attack in his truculent correspondence with Eliot in March 1925, when he claims that 'the devil has you by the heel' and notes that if his suspicions over Eliot's conduct are correct he need not 'tell you where to go for you will be there already' (Lewis, *Letters*, 154). Lewis's paranoia had now brought the pair's relationship to breaking point, with Eliot exasperatedly denying any involvement in an 'intrigue' or 'plot' and appealing to him, in an echo of Chesterton's youthful advice to Bentley, to be 'convinced by your own senses' (Eliot, *Letters*, 23 Mar. 1925, 2:612) on the matter. This dispute simmered throughout the rest of the year, while Lewis also pursued his quarrel with Pound over the latter's interference in his publishing affairs. When Pound finally initiated a *rapprochement* after three months' silence, Lewis updated him with the news that Eliot seemed 'very peculiar and ill' (Pound, *Pound/Lewis*, 12 Sept. 1925, 152). Eliot had perhaps been brooding on the degeneration of the old fraternity into a morass of private mistrust and public recrimination, as he completed work on the final version of 'The Hollow Men'. While the Vorticists of 1914 had come across as exhilarating real-life manifestations of the vivacious comedian of 'Suite Clownesque', by 1925 Lewis and Pound more closely resembled the 'haranguing spectres' that torment the vulnerable marionette of 'Humouresque'.

Other intimates were also taking public potshots. Vivien Eliot's satire of a London literary gathering, 'Fête Galante', appeared in July 1925, published by Eliot himself in the *Criterion*. Written under the Conradian pseudonym, Fanny Marlow, the sketch not only takes aim at doyens of Bloomsbury such as Roger Fry, but also includes a thinly-disguised portrait of Eliot, in the role of an 'American financier' (558) who doubles as 'the most marvellous poet in the *whole world*' (562). This 'unsatisfactory' figure 'only smiled' (558) and has a 'strange appearance': a 'thickly powdered' (558) face and 'lips a little reddened' (559). This detail would seem to allude to rumours that Eliot had lately taken to applying grey-green make-up to lend his complexion a cadaverous pallor (see Ackroyd, 136–37), in a histrionic exhibition of the dress-body-mind aggregate.

If Eliot felt that he had been plunged back into the purgatorial social nightmare of 'Humouresque' in this period, it is appropriate that when taking cryptic leave of his erstwhile comrades in 'The Hollow Men', he does so by reintroducing his old puppets, the 'weak' marionette of 'Humouresque' and the mocking 'comedian' of 'Suite Clownesque'. In doing so, he satirises the cultural endeavour upon which his friendship group had been founded, while drawing himself, his collaborators, and his bohemian audience into the range of criticism in a manner closely comparable to Lewis's contemporaneous methodology in *The Childermass*. This context comes to light when the poem's free-verse sections are read in ironic counterpoint with the two parodies of the nursery rhyme 'Here we go round the mulberry bush' that bookend the final section. These skits were the last components to be added to the poem, thus postdating Eliot's quarrel with Lewis, and the publication of Pound's 'Hell Cantos' and Vivien Eliot's 'Fête Galante'. In the first rhyme, Eliot replaces the mulberry bush with a cactus:

> Here we go round the prickly pear
> Prickly pear prickly pear
> Here we go round the prickly pear
> At five o'clock in the morning.
>
> (*PTSE* 1:83)

The timing of this dance is conventionally understood to be the hour of Christ's Resurrection, thus juxtaposing Eliot's newly discovered faith, and his consequent sense of personal regeneration, with a bathetic rendition of the cultural regeneration that he had previously thought immanent within the 'living English' of his prickly pair of associates. The 'mulberry bush' rhyme is thought originally to derive from a fertility ritual, and Eliot's recourse to the children's song has often been discussed as an allusion to his broader view of the enervation of the epoch. Chinitz argues that the poem represents the 'culmination of a recurring theme' in Eliot's work: 'The impossibility of resurrecting a defunct ritual' (87), which would merely represent 'an exotic confection for the delighted palates of literary faddists' (86), reducing 'sacred rites [...] to children's games' (123). While this assessment is convincing, there is also a strain of self-interrogation within the critique: the Men of 1914 had travestied the sacred rite of the scapegoat ritual as a game of commercial advancement, while Eliot's esoteric corpus was at increasing risk of becoming an exotic confection offered up to an exhausted literary culture: a poetic accompaniment to Marinetti's polyrhythmic salad. In Vivien Eliot's party scene, the American poet-financier looks on inscrutably as the participants are 'organis[ed] in a ring', in which '[e]ach member [... is] linked to the next by a bonbon held between them' (560). Having been implicated within Vivien's satire, Eliot found a means of manipulating her image to his own ends in his complementary critique of the circle-dancing smart set six months later.

Vivien's cadaverous rendition of the illustrious poet accords with Kenner's account of the slow drift towards calcification that seemed to grip Eliot as he became increasingly assimilated into the mainstream of literary culture: 'the vitality dwindle[s] in his prose as he grows, between the *Egoist* and the *TLS*, more and more like the thing he was pretending to be' (*Invisible*, 179). This danger would have become increasingly clear to Eliot as his visions began to be reflected back to him in the revisions of others, not only in the fairground mirror of satirical parody, but also in the inadvertently comic surplus productions of the many acolytes that he was beginning to accrue. As Ackroyd reports, in the course of the 1920s a 'cult of "The Waste Landers" developed [...] The poem was widely imitated by young or aspiring poets [...] "It became such a plague that the moment the eye encountered, in a newly arrived poem, the words 'stone', 'dust' or 'dry' one reached for the waste paper basket"' (Brian Howard qtd. in Ackroyd, 128).

Chesterton highlights an example of this phenomenon in an article on 'The New Poetry' (*ILN*, 30 Jan. 1926), which centres upon a discussion of the verses of Ernest Walsh, recently published in *This Quarter*, the same journal that had been the focus of Lewis's quarrel with Pound.[25] Chesterton is somewhat baffled to find Walsh's poetry 'bound up in the same volume with works by Mr. James Joyce and Mr. Ezra Pound, whose notions we may regard as quite false or unphilosophical, but who are men of thought and reading, who generally mean something by what they say' (*CW* 34:36). Conversely, Chesterton is nonplussed by Walsh's account of his acts of 'worship' before 'stone images' (*CW*

34:33) filled with blood, and has fun drawing out the nonsense possibilities of this conceit, listing a series of comparable category mistakes: 'the ink in icebergs, or the beer in bicycles, or the champagne in Bradshaw's railway guide' (*CW* 34:35–36). In a follow-up essay ('More about Modern Poets', *ILN*, 6 Feb. 1926), he argues that this 'sort of stone image is avowedly an Aunt Sally. Nobody could help laughing at it, unless he were morbidly careful only to laugh when he was told to by Mr. Ezra Pound' (*CW* 34:38).

Lewis went on to make precisely the same points in *Time and Western Man*, discussing *This Quarter* as a proof of the degeneration of the avant-garde, finding Walsh's verses to be 'abominably foolish' (63) and expressing astonishment at discovering 'Ezra Pound, as patron saint, at the heart of all this profuse and meaningless word bath' (59).[26] While Lewis's critical tract demotes the once vibrant 'discriminating Element' to the role of 'discriminating parasite' (85), in *Men Without Art* he withdraws even the capacity for discrimination, arguing that Pound can no longer differentiate between 'writers of very great intellectual power—say Mr. Joyce' and writers possessing 'no interest whatever' (67). Since Eliot had complained to Quinn in 1923 that he felt compelled to 'keep an attitude of discipleship' (*Letters*, 4 Oct. 1923, 2:236) towards Pound, despite reservations over his judgement, Eliot's public allegiance to the high priest of the new movement placed him in disquieting proximity to these less than flattering bedfellows.

Walsh's worship of uncertainly animate totems is also rather close to the bone in view of Pound's explanation of how he came up with Eliot's nickname, 'Old Possum', as an ironic tribute to his ability to 'appear dead while [...] still alive' (qtd. in Hofer, 480). Elsewhere, Pound argued that Eliot's success in establishing cultural authority rested upon 'disguising himself as a corpse' (qtd. in Chace, 221), an ostensibly metaphorical assessment that takes on a peculiar literalism in the light of Eliot's face-painting habits. If Eliot was coming to resemble an uncannily petrifying human statue, Pound's insistence on the point suggests that the 'Hell Cantos' might be understood as a rather Chestertonian attempt to translate psychological unease into ethical instruction, via a Bergsonian warning of the dangers of lapsing into 'a certain rigidity of body, mind and character'. If so, Eliot heeds this warning at Pound's expense in 'The Hollow Men', in which the introductory collective noun conveys a double-edged allusion both to the Men of 1914 and their subsequent copyists:

> We are the hollow men
> We are the stuffed men
> Leaning together
> Headpiece filled with straw. Alas!
>
> (*PTSE* 1:81)

Ackroyd notes that *The Waste Land* had been 'sung and chanted by undergraduates' (119) in the years immediately following its publication: in one sense, Eliot's opening lines can be read as an arch invitation to his undergraduate chorus to join in with a rather unflattering new variation on an air. However, when understood in the context of Eliot's increasing sense of distance from his former allies, this marching song for an ineffectual generation not only conveys an exasperated throwing up of the hands at the dull-wittedness of his charges, but also a retrospective sense of the futility of the machinations of the Men of 1914 themselves. The near-instantaneous decay of the chorus mocks its own invocation of community, confirming Chesterton's contention that in the modern age, '[p]oetry has become more than normally individualistic. The individualist can write a song; but not a song with a chorus' (CW 21:606). It also hints at the contemporaneous dissolution of Eliot's circle into paranoid whisperings, ironically juxtaposing the collective pronoun, the watchword of innumerable avant-garde manifestos—'we fling our challenge to the stars', 'we discharge ourselves on both sides'—with the simultaneously comradely, conspiratorial, and enervated phrase, 'Leaning together'.

The sense that Eliot's critical gaze is directed towards his immediate peers becomes still clearer when the mulberry bush rhyme's travesty of fertility ritual is read in conjunction with the subtly deprecatory allusions to Lewis and Pound inscribed within the sections preceding it. When the narrator discusses his anxiety to avoid a meeting in Part II of the poem, his account of the strategies necessary to achieve the required detachment not only includes adopting the 'deliberate disguises' that Eliot had cultivated in his earliest work, but also '[b]ehaving as the wind behaves' (*PTSE* 1:82). In 'Work in Progress', and later *Finnegans Wake*, Joyce peppers the text with references to 'wind' as an allusive means of mocking Lewis, a pun on *Wynd*ham and his 'blast' of hot air (see Glasheen, 166–68) that recalls the ribbing of 'WYNDY LEWIS' in the *New Age* in 1914.[27]

In mimicking this pun, Eliot sets up a dialogue between the former self who had spent the preceding years frequently behaving as Lewis behaved—espousing an austere Hulmean classicism while manipulating the trapdoor ironies of the Romantic grotesque—and the present Eliot who has begun to apprehend the sterility of these methods, exchanging Hulme's 'dry, hard' strictures for the vitalising rainwater that penetrates 'all impermeables' in Joyce's contemporaneous parody of *The Waste Land*. In correspondence with Strachey three years earlier, Woolf had aired her perplexity at Eliot's appreciation of the physical grotesque, placing him in league with a young man carbuncular in a scornful assessment of *Ulysses*: 'Never did I read such tosh [...] the scratching of pimples on the body of the bootboy at Claridges. [...] And this is what Eliot worships' (Woolf, *Question*, 24 Aug. 1922, 551).

If Eliot's repeated recourse to 'stone images' (*PTSE* 1:82) in 'The Hollow Men' hints at the un-regenerative endgame encoded within Hulme's arid vision of the 'properly classical poem', the phallic travesty of Eliot's invocation of the prickly pear harks back to the self-confident Vorticist era in which he had conceived the work of his friends to be the lone site of fertility in a cultural desert. This was the period in which Gaudier-Brzeska had sculpted his celebrated 'Hieratic Head' of Pound. During its composition, Pound boasted to Dorothy Shakespear that 'Brzx's column gets more gravely beautiful and more phallic each week' (Pound, *Ezra Pound and Dorothy*, 10 Mar. 1914, 323), while Lewis later termed it 'Ezra in the form of a marble phallus' (qtd in Kenner, *Pound*, 256) and recalled viewing it from the apartment in which he was first introduced to Eliot (see *Blasting*, 285).

Others perceived a less than adulatory message in the artefact's penile structure. Horace Brodzky, an acquaintance of both Gaudier-Brzeska and Pound, claimed that the piece was carved 'by way of disapproval and in contempt of Pound' (60), while Ford—its first owner—emphasised the sculptor's 'great sense of the comic' ('Henri Gaudier: the story of a low tea-shop', *English Review*, 1919, 297). When sitting for the piece, Pound had himself noticed that the artist's studio was littered with sculpted 'parodies' (Pound, *Gaudier-Brzeska*, 51). It is perhaps in this spirit that we should interpret Eliot's lines:

> This is the dead land
> This is cactus land
> Here the stone images
> Are raised, here they receive
> The supplication of a dead man's hand
> Under the twinkle of a fading star.
>
> (*PTSE* 1:82)

When read in combination with the parody of the 'mulberry bush' rhyme, also set in cactus land, the link to Gaudier-Brzeska's raising of stone images conjures up the somewhat burlesque vision of the Men of 1914 dancing around the sterile stone effigy of Pound's phallus, while a dead man's hand, presumably that of 'Old Possum' himself, proffers a grotesque parody of youthful supplication. In *Time and Western Man*, Lewis argued that Pound was not quite the embodiment of vitality that he claimed: 'an intellectual eunuch', he 'never loved anything living as he loved the dead' (87) and was perhaps 'only pretending to be alive for form's sake' (57). In this sense, Eliot implies that if he is indeed a petrified possum, it may be a result of unwisely reaching out to Pound. The word 'mulberry' comes from the Greek *moros*, meaning 'a fool' (Evans, I., 736)—a derivation of which Eliot is likely to have been aware and willing to deploy to poke fun both at Pound, in the implicit role of surrogate mulberry bush, and at himself, as capering acolyte.

With this self-implicating pratfall, Eliot embraces the role of buffoon and pointedly abjures the guise of trickster. In Aldington's later prose satire, 'Nobody's Baby: A Mystery Story' (1932), Pound is portrayed in the slang-phallic guise of Charlemagne Cox, a 'parody of a god' (*Soft*, 109)—specifically, 'a bad and rather greasy copy of the Hermes of Praxiteles' (126)—a would-be trickster who boasts of possessing '"exceptional potency"' (123). Like the primitive mercenaries of Vorticism, Cox is 'a barbarian clown' with 'a sort of dammee-I-will-NOT-be-good' demeanour (*Soft*, 133), who charges 'rich boobs' (107) extortionate fees simply for a private audience, while 'request[ing] that he shall not be annoyed by applause during the performance of Works of Art' (109). If Cox's forename conveys an air of *charl*atanry, the narrator notes that his fiancée has been charmed by the 'lanoline Hermes profile, and couldn't see the fool for the god' (*Soft*, 121).

These echoes of Chesterton's portrayal of Ezza Montano as a fraudulent travesty of Hermes' son, Autolycus, the 'King of Thieves', are more subtly mirrored in Eliot's setting of images of 'wind' and 'stone' within the 'twilight kingdom' (*PTSE* 1:82) of 'The Hollow Men'.[28] The name, Hermes, is etymologically tied to 'stone' (see Guirand, 133)—a 'herm' is a 'stone pillar with phallus and head of Hermes on it' (Glasheen, 126). Due to an etymological ambiguity, the name is also associated with 'the wind' (Glasheen, 125) and 'the idea of movement': Hermes 'was either a god of the twilight or of the wind' (Guirand, 133). Accordingly, 'Windy' Lewis also conceived himself as a descendant of Hermes. Proverbially, Hermes is the protector of Herdsmen and carries a winged staff.[29] Likewise, the authorial surrogate in Lewis's manifesto of high modernism, 'The Code of a Herdsman', is Benjamin Richard Wing.

By implanting this concatenation of imagery within the desiccated environment of 'The Hollow Men', Eliot retrospectively questions the creative fecundity of the trio's earlier self-rendering as inhuman tricksters. Whereas his contemporaneous review of *Tarr* had praised the novel's 'frigid' and 'inhuman' qualities ('Tarr', 105), the opening lines of 'The Hollow Men' implicitly challenge Frederick Tarr's conviction that an essential condition of art is '"to have no inside"' (*Tarr*, 300). They also evoke Ford's account of his first encounter with Lewis, in which the mysterious stranger proved to be stuffed with paper, leading to the mock-surmise, '[h]e must be Guy Fawkes'. Van Aelst argues that the poem's second epigraph—'A penny for the Old Guy'—implicitly recurs in the 'whimper' (*PTSE* 1:84) of the final line, which alludes to the breath 'that Guy Fawkes exhaled when he gave up his co-conspirators' (Van Aelst). If this hints at the wider accusations of treachery circulating amongst the group, as well as the traitorous repudiation enacted by the poem itself, the epigraph's aggressive demand for money in exchange for the opportunity to gaze upon a dummy also addresses the questionable probity of the trio's early commercial-aesthetic manoeuvrings.

As with Lewis's exploitation of the carnival licence of Childermass day and Chesterton's exempting of Flambeau from conventional law within the liminal spaces of the early *Father Brown* stories, Eliot situates his poem in the context of Bonfire Night in order to draw upon the special privileges of an evening on which a 'licensed "lawlessness"' conventionally pertains and 'behaviour that would be prohibited at any other time of year [is rendered] socially acceptable' (Roud, 458). In this way, Eliot cordons off his cultural transgression within a privileged festive amnesty space, unconsciously mirroring Lewis's traitorous inclusion of Joyce and Pound within the satirical range of *The Childermass*, by using Lewis and Pound as fuel for the fire of a personal regeneration enacted through a satire of a failed social fertility ritual.

With the allusion to Bonfire Night, Eliot positions himself as a more constructive manipulator of Hermes' disruptive status as 'both boundary-setter and boundary-crosser' (Eckard and Gargano, 266), while anticipating Bakhtin's vision of the carnivalesque fire that 'destroys and renews the world'. This redemptive movement is inscribed within the structure of 'The Hollow Men' in a manner comparable to that of *The Man Who Was Thursday* and 'The Queer Feet'. The poem establishes a dyadic contrast between the alienation of the nocturnal, Romantic grotesque landscape of the free-verse sections and the carnivalesque, communal folk grotesque of the nursery rhyme quatrains, set in the period around dawn. The final decay of section V produces a moment of crisis, in which language is pared to the edge of annihilation, 'refined out of existence' (Joyce, *Portrait*, 166) like the fingernails of Stephen Dedalus's artist-god:

> For thine is
> Life is
> For thine is the.
>
> (*PTSE* 1:84)

If these abortive statements suggest a paralysing Jamesian superabundance of sensibility, in a more positive sense they also offer a thematic deconstruction of the principle that 'life' can be formulated in terms of dogmatic precepts. In a further instance of vision and revision, Eliot corrodes the banally pessimistic sentiment conveyed earlier in the same section, '*Life is very long*' (*PTSE* 1:84)—an unattributed quotation from Conrad's *An Outcast of the Islands* (1896)—to suggest a speculative interrogation of the remark's emotional truth. In this way, the moment of linguistic aporia is made to simultaneously suggest new vistas of possibility: Life is…? When Eliot emerges on the other side of Conradian pessimism with a hesitant gesture towards religious conversion—a reference to the Lord's Prayer—one is reminded of Wills's observation that '[a]t the centre of Chesterton's best fiction there is always a moment of aporia, the dark seed of all his gaudy blossomings' ('Man', 339). As Long argues, the 'the failure of language' bound up with instances of literary aporia is rendered 'positive and constructive' (109) when co-aligned with 'the step of parabasis': 'rather than a dead-end' (73) it becomes 'a new step in a different direction' (108).

Step forward the comedian. Eliot's interregnum in the twilight kingdom is the dark seed that precipitates the gaudy blossoming of the final nursery rhyme, in which a parody of the refrain with which the children's rhyme often continues—'this is the way we wash our hands'—offers an appropriate, semi-effaced motto with which to close his poem of renunciation:

> This is the way the world ends
> This is the way the world ends
> This is the way the world ends
> Not with a bang but a whimper.
>
> (*PTSE* 1:84)[30]

Recall the close of 'Suite Clownesque', in which there 'falls a shadow dense, immense' as the 'comedian' surveys the departing bourgeoisie sardonically from the side of the stage. The return of this figure in 'The Hollow Men' is presaged by the 'shadow' that falls 'between the emotion / And the response' in the build-up to the final quatrain. The comedian then leaps into action with the transposition of the martial rhythm of the poem's opening lines into the burlesque song form of the nursery rhyme, an incongruous climax that encourages us to re-imagine the poem as a pantomime skit, in which the iconoclastic clown bursts in at the moment of crisis and delivers his warped nursery rhyme as a sardonic gloss, before throwing one leg forward with a clap of the hands as the curtain falls.

Eliot's recorded performance of the poem heightens this effect, via a vocalisation that brings to mind Chesterton's account of Bentley's knack of saying 'amusing things with the air of one reading the burial service' (*CW* 14:440). As Chinitz notes in a different context, Eliot's 'deadpan [is], paradoxically, the one unmistakable sign of his facetiousness' (178). The aporic passage that precedes the final quatrain is intoned in ever-more deflated fashion, suggestive of a sagging Jack-in-the-box, only for the Jack to spring back to life with gritted teeth and popping eyes for the manic *finale*. Again, the poet-financier of 'Fête Galante' lurks in the shadows of this performance: although his 'lips a little reddened' suggest a ventriloquist's dummy, Vivien's figure of fun also has the 'huge protuberant nose' (559) of Eliot's comedian. This clown-puppet duality had been primed for mobilisation from the twilight kingdom of Eliot's earliest work: the narrator of 'Humouresque' notes of his 'deceaséd' marionette that 'A jumping-jack has such a frame' (*PTSE* 1:237).

Eliot explained to Pound that he composed 'The Hollow Men' in order to have something 'post-Waste' (Eliot, *Letters*, 13 Oct. 1925 2:758) to include in the anthology, *Poems 1909—1925*, published in November 1925, an event that he described to Leonard Woolf, in characteristically abject terms, as an 'ejection' (*Letters*, 17 Dec. 1925, 2:802). Although 'Humouresque' and 'Suite Clownesque' were excluded from this survey, their protagonists make a veiled return in the final nursery rhyme of its closing poem, which might be read as a burlesque afterword to the entire collection, capping this monument to his cultural success with a comically condensed Aristophanean gloss on the tragic visions that precede it—a *reductio ad absurdum* of his career to date.

Much as the Comedian '[e]xplodes in laughter' at the conclusion of 'Suite Clownesque', 'The Hollow Men' ends with the abortive 'bang' of a comedy pistol, a weapon that Eliot ranges against himself, his erstwhile friends, and his solemnly respectful audience in an all-embracing skirl of carnivalesque laughter. This immersive strategy represents a further implied critique of Pound. In *After Strange Gods* (1934), Eliot finds fault with the 'Hell Cantos' on the grounds that the satirist exempts both himself and his projected audience from the critical laughter. Despite the text's uproarious scurrility, Pound abjures the immersive spirit of the carnivalesque:

> Mr. Pound's Hell, for all its horrors, is a perfectly comfortable one for the modern mind to contemplate, and disturbing to no one's complacency: it is a Hell for the *other people*, the people we read about in the newspapers, not for oneself and one's friends.
>
> (43)

In *The Use of Poetry and the Use of Criticism* (1933), Eliot argues that 'from one point of view, the poet aspires to the condition of the music-hall comedian' (32). This mischievous parody of Walter Pater's famous invocation of music as the aesthetic ideal of the creative artist is not conceived to ridicule the Paterian sublime, but, like Chesterton's defences of the pleasures of the *vulgaris*, to sublimate the unrefined. As Eliot goes on to explain,

> [e]very poet would like, I fancy, to be able to think that he had some direct social utility [...] He would like to be something of a popular entertainer, and be able to think his own thoughts behind a tragic or a comic mask.
>
> (154)

In other words, the poet searches for 'a part to play in society as worthy as that of the music-hall comedian' (154). The climax of 'The Hollow Men' strives to attain such a social utility by activating a pedagogically antagonistic relationship with the audience. Cavendish-Jones's view of the final rhyme's repetitive framework—it 'hectors the reader into accepting [Eliot's] conclusion' (198)—is only partly correct: for 'accepting', read 'rebutting'. If the poem's stern moral is that the dead must judge those now living 'not as lost / Violent souls, but only / As the hollow men' (*PTSE* 1:81), the misfiring conclusion is best read as a shaking of the reader's shoulders, comparable to Innocent Smith's declaration in *Manalive*:

> "I am going to hold a pistol to the head of Modern Man. But I shall not use it to kill him—only to bring him to life. I begin to see a new meaning in being the skeleton at the feast [...] the *memento mori* [...] isn't only meant to remind us of a future life, but to remind us of a present life too".
>
> (58)

Recall the purpose of the *Danse Macabre* in Chesterton's imaginative landscape: 'the dance of death [leads] the way to the dance of life'. In chivvying the reader to become an active participant, Eliot establishes a parabasic technique that once more cross-pollinates the practices of Laforgue and Chesterton. As Hannoosh notes, Laforgue's Hamlet 'constantly breaks his narrative with parenthetical asides [and] direct commentary [...] the narrator's intervention, so frequent in parody, allegedly distances him from the text but, by allying us with him, it actually incorporates us into the narrative' (*Parody*, 27–28). Of course, this is also the carnivalesque purpose of Chesterton's narratorial clowning in 'The Queer Feet', with its debts to the audience-baiting practices of Greek comedy and its reimagining of Father Brown as a Petrushka/Punch figure.

Eliot and Lewis each read F.M. Cornford's study, *The Origins of Attic Comedy* (1922), in the period preceding their construction of 'The Hollow Men' (see Matthews, 117–18) and *The Childermass* (see Caracciolo, 'Carnivals', 222–25). Cornford's text features a Punch and Judy show as its frontispiece and establishes connections 'between Aristophanes' gallery of imposters, the harlequin figures in Carnival [... and] *comemedia dell'arte* puppets' (Caracciolo, 'Carnivals', 223). Cornford also records the convention of Attic comedy whereby performers would dash 'forward and satirise persons' (qtd. in Brody, 69) in the audience during the choral 'Phallic Song' (Brody, 69) of the *komos*, a term from which 'comedy' is thought to derive. Alan Brody observes the continuities between Cornford's account of the 'action of death and revival' traceable in this 'ancient fertility ritual' (71) and the conventions of the mummers' play, in which the players improvise 'abusive caricatures of contemporary and local figures' (Brody, 71) within the ritualistic framework of the performance, and 'the final movement of the action' is initiated 'by the clown' (68).[31]

By incorporating each of these elements within 'The Hollow Men', Eliot establishes an aesthetic means of conveying his critical view that 'tragic feelings are best expressed not through "tragedy" but through farce' (qtd. in *PTSE* 1:816), instituting a hybrid structure that encourages his audience to appreciate another of Wilde's dictums in 'The Decay of Lying': 'In Falstaff there is something of Hamlet, in Hamlet there is not a little of Falstaff' (*Intentions*, 18). Although he was characteristically cautious to draw scholarly attention to the range of high-cultural influences subsequently assigned to 'The Hollow Men'—Conrad, Dante, Frazer, Stravinsky, et al.—so as to invest his corpus with a ready-made mythos, these official influences coexist throughout with the carnivalesque, unofficial subtext, which playfully subverts that same myth-making, much as Lewis's immanent juxtaposition of the giddy Bailiff and the sober Hyperides finally complicates their apparent distinction.

Ricks observes that the final section of Eliot's 'athwart' (*T.S. Eliot*, 210) text is riddled with the word 'between'. Both *The Childermass* and 'The Hollow Men' are threshold texts in several senses—each structured upon a simultaneous rehearsal and rejection of the position previously recommended by the author, each intertwining local, satirical sallies with more universal, existential anxieties, and each taking place in surrealistic limbo-realms that immerse the reader within a thoroughly modernist nightmare. Nonetheless, the texts' seriocomic structures also dramatise Chesterton's account of the more benign generic disruptions that emerge in dreams, when 'abstractions fit for an epic' become mixed up 'with fooleries not fit for a pantomime' ('Dreams', the *Speaker*, 24 Aug. 1901; collected in *Coloured*, 81–82). In his preface to a republication of *Barnaby Rudge* (1841), Chesterton argues that the particular value of Dickens's stylistic practice lies in an '[a]udacious reconciliation' of types that 'are abruptly different from each other', much as Shakespeare juxtaposes 'skulls and motley' (*CW* 15:284) in *Hamlet*. From the children's songs in the dead land of 'The Hollow Men' to the purgatorial pranks of *The Childermass*, Eliot and Lewis had begun to pursue a similar collocation of the Romantic and folk grotesques: what Lewis terms elsewhere the 'protracted comedy, which glitters against the darkness' (*Blasting*, 8).

Equally, both men were beginning to perceive the factional polarisation of 'lowbrow' and 'highbrow' literature to be bathetically reductive—the epochal confrontation of the contrary 'crowd-masters' (*Childermass*, 292) of *The Childermass* ultimately devolves into childish parody and mirror image resemblance, as outlined in an arch stage note: '(Applause from the seated audience, mock counter-applause from the Hyperideans.)' (263). Joyce considered Lewis's cultural criticism of the mid-1920s to be evidence that he was 'preparing to make a clamorous conversion' (Ellmann, R., *James*, 595). Although Joyce had a theological epiphany in mind, it might be said that Lewis was on the verge of a small-'c', cultural conversion, to an embrace of what Hulme had termed 'the infamous attitude of the person with catholic tastes'. Pullman's many personae range from Joycean hegemonic collaborator to irascible Lewisian serviceman, to a rather more Eliotic register: 'Pullman, the polite faintly-ironical professional question-mark' (58). The one continuous attribute in all of these modernist metamorphoses is his steadfast defence of the Chestertonian Bailiff: '"He's really not so black as he's painted [...] I like the beggar!"' (55/72).

Notes

1 The War Propaganda Bureau was set up by Chesterton's friend Charles Masterman, who invited a range of authors, including Chesterton, Conan Doyle, Ford, and Wells, to a meeting on 2 September 1914 to request contributions. For more details of the Bureau's work, see 'War Propaganda Bureau', Spartacus Educational, September 1997 (updated January 2015) <http://spartacus-educational.com/FWWwpb.htm>.
2 Chesterton cut his ties with the *Daily Herald* when the newspaper adopted a pacifist stance over the conflict. Thereafter, his journalistic interventions were carried out primarily in the *New Witness*. His autobiography distinguishes the *New Witness* from the *Daily Mail*, because the former was 'patriotic and pro-ally, but emphatically opposed to the jingoism of the Daily Mail' (256).
3 With characteristic indelicacy, Chesterton does refer to 'Huns' several times in *The Barbarism of Berlin* (29, 54, 81).
4 For the composition history of 'The Code of a Herdsman' (see Munton, 'Code', 8).
5 The same poem in *BLAST 2* in which Pound rails against 'Cowardly editors' includes the lament that 'Friends fall off at the pinch, the loveliest die' (22).
6 Wells's missive was prompted by intemperate criticisms of Ford Madox Ford in the *New Witness*; see Ward, *Gilbert*, 350–52.
7 Lewis is most probably referring to either David Garnett or Duncan Grant, who lived together on a fruit farm during the war and 'received a continuous stream of visitors' to their 'country outpost of Bloomsbury' (Knights, 114).
8 Edwards, 'Lewis's', 33–35, also finds this phrase to be a deliberate allusion to Dostoevsky.
9 To my knowledge, the only critical work to suggest this correspondence is William Blissett's article, 'Chesterton and English Literary Modernism'. Blissett notes, as an aside, that '[t]he exuberant, larger-than-life, grotesque figure of the Bailiff [...] reminds me of the pseudo jolly, somehow menacing figure of Chesterton as caricatured by the Men of 1914 early in their careers' (129). See Caracciolo, 'Metamorphoses', 266, for a discussion of the original crossover of material between *The Childermass* and *Time and Western Man*.
10 Chesterton once dressed up as Bacchus in an amateur theatrical, in which guise he soon 'began to knock [a] professor about' (Ffinch, 72).
11 *The Childermass* has its roots in the abandoned novel, 'Joint', in which Lewis planned to include a section titled 'The Infernal Fair' (see Edwards, *Wyndham*, 317).
12 When Pound loaned him twenty pounds in September 1925, Lewis thanked him for a gesture that would help to 'keep the bailiffs out' (12 Sept. 1925; Pound, *Pound/Lewis*, 152).
13 It is rather striking that in Burton Hatlen's account of Pound's anti-Semitism, one could seamlessly replace 'Jews' with 'Chesterton': 'Pound's conviction that the ills of the world can be ascribed to Jews and the apparently uncontrollable outbursts of scatological language that came to accompany almost any reference to Jews both suggest some sort of mental breakdown consistent with paranoia' (254).
14 See Caracciolo, 'Metamorphoses' 267, and 'Carnivals', 208, for a more detailed analysis of the Bailiff's links to saturnalia and carnival.

234   Le Mob c'est Moi

15 The rationale behind this remark is thoroughly Schopenhauerian: it would be 'either like killing yourself without being interfered with by the instinct of self-preservation—or exterminating the instinct of self-preservation itself!' (*BLAST* 1:133).
16 Jameson observes of the passage on Chesterton from *The Art of Being Ruled*, '[o]ne cannot help suspecting that with all the appropriate changes, this is something of a self-portrait' ('Wyndham', 19). However, he does not make the further connection to the Bailiff.
17 Pound conveyed his response by annotating and returning Lewis's original letter.
18 Pound also brings Chesterton and Meynell together in his review of *Tarr*. Chesterton had collaborated with Meynell in editing *Samuel Johnson: Extracts from his Writings* (1911).
19 As early as 1933, John Edgell Rickword observed that the rhetorical tone of Eliot's criticism was '[n]ot quite so paradoxical as Mr. G.K. Chesterton methodically is, but surprisingly near it' (221).
20 In his assessment of Chesterton and Meynell, Eliot acknowledges, tangentially, that '[o]ne often agrees with Mr. Chesterton' ('Professional', 61).
21 Here, the interested reader is encouraged to track down my book chapter, 'A Large Mouth Shown to a Dentist: G.K. Chesterton's Surgical Parodying of T.S. Eliot', in the essay collection, *Literary and Cultural Alternatives to Modernism: Unsettling Presences* (New York: Routledge, 2018). The material contained in this essay was originally intended for inclusion in the present work, but had to be excised for reasons of space. It focuses primarily upon a close analysis of Chesterton's verse parody of Eliot, 'To a Modern Poet' (*G.K.'s Weekly*, 31 May 1925), and provides an additional perspective on Chesterton's engagement with Eliot in the 1920s, which would result in a kind of director's cut if imaginatively reinserted at this stage of my narrative.
22 The 'Hell Cantos' were conceptualised by July 1922, though Pound continued to revise them until their publication in January 1925 (see Bush, 244).
23 Hofer argues convincingly that this is a reference to Eliot and that Eliot was aware of this (480).
24 The collection in question was *Personae: The Collected Shorter Poems of Ezra Pound* (1926).
25 Walsh was the editor of *This Quarter*. Joyce discusses his contribution for Walsh in the same letter to Weaver in which he parodies *The Waste Land*.
26 In his correspondence with Pound, Lewis refers to *This Quarter* as 'your paper, or your friend's paper', to which Pound responds tersely, 'not my paper' (Pound, *Lewis/Pound*, 151).
27 Of course, as with Pound's reference to Chesterton's 'cheek', 'wind' also bears a burlesque connotation, implying emissions of the mouth and bowels alike.
28 In a (presumable) typo in *BLAST* 2, a reproduction of Gaudier-Brzeska's sculpture is listed as the 'Head of *Eza* Pound' (84; my emphasis).
29 Glasheen notes that 'Hermes is a principal role of Shaun' (125), the Lewisian twin of the Joycean Shem in *Finnegans Wake*. In 'The Dagger with Wings', Chesterton points out that 'the rod of Hermes' is 'decorated with wings' (*CFB* 466).
30 'This is the way we wash our hands' is listed as the second verse in Alfred Moffat's *What the Children Sing* (London: Augener, 1915).
31 Rather like the Bonfire Night request for 'A penny for the Old Guy', R.J.E. Tiddy considers the modern mummers' play 'a perfunctory piece of fooling that precedes the collection of money' (qtd. in Brody, 71).

6 Audacious Reconciliation
The Human Circulating Library of Late Modernism

> It cannot be too often repeated that if we are to love our enemies we must fight them.
> —Chesterton, 'On Mrs. Eddy and a New Creed', *DN* 11 Apr. 1908 (*CDN* 5:52)

> We can sometimes arrive at a very satisfactory intimacy with our anti-masks.
> —Eliot, 'Matthew Arnold' (*Use*, 112)

When Father Brown enters the gentleman's club of 'The Queer Feet', the narrator reports that 'Mr Lever at last hit on a plan to cover, since he might not obliterate, the disgrace' (*CFB* 38) of the priest's presence. He does so by sequestering Brown within the body of the club in a manner that conceals him from the auspicious clients, while enabling him to get on with his work. With this strategy in mind, there is something suggestive about the surreptitious act of vicarious book procuration that occurs in Lewis's late novel, *Self Condemned* (1954), in which a volume of *Father Brown* is placed amongst the possessions of a character named Percy—the forename that Lewis suppressed from his own moniker. The cultural tastes of Lewis's Percy Lamport are 'orthodoxly-liberal and unusually developed for a city man' (Lewis, *Self*, 46), extending from Chesterton to W.H. Auden, G. D. H. Cole, Marie Laurençin, Katherine Mansfield, Henri Matisse, George Orwell, J.B. Priestley, and George Bernard Shaw. This eclectic catalogue suggests that while Lewis still felt compelled to find ways to cover, since he might not obliterate, the disgrace of Chesterton's influence, he had belatedly graduated towards a more nuanced approach to the wider culture, recognising that Chesterton's popular fiction might coherently share a bookshelf with a miscellany of Georgian poets, left-wing political theorists, modernist satirists, and late-modernist social commentators, in the rooms of a man who prides himself on his *'avantgardisme'* (Lewis, *Self*, 49).

Lewis's account of the contents of Lamport's bookshelf calls to mind a moral drawn half a century earlier by Chesterton in 'Some Urgent Reforms: The Human Circulating Library' (*Speaker*, 2 Nov. 1901). He proposes this initiative as a means of traversing cultural divides, in the hope that the

> vast herds of suburban citizens living perpetually among people like themselves, might [...] be rescued to some extent from ignorance of others [...] All those who were members of [the library] would hold themselves ready during certain specified months of the year to stay at the houses of any other members who had taken them out of the library. In return, of course, they would themselves have the privilege of taking other people out of the library. The subscriber would send a postcard to the librarian saying, 'Send me Mr. Smiles, Professor Puffy, and Unterbringen, the German Anarchist'.
> (BL MS Add.73381 fol.75)

'Unterbringen' translates as to 'accommodate' or 'house' (Betteridge, 502). In this sense, the imaginative impetus of 'The Human Circulating Library' accords with the practices of the parodist, who invites the alien mind into her/his textual home and attempts to get to grips with it through a process of stylistic acclimatisation. The fascination of the figures under discussion with such acts of textual hospitality was a key factor in sharpening their critical acuity. Consider Eliot's account of the characteristics of successful criticism: 'the reason why some criticism is good [...] is that the critic assumes, in a way, the personality of the author whom he criticises, and through this personality is able to speak with his own voice' (*Use*, 112). Stephen Medcalfe identifies a comparable facility in Chesterton, which he links to a productive negotiation of the tension between public and private selves that Chesterton had articulated in his pained letter to Ronald Knox:

> Chesterton was much embarrassed by the disjunction between his public self and his real person: but the disjunction is presumably connected with his ability to impersonate. And it is this ability to impersonate, modified by his awareness of a strong system of values to judge what he is impersonating, that makes his literary criticism [...] so good.
> (85)

From the late 1920s to Chesterton's death in 1936, these writers' longstanding experimentation with ambivalent forms of impersonation found a complement in their increasing urge to circumvent the demands of their public personae and establish private channels of communication. The result was a more personal rendition of Chesterton's 'audacious reconciliation' of types that 'are abruptly different from each other', as Eliot and Lewis began more frankly to accommodate aspects of popular culture, while Chesterton found himself, to his surprise, increasingly taking 'the side of the cultivated and the clever' ('The Reaction of the Intellectuals', collected in *The Well and the Shallows*, 1935; CW 3:406).

Surviving Mr Chesterton's Approval

John Dickson Carr's most famous mystery story concerns a detective conceived as an affectionate parody of Chesterton, who investigates the problem of *The Hollow Man* (1935)—a curiously serendipitous juxtaposition, since Chesterton's attempts to decode the mystery of Eliot were conducted partially in collaboration with his own most celebrated sleuth. In 1925, Chesterton published two *Father Brown* stories in which the priest is made to exercise his deductive judgement in relation to figures with decidedly Eliotic attributes. In 'The Arrow of Heaven' (*Nash's Magazine*, July 1925), an American character whose 'conversation seemed to consist of stratified layers of irony' (*CFB* 379–80) is described as being 'dressed to the nines—up to that point, indeed, where there begins to be too fine a distinction between the dandy and the dummy outside a tailor's shop' (*CFB* 389). Meanwhile, in 'The Mirror of the Magistrate' the finger of guilt falls temporarily upon a near relative of Unterbringen the German Anarchist—a writer described as '"one of the new poets, and pretty steep to read, I believe"' (*CFB* 525), whose philosophy is considered 'pessimistic [and] anarchial' (*CFB* 649).

In September 1927, 'The Mirror of the Magistrate' was collected in *The Secret of Father Brown* alongside an explanatory framing narrative in which the priest reveals that he finally succeeded in establishing the poet's innocence through an act of deductive mimicry: 'I set myself consciously down to *be* a revolutionary poet' (*CFB* 649). As Brown explains, his detective method is conceived to counter the materialist impersonality espoused by Sherlock Holmes, which involves '"treating a friend as a stranger"' (*CFB* 522). Brown's contrary practice of reimagining strangers as friends in order to grasp their true motives yielded a real-life *rapprochement* when Chesterton redoubled his investigations into Eliot in the decade that followed. Two months after the publication of *The Secret of Father Brown* came Chesterton's critical study, *Robert Louis Stevenson*, in which Eliot makes a further veiled appearance, alongside Lewis and Pound:

> There is [...] a group, we might say a family group, of poets who consider themselves, and are generally considered, the last word in experiment [...] and who are not without real qualities of deep atmosphere and suggestion. Yet all that is really deep in the best of their work comes out of those depths of garden perspective and large rooms as seen by little children [...] Many have complained,

and perhaps justly, of the almost American modernity of the artistic ambition of these artists. They announce their message through a megaphone; they shout it through pantomime masks; they hustle and push and pick quarrels; but there is something in them, for all their efforts to advertise—or to hide it. [...] what they are really after is still the same [as in Stevenson]: those lost children who are themselves; lost in the deep gardens at dusk.

(CW 18:146)

The reference to these writers' 'efforts to advertise—or to hide' the true derivation of their methods once more rehearses the exposure of misleading commercial-aesthetic self-positioning that Chesterton had first conducted in 'The Paradise of Thieves', while the image of Eliot and Co. shouting their messages through pantomime masks gestures towards the 'unhuman' strategies of their early propagandising. However, these criticisms are offset by Chesterton's more sympathetic evocation of disquiet at finding oneself lost in a childhood garden, which coheres with the wandering of his Eliotic poet in 'The Mirror of the Magistrate' through a perilous night-time garden, the chanting of nursery rhymes in the twilight kingdom of Eliot's 'The Hollow Men', and Lewis's later recollection that in his youth, he had read the Russian classics 'as a child reads "Through the Looking Glass"' (*Rude*, 147)—more saucer-eyed interloper than seasoned inhabitant of Wonderland. Of course, these motifs also recall the disorientated picaresque of Chesterton's Carrollian fairy-tale, *The Man Who Was Thursday*, the shadow presence of which serves once more to disclose the effaced narrative of Chesterton's aesthetic influence upon, and identification with, the same figures who had denounced him 'through a megaphone' as their rejected cultural antipode.

Following the publication of *Stevenson*, Eliot took up the megaphone once more in a largely negative review, disparaging his interpreter via a sustained exercise in critical *froideur* that strains to cast doubt upon Chesterton's capacity to correctly deduce the meaning of modernism—not least, his misapprehension that 'we are [...] still very much interested in the 'Nineties, and somewhat like them, only worse' (Eliot, 'There', 445).[1] While complaining that 'I have always found Mr. Chesterton's style exasperating to the last point of endurance' (444), Eliot goes on to damn the text with the faintest conceivable praise—it is a 'not at all stupid book' (445)—before ending with a further example of Chestertonian paradox being turned against its subject: Stevenson is 'an author well enough established to survive Mr. Chesterton's approval' (446).

Having heard news of Eliot's jibes at second hand, Chesterton mentally filed them away and responded in kind in the following year. In 'An Apology for Buffoons', he admits to being out of sympathy with the 'severe and classic' (CW 3:343) stylistic method articulated in the line from Eliot's 'Preludes' (1915) that refers to the 'smell of steaks in passageways' (*PTSE* 1:15).[2] Nonetheless, this temperamental antipathy 'is not a subject for these extreme controversial passions. If I were to say that the style of the line maddened me to the point of unendurance, I should be greatly exaggerating its effect on the emotions' (*CW* 3:343). While Chesterton's selection from Eliot's verse again serves to expose a certain discrepancy between the poet's 'severe and classic' precepts and the somewhat burlesque corporeality of his poetic practice, his final remarks are suffused with an impudent suavity that parodies the rhetorical tone of Eliot's criticism. By drawing attention to the unintentional paradox encoded within Eliot's phrasing, through which a stylistic critique that strains to convey arch disinterest is expressed in such intemperate terms as to intimate hysteria, Chesterton's riposte mimics his antagonist's voice in order to discredit it, much as Eliot had appropriated the Chestertonian paradox to frame his attack in the 'Henry James' essay.

Despite the precision of Chesterton's counterblow, he was not always such a poised critic himself. In his discussion of Wilde's literal handling of the world of objects Chesterton uses precisely the same intemperate term as Eliot: 'I for one cannot *endure* [...] his sensual way of speaking of dead substances' (my emphasis). In both cases, an engagement with the cultural father-figure results in an inadvertent lapse of critical distance, disclosed precisely in the haughty phraseology selected. If this flirtatious dance of disapprobation bears echoes of the mirror-image withdrawal into urbanity conducted by the young Chesterton and Bentley in response to one another's outbreaks of mental disturbance, it is striking to find Chesterton and Eliot drifting into an increasing intimacy immediately after this exchange.

This path was not without its potholes. Eliot initially replied to Chesterton's article with a bad-tempered private missive, complaining of the latter's slight misquotation of the 'steak' line from 'Preludes': 'as a humble versifier [...] I prefer my verse to be quoted correctly, if at all' (Eliot, *Letters*, 2 July 1928; 4:198). Nonetheless, the extraordinary speed with which the pair's correspondence progressed thereafter from animus to cordiality suggests that Chesterton's largely sympathetic pen portraits in *Father Brown* and *Stevenson* had given Eliot hope that a more benign critical engagement might be possible. If so, this process was considerably assisted by Chesterton's immediate reply to Eliot's crotchety correspondence, a masterclass in mollification that centres upon a self-mocking caricature as a clapped-out member of the old guard, indulging in his own particular brand of nonsense:

> I am so very sorry if my nonsense in the Mercury had any general air of hostility [...] I meant it to be quite amiable; like the tremulous badinage of the Oldest Inhabitant in the bar parlour, when he has been guyed by the brighter lads of the village.
> (Chesterton in Eliot, *Letters*, 5 July 1928; 4:201n1)

Chesterton's protestation that his satirical swordstick was merely the harmless cane of a greybeard at play drew a response from Eliot that suggests a new sense of identification, mirroring Chesterton's self-deprecating tone while empathising with his famous incapacity to render quotations accurately: 'I [...] made twelve distinct mistakes in well-known passages of Shakespeare' (Eliot, *Letters*, 6 July 1928; 4:202).

Thus began a more sustained correspondence. The following May, Eliot writes that 'I have much sympathy with your political and social views' (Eliot, *Letters*, 8 May 1929; 4:493), to which Chesterton responds with an appreciative discussion of Eliot's *For Lancelot Andrewes* (1928) and a hope that 'you will come down and see me as you suggest' (Eliot, *Letters*, 13 May; 4:493n3).[3] When Eliot explains that his original, hostile missive had merely been 'a pretext' (Eliot, *Letters*, 21 Oct. 1928; 4:283) to establish communication, with the somewhat ironic thought of offering Chesterton journalistic work in an anti-populist forum—'I should like you to think of The Criterion as a medium for making any unpopular statements' (Eliot, *Letters*, 6 July 1928; 4:202)—the scornful *Stevenson* review begins to resemble an expression of the interpersonal dynamic articulated by Chesterton in *The Ball and the Cross*:

> "I must kill you now," said the fanatic, "because..."
> "Well, because," said Turnbull, patiently.
> "Because I have begun to like you".
>
> (*CW* 6:429)

Another letter ends with a compliment to Chesterton's perspicacity as a critical reader, drawing particular attention to his ability to correctly interpret Eliot's intentions where others would mistakenly draw unflattering inferences: 'I was particularly pleased by your noticing that footnote: I wonder how many readers thought it more than an attempt at smartness' (Whit Monday, 1929; BL MS Add.73195 fol.68). From hopelessly muddled-headed antagonist, Chesterton metamorphoses into incisive, sympathetic critical reader.

Once this amicable personal relationship had been cemented by the correspondence of 1928–30, Chesterton recurred to Eliot's theme of the mulberry bush in his later public assessments of the poet, now using parody to demonstrate his sense of affinity, although—in an apt correlation with Eliot's methods—not always in a manner that rendered his meaning lucid to his audience. Critical confusion over Chesterton's attitude towards Eliot has been exacerbated by the famous parody of the final quatrain of 'The Hollow Men' that he delivered in a radio broadcast on 'The Spice of Life' (15 Mar. 1936; published in the *Listener*, 18 Mar. 1936), just three months before his death:

Some sneer, some snigger, some simper;
In the youth where we laughed, and sang.
And *they* may end with a whimper
But *we* will end with a bang.

(*Spice*, 167)

The tendency of anthologists to reproduce this parody in isolation from its original context has encouraged the inference that Chesterton remained implacably hostile towards Eliot throughout his career, and that this antagonism was inspired by a naïve assumption that 'The Hollow Men' uncomplicatedly articulated its creator's enervation.[4] However, when the full text of the broadcast is read in combination with Chesterton's other pronouncements on Eliot from the period, it becomes clear that he had successfully interpreted the ironic double-voicing of 'The Hollow Men' in a manner that has often evaded Eliot's critical interpreters.[5]

Chesterton clarifies his position in a near-contemporaneous essay on 'The Reaction of the Intellectuals'. Perhaps gesturing towards the poem's introductory marching song conceit, he notes that it is the 'bold and enquiring spirits, who were always said to be in advance of the age, who are now most doubtful about the desirability of advancing' (*CW* 3:403). He goes on to contend that the poet's true message is lost on his acolytes: 'As soon as the quite brainless mob of Bright Young Things discovers that it is really being *despised*, as a mob of dull old things [...] there will be a panic' (*CW* 3:407). Earlier in the 'Spice of Life' broadcast, Chesterton alludes to the pedagogic purpose of Eliot's self-appointed role as an embodied *memento mori*, as well as his own sense of cultural supersession, identifying himself as a 'skeleton at the feast [... with] a hollow voice from the tomb' (*Spice*, 161). Once having established this air of alliance, Chesterton's parodic quatrain comes to read not as a hostile satire but a sympathetic pastiche, reframing Eliot's message in slightly differing terms, much as his article on 'The Futurists' had expressed authentic identification with Dostoevsky's authorial intent, in contrast to the misreadings of the Russian's modernist acolytes.

The difficulty of extracting this meaning from Chesterton's skit when read in isolation results from its repetition of the sweeping, clear-cut battle lines first essayed in the *Thursday* dedication, which serve to cordon off his merry band from their pessimistic cultural antitheses. While Chesterton characteristically employs a distinction between the open 'laugh' and the closed 'sneer' as a metaphor for the positive and negative existential standpoints under consideration, a further echo of the partitioning tendency of the *Thursday* preface emerges in his recourse to the philosophical authority of Whitman—'the youth where we laughed, and sang' alludes to the lines from *Leaves of Grass*, 'I see, dance, laugh, sing' (66). Since the presence of a battle line is beyond question, Chesterton's attitude towards

Eliot's text must be determined by which side of the divide he places the poet—either holding the fort with the '*we*' or threatening its barriers as a constituent of a new band of Lear-esque '*they*' figures. Of course, this interpretive labyrinth is made particularly perilous to navigate by the ambivalent context of Eliot's own use of 'we' in the opening lines of his poem, which exemplifies the simultaneously immersive and self-extricating antimodern temperament that he shared with Chesterton.[6]

When Chesterton affirms that the 'author of The Waste Land knows all there is to know about scepticism and pessimism' (*Common*, 227), we might reflect once more that it takes one to know one. A 'somewhat opaque [...] bitter version of the quest of the Holy Grail', in which a 'note of revolt' is expressed via 'powerful lyrics [that] I can hardly venture to quote, so terrible is their pessimism' ('So Nobly', 30–31)—this is not Chesterton's *précis* of *The Waste Land*, but James Douglas's 1900 review of Chesterton's verse drama, 'The Wild Knight'. Chesterton's intuition that Eliot had passed through a crucible of doubt comparable to the 'abysses' traversed in his own youth encouraged him to identify with Eliot at a time when figureheads of conservative and progressive cultural politics alike were lining up to anathematise him—C.S. Lewis averred that Eliot's work constituted 'a very great evil' (to Paul Elmer More, 23 May 1935; qtd. in Ricks, *T.S. Eliot*, 197), while Pound warned John Drummond of 'Eliot's evil influence' (Pound, *Letters*, 18 Feb. 1932; 322).

Conversely, although Chesterton's Eliotic poet in 'The Mirror of the Magistrate', Osric Orm, shares his surname with the Miltonic villain of 'The Wild Knight', Lord Orm, this signifier of maleficence—the Old Norse, *orm*, means 'serpent, snake', or 'maggot' (Haugen, 297)—finally proves to be a red herring, thanks to Father Brown's capacity to empathise with the 'revolutionary poet'. In 'The Wheel' (collected in *Alarm and Discursions*, 1910), Chesterton discusses his own taste for 'revolt', observing that 'one cannot have a Revolution without revolving'—the 'sublime paradox' of the wheel is that 'one part of it is always going forward and the other part always going back' (87). While this 'rotary' (*Alarms*, 87) image evokes the recursive quality of Chesterton's biographical identification with Eliot, in 1939 Katherine Brégy conjured a comparable image of circularity to illustrate Eliot's unlikely resemblance to Chesterton—the exemplary modernist might seem to occupy 'the other extreme from the robust and joyous Chesterton. But in a world of transition, extremes often meet!' (399).

The Doom of Doom

Chesterton's affiliative pastiche of 'The Hollow Men' in the 'Spice of Life' broadcast encounters a sharp contrast in the portentous invocation of 'maggots' that precedes Pound's more straightforward admonishment in 'Canto LXXIV': 'say this to the Possum: a bang, not a whimper, / with a bang not with a whimper' (*Cantos*, 425).[7] In turn, Pound's reproachful rejoinder is given more explosive expression in Lewis's blasting of the 'melodious groans issued from time to time from the deliberately "hollow" carcass of Mr Eliot, at the thought of the vanishing of the Butler and the Upper Housemaid' ('The Artist as Crowd', *Twentieth Century*, Apr. 1932; collected in *Creatures*, 172). This gesture towards Prufrock's apprehension of the eternal footman and Woolf's wonder at the unorthodox manoeuvres of the housemaid fixes Eliot firmly at the heart of the effete London literary community satirised in Lewis's mammoth satire, *The Apes of God* (1930). In the opulent literary masque that brings the novel to a close, a figure dressed as 'Prufrock' is spied amongst the 'great number of variously costumed individuals' (Lewis, *Apes*, 460) engaged in the gargantuan freak dinner of 'Lord Osmund's Lenten Party'.

Lewis's disdain for a scenario in which, as Mark Perrino puts it, the 'wealthy imitate the social customs of the dispossessed, but do not forego their own privilege' (130) bears distinct echoes of the 'Slum Dinner' satirised by Chesterton in 'The Mistake of the Machine'. Likewise, although the presiding 'carnival mock-priest' (Perrino, 79) of Lewis's satire, Horace Zagreus, fulminates against the rise of detective fiction as 'symptomatic of highbrow capitulation, in face of universal pressure' (*Apes*, 401), the Harlequinesque disruption sown by this 'very good mimic' (*Apes*, 14) within an enervated aristocratic party once more suggests the clandestine influence of 'The Queer Feet'.[8] The textual similarities extend further. Lewis's narrative begins by offering the reader instructions on how to gain entry to an exclusive residence—'[s]hould a visitor, from just within the entrance, have been able to proceed at right angles to his left [...] he would have reached the gardener's tool shed...' (7)—only to introduce us to the decrepit aristocrat, Lady Fredigonde, who displays solipsistic ignorance of a servant upon whom she is completely dependent. In the concluding set piece 'anti-carnival' (Munton, 'Wyndham', 145) of the Lenten party, a character in fancy-dress disguise steals the cutlery (see Lewis, *Apes*, 406), while an air of trans-historical interclass equivalence is produced by a discussion of the outfit of a 'footman', who appears in 'a braided uniform (such as formerly worn by aristocrats, but only by poor bottom-dogs at present' (520).

However, while the novel borrows thematic motifs from the unorthodox festive comedy of 'The Queer Feet', Lewis's portrayal of 'wealth [...] as a living death' (Perrino, 126) is finally more formally and philosophically akin to 'Prufrock'. Much as Harriet Monroe complained to Pound that 'the final image of Prufrock' lacked 'a rejuvenating effect' (paraphrased by Gosden, 31), Lewis's novel countenances 'no thematic resolution, neither a return to stability nor a transformation' (Perrino, 127), instead constructing a Hankin-like, pessimistic 'parody of the conventional happy ending of the comedy of manners' (Perrino, 125): Zagreus agrees to marry Fredigonde merely for her money, and she promptly expires, as 'ced*Death the Drummer*' raps out the 'fatal step' (Lewis, *Apes*, 624) of a *Danse Macabre* in the background.

Thus, the recursive structure of this least genial of modernist texts subverts the regenerative turn of 'The Queer Feet' and the positive cyclical reawakening at dawn in *The Man Who Was Thursday*. The nightmarishly stultifying nonsense world of *The Apes of God* more closely resembles Chesterton's assessment in *Orthodoxy* of the negative strain of circularity espoused by 'moderns', 'sceptics', 'fatalists', and 'pessimists': the 'ultimate nullity' represented by 'a serpent with his tail in his mouth' (19). In the later article, 'Nothing but Negative Morality' (*ILN* 1 Oct. 1932), Chesterton presents a variation on this 'very unsatisfactory meal' (*Orthodoxy*, 19) in an account that turns Lewis's mockery of Eliot's hollowness back upon him. Despite being thought of as one of 'our modern moral satirists', Lewis's 'whirlwind of destructive criticism' has 'a hollow in [its] heart [...] as there is a hollow in the heart of the whirlpool' because it consists of 'nothing but negative morality' (*CW* 21:154). Satirists such as Lewis 'even admit they are hollow, as a hungry man would admit he was hollow. They have not enough solid sustenance; not enough food for the mind' (*CW* 21:154).

When Fredigonde shivers at the thought of being 'buried undead and sentient up to your neck in the disobliging bosom of a domestic' (Lewis, *Apes*, 16), there is an echo of Chesterton's mockery of Mr. Mandragon the Millionaire in *The Flying Inn*, who refuses to rot 'with Adam and all mankind'. Nonetheless, Lewis's satirical method mirrors this unregenerative state, enacting a Schopenhauerian withdrawal from the 'sorts of people I would sooner be dead than mixed into', reifying his contemporaries as marionettes whose strings he pulls from afar. Perhaps surprisingly, when Lewis begins talking of Michelangelo in *Time and Western Man*, it is to favour his work over that of Picasso—whereas the latter might produce 'a beautifully executed, imposing, human doll', the 'figures of Michelangelo [...] are creatures of an infectious life' (80). While the last phrase evokes the animating fingertip spark of *The Creation of Adam* (1512), Lewis's privileging of detached wit over immersive humour in *The Apes of God* leaves him incapable of performing a comparably galvanic act. As with Chesterton's account of the arid satirical 'judge' who is unwilling to be 'touched at all', the Lewisian puppet master becomes as ontologically redundant as his cast—his satire of unsatisfactory festivity inadvertently discloses an equally 'hard and frivolous' outlook, 'without fruit for God or man', as Father Brown puts it when scolding the Twelve True Fishermen back into life.

In a review of *Men without Art*, delivered in a radio broadcast shortly after its publication ('Books in General', 21 Nov. 1934, published in the *Listener*, 28 Nov. 1934), Chesterton addresses the internal tensions of Lewis's disinvested satirical doctrine, as articulated in the collection's pivotal essay, 'The Greatest Satire is Non-Moral':

surely the satirist is a fighter, whatever else he is; and he must have some reason for fighting. It may not be morality, in the sense of moralising. But this dilemma remains; either he fights for something larger including morality; a cosmic conception; religion. Or else he only fights for something he happens to like against something he happens to dislike. There are only two ultimates: God and good taste; and even then it is only the taster who decides whether the taste is good.
(BL Add MS 73283 fol.33–34)

As Orage had noted of Pound's criticisms of Chesterton in the *New Age*, these were 'a matter entirely of taste and not of judgment. [...] I listen to his remarks on Mr. Chesterton as I should hear his opinion of crab-soup' ('Readers', 17 Jan. 1918; 232).

Lewis based his defence of 'non-human [...] non-moral' satire upon a professed faith in the possibility of '"satire" *for its own sake*' (*Men*, 109), a phrase that not only mimics the ethically disengaged art for art's sake slogan of the aesthetes to whom he was ostensibly opposed, but also Chesterton's view of Carroll's work as 'nonsense for nonsense's sake'.[9] While this aporic closed circuit runs counter to Chesterton's vision of the positive possibilities of nonsense as an 'escape into a world where things are not fixed horribly in eternal appropriateness', the echoes of Bentley's deterministic fatalism and urge for withdrawal, as well as his own youthful solipsism (a delusion of 'being God'), that Chesterton discovered in Lewis's fictional and polemical work roused him to a critical engagement that ultimately enabled the pair to evade the apparent fixity of their animus.[10] In 'The Crowd Master', Lewis's narrator speculates upon the possible means through which one might achieve such an escape, observing 'the necessity of brutal and enthusiastic actions like the buying of a book [...] to keep [one] from capitulating to Fate' (*BLAST* 2:100). Something of the kind happened to Chesterton one day on a visit to his friend, Douglas Woodruff. Spotting a copy of *The Apes of God*, Chesterton took it from the shelf. Woodruff reported what followed to Maisie Ward:

> He once seized from my shelves in Lincoln's Inn, Wyndham Lewis's *Apes of God* saying it was a book he had not seen and wanted to see. [... He] opened it and stood reading it [with] a kind of sucking out of the printed contents, as though he were a vacuum cleaner and you could see the lines of type leaving the pages and being absorbed. When he put it down it was to discuss the thesis and illustrations of the book as a man fully possessed of its whole standpoint.
> (qtd. in Ward, *Gilbert*, 475)[11]

Woodruff leaves the date of this reading unspecified, but it seems probable that it may have coincided with a public exchange that Chesterton entered into with Lewis in 1931, a year after the novel's publication. Avoiding a capitulation to fate is a key theme of this intervention, which was occasioned by Lewis's publication of a series of articles on 'The Doom of Youth' in *Time & Tide* (7 Jan. to 14 Feb. 1931). In a further example of Lewis's 'fulminations against the child-actors' ('There', 445), as Eliot put it, 'The Doom of Youth' accuses the British popular press of colluding with big business to encourage a 'spellbound public' to fixate upon achieving 'a super-adolescent type of maturity' (26).[12] Despite having been the recipient of a similar critique in *The Childermass*, Chesterton found fulsome praise for Lewis's polemic in a two-part follow-up article on 'The Doom of Doom' (*Time & Tide* 1 and 8 Aug. 1931), a title that joins in with the parodic game initiated by Lewis's satirical tweaking of *The Loom of Youth* (1917), the bestselling fictional debut of Alec Waugh.[13]

Having generated a genial air of dialogic to-and-fro with his own titular emendation, Chesterton heaps extravagant praise upon 'the genius of Mr. Wyndham Lewis' (8 Aug.; 935), as revealed by his 'brilliant and stimulating articles on "Youth-Politics"' (1 Aug.; 910), affirming his 'warm admiration for [...] Lewis's penetration and sincerity', and finding him to be a 'really brilliant philosopher' (8 Aug.; 936). Nonetheless, the plaudits remain peppered with a subtle sardonic bite—in flattering Lewis's insight, Chesterton makes it clear that his some-time antagonist has simply come around to his way of thinking. Perhaps alluding to the bygone skirmishes of 'Futurism and the Flesh', in which it had been Lewis who had replied to Chesterton, and with brickbats rather than bouquets, he chides Lewis on his vaunted radicalism—'Mr. Wyndham Lewis, of course, has never seen the funny little rags in which we poor old reactionaries write our opinions'—before affirming that 'to a very large extent I agreed with him. I think he will understand that I mean no disrespect, if I even go so far as to say that he agrees with me' (1 Aug.; 910).

Chesterton goes on to articulate his principal demurral over Lewis's thesis via a puckish allusion to his shifting cultural allegiances: 'The one person for whom there is no future is the futurist; especially when the futurist is the fatalist' (911). As with the structural conceit of *The Apes of God*, Chesterton discerns a capitulation to fate in Lewis's ascription of inevitability to the degenerative processes that he diagnoses. The one-time Futurist fellow-traveller is thus reconceived as *passéiste*, espousing a deterministic 'notion of things being inevitably doomed [... that] disappeared with the nineteenth century' (1 Aug.; 911). Chesterton's proposed remedy is for Lewis not only to cultivate his temperamental leaning towards popular comic forms—'I am glad that Mr. Wyndham Lewis knows how to parody the newspapers by the usual travesty of Gray' (1 Aug.; 910)—but also to consider dramatically expanding the social circles in which he circulates, so as to gain greater perspective on the seeming centrality of the London literary world:

> He judges far too much by the changes in cliques and clubs. For instance, Mr. Lewis actually says it is no longer an insult to call a

man a coward. [...] if he will walk out of his house and go round the whole world, calling every man a coward, and carefully record the reactions in every case, from the first Irish navvy to the last Japanese nobleman, he will come back (in the improbable event of his survival) realizing his error about the proportion of the change in the fundamental ideas of mankind.

(1 Aug.; 911)

A year after Chesterton's initiation of this public dialogue, Lewis wrote privately to propose sketching him for the collection, *Thirty Personalities and a Self-Portrait* (1932). In his invitation to sit, Lewis notes that '[i]t will give me very great pleasure to make your acquaintance', before reviving Marinetti's collective future predictive: 'we will have a talk' (BL Add MS 73238 fol.68). Though no record remains of the meeting, Lewis's foreword to the portfolio of prints suggests a spirited exchange, commending 'the post-gothic fullness of the brilliant sophist and catholic, G. K. Chesterton' (3). If the uncharacteristic tact of 'post-gothic fullness' is a far rhetorical cry from the 'fatness [... and] animal violence' of Lewis's earlier imaginings, it will also be observed that there is no sign of a 'sanguine grin' either in the resulting sketch or in Lewis's accompanying self-portrait. In a further projection of symmetry, both mouths are discreetly underemphasised, with canines respectfully sheathed (Figures 6.1 and 6.2):

Figure 6.1 G.K. Chesterton Esq., Wyndham Lewis, 1932.

Figure 6.2 *Self-Portrait*, Wyndham Lewis, 1932.

Munton argues that the eccentric extremism and unconscious self-contradiction that blemish *The Art of Being Ruled* indicate that Lewis had 'never talked over his ideas with any interlocutor, that he [had] never faced measured criticism' ('From', 170–71) during his period of self-isolation in the early 1920s. That a dialogue of this kind occurred during his encounter with Chesterton is suggested by the surprising re-assessment of the erstwhile drivelling imbecile set forth in *Rude Assignment*: 'I certainly respect [Chesterton] and even share' certain 'beliefs' (93). Once more, these beliefs were perhaps not so much of a theological as a cultural nature. Although the small 'c' of 'catholic' in Lewis's foreword to *Thirty Personalities* would seem a product of his idiosyncratic orthography, it also serves subtly to emphasise appreciative eclecticism over narrow dogmatism. In placing Chesterton's image amongst a diverse array of contemporaries, from Noel Coward to Augustus John, James Joyce, J.B. Priestley, and Rebecca West, Lewis's portfolio might offer a very satisfactory catalogue for a human circulating library, a sober counterpoint to the caricature compilations made popular by artists such as Kapp, whose collection of 1919 had presented Chesterton, John, Lewis, and Epstein in direct succession.

If Lewis's heterogeneous gallery suggests an aesthetic accommodation of Chesterton's advice to adopt a more cosmopolitan outlook, a year later Pound diagnosed a comparable, if inverse, myopia in the younger Chesterton in a meditation on 'Past History' (*English Journal*, May 1933): 'the prevailing line-up in England in the 1900s to 1910s was the Wells-Bennett-Chesterton, that simply did *not perceive* more than two thirds of the human spectrum' (Pound, *Joyce/Pound*, 248). Chesterton's increasing willingness to take serious account of Pound led to a still-more surprising *entente* in the years that followed. Once more, this progress towards mutual understanding was assisted by Chesterton's consistently mollifying rhetoric—even when challenging Pound's view of world history in *The New Jerusalem* (1920), he had referred to his antagonist as 'a man of great talent and information' (218). Pound responded with characteristic irascibility on that occasion, firing off a letter to the *Daily Telegraph* ('The Crusades: A Reply to Mr. Chesterton', 17 Sept. 1920) that begins by addressing three accusations that Chesterton had not made, while portraying his adversary as a Humpty-Dumpty-like linguistic trickster: 'It is impossible to be annoyed by Mr. Chesterton's calling me a Boche, a bungler, and a blasphemer', since he 'has so long been engaged in trying to prove that no word means anything in particular' (Pound, *Ezra Pound's*, 4:94).[14]

Pound goes on to make his customary complaint about Chesterton's advocacy of amateurism, while insisting that his antagonist's apparent criticisms might actually be taken for praise: Chesterton's 'life has been one long exemplification of his early manifesto to the effect that: "If a thing is worth doing it is worth doing badly"'; therefore, one might infer that 'in calling me a bungler he had but meant to imply that I was the incarnation of his cherished ideal' (Pound, *Ezra Pound's*, 4:94). Fourteen years later, this counterintuitive reading was at least partially vindicated by the favourable notice given to Pound's *Make it New* (1934) in the same radio broadcast in which Chesterton discussed *Men Without Art*. Again, the plaudits remain double-edged. While praising Pound as a 'brilliant thinker', Chesterton gently alludes to his tendency towards immoderation: he displays a propensity for 'furious likes and dislikes, which I have but should hesitate to state so furiously' (Pound, *Ezra Pound: The Critical*, 288/87).

Pound promptly grasped this olive branch, writing to thank Chesterton for the broadcast, while attempting to graft himself to the Chesterbelloc: 'we are all three definitely against Shaw, Wells etc' (qtd. in Stock, 329). Four months later, he wrote an open letter to the *New English Weekly* regretting an 'unmannerly swat at Mr Chesterton' in an earlier edition, which had 'failed to dissociate Chesterton's early playful style [...] from his present, perfectly straightforward writing on social infamies' (Pound, *Ezra Pound's*, 7 Mar. 1935; 6:256). As this suggests, Pound's new air of amiability was guided in part by the belief that he might have found a valuable venue of support for his economic views. His eye for an influential backer was undimmed, and if it is amusing to find him hoping to exploit Chesterton's influence over his acolytes—the precise grounds of his previous criticisms in the *New Age*—it is equally ironic to find him admonishing a fellow advocate of social credit that '[f]ailure to mention Chesterton *politely*' was a 'great mistake' (qtd. in Surette, 32; my emphasis). Pound's overtures were rewarded: from November 1934 onwards, *G.K.'s Weekly* presented him with an occasional platform for articles on economics (see Stock, 328). Six months later, the pair finally met, dining together in Rapallo while the Chestertons were in town to visit Beerbohm, at which point the baleful prediction made to John Quinn eighteen years earlier was finally realised: 'Pound discovered that he liked him' (Stock, 328).

This revelation of affinity might appear less than salutary in view of Pound's political progress through the 1930s. His dissenting parody of 'The Hollow Men' in the *Pisan Cantos* arises in the context of a eulogy to Mussolini, a figure with whom he increasingly allied himself after having had 'amiable jaw with Marinetti' in 1932, a meeting at which the latter had furnished Pound with 'futurist and fascist licherchoor' (Pound qtd. in Carpenter, 489). Nonetheless, Chesterton was set on a reverse trajectory over the same period. Although *G.K.'s Weekly* had evinced a tentative sympathy towards Mussolini in his early years as Italian prime minister, taking him for a fellow scourge of plutocracy, the democratic humanism that had inured Chesterton against Futurism ultimately preserved him from Pound's uncritical embrace of Fascism. His otherwise equivocal tract, *The Resurrection of Rome* (1930), ends with a 'warning against fascism' (345), and his deepening accord with the Men of 1914 remained tempered with the complaint that '[n]obody is less in the spirit of Walt Whitman than Wyndham Lewis or T.S. Eliot [...] Lewis seems to prefer a Dictatorship, in so far as he may be said to prefer anything' ('The Last Turn', collected in *The Well and the Shallows*; CW 3:432).

Pound's obituary of Chesterton, 'A Late Friend' ('*Un Compianto Amico*', *Il Mare* 20 June 1936), ends by observing that '[f]or his sympathetic manner, he merited not only honour but affection [...] Wherever there was injustice, it had Gilbert Chesterton for an enemy' (Pound, *Ezra Pound's*, 7:63).[15] This affirmation is borne out by an interview with the *Jewish Chronicle* in 1933, which places Chesterton at the vanguard of British social critics alive to the threat posed by Hitler, a demagogue 'driven to finding a scapegoat', who 'has found, with relief, the most famous scapegoat in European history—the Jewish people' ('Hitler', 22 Sept. 1933; 100). While declaring his willingness to 'die defending the last Jew in Europe' from the Nazis, Chesterton concedes, with rueful self-irony, '[t]hus does history play its ironical jokes upon us' ('Hitler', 100). One thinks of his observation on the moral character of his foundational journalistic inspiration, Samuel Johnson: 'There is no better test of a man's ultimate [...] integrity than how he behaves when he is wrong' ('The Real Dr. Johnson', collected in *Common*, 120–21).

Recall Chesterton's exposition of the virtues of trans-temporal integrity in 'A Defence of Rash Vows', in which he contrasts the 'horrible fairy tale of a man constantly changing into other men' with the positive vision of the 'man who makes a vow' and, in so doing, 'makes an appointment with himself at some distant time or place'. The 'Hitler' interview keeps an appointment made by 'To a Certain Nation' (*Speaker*, 7 Jan. 1899), a youthful poem in which Chesterton had mounted a passionate defence of Dreyfus against the French establishment, long before his identification with Belloc occasioned his metamorphosis into another man. A curious kinship pertains between Beerbohm's satirical portrayal of the resulting breach of integrity and Chesterton's private complaint that Belloc's unreflective dogmatism tended to provoke the irremediable ruptures of which Chesterton was so apprehensive: 'There is always such a *sundering* quality about Belloc's quarrels' (qtd. in Ward, *Gilbert*, 472).

In a circuitously revealing article 'On Courage and Independence' (collected in *The Thing: Why I Am a Catholic*, 1929), Chesterton begins by defending Belloc's comprehension of the Dreyfus case, before unnecessarily supplying a list of topics on which his friend's opinion is 'opposed to mine', amongst which is Belloc's view 'that wit is superior to humour' (CW 3:264). This divergence helps to account for Chesterton's ultimate recovery of psychological and ethical integrity. If the sentiment of Lear's Pelican chorus unexpectedly holds true between 'To a Certain Nation' and the 'Hitler' interview—'We think so then and we thought so still!'—these intuitive expressions of revolt against injustice are distinguished by a telling modification of tone: while the youthful exposition is humourlessly self-righteous, the mature response is measuredly self-mocking. Chesterton's belated acknowledgement that history had slipped him a butter-slide reflects his lifelong refinement of the conscious dual-mindedness of the humourist, confessedly 'caught in the entanglements and contradictions of human life' (*Spice*, 29). By abandoning the detached juridical certitudes of his friend and embracing the ties of buffoonish entanglement, Chesterton finally safeguarded himself against sundering the vows of his youthful self.[16]

Lewis's progress through the 1930s presents a remarkably similar portrait of ethical recovery. Having begun the decade by advocating appeasement of the Nazis in a series of bowdlerised accounts that confidently assured his readers that any concern over Hitler's expansionist aims could 'be entirely dismissed from the most apprehensive mind' (qtd. in Meyers, 188–89), he ended by recanting his earlier anti-Semitism with *The Jews: Are They Human?* (1939). The apparent offensiveness of Lewis's tin-eared title overshadows its status as another parody, this time entangling the projected cultural other with the national self, via an emendation of G.J. Renier's 1931 best-seller, *The English, Are They Human?* The parodic juxtaposition of 'Jews'/'English' gestures towards the culture of the melting-pot that Lewis considered to have rendered such distinctions obsolete, and any attendant prejudice embarrassingly *passé*: 'Bellocian antisemitism dates as heavily as a poke-bonnet [...] "the Jews" are an anachronism [...] just as much out-of-date as "John Bull"!' (22/108).

That Lewis was now capable of contemplating such immersive conceits with sanguinity reflects his increasing consciousness that the urge to attain unhuman satirical detachment was both psychologically and ethically unsustainable: 'it is extremely unintelligent [...] not to be humane' (9), as he belatedly reflects in the same text. A year earlier, he had amended his position on satire in *The Mysterious Mr Bull* (1938), a title that implies an extended detective enquiry into a figure long conceived as a synonym of Chesterton in Lewis's writing. In contrast to the 'chronic ailment' ascribed to the human condition in *Men without Art*, we are now told that '[s]atire is a criticism of human society [...] undertaken with the deliberate purpose of changing what is criticized' (*Mysterious*, 144). Lewis's fourth chapter is dedicated to an analysis of John Bull's 'Sense of Humour', characterising '[s]atire and humour' as respective signifiers of order and chaos, or 'the few and the many' (148), and setting out to establish whether '"satire" and "humour"' [can] exist 'upon equal terms' or are 'inimical to [each] other' (138). While Chesterton had preferred humour to wit while attributing value to both, the same ultimately proves true in reverse of Lewis. He acknowledges that there is 'no such thing as straight satire [...] mostly it is touched, and softened, with humour' (145), a dynamic that involves the satirist in a simultaneous criticism of the other and the self that bears the capacity to change both: '"satire" [...] does something to somebody else, whilst "humour" is rather a something that is done to [one]self [...] it is not directed outward, but inward' (146).

Many years later, Pound repented his Bellocian silencing of inward self-criticism, lamenting the 'harm I have done' from having 'arrived too late at ultimate uncertainty' (qtd. in Carpenter, 879/81). As Ackroyd observes, 'on a private level, it was Pound's very lack of scepticism and relativism which destroyed him' (119). For Chesterton, measured scepticism possessed an intermediate merit: 'It is the very definition of a madman that he is a man who can explain everything [...] there is one thing a madman never is, and that is a sceptic' ('A Glimpse of Paganism', *DN* 17 Mar. 1906; *CDN* 3:325). The suspicion that the conspiratorial certitudes of Belloc inform this account is bolstered by Chesterton's rueful reflection, a month later, that '[m]y best friends are all either bottomless sceptics or quite uncontrollable believers' ('The Extraordinary Cabman', *DN* 7 Apr. 1906; *CDN* 3:337), phrasing that implies the desirability of settling upon a moderating balance of the two extremes.

Eliot ultimately came to a similar conclusion. Whereas Pound had declared '[p]erhaps be damned' (qtd. in Liebregts, 133) in the margins of the draft of *The Waste Land*, the mature 'Mr. Eliot' of 1933 claimed to restrict himself to 'If and Perhaps and But' (*PTSE* 1:143). This self-mocking account suggests a performative accommodation of Lewis's criticism that Eliot was the bottomless sceptic to Pound's uncontrollable believer, seemingly bereft of 'sincerity in the sense of integral belief of any sort' (*Men*, 81).[17] The 'Mr Eliot' persona possesses the same function that Hutcheon attributes to intentional self-parody: 'disowning earlier mannerisms by externalisations' (10). By drawing ironic attention to his reputation for equivocation, Eliot's histrionic buffoonery is conceived as a means of inducting a new atmosphere of cultural candour: 'I no longer pretend that I am pretending' (qtd. in Ricks, *T.S. Eliot*, 187), as he later explained to Pound.

In 'The Reaction of the Intellectuals', Chesterton detects a comparable about-turn in Eliot, discussing the very ontological scepticism that had characterised the poet's early verse as the engine of a recent change in his worldview: 'Mr. Eliot [has] the sense to see that the half-truths of the sceptic are not only edged tools, but double-edged tools. [... In] the last resort they can inoculate the mind with doubts about doubt itself' (*CW* 3:407). Eliot later formulated a similar argument with reference to the same form of scepticism that Bentley's youthful withdrawal into *ataraxia* had resembled: 'Scepticism is a highly civilised trait', but 'when it declines into pyrrhonism, it is one of which civilisation can die. Where scepticism is strength, pyrrhonism is weakness: for we need not only the strength to defer a decision, but the strength to make one' (*Notes*, 29).

The most decisive instance of Eliot acting upon this principle—his religious conversion—is the context for another of Chesterton's parodic accounts of the mid-1930s. 'The New Bigotry' (*G.K.'s Weekly*, 13 Sept. 1934) elaborates upon the schism between the poet and his followers, combining an exuberant parody of the excesses of Eliot's early stylistics with a mocking account of the bafflement of his acolytes at their hero's recent *volte-face*:

> A young idealistic poet, full of the new visions of beauty, writes verses appropriate to such a vision; as, for instance:
>
> Bug-house underbogies belch daybreak back-firing.
> Daylight's a void-vomit; steadying legs to stump.
>
> And all the young critics know he is all right.
>
> (*Common*, 227)

While the references to belching and vomit once more invoke an abject physical evacuation, 'bug' forms a punning allusion to the spread of infection.[18] As with the gruesome underworld of Pound's 'Hell Cantos' and the 'bighorror' that Lewis encodes within his parodies of Joyce, the subconscious anxieties, or 'underbogies', of the parodist are thus revealed by the air of automatic writing, which complements Eliot's own artistic process in constructing the final section of *The Waste Land*. These apparitions dissipate when Chesterton continues his narrative of the poet's spiritual progress, which we are assured 'is a strictly correct biography of a man of genius who has come to us from America—Mr. T.S. Eliot' (*Common*, 227):

> a horrid whisper goes round that he was seen outside an Episcopal Church near Vermont. The whole horrid truth is soon known. He has admitted to a newspaper man that he believes in God. Then the young critics go back gloomily and stare at his poetry; and, strangely enough, see for the first time that there was something awfully old-fashioned in saying "daylight" when Binx might have said "sky-blank".
>
> (*Common*, 227)

The ironic motif of impropriety that Chesterton injects into this account is fitting in view of Woolf's arch response to the news of Eliot's conversion: 'I have had a most shameful and distressing interview with poor dear Tom Eliot [...] there's something obscene in a living person sitting by the fire and believing in God' (Woolf, *Change*, 11 Feb 1928, 3:457–58). Chesterton's parody of biographical prose perhaps also aims a blow at Aldington's satire, 'Stepping Heavenward: A Record' (1931), a mock-hagiography of Jeremy Cibber, an Eliotic historian 'with a faint trace of satire in his voice' (*Soft*, 214) whose accession to cultural sainthood from obscure beginnings in 'Colonsville' (199) USA, is savagely lampooned as 'a case of chronic constipation' (198) turned to literary purpose. Cibber's eventual religious conversion entails doing 'violence to his nature' by making 'a decision' (*Soft*, 240), after which he becomes 'the acknowledged if unofficial Social-intellectual Dictator of England' (241), though his personality remains 'a vacuum' (243).

Although Aldington's narrator affects to lament the 'fashionable spirit of belittlement' that has gripped modern biography as a consequence of 'secular bigotry' (*Soft*, 198), the Stracheyan irreverence of the satire perhaps tacitly informs Chesterton's parody of the format in 'The New Bigotry'. If so, Chesterton satirises the satirist, situating Aldington—a signatory of the original Vorticist manifesto now bent upon belittling his former associates—as the dull-witted conformist to cultural fashion. Since Eliot had been wounded by what he later termed Aldington's 'cruel and unkind lampoon' (qtd. in Gates, 91), Chesterton's intervention would have offered welcome public evidence of his sympathetic support.

In an earlier article on 'Progress in the Arts' (*ILN* 27 Nov. 1926), Chesterton had identified a more enduring movement towards aesthetic conformity in those 'modern artists' who have 'return[ed] to a more normal manner', affirming that 'the moment when artists become intelligible is the moment when they become truly and triumphantly individual' (*CW* 34:209). Looking back from the vantage point of 1953, Lewis explained his comparable career path to Kenner: while he had been 'an extremist' in his youth, his 'later novels (post Apes of God)' were energised by a quasi-parodic stress upon 'avoiding eccentricity—not acting oneself, but tacitly impersonating someone' else, in order 'to tell a story' (*Letters*, 23 Nov.; 552).

In 'Progress in the Arts', Chesterton contrasts this authentic creative evolution with a scenario that uncannily anticipates the titular conceit of *The Apes of God*: 'there is [also] a sort of bad parody of this good process [...] *diabolus simius Dei*' ('the devil is an ape of God'; *CW* 34:209). In an appropriately circular movement, almost thirty years later, Lewis added a diabolic prefix to Chesterton's essay title with *The Demon of Progress in the Arts* (1954), a comprehensive repudiation of 'the glamour of the extreme' (68) in art. Lewis warns of the enticements of abstraction in terms that recall Chesterton's account of the pure nonsense-writer 'passing the borderland' and crashing 'through the floor of sense' into a 'starry abyss': 'in the arts as in everything else' there exists 'a certain well-defined line [...] beyond that limit there is nothing. Nothing, zero, is what logically you reach past a line, of some kind, laid down by nature' (32). The artist who progresses 'over the side of the precipice' (33) risks a bathetic self-annihilation: in crossing 'the line beyond which the extreme [becomes] the nonsensical' (35), the artist 'commit[s] a clownish suicide' (92).

If this imagery is suggestive of the 'sky-blank' into which Binx descends in his pursuit of novelty, one thinks once more of Pound's unwise collaboration with the would-be avant-gardist, Ernest Walsh, conducted in the same period as the publication of 'The Hollow Men'. In 'The Romance of Rhyme', Chesterton had contrasted the 'proud [...] unpopularity' of the *vers libres* of 'the aristocrats of the New Learning' (*Fancies*, 18) with the 'huge popular power' of 'the human love of a song, a riddle, a proverb, a pun or a nursery rhyme; the sing-song of innumerable children's games, the chorus of a thousand camp-fires' (*Fancies*, 17). The comprehensive applicability of this taxonomy of popular forms to the parodic quatrains of 'The Hollow Men' reflects Eliot's mobilisation of the 'positive network of notions and allusions' ('The Meaning of Mock Turkey', collected in *Fancies*, 35) that Chesterton discovered in the nursery rhyme form, thus happily disproving his thesis that 'the enlightened disapprove' of such rhymes and might ultimately 'destroy' (*Fancies*, 35) them. By picking up the baton in turn with his parody of Eliot's parody, Chesterton brought to a close a forty-year fascination with the network of notions and allusions that he particularly attached to the mulberry bush rhyme as a metaphor of cultural integration.

The Meaning of the Mulberry Bush

In the 'Spice of Life' broadcast, Chesterton's encomium to Eliot as 'a man of genius [...] for whom I have a very special admiration' (*Spice*, 165) is offset by a projected point of departure: 'I recognize the great realities Mr. Eliot has revealed; but I do not admit that this is the deepest reality'; perhaps 'Mr. Eliot described the desolation he found more than the desolation he felt. But I think that "The Waste Land" was at least a world in which he had wandered' (*Spice*, 166). In setting out to establish his own position, Chesterton prefaces his parody of 'The Hollow Men' by invoking a more ingenuous, unworldly conceit first explored in the title of his literary debut, *Greybeards at Play*, thirty-six years earlier:

> It is doubtless a grotesque spectacle that the great-grandfathers should still be dancing with indecent gaiety, when the young are so grave and sad; but [...] I will defend the spiritual appetite of my own age. I will even be so indecently frivolous as to break into song....
>
> (*Spice*, 166–67)

As this echo of *Greybeards* suggests, in Chesterton's combustive 'end' is his beginning.[19] The *Greybeards* preface pre-empts Eliot's allusion to 'Here we go round the mulberry bush', employing the rhyme to symbolise Chesterton's utopian conception of friendship via a literal rendition of what he termed elsewhere 'the cosmic camaraderie of the child' ('George MacDonald and His Work', *DN* 11 June 1901; *CDN* 1:102):

> Behold the simple sum of things,
> Where in one splendour spun,
> The stars go round the Mulberry Bush,
> The Burning Bush, the Sun.
>
> (*Collected Nonsense*, 4)

Recall that Chesterton's view of the impossibility of the 'sum of all things being barren' was the message that he sought to convey in his correspondence with Bentley. In Bentley's diary of 1894, he writes, on two consecutive days, 'I am feeling like a stuffed man' and '[h]ow fares it, I wonder, among the dwellers in Kensington. Do they laugh and sing?' (14–15 Nov.; Bod MS Eng.misc.e.862).[20] These rather extraordinary anticipations of both Eliot's poem and Chesterton's parody help to explain the alacrity with which Chesterton attempted to establish a sympathetic dialogue with Eliot, as a means of positively resolving a relationship that bore such striking similarities to the friendship that had accompanied the traumas of his youth.

Chesterton's first textual reference to the mulberry bush rhyme dates back to the mid-1890s in 'Shipwrecked off Fairyland', a play in verse and prose, or 'a sort of fairy farce' (*CW* 10:201), as he terms it. This sketch includes an interlude of 'The Song of the Mulberry Bush', in which 'three old gentlemen' resolve to 'reestablish the sports of their childhood' (*CW* 10:206), thus prefiguring the 'indecent gaiety' of the 'great-grandfathers' in the 'Spice of Life' broadcast. Astonishingly, this pursuit finds expression in the old gentlemen chanting:

> They can snigger, but we can sing—
> Here we go round the Mulberry Bush,
> Three old fools in the staring sun.
>
> (*CW* 10:206)

While Chesterton's conjoining of 'fools' to mulberries demonstrates his consciousness of the etymological kernel later ingrained tacitly within 'The Hollow Men', the almost exact correspondence between Chesterton's terms in 'Shipwrecked off Fairyland' and in his parody of Eliot—texts separated by forty years—suggests that Eliot's manipulation of the nursery rhyme had rekindled Chesterton's memories of the earliest stirrings of his own rebellion against the pessimistic culture of the age.

A year after *Greybeards at Play*, Chesterton revisited the rhyme at the outset of his journalistic career, this time investing it with a utopian social moral in the same series of articles that produced the 'Human Circulating Library'. In 'Some Urgent Reforms: Playgrounds for Adults II' (*Speaker*, 30 Nov. 1901), he notes that amongst the various forms of 'strictly ceremonial rejoicing' undertaken by children, '[o]ne of the most universal and popular forms [...] is that represented by "Here we go round the mulberry-bush," which consists of nothing but running round in a ring. It consists of the circle, the very type of equality and communism, the figure in which all points are equally distant from the centre' (BL MS Add.73381 fol.77). Alluding to the cultural influence of *The Golden Bough*, he goes on to discuss the curious fact that while

> games [such] as 'Here we go round the mulberry-bush' may be said to constitute the first class of children's games, the purely ritualistic [... in] an age when the sense of ritual is supposed to have been revived it is nothing short of scandalous that human beings in the fulness of life and strength have not revived these elementary and beautiful movements.
>
> (BL MS Add.73381 fol.77)

Chesterton crystallises the point with a parody, in the form of a reverse travesty, arguing that if this sublime ideal of play could be achieved in the adult world,

> [t]he rude rhymes which are sung to them might blossom, as the ancient legends have blossomed, into elevated poetry. [...] The song
>
> "Here we go round the mulberry-bush
> On a cold and frosty morning."
>
> might take the form of
>
> "Though the pale day be paler with snow,
> Yet round the mulberry laden boughs we go."
>
> (BL MS Add.73381 fol.77)

The argument conveyed by this parody recalls Eliot's view in the period immediately preceding 'The Hollow Men', as paraphrased by Kenner: 'an aristocratic art [...] is the refinement, not the antithesis, of folk art' (*Invisible*, 161). This standpoint has an affinity with Chesterton's foundational argument in 'A Defence of Farce' that popular forms simply require a 'gust of generous artistic pride to lift them up' to the status of high art—people must begin to speak 'of "sonnets" with the same accent with which they speak of "music-hall songs"' (*Defendant*, 122). This generic egalitarianism finds further expression in Chesterton's assessment of Edward Lear as 'one of the great masters of English literature' ('How Pleasant to Know Mr. Lear', *Nation* 1908, collected in *Handful*, 123), a mischievous confounding of 'high' and 'low' culture later echoed in Eliot's observation to Stravinsky 'that he considered Edward Lear to be a great poet and compared him with Mallarmé' (Ackroyd, 252).

In addition to the 'unpleasant [...] Mr. Eliot' encountered in 'Lines for Cuscuscaraway and Mirza Murad Ali Beg', Eliot's self-reflexive pastiches of Lear include 'How to Pick a Possum' (1939), in which the poet's transformation into a character from popular children's literature leads him to become a more welcome guest: 'How delightful to meet the O'Possum' (*PTSE* 2:211–12). Long before the emergence of Eliot and Pound as the modernist Old Possum and Br'er Rabbit, Chesterton had noted that 'the Uncle Remus stories reveal, what all real folklore reveals'—the falsity of any belief in the 'cool superiority of one section of life over another' ('American Slaves and Female Emancipation', *ILN* 1 Aug. 1908; *CW* 28:152). A comparable ethos informs Eliot's request that Groucho Marx should send him a signed photograph that he might place 'next to Paul Valéry [...] snuggled up to Yeats's (letter of 1961; *PTSE* 2:203). In *The Jews: Are They Human?* Lewis affirms his own allegiance to the Marx Brothers, in a passage that ascribes a beneficent spirit of carnivalesque disruption to Jewish transnational finance:

> Commercially they are said to be a disintegrating element. Amongst our stately business institutions to have a lot of them knocking about is like letting loose a troupe of Marx Brothers [...] like having a Poltergeist in the bank vaults [...] I have always been attracted by Poltergeists. As in watching those American-Jewish comedians, Groucho and Harpo, my sympathy is always with them [...] so my sympathy is with their counterparts in the real world.
>
> (74)

Lewis's increasingly candid appreciation of knockabout comedy is mirrored in Eliot's profession of a taste for the more 'simple [...] kinds of practical joke' (Eliot qtd. in Ackroyd, 234). An example occurs in a letter sent to the *Times* in 1935, in which the poet advances a poker faced proposal for 'the formation of a Society for the Preservation of Ancient Cheeses' (qtd. in Chinitz, 177). As with the delightful qualities of the hero of 'How to Pick a Possum', which include the revelation that 'he eats almost nothing but cheese' (*PTSE* 2:212), Eliot's scheme is both staged and sincere, echoing the ethos of Chesterton's 'Sonnet to a Stilton Cheese', in which a burlesque account of the author's feats of gluttony had offset the accompanying article's sober critique of the decline of localised food production.

On another occasion, Eliot engaged in a more private performance of cheese connoisseurship, farcically reapplying his famously fastidious literary persona to the painstaking examination of a Stilton, after which he informed his interlocutor, 'I am afraid I cannot recommend it' (Kenner, *Pound*, 441). In the context of Eliot's wariness of calcification, consider once more Chesterton's observation that '[b]ad cheese symbolises the startling prodigy of matter taking on vitality'. By satirising the air of exquisite refinement that he had established early in his career, Eliot finally attained Chesterton's ideal of the 'genial grotesque', displaying a gift for self-revitalisation to which Chesterton perhaps alludes in his panegyrics to the poet's 'genius', a term connotative of exceptional generative mastery.

Auden noted that there was within Eliot 'a conscientious churchwarden [... but] there was also a twelve-year-old boy, who liked to surprise over-solemn wigs by offering them explosive cigars' (qtd. in Eliot, *Letters*, 4:384n1). The two strands come together in a further anecdote that reveals the mature Eliot to be not so much a direct descendant of Chesterton as a one-man Chesterbentley, balancing his academic and popular inclinations in dynamic opposition. At meetings of the Christian sociology society, the Chandos Group, Phillip Mairet recalled Eliot's assumption of a certain 'detachment'; at one particular meeting he 'lampooned' everyone present 'with clerihews' (qtd. in Ackroyd, 222). A surviving example from 1937 turns upon a suggestive juxtaposition of burlesque corporeality and modernist statuary, the second couplet presenting an exemplary image of sublime vulgarity:

Mr. Hilderic Cousens
Ordered oysters by dozens,
And after fifteen Guinesses
Resembled Epstein's *Genesis*.

(*PTSE* 2:183)

Eliot's achievement of a balance in duality calls to mind Chesterton's conclusion to *Manalive*, in which the sober professional, Dr. Cyrus Pym, and the disillusioned ironist, Michael Moon, finally agree on the benignity of the Chestertonian figure, Innocent Smith, after which each assumes a more genial air. Appropriately enough, *Manalive* incorporates a further circuit around the mulberry bush, instigated by Moon:

"let's dance round that bush!"
 "Why, what bush do you mean?" asked Rosamund, looking round with a sort of radiant rudeness.
 "The bush that isn't there," said Michael—"the Mulberry bush".
(28)

This reprise of the rhyme, articulated through the Bentleyan voice of Moon, forms another of Chesterton's attempts to compel life to imitate art in the hope of engendering an alteration in his friend's temperament. Nicolas Bentley later wrote of his father in terms that echo the internal contradictions of Chesterton's fictional renderings:

> [He] was a complicated man, much more complicated than you would have imagined from his manner, which was shy, although it was open and interested. He was extraordinarily reserved, and yet he was capable of being extremely affectionate. He valued friendship, and yet often seemed deliberately to discourage it.
>
> (20)

When the son goes on to chart his father's ultimate decline into hypochondria and alcoholism (see Bentley, N., 20), the account offers a melancholy postscript to the hopes for positive resolution that Chesterton had inscribed within his fiction.

In recording his grief at Chesterton's death, Bentley particularly mourned the conclusion of a lifelong 'conversation', the termination of which had 'put an end to [...] much of my pleasure in existence' (*Those*, 46). The consequences of this loss of dialogic grounding are rendered dispiritingly vivid in his final published work, *Far Horizon: A Biography of Hester Dowden, Medium and Psychic Investigator* (1951), a bizarre hagiographic testimony that represents Bentley's ultimate expression of withdrawal from engagement with the material world. *Far Horizon* recurs to the conflicts of the *fin de siècle*, in which he and Chesterton had dabbled in the planchette (see Chesterton, *Autobiography*, 82–85; Bod MS.Eng. misc.e.864, 16–17 Jan. 1896), while replacing the vision of cosmic camaraderie that Chesterton derived from the song of the mulberry bush with a comprehensively contra-Chestertonian system of metaphysical Idealism, based upon the 'evolution of the soul upwards [...] to an eventual mergence in the great cosmic ocean of the God-spirit' (Bentley, *Far*, 95). As this snippet suggests, the text is invested throughout with an inadvertent air of bathos, expressed at times through an awkward marriage of the material and the sublime—Bentley explains that his information must be 'painfully digested by all who wish to become students of cosmic philosophy' (95).

One begins to wonder if this could be a final, inscrutable practical joke on Bentley's part, akin to the burlesque 'bad cold' (*PTSE* 1:56) that afflicts Eliot's dubious mystic, Madame Sosostris, or the screwball supernaturalism of Lewis's Marxian poltergeist.[21] However, Bentley's rhetoric proves all too earnest—the earlier dedication of *Trent's Last Case* to Chesterton is now replaced with a dedication to 'the spirit of Carneades' (Bentley, *Far*), the Greek Academic Sceptic philosopher, whom Bentley believed he had successfully channelled following Dowden's death.[22] Over half a century after their earliest intellectual sparring, the divide between Bentley and Chesterton remains drawn upon the popular and the academic. Bentley's identity-confounding communion with Carneades forms a sharp contrast with the more self-possessed scepticism displayed by Chesterton in 'The Vulgar Ghost' (*DN* 15 Aug. 1908), in which he had argued that a 'fraud effected by phosphorescent lights is a thing that stinks in the nostrils like phosphorous. But a turnip ghost is as healthy and sustaining as a turnip', a distinction that attests to '[t]he superiority of the vulgar ghost' (*CDN* 5:128).

Bentley's withdrawal into discourse with the dead of antiquity starkly illustrates his disengagement from a modernity with which Chesterton never ceased to grapple. The constructiveness of the latter approach is illustrated by the expression of amended allegiance affixed to Chesterton's final essay collection, *The Well and the Shallows*—'I should be proud to dedicate this book to T.S. Eliot' (*CW* 3:340)—thirty-five years after his first publication had been dedicated to Bentley. The pair's dedicatory divergence suggests that Chesterton had been wise to respond warily to the detachment of pure nonsense. In 'A Defence of Nonsense', he argues that Lewis Carroll was 'something of a Philistine' (*Defendant*, 65). Likewise, Nicolas Bentley's list of his father's paradoxes includes the observation that although he 'was cultivated and was widely read [...] in most matters of taste he was a Philistine'; he 'grew more and more out of sympathy with the age he lived in', displaying 'an extraordinarily meagre [...] interest in contemporary literature' (20). This contention is corroborated by *Far Horizon*, in which Bentley authenticates Dowden's notorious claim to have acted as a literal ghost writer to Wilde, whose dispatches from the spirit-world included criticisms of contemporary literature, most notably the news that he 'abhor[red] James Joyce' (*Far*, 70).

Although Chesterton was sceptical of the value of Joyce's late excursions into 'heavy nonsense', he affirmed nonetheless that '[o]n an all-round view of cultural traditions and spiritual potentialities, I think it probable that I should very much prefer Mr. Joyce to Mr. Dodgson' ('On Phases of Eccentricity', collected in *All I Survey*, 53). He demurred at *Ulysses* primarily on the grounds that it was insufficiently dialogic and, consequently, not as Rabelaisian as frequently thought: 'Rabelais sometimes seems confusing, because he is like twenty men talking at once; but Joyce is rather inaudible, because he is talking to himself' (*CW* 21:607–608). Chesterton's counterintuitive reading closely mirrors that of Lewis in *Time and Western Man*, in which he avers that 'it is the manner of Rabelais that is parodied' in *Ulysses*, 'and the matter of that unusually profound writer is not very much disturbed' (122), while contending that Joyce's dyadic protagonists merely represent two sides of 'the author, thinly disguised' (117), rather than an authentic dialogue between self and other.

In an article designed to articulate the guiding principles of *G.K.'s Weekly* ('How I shall Deface this Paper', 4 Apr. 1925), Chesterton stresses the value of cross-cultural dialogue, beginning by urging that there is no reason 'why a thing should not be popular and serious', before explaining that the periodical will be built upon the principle of 'contrast' and 'combination': 'I should like a man to pick up this paper for amusement and find himself involved in an argument' (Chesterton, 'How', 81). Accordingly, while he published Bernard Gilbert's ambiguously jocular proposal to put 'Shaw or Joyce to death' Gilbert, (84), he also gave Shaw a platform to issue 'Provocations' (21 Mar. 1935). This enduring enthusiasm for dialogic exchange ultimately provided the impetus for his *rapprochement* with Eliot, Lewis, and Pound. As with Bentley's lamentation at the loss of Chesterton's 'conversation', Eliot's obituary emphasised the sense of 'personal loss and isolation' ('Obituary', 531) that he experienced upon hearing the news of Chesterton's death, despite never having met his sometime public adversary.

In 'Doppelgänger' (*Encounter*, Jan. 1954), a late satire of Pound, Lewis addresses the danger of capitulating entirely to the demands of one's public reputation. The central premise of Beerbohm's satire of Wilde, 'The Happy Hypocrite', lurks behind the narrator's comparison of the persona of the Poundian protagonist, Thaddius Trunk, to 'the extraordinary grimaces some men affect, until, two-thirds of the way through life, the face integrally includes the grimace' (27). As he explains, '[n]o poet as fine as he is should maintain so compromising a parasite' as the 'publicity figure' that the reclusive, mountain-bound Trunk has allowed to take possession of his later years, '[f]or a man's publicity is a caricature of himself' (24). When the narrator speculates that this Trunk might possess a 'false bottom' (23), the textual correspondences extend to Chesterton's satire of Ezza Montano, whose declaration, '"if I ever had a private character, I have forgotten it"', had reflected his status as a mere '"bundle of masks"'.[23]

Lewis's high-modernist manifesto, 'The Code of a Herdsman', had advised that a range of 'masks' should be adopted when circulating amongst the masses who dwell at the foot of the cultural mountainside: 'Above all this sad commerce with the herd, let something veritably remain "un peu sur la montagne"' ('Imaginary', 7). In 'The Paradise of Thieves', Ezza's surname, Montano, derives from the Latin *montanus*, or 'dweller in the mountains' (Ripman, 289), while Vivien Eliot's protagonist in 'Fête Galante' remarks of the Eliotic poet-financier, 'the devil took him up a high mountain and showed him all the kingdoms of the world—unfortunately for him! [...] He's still up on the mountain, so far as I know' (562). In a similar manner, Lewis's portrayal of Trunk's residence *sur la montagne* serves belatedly to interrogate the value system of 'The Code of a Herdsman'—Trunk's stately retreat is conceived not so much an act of fidelity to high-modernist ethics as a metaphor of the movement's cultural exhaustion: 'Would Trunk die if he stepped down from this lofty mountain site? Probably' (26).

Despite Lewis's monitory account, both he and Eliot ran a comparable risk of being overwhelmed by their self-created public personae, just as Chesterton and Shaw had threatened to be 'swallowed up' by G.K.C.

and G.B.S. a generation earlier. Edmund Wilson considered Eliot 'a genuine person, whose work is of exceptional interest, but [...] the public "Mr. Eliot" is a fictional character, a creation of T.S. Eliot's' (qtd. in Chinitz, 175). Likewise, Chapman argues that Lewis's 'public image' increasingly crossed over into 'his writing and drawing and began to lead a dual life with the private person. Wyndham Lewis left the stage to "Mr. Wyndham Lewis"' (27). As we have seen, 'The Hollow Men' pursues a self-regenerative agenda by satirising the public monument into which Eliot threatened to petrify; similarly, Lewis protests in 'Doppelgänger' that he is conducting an ethical travesty; the purpose of his 'debunking' is to enact a galvanic transformation scene: to 'reduce poor old Trunk from the Greek statue he has become, back into flesh and blood again' (24).

In 'A Defence of Rash Vows', Chesterton deprecates the Decadent movement's programmatic espousal of artifice, arguing that the 'most hellish' situation imaginable 'is to be eternally acting a play without even the narrowest and dirtiest greenroom in which to be human' (*Defendant*, 34). Prior to his construction of the 'inhuman [...] mask' of Evan Royal from the refashioned materials of the Harlequinade, the young Lewis had established a greenroom of his own in the realm of popular culture. As Augustus John recalled, although his youthful behaviour resembled 'a perpetual performance' (paraphrased in Munton, 'Wyndham', 141), Lewis displayed a more ingenuous response to the stimulus of 'popular art' in the form of the *Commedia dell'Arte*: 'overcome with satisfaction, he would drop his mask and howl with laughter like a human being!' (qtd. in Munton, 'Wyndham', 141).

In the 1930s, Eliot's decampment from the mountain to reengage with popular culture was the occasion of some alarm amongst his critical adherents. John Holmes's view that the publication of *Old Possum's Book of Practical Cats* (1939) should have somehow been 'prevented' (qtd. in Chinitz, 179) speaks to the widespread critical 'embarrassment' (Chinitz, 179) caused by the poet's trampling upon his former strictures. To return to Pound's criticism of Chesterton's relationship to his followers, Eliot was 'the man who [had] taught them how to do it', and he later acknowledged his responsibility for this stifling dynamic with rueful candour:

> In my earlier years I obtained, partly by subtlety, partly by effrontery, and partly by accident, a reputation amongst the credulous for learning and scholarship, of which (having no further use for it) I have since tried to *disembarrass* myself.
> (Eliot qtd. in Sullivan, 170; my emphasis)

In *The Ball and the Cross*, a contributory factor in the protagonists' final reconciliation is their increasing sense that they possess a common foe in the massed audience of acolytes and critics who perpetually interfere in their disagreement. This conception of an intellectual hierarchy that transcends ideological difference, and ultimately bonds the disputants, is present in Chesterton's cautious demarcation of the work of Joyce and Pound from that of Walsh, and Lewis's dismay that 'a great poet' like Trunk should be discovered consorting with what Chesterton had termed the 'mob' of modernist bandwagon-jumpers, the 'hordes of warblers [who] poison him with their dullness' (Lewis, 'Doppelgänger', 27). A comparable differentiation of true coin from counterfeit is present in Eliot's affirmation that

> [n]o one admires and enjoys [...] such delightful fiction as Mr. Chesterton's *The Man Who Was Thursday*, or his *Father Brown* [...] more than I do; I would only remark that when the same effect is aimed at by zealous persons of lesser talent [...] the effect is negative.
> ('Religion and Literature', 1935; collected in *Selected*, 100)

In a chapter of *The Writer and the Absolute* (1952) concerned with 'The Community of Writers', Lewis addresses the importance of establishing solidarity between authors of significance irrespective of cultural affiliation, proposing that 'what used to be called the "Republic of Letters"' (52) must be re-established and, with it, 'a reinforcement of the writer's corporate consciousness' (54) in order to counter the critical tendency to pit authors against one another along cultural fault lines of suspect motivation and acuity. As Eliot belatedly acknowledged, when 'groups of writers and artists give themselves' labels that appeal to 'professors' such as '"romanticists" or "classicists"', they 'should not be taken very seriously; their chief value is temporary and political' (*After*, 25). Faced with an increasingly falsifying public narrative of their own invention, the disputants in the culture wars of modernism finally dropped their pantomime masks and began engaging with one another in human terms. As Eliot explained to Chesterton, he had initiated their correspondence because 'I did not like to be judged by anyone of your importance at second hand' (Eliot, *Letters*, 21 Oct. 1928; 4:283).

As with Chesterton's greenroom in which to be human, Lewis's Republic of Letters represents a conceptual amnesty space: 'a kind of Switzerland' (Lewis, *Writer*, 54), allowing 'for its members that unimpeded latitude of expression which' would produce a 'master prophylactic against obsessional contagions' (53) both within its ranks and its audience. Like the Human Circulating Library, this heterogeneous collective is conceived as a means of moderating bias through exposure to alternative thought. One thinks once more of the dialogic arena of the domestic courtroom of *Manalive*, in which the community establishes a benign means of reining in extremism while accommodating eccentricity. In this sense, Lewis's communitarian proposition possesses an ethical value comparable to that which Chesterton attributed to Dickens's espousal of 'a grotesque democracy. By that is more properly meant a vastly varying democracy' (*Charles*, 126).

The enduring symbol of the grotesque in Chesterton's imaginative landscape was the cross, which he discusses in *The Ball and the Cross* as 'primarily and above all things at enmity with itself. The cross is the conflict of two hostile lines, of irreconcilable direction' (*CW* 7:41). If this presents an apt analogy of the curiously contrapuntal confrontation between Chesterton and literary modernism, it is appropriate that the unresolved duel between his ideological adversaries, MacIan, the uncontrollable believer, and Turnbull, the bottomless sceptic, finds repeated symbolic expression in their swords meeting in the shape of a cross—an image that conveys conjunction as much as conflict. At one perilous stage, 'the two bright, bloodthirsty weapons made the sign of the cross in horrible parody upon each other' (*CW* 7:152); at the novel's close, this image is transmuted into a benign symbol of reconciliation: the combatants finally abandon the field of battle, leaving their swords discarded 'haphazard in the pattern of a cross' (*CW* 7:258).

Notes

1 Ricks has observed that Stevenson is a possible further influence upon the mulberry bush parody of 'The Hollow Men'. See 'A Note on "The Hollow Men" and Stevenson's *The Ebb-Tide*.' *Essays in Criticism* 51:1 (2001): 8–17.
2 First published in *Blast* 2 (48) and later collected in *Prufrock*.
3 No such meeting transpired.
4 As recently as April 2015, an otherwise incisive article in the *Atlantic* states baldly that Chesterton 'hated Eliot's "The Hollow Men"' (Parker).
5 See, for example, Bernard Bergonzi's description of 'The Hollow Men' as 'a literally hopeless poem, though stylish in its despair' (104).
6 In 'The Spirit of the Age in Literature', Chesterton places Lawrence on both sides of the divide, in an approving account of his 'childlike and honourable seriousness [...] He did not always sneer. But the moral chaos of his time delayed the self-education of his genius' (*CW* 21:608–09).
7 Pound reflects 'That maggots shd/ eat the dead bullock' three lines before correcting 'the Possum' (*Cantos*, 425) on the auditory qualities of the apocalypse.
8 Zagreus has been interpreted as a satirical composite of Pound and Horace de Vere Cole (see O'Keefe, 290).
9 Joyce associates Lewis with both Carroll and Alice throughout *Finnegans Wake* (see Glasheen, 167).
10 As Pullman had remarked of the Bailiff, '"I doubt if [he] would admit it as an allowable opinion that we were behaviourist machines addressed to a static millennium of suffering [...] He's dead against the famous stoic apathy he won't hear of it. Epicurus's ataraxia he hates even more"' (*Childermass*, 78–79).
11 In contrast, Beerbohm reported to William Rothenstein that he 'did once look into' *The Apes of God*, 'but it disgusted me so much that I only read a few pages' (Beerbohm, *Max and Will*, 20 July 1939; 154).

12 These articles were republished as *Doom of Youth* by Chatto and Windus in 1932. My citations are from this edition.
13 Similarly, the title of *Men without Art* parodies Ernest Hemingway's *Men without Women* (1927).
14 Chesterton's original article, 'The New Jerusalem. The Crusade. Chapter XI', appeared in the *Daily Telegraph* (10 Sept. 1920). His discussion of Pound came in response to a 'pastiche' column in the *New Age* ('The Regional. XVIII', 20 Nov. 1919).
15 This is my translation. The original reads, '*Per I suoi modi simpatico, egli meritava non soltanto onore, ma affetto [...]Dove fu ingiustizia, questa ingiustizia trovo in Gilbert Chesterton un nemico*'.
16 Although Chesterton assures the *Jewish Chronicle* that he 'and Belloc' ('Hitler', 100) would both be willing to lay down their lives in defense of Jewish freedoms, this looks very much like a further example of his adherence to Whitman's maxim, 'what I assume you shall assume', much as Bentley remarked to Christopher Hollis that the *Thursday* dedication had 'ascribed to him a far more definite creed than any he in fact possessed' (Hollis, 62).
17 Perhaps conscious of his reputation preceding him, Eliot signs off one letter to Chesterton with the emphatic assurance that he is '[y]ours very sincerely' (Eliot, *Letters*, 8 Mar. 1929; 4:463).
18 It is striking that the 'bug-house' to which Chesterton refers is the same slang term for a psychiatric hospital that Pound later used to describe the place of detention to which his pro-fascist wartime broadcasts led (see Carpenter, 793).
19 Four years before the famous final line of Eliot's 'East Coker', Chesterton noted that 'for me my end is my beginning' (*Autobiography*, 342). In both cases the allusion is to the phrase embroidered by Mary Queen of Scots on her cloth of estate while in prison.
20 Chesterton's family lived in the Kensington area.
21 In *Those Days*, Bentley jokingly ascribes his invention of the clerihew to an uncanny experience of automatic writing: 'The pen was in my hand. Musing, I hardly knew what it was tracing on the page. Then, with a start, I saw that I had written' the Davy clerihew (*Those*, 153).
22 The dedication is in the un-paginated front matter.
23 Lewis's story is also a pastiche of Dostoevsky's novella, *The Double* (1846), a text that had helped to inspire the motif of identity theft that animates *Mrs. Dukes' Million*. As with Chesterton and Eliot, in Lewis's literary end was his beginning.

Works Cited

Ackroyd, Peter. *T.S. Eliot*. London: Abacus, 1985. Print.
Aldington, Richard. 'Blast.' *Egoist* 15 July 1914: 272–73. *Modern Journals Project*. Web. 8 June 2017.
_____. *Soft Answers*. Harmondsworth: Penguin, 1949. Print.
Anon, 'Picture Shows. The Camden Town Group' *Times* 11 Dec. 1911. 12. *The Camden Town Group in Context*. Tate Research Publication. Ed. Helena Bonett, Ysanne Holt, Jennifer Mundy. May 2012. Web. 8 June 2017.
Anon. Unsigned Review. *New York Times* 7 Apr. 1912. *G.K. Chesterton: The Critical Judgments 1900–1937*. Ed. D.J. Conlon. Antwerp: Antwerp UP, 1976. 295–96. Print.
Anspaugh, Kelly. 'Jean qui rit and Jean qui pleure: James Joyce, Wyndham Lewis and The High Modern Grotesque.' *Literature and the Grotesque*. Ed. Michael J. Meyer. Amsterdam: Rodopi, 1995. 129–52. Print.
Apollinaire, Guillaume. *The Cubist Painters*. Berkeley: California UP, 2004. Print.
Archer, William Earnest. Signed Review. *World* 20 Feb. 1895. *Oscar Wilde: The Critical Heritage*. Ed. Karl Beckson. London: Routledge, 1970. 189–91. Print.
Arnold, John. 'An Unholy Trinity.' *New Age* 30 July 1914. 311. *Modern Journals Project*. Web. 8 June 2017.
Asquith, Michael. 'G.K. Chesterton: Prophet and Jester.' *Listener* 6 Mar. 1952. *G.K. Chesterton: A Half-Century of Views*. Ed. D.J. Conlon. Oxford: Oxford UP, 1987. 118–22. Print.
Auden, W.H. Notes on the Comic. *The Dyer's Hand and Other Essays*. London: Faber, 1963. Print.
Bakhtin, Mikhail. *The Dialogic Imagination: Four Essays*. Ed. Michael Holquist; trans. Carol Emerson and Michael Holquist, Michael. Austin: Texas UP, 2008. Print.
_____. *Problems of Dostoevsky's Poetics*. Ed. and trans. Caryl Emerson. Minneapolis: Minnesota UP, 2006. Print.
_____. *Rabelais and His World*. Trans. Helene Iswolsky. Bloomington: Indiana UP, 1984. Print.
Baldick, Chris. *The Modern Movement*. Oxford: Oxford UP, 2004. Print.
Balla, Giacomo. 'Futurist Men's Clothing: A Manifesto.' 20 May 1914. *Futurism: An Anthology*. Ed. Lawrence Rainey, Christine Poggi, and Laura Wittman. New Haven: Yale UP, 2009. 194–95. Print.
Barker, Dudley. *G.K. Chesterton: A Biography*. London: Constable, 1973. Print.

Works Cited

Barnhart, Robert K, ed. *Chambers Dictionary of Etymology*. London: Chambers Harrap, 2011. Print.

Barr, Donald. Introduction. *The Collected Works of G.K. Chesterton. Vol. VIII*. By G.K. Chesterton. Gen. eds. George J. Marlin, Richard P. Rabatin, and John L. Swan. San Francisco: Ignatius, 1999. 15–43. Print.

Barthes, Roland. *Critical Essays*. Trans. Richard Howard. Evanston: Northwestern UP, 1972. Print.

Baudelaire, Charles. *The Painter of Modern Life, and Other Essays*. Trans. Jonathan Mayne. London: Phaidon, 1995. Print.

Bechhöfer, Carl Erich. 'More Contemporaries.' *New Age* 30 July 1914: 308. *Modern Journals Project*. Web. 8 June 2017.

Beerbohm, Max. *A Christmas Garland*. Coln St. Aldwyns: Echo Library, 2005. Print.

———. *Conversations with Max*. London: Hamish Hamilton, 1960. Print.

———. *The Happy Hypocrite: A Fairy Tale for Tired Men*. New York: John Lane, 1922. Print.

———. *Max and Will: Max Beerbohm and William Rothenstein, their Friendship and Letters, 1893–1945*. Ed. Mary Lago and Karl Beckson. London: John Murray, 1975. Print.

Benstock, Shari. *Women of the Left Bank: Paris, 1900–1940*. Austin: Texas UP, 2008. Print.

Bentley, E.C. *The Complete Clerihews*. Oxford: Oxford UP, 1981. Print.

———. *Far Horizon: A Biography of Hester Dowden, Medium and Psychic Investigator*. London: Rider, 1951. Print.

———. *The First Clerihews*. Oxford: Oxford UP, 1982. Print.

———. 'G.K.C.' *Spectator* 19 June 1936. *G.K. Chesterton: The Critical Judgments 1900–1937*. Ed. D.J. Conlon. Antwerp: Antwerp UP, 1976. 525–27. Print.

———. 'Introduction'. *Chesterton as Seen by His Contemporaries*, Ed. Cyril Clemens. New York: Gordon Press, 1972. i–iv. Print.

———. 'A Novel of the Moment.' *Bystander* 27 Apr. 1904. *G.K. Chesterton: The Critical Judgments 1900–1937*. Ed. D.J. Conlon. Antwerp: Antwerp UP, 1976. 97–99. Print.

———. *Those Days*. London: Constable, 1940. Print.

———. *Trent's Last Case*. London: Thomas Nelson, 1913. Print.

Bentley, Nicolas. *A Version of the Truth*. London: Andre Deutsch, 1960. Print.

Bergonzi, Bernard. *T.S. Eliot*. London: Macmillan, 1972. Print.

Bergson, Henri. *Laughter: An Essay on the Meaning of the Comic*. Trans. Cloudesley Brereton and Fred Rothwell. London: Macmillan, 1921. Print.

Betteridge, Harold T, ed. *Cassell's German & English Dictionary*. London: Cassell, 1966. Print.

Black, Jonathan, ed. *Blasting the Future: Vorticism and the Avant-Garde in Britain 1910–20*. London: Philip Wilson, 2004. Print.

Blake, Kathleen. *Play, Games, and Sport: The Literary Works of Lewis Carroll*. Ithaca: Cornell UP, 1974. Print.

Blissett, William. 'Chesterton and English Literary Modernism.' *Chesterton Review* 34.1&2 (2008): 113–46. Print.

———. 'G.K. Chesterton and Max Beerbohm.' *G.K. Chesterton and C.S. Lewis: The Riddle of Joy*. Ed. Michael H. MacDonald and Andrew A. Tadie. Grand Rapids: William B. Eerdmans, 1989. 100–14. Print.

Bloom, Harold. *The Anxiety of Influence: A Theory of Poetry*. Oxford: Oxford UP, 1997. Print.
Boccioni, Umberto, et al. 'Futurist Painting: Technical Manifesto.' 11 Apr. 1910. *Futurism: An Anthology*. Ed. Lawrence Rainey, Christine Poggi, and Laura Wittman. New Haven: Yale UP, 2009. 64–67. Print.
Borges, Jorge Luis. *Other Inquisitions: 1937–1952*. Trans. Ruth L.C. Simms. London: Souvenir Press, 1973. Print.
Boyd, Ian. *The Novels of G.K. Chesterton: A Study in Art and Propaganda*. London: Paul Elek, 1975. Print.
Bradbury, Malcolm. *No, Not Bloomsbury*. London: Andre Deutsch, 1987. Print.
Brégy, Katherine. 'T.S. Eliot: A Study in Transition.' *America* 15 July 1939. *T.S. Eliot: The Contemporary Reviews*. Ed. Jewel Spears Brooker. Cambridge: Cambridge UP, 2004. 397–99. Print.
Brody, Alan. *The English Mummers and Their Plays: Traces of Ancient Mystery*. Philadelphia: Pennsylvania UP, 1970. Print.
Brodzky, Horace. *Henri Gaudier-Brzeska, 1891–1915*. London: Faber, 1933. Print.
Brown, Dennis. *Intertextual Dynamics within the Literary Group - Joyce, Lewis, Pound and Eliot: the Men of 1914*. Basingstoke: Macmillan, 1990. Print.
———. 'James Joyce's Fable of the Ondt and the Gracehoper: "Othering", Critical Leader-Worship and Scapegoating.' *Wyndham Lewis Annual* 7 (2000): 32–42. Web. 8 June 2017.
Burgess, Anthony. 'The Level of Eternity.' *G.K. Chesterton: A Half-Century of Views*. Ed. D.J. Conlon. Oxford: Oxford UP, 1987. 251–54. Print.
———. 'Nonsense.' *Explorations in the Field of Nonsense*. Ed. Wim Tigges. Amsterdam: Rodopi, 1987. 17–22. Print.
Bush, Ronald. *The Genesis of Ezra Pound's Cantos*. Princeton: Princeton UP, 1976. Print.
Butler, Christopher. *Early Modernism: Literature, Music and Painting in Europe 1900—1916*. Oxford: Clarendon Press, 1994. Print.
Caesar, Terry P. 'Betrayal and Theft: Beerbohm, Parody, and Modernism.' *Ariel* 17.3 (1986): 23–37. Web. 8 June 2017.
Canovan, Margaret. *G.K. Chesterton: Radical Populist*. New York: Harcourt Brace Jovanovich, 1977. Print.
Caracciolo, Peter L. '"Carnivals of Mass-Murder": The Frazerian Origins of Wyndham Lewis's *The Childermass*.' *Sir James Frazer and the Literary Imagination: Essays in Affinity and Influence*. Ed. Robert G. Fraser and Carol Pert. Basingstoke: Macmillan, 1990. 207–31. Print.
———. 'The Metamorphoses of *The Human Age*.' *Modernist Writers and the Marketplace*. Ed. Warren Chernaik, Warren Gould, and Ian Willison. London: Macmillan, 1996. 258–86. Print.
Carew Hazlitt, William. *A Dictionary of National Beliefs, Superstitions, and Popular Customs, Past and Current, with their Classical and Foreign Analogues, Described and Illustrated: Vol. 1*. London: Reeves and Turner, 1905. Print.
Carpenter, Humphrey. *A Serious Character: The Life of Ezra Pound*. London: Faber, 1988. Print.

Works Cited

Carrà, Carlo. 'The Painting of Sounds, Noises, and Smells.' 11 Aug. 1913. *Futurism: An Anthology*. Ed. Lawrence Rainey, Christine Poggi, and Laura Wittman. New Haven: Yale UP, 2009. 155–59. Print.

Carroll, Lewis. *The Annotated Alice*. Ed. Martin Gardner. Harmondsworth: Penguin, 1970. Print.

———. *The Works of Lewis Carroll*. Ed. Roger Lancelyn Green. Feltham: Hamlyn, 1968. Print.

Carter, Huntly. 'Schönberg, Epstein, Chesterton, and Mass-Rhythm.' *Egoist* 16 Feb. 1914: 75–76. *Modern Journals Project*. Web. 8 June 2017.

Caserio, Robert. 'G. K. Chesterton and the Terrorist God Outside Modernism.' *Outside Modernism: In Pursuit of the English Novel, 1900–30*. Ed. Lynne Hapgood and Nancy L. Paxton. London: Macmillan, 2000. 63–82. Print.

Cavendish-Jones, Colin. 'Estranging the Everyday: G.K. Chesterton's Urban Modernism.' *G.K. Chesterton, London and Modernity*. Ed. Matthew Beaumont and Matthew Ingleby. London: Bloomsbury, 2013. 183–202. Print.

Chace, William M. *The Political Identities of Ezra Pound & T.S. Eliot*. Stanford: Stanford UP, 1973. Print.

Chamberlain, Lesley. 'Introduction.' *The Futurist Cookbook*. Ed. Lesley Chamberlain. Trans. Suzanne Brill. London: Trefoil, 1989. 7–20. Print.

Chapman, Robert Turnbull. *Wyndham Lewis: Fictions and Satires*. San Ramon: Vision, 1973. Print.

Chesterton, Cecil. Unsigned review of *The Napoleon of Notting Hill*. *Vanity Fair* 7 Apr. 1904. *G.K. Chesterton: The Critical Judgments 1900–1937*. Ed. D.J. Conlon. Antwerp: Antwerp UP, 1976. 92. Print.

Chesterton, Gilbert Keith. *Alarms and Discursions*. Gloucester: Dodo Press, 2008. Print.

———. *All I Survey*. London: Methuen, 1934. Print.

———. *All Things Considered*. New York: John Lane, 1909. Print.

———. *The Annotated Innocence of Father Brown*. Ed. Martin Gardner. Mineola: Dover, 1998. Print.

———. 'The Asceticism of the Futurists.' *T.P.'s Weekly* 4 July 1914: 5–6. Print.

———. *Autobiography*. London: Hutchinson, 1936. Print.

———. *Avowals and Denials*. New York: Dodd, 1935. Print.

———. *Barbarism of Berlin*. London: Cassell, 1914. Print.

———. *Charles Dickens*. Ware: Wordsworth Editions, 2007. Print.

———. *Collected Nonsense and Light Verse*. Ed. Marie Smith. London: Methuen, 1989. Print.

———. *The Coloured Lands*. Paulton: Purnell, 1938. Print.

———. *The Common Man*. Ed. Dorothy Collins. London: Sheed and Ward, 1950. Print.

———. *The Defendant*. London: J.M. Dent, 1940. Print.

———. 'The Doom of Doom.' *Time & Tide* 1 Aug. 1931: 910–11. Print.

———. 'The Doom of Doom.' *Time & Tide* 8 Aug. 1931: 935–36. Print.

———. *Fancies versus Fads*. London: Methuen, 1923. Print.

———. *The Flying Inn*. Harmondsworth: Penguin, 1958. Print.

———. *G.F. Watts*. Chicago & New York: Rand, McNally, 1904. Print.

———. *G.K.C as M.C.: Being a Collection of Thirty-Seven Introductions*. London: Methuen, 1929. Print.

———. *A Handful of Authors*. Ed. Dorothy Collins. London: Sheed and Ward, 1953. Print.
———. *Heretics*. Guildford: White Crow, 2009. Print.
———. 'Hitler Branded a Barbarian: "A Menace to Europe."' *Chesterton Review* 31.1&2 (2005): 100–01. Print.
———. 'How I shall Deface this Paper.' *G.K.'s Weekly* 4 Apr. 1925. *G.K.'s Weekly: A Sampler*. Ed. Lyle W. Dorsett. Chicago: Loyola University Press, 1986. 81. Print.
———. *The Man Who Was Orthodox: A Selection from the Uncollected Writings of G.K. Chesterton*. Ed. A.L. Maycock. London: Dennis Dobson, 1963. Print.
———. *Manalive*. Stilwell: Digireads.com, 2008. Print.
———. *A Miscellany of Men*. New York: Dodd, Mead, 1912. Print.
———. *The New Jerusalem*. London: Hodder & Stoughton, 1920. Print.
———. *Orthodoxy*. Mineola: Dover, 2004. Print.
———. *The Resurrection of Rome*. London: Hodder & Stoughton, 1930. Print.
———. *Robert Browning*. London: Macmillan, 1964. Print.
———. *The Spice of Life and Other Essays*. Ed. Dorothy Collins. Beaconsfield: Darwen Finlayson, 1964b. Print.
———. *Tremendous Trifles*. New York: Dodd, Mead, 1909. Print.
———. *Twelve Types*. London: Arthur L. Humphreys, 1902. Print.
———. *The Uses of Diversity: A Book of Essays*. London: Methuen, 1920. Print.
———. *Varied Types*. New York: Dodd, Mead, 1903. Print.
———. *William Blake*. Kelly Bray: Stratus, 2008. Print.
———. *William Cobbett*. London: Hodder and Stoughton, 1931. Print.
Chinitz, David E. *T.S. Eliot and the Cultural Divide*. Chicago: Chicago UP, 2003. Print.
Churchill, R.C. 'The Man Who Was Sunday.' *Contemporary Review* 1974. *G.K. Chesterton: A Half-Century of Views*. Ed. D.J. Conlon. Oxford: Oxford UP, 1987. 300–04. Print.
Cianci, Giovanni. 'Reading T. S. Eliot Visually: Tradition in the Context of Modernist Art.' *T.S. Eliot and the Concept of Tradition*. Ed. Giovanni Cianci and Jason Harding. Cambridge: Cambridge UP, 2007. 119–30. Print.
Clark, Katerina and Michael Holquist, eds. *Mikhail Bakhtin*. Cambridge: Harvard UP, 1984. Print.
Clemens, Cyril. *Chesterton as Seen by His Contemporaries*. New York: Gordon Press, 1972. Print.
Coates, John. *Chesterton and the Edwardian Cultural Crisis*. Hull: Hull UP, 1985. Print.
———. *G.K. Chesterton as Controversialist, Essayist, Novelist, and Critic*. Lewiston: Edwin Mellen, 2002. Print.
Connolly, John J. 'Notes on Chesterton's Notre Dame Lectures on Victorian Literature. Lecture Seventeen: Matthew Arnold: November 12, 1930.' *Chesterton Review* 4.2 (1978): 294–95. Print.
Coyle, Michael. *Ezra Pound, Popular Genres, and the Discourse of Culture*. University Park: Pennsylvania State UP, 1995. Print.
Dentith, Simon. *Parody*. London: Routledge, 2000. Print.
Docker, John. *Postmodernism and Popular Culture: A Cultural History*. Cambridge: Cambridge UP, 1995. Print.

Dostoevsky, Fyodor. *Devils*. Oxford: Oxford UP, 1992. Print.

Douglas, James. 'Signed review', The *Throne* 8 Sept. 1906. *G.K. Chesterton: The Critical Judgments 1900–1937*. Ed. D.J. Conlon. Antwerp: Antwerp UP, 1976. 125–27. Print.

———. 'So Nobly Fierce a Singer.' *Star* 5 Jan. 1901. *G.K. Chesterton: The Critical Judgments 1900–1937*. Ed. D.J. Conlon. Antwerp: Antwerp UP, 1976. 30–31. Print.

Dove, George N. *The Reader and the Detective Story*. Madison: Wisconsin UP, 1997. Print.

Downer, Martyn. *The Sultan of Zanzibar: The Bizarre and Spectacular Hoaxes of Horace de Vere Cole*. London: Black Spring, 2010. Print.

Eckard, Bonnie Jean, and Gargano, Cara. 'The Hermes-Aphrodite Correspondence: Creative Collaboration in Archetypal Theater.' *Hermes and Aphrodite Encounters*. Ed. Metka Zupančič. Vestavia Hills: Summa, 2004. 265–80. Print.

Ede, Lisa. 'An Introduction to the Nonsense Literature of Edward Lear and Lewis Carroll.' *Explorations in the Field of Nonsense*. Ed. Wim Tigges. Amsterdam: Rodopi, 1987. 47–60. Print.

Edgell Rickard, John. Untitled Review. *Scrutiny* Mar. 1933. *T.S. Eliot: The Contemporary Reviews*. Ed. Jewel Spears Brooker. Cambridge: Cambridge UP, 2004. 220–22. Print.

Edwards, Paul. 'Lewis's Myth of the Artist: from Bohemia to the Underground.' *Volvanic Heaven: Essays on Wyndham Lewis's Painting and Writing*. Ed. Paul Edwards. Santa Rosa: BlackSparrow, 1996. 25–39. Print.

———. *Wyndham Lewis: Painter and Writer*. New Haven: Yale UP, 2000. Print.

———. 'The Apes of God and the English Classical Tradition.' *Wyndham Lewis the Radical: Essays on Literature and Modernity*. Ed. Carmelo Cunchillos Jaime. Bern: Peter Lang, 2007. 91–108. Print.

Eliot, George. *Impressions of Theophrastus Such: Essays and Leaves from a Notebook*. Edinburgh: William Blackwood, 1901. Print.

Eliot, Thomas Stearnes. *After Strange Gods: A Primer of Modern Heresy*. London: Faber, 1934. Print.

———. 'In Memory of Henry James.' *Egoist* Jan. 1918: 1–2. *Modern Journals Project*. Web. 8 June 2017.

———. *Inventions of the March Hare: Poems 1909–1917*. Ed. Christopher Ricks. London: Faber, 1996. Print.

———. *The Letters of T.S. Eliot: Volume 1, 1898–1922*. Ed. Valerie Eliot. San Diego: Harcourt Brace Jovanovich, 1989. Print.

———. *The Letters of T.S. Eliot: Volume 2, 1923–1925*. Ed. Hugh Haughton. London: Faber, 2009. Print.

———. *The Letters of T.S. Eliot: Volume 4, 1928–1929*. Ed. Valerie Eliot & John Haffenden. London: Faber, 2013. Print.

———. *Notes towards the Definition of Culture*. London: Faber, 1962. Print.

———. 'Obituary of G.K. Chesterton.' *Tablet* 20 June 1936. *G.K. Chesterton: The Critical Judgments 1900–1937*. Ed. D.J. Conlon. Antwerp: Antwerp UP, 1976. 531–32. Print.

———. 'Observations.' *Egoist* May 1918: 69–70. *Modern Journals Project*. Web. 8 June 2017.

———. 'Professional, or...' *Egoist* Apr. 1918: 61. *Modern Journals Project*. Web. 8 June 2017.
———. *The Sacred Wood: Essays on Poetry and Criticism*. London: Methuen, 1936. Print.
———. *Selected Prose of T.S. Eliot*. Ed. Frank Kermode. London: Faber, 1975. Print.
———. 'Tarr.' *Egoist* September 1917: 105–06. *Modern Journals Project*. Web. 8 June 2017.
———. 'There Must Be People Who Like It.' *Nation and Athenaeum* 31 Dec. 1927. *G.K. Chesterton: The Critical Judgments 1900–1937*. Ed. D.J. Conlon. Antwerp: Antwerp UP, 1976. 444–46. Print.
———. 'Ulysses, Order, and Myth.' *Modernism: An Anthology*. Ed. Lawrence Rainey. Malden: Blackwell, 2005. 165–67. Print.
———. *The Use of Poetry and the Use of Criticism: Studies in the Relation of Criticism to Poetry in England*. London: Faber, 1969. Print.
Eliot, Vivian. 'Fête Galante.' *Criterion* July 1925: 557–63. Print.
Ellmann, Maud. *The Poetics of Impersonality: T.S. Eliot and Ezra Pound*. Cambridge: Harvard UP, 1987. Print.
Ellmann, Richard. *The Identity of Yeats*. London: Faber, 1964. Print.
———. *James Joyce*. Oxford: Oxford UP, 1983. Print.
Eltis, Sos. *Revising Wilde: Society and Subversion in the Plays of Oscar Wilde*. Oxford: Oxford UP, 1996. Print.
Evans, Frederick. H. 'Letters to the Editor.' *New Age* 14 Dec. 1911. 166. *Modern Journals Project*. Web. 8 June 2017.
Evans, Ivor H, ed. *The Wordsworth Dictionary of Phrase and Fable*. Ware: Wordsworth Editions, 1993. Print.
Felstiner, John. *The Lies of Art: Max Beerbohm's Parody and Caricature*. London: Victor Gollancz, 1973. Print.
Ferrell, Charles. *Modernist Writing and Reactionary Politics*. Cambridge: Cambridge UP, 2001. Print.
Ffinch, Michael. *G.K. Chesterton: A Biography*. London: George Weidenfeld & Nicolson, 1988. Print.
Ford, Ford Madox. *The Bodley Head Ford Madox Ford, Volume Five: Memories and Impressions*. London: William Clowes, 1971. Print.
———. 'Henri Gaudier: The Story of a Low Tea-Shop.' *English Review* Oct. 1919: 297–304. Print.
Foster, Hal. *Prosthetic Gods*. London: MIT Press, 2004. Print.
Freud, Sigmund. *Jokes and Their Relation to the Unconscious*. Trans. James Strachey. Harmondsworth: Penguin Books, 1976. Print.
———. *The Uncanny*. Trans. David McLintock. London: Penguin, 2003. Print.
Furbank, P.N. 'Chesterton the Edwardian.' *G.K. Chesterton: A Centenary Appraisal*. Ed. John Sullivan. London: Paul Elek, 1974. 16–27. Print.
Gates, Norman T. 'The Stereotype as Satire in the Fiction of Richard Aldington'. *Exploring Stereotyped Images in Victorian and Twentieth-century Literature and Society*. Ed. John Morris. Lewiston: Edwin Mellen, 1993. 77–98. Print.
Gifford, Don. *Notes for Joyce: An Annotation of James Joyce's Ulysses*. New York: E. P. Dutton, 1974. Print.

274 Works Cited

Gilbert, Bernard. 'The Tragedy of James Joyce.' *G.K.'s Weekly* 4 Apr. 1925. *G.K.'s Weekly: A Sampler.* Ed. Lyle W. Dorsett. Chicago: Loyola University Press, 1986. 82–84. Print.

Glasheen, Adeline. *Third Census of Finnegans Wake.* Berkeley: California UP, 1977. Print.

Gordon, Lyndall. *Eliot's Early Years.* Oxford: Oxford UP, 1988. Print.

———. *T.S. Eliot: An Imperfect Life.* New York: W.W. Norton, 2000. Print.

Gosden, Serena. 'The Degenerate Muse.' *Times Literary Supplement* 6 Dec. 2013: 31. Print.

Greene, Graham. *Collected Essays.* Harmondsworth: Penguin, 1981. Print.

Gross, John. *The Rise and Fall of the Man of Letters: English Literary Life since 1800.* London: Penguin, 1991. Print.

Guirand, Felix. 'Greek Mythology.' *Larousse Encyclopedia of Mythology.* Ed. Felix Guirand. London: Paul Hamlyn, 1960. 87–212. Print.

Gutkin, Len. 'The Childermass.' *The Modernism Lab.* Yale University. 2010. Web. 8 June 2017.

Habib, Rafey *The Early T.S. Eliot and Western Philosophy.* Cambridge: Cambridge UP, 2008. Print.

Hallam, Michael. 'In the "Enemy" Camp: Wyndham Lewis, Naomi Mitchison and Rebecca West.' *Wyndham Lewis and the Cultures of Modernity.* Ed. Nathan Waddell, Alice Reeve-Tucker, and Andrzej Gasiorek. Farnham: Ashgate, 2011. 57–76. Print.

Hammerton, J.A. *English Humorists of Today.* London: Hodder and Stoughton, 1907. Print.

Hannoosh, Michele. *Baudelaire and Caricature: From the Comic to an Art of Modernity.* University Park: Pennsylvania State UP, 1992. Print.

———. *Parody and Decadence: Laforgue's* Moralités légendaires. Columbus: Ohio State UP, 1989. Print.

Harriman, Lucas H. 'Betrayals, Secrets, and Lies: Unfaithful Readings in Modernist Undecidability.' Diss. University of Miami, 2010. *University of Miami Scholarly Repository.* Web. 8 June 2017.

Hastings, Beatrice (alias 'Ninon de Longclothes'). 'Higgledy-Piggledies.' *New Age* 2 Sept. 1915: 435. *Modern Journals Project.* Web. 8 June 2017.

Hatlen, Burton. 'Racism and Anti-Semitism.' *The Ezra Pound Encyclopedia.* Ed. Demetres P. Tryphonopoulos and Stephen J. Adams. Westport: Greenwood, 2005. 251–54. Print.

Haugen, Einar, ed. *Norwegian English Dictionary.* Madison: Wisconsin UP, 1967. Print.

Heady, Chene. 'A Tenant in the House of Fiction: G. K. Chesterton's Attempt to Evict Henry James from British Culture.' *The Journal of the Midwest Modern Language Association* 39.1 (2006): 25–35. Web. 8 June 2017.

Hitchens, Christopher. 'The Reactionary.' *Atlantic.* Atlantic Monthly Group. Mar. 2012. Web. 8 June 2017.

Hofer, Matthew. 'Modernist Polemic: Ezra Pound v. "The Perverters of Language."' *Modernism/Modernity* 9.3 (2002): 463–489. Web. 8 June 2017.

Hollis, Christopher. *The Mind of Chesterton.* London: Hollis & Carter, 1970. Print.

Hulme, T.E. *The Collected Writings of T. E. Hulme.* Ed. Karen Csengeri. Oxford: Oxford UP, 1997. Print.

_____. 'Modern Art—III. The London Group'. *New Age* 26 Mar. 1914: 661–62. *Modern Journals Project*. Web. 8 June 2017.

_____. *Speculations: Essays on Humanism and the Philosophy of Art*. London: Routledge, 1960. Print.

Hurley, Michael D. *G.K. Chesterton*. Tavistock: Northcote House, 2012. Print.

Hutcheon, Linda. *A Theory of Parody: The Teachings of Twentieth-Century Art Forms*. Urbana: Illinois UP, 2000. Print.

Hynes, Samuel. *Edwardian Occasions: Essays on English Writing in the Early Twentieth Century*. London: Routledge & Kegan Paul, 1972. Print.

James, William. *The Principles of Psychology*. New York: Henry Holt, 1918. Print.

Jameson, Fredric. *Fables of Aggression: Wyndham Lewis, the Modernist as Fascist*. Berkeley: California UP, 1979. Print.

_____. 'Wyndham Lewis's Timon: The War of Forms', in *Vorticism: New Perspectives*. Ed. Mark Antliff and Scott Klein. Oxford: Oxford UP, 2013. 18–19. Print.

Jepson, Edgar. *Memories of an Edwardian and Neo-Georgian*. London: Richards, 1937. Print.

Johnson, Sheri L., and Ann M. Kring, eds. *Abnormal Psychology: Twelfth Edition*. Hoboken: Wiley, 2013. Print.

Johnston, Freya. *Samuel Johnson and the Art of Sinking 1709–1791*. Oxford: Oxford UP, 2005. Print.

Joyce, James. *A Portrait of the Artist as a Young Man*. Ware: Wordsworth Editions, 1993. Print.

_____. *Selected Letters of James Joyce*. Ed. Richard Ellmann. London: Faber, 1975. Print.

_____. *Ulysses*. London: Penguin, 1992. Print.

Kane, Louise. 'Pre-War Writing.' *Wyndham Lewis: A Critical Guide*. Ed. Andrzej Gąsiorek and Nathan Waddell. Edinburgh: Edinburgh UP, 2015. 5–19. Print.

Kapp, Edmond. *Personalities: Twenty-Four Drawings*. New York: Robert M. McBride, 1919. Print.

Kaye, Peter. *Dostoevsky and English Modernism 1900-1930*. Cambridge: Cambridge UP, 1999. Print.

Kayser, Wolfgang. *The Grotesque in Art and Literature*. Trans. Ulrich Weisstein. New York: Columbia UP, 1981. Print.

Kenner, Hugh. *The Invisible Poet: T.S. Eliot*. London: Methuen, 1965. Print.

_____. 'Mrs. Dukes' Million: The Stunt of an Illusionist.' *Wyndham Lewis: A Revaluation, New Essays*. Ed. Jeffrey Meyers. London: Athlone, 1980. Print.

_____. *Paradox in Chesterton*. London: Sheed & Ward, 1948. Print.

_____. *The Pound Era*. London: Faber, 1975. Print.

_____. 'The Satirist as Barbarian.' *English Satire and the Satiric Tradition*. Oxford: Blackwell, 1984. Print.

_____. *Wyndham Lewis*. London: Methuen, 1954. Print.

Ker, Ian. *G.K. Chesterton*. Oxford: Oxford UP, 2011. Print.

Kindley, Evan. 'Ismism.' *London Review of Books*. 23 Jan. 2014: 33–35. Print.

Kiremidjian, G.D. 'The Aesthetics of Parody.' *Journal of Aesthetics and Art Criticism* 28.20 (1969): 231–242. Web. 8 June 2017.

_____. *A Study of Modern Parody: James Joyce's Ulysses; Thomas Mann's Doctor Faustus*. New York: Garland, 1985. Print.

Works Cited

Kirk, Russell. 'Chesterton and T.S. Eliot.' *Chesterton Review* 2.2 (1976): 184–96. Print.

Klein, Scott W. *The Fictions of James Joyce and Wyndham Lewis: Monsters of Nature and Design.* Cambridge: Cambridge UP, 1994. Print.

Knight, Mark. *Chesterton and Evil.* New York: Fordham UP, 2004. Print.

Knights, Sarah. *Bloomsbury's Outsider: A Life of David Garnett.* London: Bloomsbury, 2015. Print.

Kristeva, Julia. *The Kristeva Reader.* Ed. Toril Moi. Oxford: Basil Blackwell, 1986. Print.

———. *Powers of Horror: An Essay on Abjection.* New York: Columbia UP, 1982. Print.

Laertius, Diogenes. *The Lives and Opinions of Eminent Philosophers.* Trans. C.D. Yonge. London: Henry G. Bohn, 1853. Print.

Lawrence, David Herbert. *The Letters of D.H. Lawrence: Volume I, September 1901—May 1913.* Cambridge: Cambridge UP, 1979. Print.

Lear, Edward. *Complete Nonsense.* Ware: Wordsworth Editions, 1994. Print.

Leatherbarrow, W.J. *A Devil's Vaudeville: The Demonic in Dostoevsky's Fiction.* Evanston: Northwestern UP, 2005. Print.

Lecercle, Jean-Jacques. *Philosophy of Nonsense: The Intuitions of Victorian Nonsense Literature.* London: Routledge, 1994. Print.

Lechte, John. *Fifty Key Contemporary Thinkers.* London: Routledge, 1994. Print.

Lewis, Wyndham. *The Apes of God.* New York: Robert McBride, 1932. Print.

———. Ed. *BLAST 1.* Santa Rosa: Black Sparrow Press, 1989. Print.

———. Ed. *Blast 2: War Number.* July 1915. Modern Journals Project. Web. 8 June 2017.

———. *Blasting and Bombardiering: An Autobiography, 1914–1926.* London: John Calder, 1982. Print.

———. *The Childermass.* London: John Calder, 1965. Print.

———. *Creatures of Habit and Creatures of Change: Essays on Art, Literature & Society 1914–1956.* Santa Rosa: Black Sparrow Press, 1989. Print.

———. *The Demon of Progress in the Arts.* London: Methuen, 1954. Print.

———. *Doom of Youth.* London: Chatto & Windus, 1932. Print.

———. 'Doppelgänger.' *Encounter,* January 1954: 23–33. UNZ.org. 2003. Web. 8 June 2017.

———. 'Imaginary Letters: Six Letters of William Bland Burn to His Wife—III: The Code of a Herdsman.' *Little Review* July 1917: 3–7. Modern Journals Project. Web. 8 June 2017.

———. *The Jews: Are They Human?* London: George Allen & Unwin, 1939. Print.

———. *The Letters of Wyndham Lewis.* Ed. W.K. Rose. London: Methuen, 1963. Print.

———. *Men Without Art.* New York: Russell & Russell, 1964. Print.

———. *Mrs. Dukes' Million.* London: George Prior, 1980. Print.

———. *The Mysterious Mr. Bull.* London: Robert Hale, 1938. Print.

———. *The Revenge for Love.* Harmondsworth: Penguin, 1983. Print.

———. *Rude Assignment: A Narrative of my Career Up-to-Date.* London: Hutchinson, 1951. Print.

———. *Self Condemned.* London: Methuen, 1954. Print.

———. *Tarr: The 1918 Edition*. Ed. Paul O'Keefe. Santa Rosa: Black Sparrow Press, 1990. Print.

———. *Thirty Personalities and a Self-Portrait*. London: Desmond Harmsworth, 1932. Print.

———. *Time and Western Man*. London: Chatto and Windus, 1927. Print.

———. Ed. *The Tyro: A Review of the Arts of Painting Sculpture and Design*. 1, 1921. *Modern Journals Project*. Web. 8 June 2017.

———. *The Wild Body*. London: Penguin, 2004. Print.

———. *The Writer and the Absolute*. London: Methuen, 1952. Print.

———. *Wyndham Lewis: An Anthology of His Prose*. London: Methuen, 1969. Print.

Liebregts, Peter. *Ezra Pound and Neoplatonism*. Madison: Fairleigh Dickinson UP, 2004. Print.

Lodge, David. *The Novelist at the Crossroads, and other Essays on Fiction and Criticism*. London: Routledge & Kegan Paul, 1971. Print.

Long, Maebh. 'Derrida and a Theory of Irony: Parabasis and Parataxis.' Diss. Durham University, 2010. *Durham E-Theses*. Web. 8 June 2017.

Lynch, Sandra. 'Aristotle and Derrida on Friendship.' *Contretemps* 3 (2002): 98–108. Web. 8 June 2017.

Maes-Jelinek, Hena. *Criticism of Society in the English Novel between the Wars*. Liége: Les Belles Lettres, 1970. Print.

Magalini, Sabina C., and Sergio I. Magalini, eds. *Dictionary of Medical Syndromes: Fourth Edition*. Philidelphia: Lippincott—Raven, 1997. Print.

Malcolm, Noel. *The Origins of English Nonsense*. London: Fontana Press, 1997. Print.

Mansfield, Katherine. *Collected Letters Volume Two, 1918–1919*. Oxford: Clarendon, 1987. Print.

———. 'A P.S.A.' *New Age* 25 May 1911: 95. *Modern Journals Project*. Web. 8 June 2017.

Marinetti, Filippo. 'Destruction of Syntax—Radio Imagination—Words-in-Freedom.' 11 May 1913. *Futurism: An Anthology*. Ed. Lawrence Rainey, Christine Poggi, and Laura Wittman. New Haven: Yale UP, 2009. 143–51. Print.

———. 'The Founding and Manifesto of Futurism.' *Le Figaro* 20 Feb. 1909. *Futurism: An Anthology*. Ed. Lawrence Rainey, Christine Poggi, and Laura Wittman. New Haven: Yale UP, 2009. 49–53. Print.

———. *The Futurist Cookbook*. Ed. Lesley Chamberlain. Trans. Suzanne Brill. London: Trefoil, 1989. Print.

———. 'The Pleasure of Being Booed.' 1911. *Futurism: An Anthology*. Ed. Lawrence Rainey, Christine Poggi, and Laura Wittman. New Haven: Yale UP, 2009. 96–98. Print.

———. 'Technical Manifesto of Futurist Literature.' 11 May 1912. *Futurism: An Anthology*. Ed. Lawrence Rainey, Christine Poggi, and Laura Wittman. New Haven: Yale UP, 2009. 119–25. Print.

———. 'We Abjure our Symbolist Masters, the Last Lovers of the Moon.' *Futurism: An Anthology*. Ed. Lawrence Rainey, Christine Poggi, and Laura Wittman. New Haven: Yale UP, 2009. 93–95. Print.

Marinetti, Filippo, and Nevinson, Christopher. 'Futurism and English Art.' *Observer* 7 June 1914. *Futurism: An Anthology*. Ed. Lawrence Rainey, Christine Poggi, and Laura Wittman. New Haven: Yale UP, 2009. 196–98. Print.

Marinetti, Filippo, Puma, Marcello, and Masnata, Pino. 'Qualitative Imaginative Futurist Mathematics.' June 1941. *Futurism: An Anthology.* Ed. Lawrence Rainey, Christine Poggi, and Laura Wittman. New Haven: Yale UP, 2009. 298–301. Print.

Marsh, E.C. 'Mr. Chesterton and Neo-Romanticism' *Forum* 40, 1908. *G.K. Chesterton: The Critical Judgments 1900–1937.* Ed. D.J. Conlon. Antwerp: Antwerp UP, 1976. 190–95. Print.

Marsden, Dora. 'Views and Comments.' *Egoist* 1 Nov. 1915: 165–66. *Modern Journals Project.* Web. 8 June 2017.

Martin, Robert Bernard. *The Triumph of Wit: A Study of Victorian Comic Theory.* Oxford: Clarendon Press, 1974. Print.

Mason, Michael. *The Centre of Hilarity: A Play upon Ideas about Laughter and the Absurd.* London: Sheed and Ward, 1959. Print.

Mates, Benson. *The Skeptic Way: Sextus Empiricus's Outlines of Pyrrhonism.* New York: Oxford UP, 1996. Print.

Matthews, Steven. *T.S. Eliot and Early Modern Literature.* Oxford: Oxford UP, 2013. Print.

Maycock, A.L. Introduction. *The Man Who Was Orthodox: A Selection from the Uncollected Writings of G.K. Chesterton.* By G.K. Chesterton. Ed. A.L. Maycock. London: Dennis Dobson, 1963. 13–80. Print.

Mayer, John T. '*The Waste Land* and Eliot's Poetry Notebook.' *T. S. Eliot: The Modernist in History.* Ed. Ronald Bush. Cambridge: Cambridge UP: 1991. 67–90. Print.

Medcalf, Stephen. 'The Achievement of G.K. Chesterton.' *G.K. Chesterton: A Centenary Appraisal.* Ed. John Sullivan. London: Paul Elek, 1974. 81–124. Print.

Mead, Henry. 'The Evolution of T. E. Hulme's Thought.' *Modernist Journals Project.* Brown University and the University of Tulsa. Web. 8 June 2017.

Meyers, Jeffrey. *The Enemy: A Biography of Wyndham Lewis.* London: Routledge & Kegan Paul, 1980. Print.

Moody, A. David. *Ezra Pound: Poet, A Portrait of the Man and His Work: Vol. I: The Young Genius 1885–1920.* Oxford: Oxford UP, 2007. Print.

Morris, Leon. *Revelation: An Introduction and Commentary.* Downers Grove: InterVarsity Press, 1987. Print.

Morson, Gary Saul. 'Parody, History, and Metaparody.' *Rethinking Bakhtin: Extensions and Challenges.* Ed. Gary Saul Morson, and Caryl Emerson. Evanston: Northwestern UP, 1989. 63–86. Print.

Munton, Alan, ed. 'The Code of a Herdsman.' Glasgow: The Wyndham Lewis Society, 1977. Print.

———. 'From Charlie Chaplin to Bill Haley: Popular Culture and Ideology in Wyndham Lewis.' *Wyndham Lewis the Radical: Essays on Literature and Modernity.* Ed. Carmelo Cunchillos Jaime. Bern: Peter Lang, 2007. 159–186. Print.

———. 'Lewis, Anarchism, and Socialism.' *The Cambridge Companion to Wyndham Lewis.* Ed. Tyrus Miller. Cambridge: Cambridge UP, 2016. 87–99. Print.

———. 'Wyndham Lewis: The Transformations of Carnival.' *Wyndham Lewis: Litteratural Pittura.* Ed. Giovanni Cianci. Palermo: Sellerio Editore, 1982. 141–57. Print.

Murry, John Middleton. 'The Art of Pablo Picasso.' *New Age* 30 Nov. 1911: 115. *Modern Journals Project.* Web. 8 June 2017.

———. Untitled review of *Ulysses. Nation & Athenaeum* 22 Apr. 1922. *James Joyce: The Critical Heritage, Volume One 1902–1927*. Ed. Robert H. Deming. London: Routledge & Kegan Paul, 1970. 195–98. Print.

Noyes, Alfred. 'The Centrality of Chesterton.' *Quarterly Review* Jan. 1953. *G.K. Chesterton: A Half-Century of Views*. Ed. D.J. Conlon. Oxford: Oxford UP, 1987. 126–32. Print.

O'Brien, John. *Harlequin Britain: Pantomime and Entertainment, 1690–1760*. Baltimore: John Hopkins UP, 2004. Print.

O'Connor, Fr. John. *Father Brown on Chesterton*. London: Frederick Muller, 1937. Print.

Oddie, William. *Chesterton and the Romance of Orthodoxy: The Making of GKC 1874–1908*. Oxford: Oxford UP, 2008. Print.

O'Keefe, Paul. *Some Sort of Genius: A Life of Wyndham Lewis*. London: Jonathan Cape, 2000. Print.

Oliver, Kelly. *Reading Kristeva: Unraveling the Double-Bind*. Bloomington: Indiana UP, 1993. Print.

Orage, Alfred Richard. 'Notes of the Week.' *New Age* 20 Feb. 1913: 225–227. *Modern Journals Project*. Web. 8 June 2017.

———. 'Readers and Writers.' *New Age* 23 Oct. 1913: 761–63. *Modern Journals Project*. Web. 8 June 2017.

———. 'Readers and Writers.' *New Age* 25 Dec. 1913: 240–41. *Modern Journals Project*. Web. 8 June 2017.

———. 'Readers and Writers.' *New Age* 26 Nov. 1914: 97–98. *Modern Journals Project*. Web. 8 June 2017.

———. 'Readers and Writers.' *New Age* 17 Jan. 1918: 231–32. *Modern Journals Project*. Web. 8 June 2017.

Oser, Lee. *The Return of Christian Humanism: Chesterton, Eliot, Tolkien, and the Romance of History*. Columbia: Missouri UP, 2007. Print.

Parker, James. 'A Most Unlikely Saint.' *Atlantic*. Atlantic Monthly Group. Apr. 2015. Web. 8 June 2017.

Parsons, Marnie. *Touch Monkeys: Nonsense Strategies for Reading Twentieth-Century Poetry*. Toronto: Toronto UP, 1994. Print.

Pavlock, Barbara. *The Image of the Poet in Ovid's* Metamorphoses. Madison: Wisconsin UP, 2009. Print.

Pearson, Hesketh. 'Gilbert Keith Chesterton.' *Listener* 28 June 1956. *G.K. Chesterton: A Half-Century of Views*. Ed. D.J. Conlon. Oxford: Oxford UP, 1987. 142–44. Print.

Perl, Jeffrey M. *Skepticism and Modern Enmity: Before and After Eliot*. Baltimore: John Hopkins UP, 1989. Print.

Perrino, Mark. *The Poetics of Mockery: Wyndham Lewis's* The Apes of God *and the Popularization of Modernism*. London: Maney, 1995. Print.

Peterson, Thomas Erling. *The Rose in Contemporary Italian Poetry*. Gainesville: Florida UP, 2000. Print.

Phillips, William H. *St. John Hankin: Edwardian Mephistopheles*. London: Associated UP, 1979. Print.

Pope, John C. 'Prufrock and Raskolnikov Again: A Letter from Eliot.' *American Literature* 18.4 (1947): 319–21. Web. 8 June 2017.

Porter, Dennis. 'Backward Construction and the Art of Suspense.' *The Poetics of Murder: Detective Fiction and Literary Theory*. Ed. Glen W. Most and

William W. Stowe. San Diego: Harcourt Brace Jovanovich, 1983. 327–40. Print.

Pound, Ezra. *The Cantos of Ezra Pound*. London: Faber, 1975. Print.

———. *Ezra Pound: The Critical Heritage*. Ed. Eric Homberger. London: Routledge & Kegan Paul, 1972. Print.

———. *Ezra Pound and Dorothy Shakespear, Their Letters: 1909–1914*. New York: New Directions, 1984. Print.

———. *Ezra Pound to his Parents: Letters 1895–1929*. Ed. Mary de Rachewiltz, A. David Moody, and Joanna Moody. Oxford: Oxford UP, 2010. Print.

———. *Ezra Pound's Poetry and Prose Contributions to Periodicals in Ten Volumes: Volume IV 1920—1927*. Ed. Lea Baechler, A. Walton Litz, and James Longenbach. New York: Garland, 1991. Print.

———. *Ezra Pound's Poetry and Prose Contributions to Periodicals in Ten Volumes: Volume VI 1933—1935*. Ed. Lea Baechler, A. Walton Litz, and James Longenbach. New York: Garland, 1991. Print.

———. *Ezra Pound's Poetry and Prose Contributions to Periodicals in Ten Volumes: Volume VII 1936–1939*. Ed. Lea Baechler, A. Walton Litz, and James Longenbach. New York: Garland, 1991. Print.

———. *Gaudier-Brzeska: A Memoir*. London: John Lane, 1916. Print.

———. 'I Gather the Limbs of Osiris.' *New Age* 30 Nov. 1911: 107. *Modern Journals Project*. Web. 8 June 2017.

———. *The Letters of Ezra Pound: 1907–1941*. Ed. D.D. Paige. London: Faber, 1951. Print.

———. 'Letters to the Editor.' *New Age* 10 Jan. 1918: 219. *Modern Journals Project*. Web. 8 June 2017.

———. *New Selected Poems and Translations*. Ed. Richard Sieburth. New York: New Directions, 2010. Print.

———. *Pound/Joyce: The Letters of Ezra Pound to James Joyce, with Pound's Essays on Joyce*. Ed. Forrest Read. New York: New Directions, 1967. Print.

———. *Pound/Lewis: The Letter of Ezra Pound and Wyndham Lewis*. Ed. Timothy Materer. London: Faber, 1985. Print.

———. 'The Revolt of Intelligence IV.' *New Age* 1 Jan. 1920: 139–40. *Modern Journals Project*. Web. 8 June 2017.

———. 'Studies in Contemporary Mentality XVII—The Slightly Shop-Worn.' *New Age* 27 Dec. 1917: 167–68. *Modern Journals Project*. Web. 8 June 2017.

———. 'Tarr, by Wyndham Lewis.' *Literary Essays of Ezra Pound*. Ed. T.S. Eliot. London: Faber, 1968. 424–30. Print.

Pritchett, V.S. 'Secret Terrors.' *New Statesman* 7 June 1974. *G.K. Chesterton: A Half-Century of Views*. Ed. D.J. Conlon. Oxford: Oxford UP, 1987. 324–26. Print.

Quema, Anne. *The Agon of Modernism: Wyndham Lewis's Allegories, Aesthetics, and Politics*. Lewisburg: Bucknell UP, 1999. Print.

Resseguie, James L. *The Revelation of John: A Narrative Commentary*. Grand Rapids: Baker Academic, 2009. Print.

Ricks, Christopher. Preface. *Inventions of the March Hare: Poems 1909–1917*. By T.S. Eliot. Ed. Christopher Ricks. London: Faber, 1996. xi–xxxiii. Print.

———. *T.S. Eliot and Prejudice*. London: Faber, 1988. Print.

Ripman, Walter. *A Handbook of the Latin Language: Being a Dictionary, Classified Vocabulary, and Grammar*. London: J.M. Dent, 1930. Print.

Rohdie, Sam. 'A Note on F.T. Marinetti's Futurist Cooking.' *Screening the Past*. The Screening the Past Publications Group. 5 Sept. 2010. Web. 8 June 2017.

Rose, June. *Demons and Angels: a Life of Jacob Epstein*. New York: Constable, 2002. Print.

Rose, Margaret. *Parody: Ancient, Modern, and Post-Modern*. Cambridge: Cambridge UP, 1993. Print.

Rother, James. 'Modernism and the Nonsense Style.' *Contemporary Literature* 15. 2 (1974): 187–202. Web. 8 June 2017.

Roud, Steve. *The English Year: A Month-by-Month Guide to the Nation's Customs and Festivals, from May Day to Mischief Night*. London: Penguin, 2008. Print.

Rulo, Kevin. 'Modernism and the Antimodern in the "Men of 1914"'. *Neohelicon* 43.1 (2016): 251–78. Web. 8 June 2017.

Schenker, Daniel. *Wyndham Lewis: Religion and Modernism*. Tuscaloosa: Alabama UP, 1992. Print.

Schopenhauer, Arthur. *Essays and Aphorisms*. Ed. and Trans. R.J. Hollingdale. London: Penguin, 2004. Print.

―――. *The World as Will and Idea*. Ed. David Berman. Trans. Jill Berman. London: J.M. Dent, 2004. Print.

Schock, Peter. *Romantic Satanism: Myth and the Historical Moment in Blake, Shelley, and Byron*. Houndmills: Palgrave, 2003. Print.

Schuchard, Ronald. *Eliot's Dark Angel: Intersections of Life and Art*. Oxford: Oxford UP, 1999. Print.

Scott, Dixon. 'The Guilt of Mr. Chesterton' *Manchester Guardian* July 1911. *G.K. Chesterton: The Critical Judgments 1900–1937*. Ed. D.J. Conlon. Antwerp: Antwerp UP, 1976. 265–68. Print.

Seaber, Luke. *G.K. Chesterton's Literary Influence on George Orwell: A Surprising Irony*. Lewiston: Edwin Mellen Press, 2012. Print.

―――. 'The Meaning of Margate: G. K. Chesterton and T. S. Eliot.' *English* 59.225 (2010): 194–211. Web. 8 June 2017.

Sewell, Elizabeth. *The Field of Nonsense*. London: Chatto and Windus, 1952. Print.

―――. 'G.K. Chesterton: The Giant Upside-Down.' *Thought* 30.4 (1955/56): 555–76. Web. 8 June 2017.

―――. 'Nonsense Verse and the Child.' *Explorations in the Field of Nonsense*. Ed. Wim Tigges. Amsterdam: Rodopi, 1987. 135–148. Print.

Shaw, George Bernard. 'The Case against Chesterton.' 13 May 1916. *Bernard Shaw's Book Reviews, Volume Two: 1884 to 1950*. Ed. Brian Tyson. University Park: Pennsylvania State UP, 1996. Print.

―――. 'The Chesterbelloc: A Lampoon.' *New Age* 15 Feb. 1908. *G.K. Chesterton: The Critical Judgments 1900–1937*. Ed. D.J. Conlon. Antwerp: Antwerp UP, 1976. 135–43. Print.

―――. 'The Importance of Being Earnest.' *Saturday Review* 23 Feb. 1895. *Oscar Wilde: The Critical Heritage*. Ed. Karl Beckson. London: Routledge, 1970. 194–95. Print.

―――. 'A Tribute to a Great Churchman.' 13 Jan. 1950. *Bernard Shaw's Book Reviews, Volume Two: 1884 to 1950*. Ed. Brian Tyson. University Park: Pennsylvania State UP, 1996. Print.

Sheinberg, Esti. *Irony, Satire, Parody and the Grotesque in the Music of Shostakovich: A Theory of Musical Incongruities*. Aldershot: Ashgate, 2000. Print.

Sherry, Vincent. *Modernism and the Reinvention of Decadence*. Cambridge: Cambridge UP, 2014. Print.
Sinclair, May. 'Prufrock: A Criticism'. *Little Review* Dec. 1917: 8–14. *Modern Journals Project*. Web. 8 June 2017.
Smith, John (alias 'Mimnermus'). 'A Licenced Jester.' *Freethinker* 16 Oct. 1910. *G.K. Chesterton: The Critical Judgments 1900–1937*. Ed. D.J. Conlon. Antwerp: Antwerp UP, 1976. 240–42. Print.
Soldo, John J. 'T. S. Eliot and Jules LaForgue.' *American Literature* 55.2 (1983): 137–50. Web. 8 June 2017.
Stansky, Peter. *On or About December 1910: Early Bloomsbury and its Intimate World*. Cambridge: Harvard UP, 1996. Print.
Stapleton, Julia. *Christianity, Patriotism, and Nationhood: the England of G.K. Chesterton*. Plymouth: Lexington, 2009. Print.
Stewart, Susan. *Nonsense: Aspects of Intertextuality in Folklore and Literature*. Baltimore: John Hopkins UP, 1989. Print.
Stillman, Anne. 'Ezra Pound.' *T.S. Eliot in Context*. Ed. Jason Harding. Cambridge: Cambridge UP, 2011. 241–51. Print.
Stock, Noel. *The Life of Ezra Pound*. London: Routledge, 1970. Print.
Sugg Ryan, Deborah. 'Spectacle, the Public and the Crowd: Pageants and Exhibitions in 1908.' *The Edwardian Sense: Art, Design and Spectacle in Britain, 1901–1910*. Ed. Michael Hatt, and Morna O'Neill. New Haven: Yale UP, 43–71. Print.
Sullivan, Hannah. 'Classics.' *T.S. Eliot in Context*. Ed. Jason Harding. Cambridge: Cambridge UP, 2011. 169–79. Print.
Sumner, Charles. 'Wyndham Lewis's Theory of Mass Culture.' *The Space Between: Literature and Culture, 1914–1945* 3.1 (2007): 29–45. Web. 8 June 2017.
Surette, Leon. *Pound in Purgatory: From Economic Radicalism to Anti-Semitism*. Chicago: Illinois UP, 1999. Print.
Symons, Arthur. *Selected Writings*. Ed. Roger Holdsworth. Manchester: Carcanet, 2003. Print.
———. *The Symbolist Movement in Literature*. New York: AMS Press, 1980. Print.
Taylor, Alan. 'The Battle of Enfarinats.' *Atlantic*. Atlantic Monthly Group. 28 Dec. 2015. Web. 8 June 2015.
Thompson, Della, ed. *The Concise Oxford Dictionary*. Oxford: Clarendon, 1995. Print.
Thomson, Philip. *The Grotesque*. London: Methuen, 1972. Print.
Trilling, Lionel. *Matthew Arnold*. London: George Allen & Unwin, 1955. Print.
Van Aelst, Heather. 'T.S. Eliot's "The Hollow Men": a Hypertextual Study of Allusion.' ADUni.org: ArsDigita University Alumni Website. Web. 8 June 2017.
Walkley, A.B. 'The Importance of Being Earnest.' *Speaker* 23 Feb. 1895. *Oscar Wilde: The Critical Heritage*. Ed. Karl Beckson. London: Routledge, 1970. 196–99. Print.
Ward, Maisie. *Gilbert Keith Chesterton*. London: Sheed and Ward, 1945. Print.
———. 'The Man Who Was Thursday' (1947). *G.K. Chesterton: A Half-Century of Views*. Ed. D.J. Conlon. Oxford: Oxford UP, 1987. 72–74. Print.
———. *Return to Chesterton*. London: Sheed and Ward, 1952. Print.

Wells, H.G. 'About Chesterton and Belloc.' *New Age* 11 Jan. 1908. *G.K. Chesterton: The Critical Judgments 1900–1937*. Ed. D.J. Conlon. Antwerp: Antwerp UP, 1976. 131–35. Print.

Welsford, Enid. *The Fool: His Social and Literary History*. Gloucester: Peter Smith, 1966. Print.

West, Rebecca. 'Manalive.' *Freewoman* 14 Mar. 1912. *G.K. Chesterton: The Critical Judgments 1900–1937*. Ed. D.J. Conlon. Antwerp: Antwerp UP, 1976. 291–93. Print.

_____. 'Mr Chesterton in Hysterics: A Study in Prejudice.' *Clarion* 14 Nov. 1913: 5. *Marxists Internet Archive*. Web. 8 June 2017.

Wetzsteon, Ross. *Republic of Dreams: Greenwich Village: The American Bohemia, 1910–1960*. New York: Simon & Schuster, 2003. Print.

Whelpton, Vivien. *Richard Aldington: Poet, Soldier and Lover 1911–1929*. Cambridge: James Clark, 2014. Print.

Whitman, Walt. *The Complete Poems*. Harmondsworth: Penguin, 1975. Print.

Wilde, Oscar. *Complete Works of Oscar Wilde*. London: Collins, 1976. Print.

_____. *Intentions*. London: The Unicorn Press, 1945. Print.

Williams, Paul. *The Fool and the Trickster: Studies in Honour of Enid Welsford*. Cambridge: D.S. Brewer, 1979. Print.

Wills, Garry. *Chesterton: Man and Mask*. New York: Sheed & Ward, 1961. Print.

_____. 'The Man Who Was Thursday.' *G.K. Chesterton: A Half-Century of Views*. Ed. D.J. Conlon. Oxford: Oxford UP, 1987. 335–42. Print.

Wilson, A.N. *Hilaire Belloc*. London: Hamish Hamilton, 1984. Print.

Wood, Michael. 'A Preference for Torquemada.' *London Review of Books* 9 Apr. 2009: 8–10. Print.

Woolf, Virginia. *The Diary of Virginia Woolf, Volume III: 1925–1930*. Ed. Anne Olivier Bell. London: Hogarth, 1980. Print.

_____. *The Essays of Virginia Woolf, Volume II: 1912–1918*. Ed. Andrew McNeillie. London: Hogarth, 1987. Print.

_____. *Mrs Dalloway*. Ware: Wordsworth Editions, 2003. Print.

_____. *The Question of Things Happening: The Letters of Virginia Woolf, Volume II: 1912–1922*. Ed. Nigel Nicolson. London: Hogarth, 1976. Print.

_____. *A Change of Perspective: The Letters of Virginia Woolf, Volume III: 1923–1928*. Ed. Nigel Nicholson. London: Hogarth, 1977. Print.

_____. *Virginia Woolf: Selections from her Essays*. Ed. Walter James. London: Chatto and Windus, 1966. Print.

Wootten, William. 'Fame and Fleabites.' *Guardian*. Guardian News and Media. 26 Feb. 2005. Web. 8 June 2017.

Wordsworth, William. *The Letters of William Wordsworth: A New Selection*. Ed. Alan G. Hill. Oxford: Clarendon, 1984. Print.

Index

abjection 166–67; Bloomsbury and 107–08; Chesterton and 62, 66–67, 167–68, 185, 190–91, 253; Eliot and 123, 125–26, 165–67, 169, 176, 178, 218, 230; Joyce and 168–69, 220; Lewis and 136, 139, 169–70, 176–178, 197, 203, 218; Pound and 169, 171–72, 176, 218, 220
Aiken, Conrad 12, 121, 124, 162
Aldington, Richard 11, 155, 171, 176, 227, 254; 'Nobody's Baby: A Mystery Story' 227; 'Stepping Heavenward: A Record' 254
Alice in Wonderland syndrome 39
Andersen, Hans Christian 38
Antheil, George 133
antimodernism 4–5, 7, 13, 20, 68, 167, 206, 242
Apollinaire, Guillaume 142, 150, 166
aporia 182, 187, 228–29, 245
Aristophanes 13–14, 26, 67, 230
Aristotle 20, 46, 67
Arkell, Reginald 181–82
Arnold, Matthew 75
Attic comedy 88, 231
Auden, Wystan Hugh 51, 153, 181, 188, 214, 235, 259
Autolycus 147–48, 227

Bacchus 84, 201, 233n10
Bakhtin, Mikhail: carnivalesque theorised by 13–15, 41–42, 73–76, 84–85, 90–91, 97, 99, 101, 123, 137, 164, 167, 220, 228; dialogism theorised by 14, 16; Dostoevsky and 137; marionettes and 119; masks and 41–42, 44; official feast, the 95; Romantic grotesque theorised by 41–42, 44, 54n25, 75, 119, 178; skaz theorised by 90

Baring, Maurice 141n5, 161
Barthes, Roland 55–56
bathos 21, 232; Bentley, unintentional 260; Chesterton identifies in Wilde 59–60, 63, 69, 91, 167–68, 170; Chesterton identifies in Futurism 116, 157; Chesterton's manipulation of 57–58, 77; Eliot, intentional 120, 122, 223; Lewis discusses 255
Baudelaire, Charles 67–69, 71, 76–77, 120–22, 132
Bechhöfer, Carl Erich 10–11, 155, 161, 204
Beerbohm, Max: Baudelaire's influence upon 68; Belloc discussed by 194n22; Bentley's temperamental affinity with 24, 61; buffoonery of 62, 92; Chesterton caricatured by 74, 166, 178, 181, 250; Chesterton discussed by 194n22; Chesterton influenced by 59–62; Chesterton parodied by 70, 181, 250; Chesterton's fictional portrayal of 120; Chesterton's friendship with 249; *Christmas Garland, A* 70; costuming of 82, 214; 'Defence of Cosmetics, A' 60, 68; Eliot influenced by 120–21, 214; 'Happy Hypocrite, The' 70, 262; Lewis discussed by 266n11; Wilde caricatured and parodied by 59–60, 62, 70, 82, 262
Beit, Alfred 186–88, 191
Bell, Clive 218
Belloc, Hilaire 13, 17n8, 249; anti-Semitism of 181–82, 190, 193n16, 193n19, 194n22, 251, 266n16; Beerbohm discusses 194n22; Chesterton's friendship with 161,

186, 193n19, 220; Chesterton's temperamental dissimilarity to 19, 250; Chesterton's urge to emulate 181, 190, 250; dogmatism of 188, 190, 221, 250, 252; Lewis's criticism of 251; Shaw's 'Chesterbelloc' 13, 19, 181, 221
Bennett, Arnold 248
Bentley, Edmund Clerihew 3, 18, 21, 42, 51–52, 58, 135, 143, 171, 188, 192n3, 196, 220–21, 262; anti-Semitism of 193n19; attachment to Chesterton 19, 37, 47, 50, 260; attraction to, and practising of, nonsense 23–26, 163, 186–88, 261; attraction to Decadence 22–23, 26, 43; Chesterton's disagreements with 22–23, 27, 47–49; Chesterton's fictional portrayals of 45–46, 49–50, 134, 167–68, 266n16; Chesterton's psychological disturbance, recorded by 36–37, 39; Chesterton's public reception, discussed by 67, 72; clerihew composition *see* clerihew; determinist worldview of 34, 47, 245; dislike of Frances Blogg 22–23, 53n8; *Far Horizon: A Biography of Hester Dowden, Medium and Psychic Investigator* 260–61; psychological disturbance of 31–35, 37; snobbery of 20, 22; spiritualist beliefs of 260–61; temperamental affinity with Beerbohm 24, 61; temperamental detachment of 18, 20, 27, 31, 36–37, 47, 50, 61, 153, 239, 245, 252, 261; temperamental resemblance to Eliot and Lewis 162, 178, 229, 256, 259; *Those Days* 18–19, 25, 33, 46, 141n2; *Trent's Last Case* 34, 103, 260
Bentley, Nicolas 52n1, 190, 260–61
Bergson, Henri 69–70, 94–95, 102n7, 113, 153, 160, 174, 206, 224
Blake, William 199
Blatchford, Robert 7, 77, 101n5
Blogg, Frances 22–23, 36–37, 53n8, 55, 65, 78–80
Bloomsbury 104–05, 107–08, 131, 144, 198, 214, 218, 222, 233n6
Boer War 107, 186–89
Bonfire Night 99, 129, 227–28, 234n31

Borges, Jorge Luis 109, 190
Brodzky, Horace 11, 221, 226
Browning, Robert 69, 218
buffoon *see* fool
Burgess, Anthony 69, 216
burlesque 19, 130, 144; aesthetic technique 5–7, 21, 38, 46, 50, 55, 85, 96, 115, 120, 122–23, 138–39, 159, 184, 216, 226, 229–30, 234n27, 239, 258–60; Bloomsbury and 109, 111; Chesterton and 7–8, 18, 21, 38, 46, 50, 55, 84–85, 96, 113, 115, 123, 159, 169, 184, 216, 258; Eliot and 120, 122–23, 213, 226, 229–30, 239, 259–60; Joyce and 5–6; Lewis and 11, 138–39; negative cultural perception of 63
Byron, George Gordon 75

Cadbury, George 142, 145, 149, 160, 191
Calverley, Charles Stuart 24–25
Camden Town Group 109, 156, 174
caricature 7, 51, 75, 108, 183, 231, 248, 262; Beerbohm's caricatures 59–60, 74, 166, 178, 181; Bentley caricatured by Chesterton 48–49, 51; Chesterton caricatured 3, 55, 62, 66, 74, 165–66, 178, 181, 201, 233n9; Chesterton's caricatures 48–49, 51, 188; Chesterton's self-caricaturing 82, 239; Chesterton's theorising of 78, 100; Eliot's self-caricaturing 214; Kapp's caricatures 166, 175, 178, 248; Lewis caricatured 144, 175, 178; Wilde caricatured 59–60
carnivalesque, the 13–15; abjection distinguished from 167; Chesterton's aesthetic methods and 7, 41–42, 67, 88–90, 95–101, 127, 137, 231; Chesterton's historical understanding of 85; Chesterton's materialist philosophy and 73–76, 90–92, 96, 98–99, 119, 180; Chesterton's pastimes and 84; Chesterton's social politics and 77, 90–92, 96, 99–101, 106, 119, 243; Chesterton's view of Futurism and 151–53, 184; Eliot's aesthetic methods and 122, 125, 228, 230–32; Eliot's cultural criticism and 164–65; Lewis's aesthetic

methods and 132–33, 210–11, 228, 231–32, 243; Lewis's cultural criticism and 201, 205, 208, 210, 243, 258; masks and 42; parody and 15; Pound's aesthetic methods and 219, 230; Romantic grotesque distinguished from 41–42
Carr, John Dixon 237
Carroll, Lewis 23, 29; *Alice's Adventures in Wonderland* 38–39, 111, 117, 120, 123, 189, 216–17; aporia and 187; Bentley influenced by 23–24, 26–27; Chesterton influenced by 39, 42–43, 45, 111, 117, 238; Chesterton's criticisms of 26, 38, 245, 261; Decadence influenced by 28; Eliot influenced by 120, 124, 216; Futurism influenced by 117; *Game of Logic, The* 26; *Hunting of the Snark, The* 187; Joyce compares Lewis to 265n9; Lewis influenced by 128, 134, 238; *Through the Looking Glass, and What Alice Found There* 26–27, 109, 120, 124, 216, 238
Carter, Huntly 9
Cervantes, Miguel de 14
Chandos Group 259
Chaplin, Charlie 206, 215
Chaucer, Geoffrey 5, 14, 75
Chesterton, Cecil 17n8, 57, 59, 183, 192n4, 198
Chesterton, Frances *see* Blogg, Frances
Chesterton, Gilbert Keith: alienation from public persona 66, 236; *All Things Considered* 214; ambivalent relationship with readership 64, 67–68, 76, 88; analogic imagination of 15, 174; anti-academicism of 24, 152; antimodernism of 3–4, 13, 205; anti-populist statements in youth 3, 44; anti-Semitism of 181, 183–86, 190, 193n15, 198, 250; apocalyptic imagination of 29–31, 167; 'Apology for Buffoons, An' 63–64, 74, 238; attraction to nonsense 24, 84, 245; *Autobiography* 16, 18–19, 23, 35, 43, 45–47, 51, 53n7, 54n17, 55, 78, 92–93, 189, 192n1, 196, 233n2; *Ballad of the White Horse, The* 164, 202; *Ball and the Cross, The* 51, 63, 117, 141n11, 152, 214, 240, 264–65; *Barbarism of Berlin, The* 195–96, 233n3; Beerbohm's influence upon 59–62; Bentley admired by 19–20; Bentley caricatured by 48–49, 51; Bentley criticised by 21–22, 47; 'Blue Cross, The' 85, 105, 114, 123, 139, 148–49, 185; 'Bret Harte' 12, 17n11, 56, 63, 161; buffoonery theorised and practised by 56, 63–67, 73, 76–77, 79, 81–82, 96, 110, 113, 121–22, 133, 175, 178, 180, 251; capitalism increasingly stringently criticised by 142, 144, 149, 180–81, 249; *Charles Dickens* 3, 8, 20, 101; cheese enthusiastically consumed by 6–7, 258–59; class exclusivity criticised by 87–88, 91–94, 96, 101, 104–05, 109; *Club of Queer Trades, The* 1, 3–4, 132; community cohesion highly valued by 51, 64, 109, 236, 255; costuming theorised and practiced by 55, 78–81, 89, 92, 114, 127–28, 214–15; criminality, identification with 77–79, 101n4; cross, conceived as symbol of dualism 49, 71, 265; Decadence opposed by 22–23, 42, 58, 79, 167; *Defendant, The* 4, 13, 26, 40, 44, 56–58, 60–61, 68, 72, 76, 80–81, 91, 98, 103, 112–13, 142, 145, 188, 250, 257, 261, 263; demagoguery of 63–64, 81, 110; democracy advocated by 57, 59, 61, 75, 250; determinism opposed by 34, 50, 54n17, 245–46; dialogic sensibility of 16, 37, 41, 45–46, 51, 67, 76, 137, 246, 261–62, 264; 'Doom of Doom, The' 246; Dostoevsky, aesthetic and ideological affinity with 137, 112, 115, 139, 147, 241; dualistic ethos of 4, 16, 52, 71; 'Duel of Dr Hirsch, The' 1, 182–83, 185, 192, 207; 'E.C.B' 47; Eliot parodied by 234n21, 237, 239–41, 253, 255; Eliot praised by 240–41, 252–55, 259, 261; *Father Brown* 1, 13, 16, 40, 49, 65, 85–101, 102n6, 103–07, 109, 114, 123, 125–26, 132–33, 138–40, 144–51, 181, 183–85, 187, 189, 191–92, 194n23, 195, 203, 227–28, 231, 234n29, 235, 237, 239, 242–44, 264; financial reliance

upon journalism and fiction 64–67, 72, 80, 190–92; First World War supported by 195–96, 202; *Flying Inn, The* 6, 67, 96, 101, 112–13, 116–18, 142, 181, 190, 192n6, 244; friendship highly valued by 34, 57, 73, 75, 86, 101, 180, 256; Futurism criticised by 112–13, 115, 145, 147, 149, 151, 154; 'Futurists, The' 115–17, 135, 147, 207, 241; *George Bernard Shaw* 30, 61, 168; *Greybeards at Play* 19, 21–22, 29, 32, 37, 50, 105–06, 111, 220, 255–57; 'Head of Caesar, The' 183–85, 188–89, 191; *Heretics* 9, 54n19, 61; 'Humour' 14, 26, 28, 67, 70–71, 89, 117, 251; imperialism criticised by 96–97; *Innocence of Father Brown, The* 149; Joyce discussed by 12, 223, 261; laughter and smirk distinguished by 75, 126, 144, 241; Lewis praised by 246; Lewis publicly engaged with 244–47, 250; *Magic* 9; *Manalive* 10, 49–52, 231, 259, 264; *Man Who Was Thursday, The* 12–13, 29, 37–38, 40–46, 50, 56–58, 64, 70, 78–79, 83, 94–95, 103, 110, 118, 123, 127, 130, 134–38, 141, 152–53, 167–68, 184, 186, 204, 220, 228, 238, 241, 244, 264, 266n16; masses/mob praised by 64, 73, 80–81, 111, 157, 206; materialism philosophically espoused by 73–76, 90–92, 96, 98–99, 113–14, 119, 152, 155, 174, 180; 'Mirror of the Magistrate, The' 99, 237–38, 242; modernism criticised by 2, 103, 139, 223; monocle employed as negative symbol by 48–49, 51, 71; *Napoleon of Notting Hill, The* 12, 49, 52, 67, 72, 78, 81, 120, 220; *New Jerusalem, The* 248; nonsense distrusted by 25–26, 261; *Orthodoxy* 28, 31, 37–38, 42, 49, 71, 101n3, 180, 244; 'Painful Fall of a Great Reputation, The' 1, 3, 63; 'Paradise of Thieves, The' 144–50, 154, 158–60, 164, 169, 171, 173, 176, 179, 185, 191, 210, 212, 221, 227, 238, 262; parodied 10, 70, 181, 193n15; parodies composed by 7, 34, 61, 66–67, 75, 116–17, 147, 151, 161, 193n9, 207–08, 241, 253–55, 257; parody theorised by 15, 17n11, 63, 207; populism of 1, 4, 35, 38, 59, 64, 157, 202; Pound criticised by 3, 224; Pound publicly engaged with 248–49; psychological disturbance of 35–37, 39, 64, 66, 78; 'Queer Feet, The' 86–101, 104–05, 114, 119, 123, 125–26, 132–33, 138, 145, 149, 165, 203, 228, 231, 235, 243–44; *Resurrection of Rome, The* 249; *Return of Don Quixote, The* 55, 75, 108; *Robert Browning* 69–70; *Robert Louis Stevenson* 237–40; satire theorised by 28, 100, 245; *Secret of Father Brown, The* 237; self-parodying, intentional 7, 69, 72, 148–49, 239, 258; Shaw, notoriety of opposition to 61–62, 65; solipsism criticised by 106, 118; solipsism experienced in youth 35, 37, 39, 45–46, 51, 245; 'Some Urgent Reforms: The Human Circulating Library' 235–36, 257, 264; 'Sonnet to a Stilton Cheese' 7, 69, 120, 258; 'Spice of Life, The' 240–41, 255–56; 'To a Certain Nation' 250–51; 'To a Modern Poet' 234n21; *Tremendous Trifles* 57, 61, 183; *Utopia of Usurers, The* 184; *Victorian Age in Literature, The* 43, 59, 167, 216; *Well and the Shallows, The* 261; *What's Wrong with the World* 73, 93, 97; Wilde criticised by 3, 26, 59, 69, 167, 239; Wilde's influence upon 42–46, 52, 148; *Wild Knight and Other Poems, The* 47; 'Wild Knight, The' 242; *William Blake* 185; *William Cobbett* 13; *Wisdom of Father Brown, The* 149, 184

Childermass festival 202, 204–05, 228
classicism, modernist interpretation of 6, 11, 173–74, 176–77, 190, 200, 225–26, 238–39, 264
clerihew 24–25, 27, 29, 31, 53n10, 163, 186–87, 259
clown *see* fool
Cobbett, William 2
Cole, George Douglas Howard 235
Cole, Horace de Vere 105–06, 198, 265n8

Commedia dell'Arte *see* pantomime
Conrad, Joseph 127, 141n4, 222, 228, 232
Cornford, Francis 231
Coward, Noel 248
Criterion 104, 218, 222, 240
Cubism 155, 196

Daily Herald 104–05, 142, 233n2
Daily News 10, 26, 52, 64, 70, 79, 85, 142–43, 156, 160, 180, 183, 191, 218
d'Annunzio, Gabriele 145, 149, 179, 192n4
Danse Macabre 76, 99, 119, 126, 195, 231, 244
Dante 219, 232
Decadence 53n6, 58, 130; Beerbohm's satirising of 60; Bentley's attraction to 22; Chesterton's association with nonsense 26, 28, 39, 96, 108–09, 112; Chesterton's opposition to 22–23, 26, 28–31, 81, 96, 161, 165, 167–68, 263; Chesterton's satirising of 29, 105, 111; Eliot influenced by 118, 121–22; Lewis influenced by 146–47, 176; Pound influenced by 146–47, 176; sartorial theatricality of 81, 146–47; suicidal impetus of 31; Wilde as embodiment of 42–43, 45
dédoublement 68–69, 71, 121
derealisation 39
detective fiction 13, 88, 90, 143, 185, 243; Bentley's parodic approach to 103; Chesterton's advocacy of 103; Chesterton's parodic approach to 45; generic connection to fairy tale 93; modernists' enthusiasm for 104
Dickens, Charles 14, 18, 24, 80, 84, 157, 232, 265
Dodgson, Charles *see* Carroll, Lewis
Dostoevsky, Fyodor 112, 115–16, 128–31, 136–37, 139–40, 147, 176, 199, 233n8, 241, 266n23; *Crime and Punishment* 112, 128, 136, 140; *Devils* 115, 128–30, 136–38, 147; *Double, The* 266n23; *Idiot, The* 128, 130, 141n11
Dowden, Hester 260–61
Doyle, Arthur Conan 233n1; *Sherlock Holmes* 103–04, 237
Dreadnought Hoax 105–06, 108, 198

Dreyfus, Alfred 182, 187, 193n16, 193n19, 250

Egoist 6, 11, 140, 164, 176, 179–80, 197, 213, 215, 223
Eliot, George 63
Eliot, Thomas Stearns 4, 5, 11–12, 15, 146, 236, 262; *After Strange Gods* 230; apocalyptic imagination of 164–66, 168, 218; cheese connoisseurship of 258–59; Chesterton criticised by 164–65, 198, 200, 213–16, 238–39; Chesterton praised by 264; Chesterton sympathised with 217, 234n20, 240, 242; comedian figures in the poetry of 104, 121–22, 124–26, 133, 184, 229–30; costuming practised by 7, 214–15, 222, 224; detective fiction enjoyed by 104, 264; Dostoevsky's influence upon 140; 'East Coker' 266n19; employment 139, 213–15, 222; *For Lancelot Andrewes* 240; 'Hollow Men, The' 118, 121, 218, 220, 222–32, 238, 240–42, 249, 255–57, 263, 265n1, 265n4, 265n5; 'Humouresque' 118–22, 136, 140, 217, 222, 229–30; 'Hysteria' 123; 'In Memory of Henry James' 215–17, 239; inscrutable irony of 119–21, 217; *Inventions of the March Hare* 120, 216; Lewis imitated by 162, 225; Lewis satirised by 225, 227–28; 'Lines for Cuscuscaraway and Mirza Murad Ali Beg' 8, 258; 'Little Gidding' 165; 'Love Song of J. Alfred Prufrock, The' 118, 122–27, 138, 140, 177–79, 243; moral relativism in youth 162–63, 165; nonsense literature's influence upon 120; obituary of Chesterton 2, 89, 262; *Old Possum's Book of Practical Cats* 263; parodied 6, 219, 222, 225, 241, 254; pastiched 223–24; *Poems 1909–1925* 229; 'Preludes' 238–39; Pound criticised by 224, 230; Pound imitated by 162; Pound satirised by 226–28; 'Professional, or…' 213; *Prufrock and Other Observations* 6, 154, 165, 213, 265n2; religious conversion of 219, 222, 228, 253; Romantic grotesque temperament in youth 119, 162; self-parodying,

intentional 8, 214, 252, 258–59, 263; 'Suite Clownesque' 121–22, 124, 126, 184, 222, 229–30; *Tarr* review 139, 154; *Use of Poetry and Use of Criticism, The* 230; *Waste Land, The* 5–6, 12, 212, 217, 219–20, 223, 225, 242, 252, 255, 260
Eliot, Vivien 217, 222–23, 229, 262; 'Fête Galante' 222–23, 229, 262
English Review 128–29, 140, 173
Epstein, Jacob 9, 197–98, 202, 219, 248, 259

fairy tale 10, 38, 79, 93, 238
fancy dress party 84, 95, 107–09, 130, 195, 243
farce 10–11, 13, 40, 56, 59, 98, 137–38, 203, 232, 256–57
Fawkes, Guy *see* Bonfire Night
fertility rite 98, 225–26, 228, 231
festive comedy 93, 98, 134, 243
Fielding, Henry 143, 192n3
flyting 153, 207
folk grotesque *see* carnivalesque, the
fool 67, 92, 98, 142, 145, 203, 255–56; artificial and natural distinguished 68, 72, 120, 123, 211; Chesterton portrays Marinetti as 115, 151–52; Chesterton's self-portrayal as 42, 62–64, 66, 72–73, 110, 163, 178, 231; costume of 82–83, 178; Eliot portrayed as 12, 229; Eliot's literary use of 120–26, 184, 226–27, 229–30; Eliot's self-portrayal as 215; holy fool 117, 141n11; Lewis portrays Chesterton as 153, 184, 200–01; Lewis portrays Pound as 211–12; Lewis's self-portrayal as 177, 207, 210–11; negative cultural perception of 63–64, 78, 148; outlawry of 67, 77, 79; social disempowerment of 64, 77; trickster and fool distinguished 148, 227
Ford, Ford Madox 127–31, 136, 141n8, 143–44, 155, 173, 226–27, 233n1, 233n6
Frazer, James 163, 232, 257
freak dinners 95, 107–08, 114, 243
Freud, Sigmund 33, 95, 97
friendship, dynamics of 20, 161–62, 171, 220

Futurism 104, 111–18, 123–26, 144–45, 147, 149–54, 156, 166, 171, 177, 212, 246, 249
Fry, Roger 109–10, 145, 174, 222

Gardiner, Alfred George 79–80, 84, 142, 193n8
Gaudier-Brezska, Henri 11, 17n10, 198–99, 226, 234n28
Gauguin, Paul 108
Gilbert, William Schwenck 24
G.K.'s Weekly 62, 75, 192, 249, 261
Goldring, Douglas 143
Grant, Duncan 105, 108, 131, 233n7
Greene, Graham 15
grotesque *see* carnivalesque, Romantic grotesque
Guy Fawkes Night *see* Bonfire Night

Hankin, St John 22–23, 25, 28, 31, 35, 53n7, 78, 126, 163, 243
Harlequin *see* trickster
Harlequinade *see* pantomime
Hastings, Beatrice 10, 179
'Here we go round the mulberry bush' 222–23, 225–26, 229–30, 234n30, 240, 255, 256–57, 259–60, 265n1
Hermes 147–48, 227–28, 234n29
Hitler, Adolf 250–51, 266n16
Homer 5, 12
Hueffer, Ford Madox *see* Ford, Ford Madox
Hulme, Thomas Ernest 6, 143, 173–74, 176–77, 190, 194n21, 198, 211, 225, 232
Huysmans, Joris-Karl 130

Ibsen, Henrik 9, 34, 54n19
Imagism 160–61, 179
Inge, William 63–64, 113, 178

Jackson, Holbrook 80–81, 131, 144, 193n7
James, Henry 8–9, 15, 216–17, 228
James, William 8, 13
Jepson, Edgar 143, 172, 179, 192n3
jester *see* fool
John, Augustus 132, 135, 248, 263
Johnson, Samuel 57, 60, 79, 84, 89–90, 142, 155, 201, 250
Joyce, James 4, 150, 161, 248, 262; Chesterton compared to 12–15, 188, 206–08; Chesterton criticised

by 9; Chesterton discusses 12, 223, 261, 264; Eliot parodied by 6, 225; Eliot's praise of 164, 225; *Finnegans Wake* 12, 169, 225, 234n29, 265n9; Lewis satirised by 225, 232, 234n29, 265n9; Lewis's criticisms of 205–08; Lewis's parodying of 206–08, 219, 253; Lewis's praise of 224; Lewis's rivalry with 207–08, 210; *Portrait of the Artist as a Young Man, A* 6, 9, 208, 228; Pound's criticisms of 12, 169, 220; *Ulysses* 5, 9, 12–14, 168, 188, 206, 212, 225, 261; Woolf's criticisms of 225; 'Work in Progress' 225

Kapp, Edmond 166, 174–75, 178, 248
Kenner, Hugh 7, 14, 75, 127, 132, 139–40, 207, 210, 223, 257
Kingston, William Henry Giles 3, 44
Knox, Ronald 12, 65, 236
Kristeva, Julia 166–70, 176, 185, 190–91, 218

Laforgue, Jules 118–19, 121–23, 140, 231; 'Hamlet' 123, 231
Laurençin, Marie 235
Lawrence, David Herbert 3, 10, 265n6
Lear, Edward 8, 26, 28, 125, 140, 163, 187, 189, 242, 250, 258
Lever, William 160, 183
Lewis, Clive Staples 242
Lewis, Percy Wyndham 5, 11–12, 16, 159, 262; *Apes of God, The* 243–46, 254, 266n1; *Art of Being Ruled, The* 157, 200–02, 205, 208, 234n16, 248; antimodernism of 4, 205–06; anti-populism of 139, 159, 197, 203, 205; anti-romanticism of 177, 203, 205; anti-Semitism of 203, 251; asceticism of 155, 174, 196; *BLAST* 10–11, 16, 17n10, 150–57, 160–62, 165, 170–71, 176–79, 192, 196–97, 203–04, 208, 220, 234n28, 265n2; *Blasting and Bombardiering* 16n5, 195, 198–200, 211; Chesterton criticised by 2, 152–53, 160, 169–70, 178, 180, 200, 220; Chesterton discussed favourably by 247–48; Chesterton's fiction parodied by 134, 136; Chesterton's fiction pastiched by 131–33; Chesterton's influence upon 127, 132, 159, 169, 235; *Childermass, The* 200–13, 218–19, 222, 228, 231–32, 233n9, 233n11, 233n14, 246; 'Code of a Herdsman, The' 128, 197, 233n4, 262; comedian figures in the prose of 104, 132, 134–35; costuming theorised and practised by 127–33, 136, 139, 143, 174, 199, 214; 'Crowd Master, The' 197, 245; *Demon of Progress in the Arts, The* 254; dental fixation of 170, 188, 208, 210, 220; *Doom of Youth, The* 246; 'Doppelgänger' 262–64; Dostoevsky's fiction parodied by 136; Dostoevsky's influence upon 128, 233n8, 238, 266n23; Eliot criticised by 217, 243–44, 252; Eliot quarrelled with 218, 221–22; ethical unscrupulousness in youth 133, 138, 155–56; 'Futurism and the Flesh' 152–53, 155–56, 169–70, 174, 184, 200, 204, 208, 246; infantilism criticised by 199–201, 205–06, 208, 211, 245; *Jews: Are They Human, The* 251, 258; John Bull criticised by 157, 170, 200–01, 251; Joyce parodied by 206–08, 253; *Lion and the Fox, The* 164; *Man of the World, The* 200, 212; *Men Without Art* 210, 224, 244, 249, 251, 266n13; moral relativism in youth 162–63; *Mrs. Dukes' Million* 103–04, 131–39, 146, 156, 191, 192n6, 204–05, 207, 209, 213, 263, 266n23; *Mr. Wyndham Lewis as a Tyro* 208; *Mysterious Mr Bull, The* 251; 'Note on Tyros' 209–10; paranoia of 207, 218, 221; parodied 10–11, 161, 204, 225, 227; 'Pole, The' 129, 131; popular culture increasingly accepted by 232, 235–36, 246, 248; popular fiction unsuccessfully attempted by 138–39, 159; popular press criticised by 156–57; Pound parodied and satirised by 211–12, 262, 265n8; Pound quarrelled with 212, 221, 223; Romantic grotesque temperament in youth 135–36, 162; romanticism effaced by 147, 175–76, 190; *Rude Assignment*

128; satire theorised by 148, 162–63, 244–45, 251–52; *Self Condemned* 235; self-parodying, intentional 209, 211; *Tarr* 2, 6, 131, 135–40, 146, 156–57, 162, 165, 172, 178, 197, 207, 227; *Thirty Personalities and a Self-Portrait* 247; *Time and Western Man* 170, 175, 177, 200, 205–06, 208, 211–12, 224, 226, 233n9, 244, 261; *Tyros (Showmen) Breakfasting* 210; war trauma of 192, 197, 199–200, 202; *Wild Body, The* 11, 210; *Writer and the Absolute, The* 264
Little Review 2, 139, 154, 165, 179, 197
Loki 135, 176, 210
Lombroso, Cesare 50

MacDonald, George 90
Maeterlinck, Maurice 58–59, 101n1
Mallarmé, Stéphane 165, 258
Mansfield, Katherine 10, 143, 235
Marconi, Guglielmo 145, 183, 192n4
Marinetti, Filippo 112, 114, 141, 155, 159, 192n4, 247; Chesterton's criticisms of 112–13, 115–18, 144–47, 154; Chesterton's increasing leniency towards 151–52, 157, 184; Chesterton's parodying of 116–17, 147, 207; Eliot's allusive gesturing towards 124–25; 'Founding and Manifesto of Futurism, The' 112, 115–17, 124–25, 134, 145, 225 Lewis influenced by 128, 134–35, 156; Lewis's criticisms of 150–53, 156, 199, 205, 208; Lewis's praise of 150; Pound influenced by 166, 212, 249; Pound's mockery of 170–71; marionette 95, 99, 119–24, 136, 203, 209–10, 215, 217, 222, 229, 231, 244
Marsden, Dora 180
Marx, Groucho 258, 260
mask, symbol of 41–42, 44–45, 118–19, 127, 135–36, 183, 197, 207, 238, 262–64
Matisse, Henri 235
memento mori 178, 231, 241
Men of 1914, The 4, 144, 154, 161–63, 177, 179, 190, 192, 198, 212–13, 221, 223–26, 233n9, 250
Meynell, Alice 213, 234n18, 234n20
Michelangelo 125, 244

Milton, John 7, 80, 136
Mitchison, Naomi 199
mock-trial 84, 201–02
Monro, Harold 155
Monroe, Harriet 12, 243
Moore, George 9
Moore, Marianne 104
Moore, Thomas Sturge 155
moral relativism 149, 162–63, 165
mummery 81, 89, 215, 231, 234n31
Murry, John Middleton 10, 12, 17n8, 110, 137
Music Hall 121–22, 124, 214, 230, 257
Mussolini, Benito 249
mystery play 85, 204

Nevinson, Christopher Richard Wynne 150, 152
New Age 4, 10–11, 13, 73, 109–10, 143, 147, 155, 157–58, 172, 174, 179, 204–05, 225, 245, 249, 266n14
New Witness 10, 17n8, 142, 183, 198, 233n2, 233n6
Nietzsche, Friedrich 117–18
nonsense 30, 32, 130; Bloomsbury and 106–09; category mistake as stylistic device of 29, 40, 58, 108, 111–12, 117, 125, 217, 224; Chesterton and Bentley bond over 23–24; Chesterton's criticisms of 26, 29, 38, 96, 108, 261; Chesterton's critical application of 111, 117, 224; Chesterton's literary manipulation of 29, 38, 40–41, 86, 95–96, 101, 105; Chesterton's praise of 38–39, 84; Decadence and 28, 109; distinction between academic and popular forms of 24, 38, 60, 106, 151; Eliot's critical application of 216–17; Eliot's literary application of 123–26; formal and philosophical attributes of 27–28, 37, 43, 163–64; Futurism and 112–14, 123–25; Lewis's criticisms of 254–55; Lewis's literary application of 132, 135, 244; ontological scepticism and 27, 29–30, 119
nursery rhyme 24, 54n24, 222, 228–30, 238, 255–56

O'Connor, John 89, 127
Orage, Alfred Richard 4, 10–11, 143, 147, 158, 205, 245
Orwell, George 173, 235

pageant play 84, 117, 215
pantomime 19, 77; Chesterton compares activities of Men of 1914 to 238; Chesterton discusses 204, 232; Chesterton's literary application of 92, 125–26, 98, 100; Eliot's literary application of 121–22, 126, 229; Lewis's affinity with 11, 131–32, 263; Lewis's literary application of 133, 136; transformation scene and 76, 180, 202
parabasis 88, 125–26, 132, 138, 229, 231
parody 4, 69, 76, 105, 107, 151, 165, 203; Chesterton's critical application of 59, 61, 111, 116–17, 147, 186, 241, 253, 255; Chesterton parodied 10, 70, 181–82, 216; Chesterton's literary application of 6–7, 46, 50, 61, 75, 86, 92, 94, 97, 134, 145, 161, 265; class division reflected by 92, 107, 243; Eliot parodied by his fellow Men of 1914 5–6, 219, 243; Eliot's critical application of 216; Eliot's literary application of 5, 122–23, 222, 255; formal and philosophical attributes of 5, 15, 20, 68, 167, 183, 217, 236; Joyce's literary application of 5–6, 261; Lewis parodied 11; Lewis's critical application of 197, 199, 206–08, 246, 251; Lewis's literary application of 131–34, 136, 138, 201, 206–08, 232, 254; negative cultural perception of 63; nonsense and 24–26; Pound parodied 179, 226; Pound's literary application of 219
pastiche 5; as uncritical imitation 20, 119, 162; Chesterton's literary application of 60, 116, 135, 137, 241–42; Eliot's literary application of 119, 123, 258; Joyce's literary application of 6, 13; Lewis's literary application of 131, 133, 135–36, 266n23; Lewis's sartorial application of 128; Pound's literary application of 11, 173, 180
Pater, Walter 54n29, 230
performance 4, 68; as characteristic feature of the age 7; carnivalesque and 73; Chesterton and 7–8, 55–56, 77, 80–82, 84–85, 108, 214; Chesterton approaches literary composition as 90; Chesterton's discomfort with 66, 70, 236; Chesterton, Shaw and 61–62, 65; Lewis criticises Chesterton for 201; Lewis criticises Pound for 262; Marinetti and 124; modernism and 7–8, 147, 161, 174, 263
pessimism, ontological 23, 29–30, 33–35, 43–44, 51, 57, 119, 135, 152, 228, 237, 242, 244, 256
Petrushka *see* Punch
Picasso, Pablo 109–10, 156, 244
Poe, Edgar Allan 86, 89
Pope, Alexander 155
Post-Impressionist exhibition 109–111, 174
Post-Impressionist fancy dress ball 108–111, 130
Pound, Ezra 4, 145, 150, 163, 166, 229, 243, 255, 264; anti-Semitism of 233n13; 'Ballad of the Goodly Fere' 173; Chesterton criticised by 2, 9, 157, 158, 160, 164, 171, 178, 180, 198, 202–03, 219–20, 245, 248, 263; Chesterton sympathised with 172–73, 249; commercial unscrupulousness of 146, 155, 159–61; dogmatism of 221, 252; Eliot satirised by 219, 234n23, 242–43, 265n7; 'Hell Cantos' 219–22, 224, 230, 234n22, 253; *Hugh Selwyn Mauberley* 171; 'In a Station of the Metro' 179; Joyce criticised by 12, 169, 220; Lewis imitated by 143; Lewis's friendship with 129, 197, 233n12; Lewis's quarrel with 212, 234n17; Lewis's satirising of 211, 262; *Make it New* 249; masses/mob disdained by 11, 157, 159, 197; 'New Cake of Soap, The' 159–60, 171–72, 193n12, 220; obituary of Chesterton 250; parodied 161, 179; *Personae* 146; *Pisan Cantos* 171, 242, 249; popular press criticised by 156–58, 219; psychological disturbance of 179, 252, 266n18; romanticism effaced by 147, 173, 176, 190; *Tarr* review 139, 154, 165, 234n18; temperamental affinity with Belloc 221, 249, 252; theatricality of 143–44, 146–47, 214

practical joke 25, 169, 204, 260;
  Bergson's theorising of 69–70, 94;
  Bloomsbury and 105–07, 109;
  Chesterton's literary application
  of 94, 104, 106, 132; Chesterton's
  theorising of 76, 178; Eliot's
  enthusiasm for 258; Futurism and
  114, 151, 157; Lewis criticises
  Chesterton's enthusiasm for
  153, 155, 171; Lewis's artwork
  conceived as 156–57; Lewis's
  literary application of 204
Priestley, John Boynton 235, 248
Proudhon, Pierre-Joseph 136
Punch 99–100, 201, 203, 206,
  213, 231
puppet *see* marionette
Pyrrhonism 33, 252

Quinn, John 157, 171–72, 176, 198,
  224, 249

Rabelais, Francois 8, 13–14, 25–26,
  40, 58, 79, 134, 176, 261
Renier, Gustaaf Johannes 251
Romantic grotesque 178, 190,
  218, 224; distinguished from the
  carnivalesque 41–42, 44, 122, 184;
  symbolism of in Chesterton's work
  41–42, 44, 48, 75, 95, 146, 184,
  188, 228, 262; symbolism of in
  Eliot's work 119, 122, 127, 136,
  178, 225, 228, 232; symbolism of
  in Lewis's work 127, 135–36, 178,
  210, 225, 232, 262
romanticism 44, 54n25, 173–74,
  176–77, 203, 205–06, 211, 264

satire 24, 43, 179, 181, 222;
  Chesterton's practicing of 29, 84,
  86, 95–96, 99, 101, 111–14, 117,
  134, 146, 150, 159, 170, 186,
  212; Chesterton's theorising of 26,
  28, 85, 100, 155, 172; conceptual
  similarity to detective fiction 88;
  Eliot's practicing of 223, 225–26,
  232; Eliot's theorising of 230;
  grotesque distinguished from
  28, 95, 99, 101, 119–20, 162,
  188; humour distinguished from
  71; 251–52; Lewis's practicing
  of 133, 199, 204, 232, 244;
  Lewis's theorising of 148, 162,
  207, 210, 245, 251–52; nonsense
  distinguished from 26, 28, 29, 95,
  107–08, 113–14, 163; pastiche
  distinguished from 5, 241; Pound's
  practicing of 160, 219; Pound's
  theorising of 171–72, 176
scapegoat ritual 163–64, 176, 204,
  208, 211, 223, 250
scepticism, ontological 23, 29–30, 33,
  35, 39, 51, 112, 119, 135, 188, 242,
  244, 252, 260
Schönberg, Arnold 9
Schopenhauer, Arthur 30–34, 44, 46,
  52, 57, 119–21, 125, 128, 134–35,
  177, 234n15, 244
self-parody, half-conscious 70–71,
  182–83, 191, 207
self-parody, intentional 62, 68–69,
  71–72, 77, 120, 122
self-parody, unintentional 59, 68,
  70–71, 83, 116, 120, 155, 168,
  181–82
Shakespear, Dorothy 226
Shakespeare, William 123, 232, 240;
  Falstaff, John 71, 79, 232; *Hamlet*
  44, 91, 123, 140, 232
Shaw, George Bernard 8, 70, 235,
  262; Chesterton discussed by 3,
  13, 19, 160, 181, 193n8, 221;
  Chesterton discusses 61–62, 71, 83,
  192; Chesterton's public association
  with 62, 65–66, 207, 214, 262;
  costuming of 82–83; Pound
  discusses 249; Wilde criticised by 28
Shelley, Percy Bysshe 56, 60, 66–67, 73
Sidney, Philip 56, 60
Sinclair, May 154
Speaker 28, 56, 64, 186, 190
Square Club 143–44, 193n6
Stein, Gertrude 205–06
Sterne, Laurence 14, 26
Steven, Adrian 105, 108
Stevenson, Robert Louis 128, 265n1
Strachey, Lytton 129–31, 181, 225,
  254
Stravinsky, Igor 133, 159, 232, 258
Swift, Jonathan 14, 107, 155
Swinburne, Algernon 28
Symons, Arthur 118, 121–22

Tennyson, Alfred 3
This Quarter 212, 223–24, 234n25,
  234n26

Tramp 134
transformation scene 38, 76, 98, 146, 180, 202, 263
travesty, reverse 61, 82, 151–52, 257
travesty, rhetorical 12, 55, 121, 153, 219, 246
travesty, sartorial: Chesterton's literary portrayal of 89, 107–08, 132, 144, 146; Chesterton's practicing of 55–56, 77, 92, 127–28; Lewis's literary portrayal of 131, 133, 139, 201, 243; Lewis's practicing of 127–29, 131, 144; Woolf's practicing of 105, 107–08
trickster 231; amorality of 148, 163; Chesterton's criticisms of 145–49; Chesterton's literary representations of 13, 85, 92, 94, 141, 146–49; Chesterton's positive portrayals of 13, 85, 92, 94; Lewis's literary representations of 132–33, 135–36, 243; Lewis's self-image as 135, 210, 227; Pound portrays Chesterton as 248; Pound's self-image as 216, 227; reputed regenerative powers of 98, 216

'Uncle Remus' stories 216, 219, 224, 226, 258

Valéry, Paul 258
vers libre 112, 116, 255
Vorticism 17n10, 150, 170–71, 196, 198, 208, 214, 221–22, 226–27, 254

Walsh, Ernest 223–24, 234n25, 255, 264
Waugh, Alec 246
Waugh, Evelyn 37
Weaver, Harriet Shaw 6, 179, 234n25

Weismann, August 34
Wells, Herbert George 8, 16n6, 198, 221, 233n1, 233n6, 248–49
West, Rebecca 9, 136–37, 183, 193n17, 248
Whitman, Walt 30, 46, 56–58, 60, 69, 81–82, 241, 250, 266n16; *Leaves of Grass* 57, 81–82, 241
Wilde, Oscar 22, 24, 31, 65, 109, 147, 214; Beerbohm's caricaturing and parodying of 60, 62, 70, 262; Bentley influenced by 23, 261; Chesterton compared to 3, 167; Chesterton influenced by 42–46, 52, 148; Chesterton's criticisms of 26, 57, 59, 69, 166–70, 208, 239; costuming of 81–82; *Critic as Artist, The* 42, 45; *Decay of Lying, The* 43–44, 59, 131, 232; *Importance of Being Earnest, The* 23, 27–28, 148; Lewis influenced by 128, 131, 148; *Picture of Dorian Gray, The* 30, 46, 127, 130
wit and humour distinguished 28, 71, 75–76, 244, 250–51
Woodruff, Douglas 84, 245
Woolf, Leonard 230
Woolf, Virginia 7, 10, 16n6, 100, 103–09, 121, 126, 131, 142, 225, 243, 253; *Mrs Dalloway* 104, 106, 108, 178
Wordsworth, William 7, 72, 75
Worringer, Wilhelm 174, 178, 190

Yeats, William Butler 6, 168, 173, 188, 258
Yellow Book 22, 60

Zola, Emile 34, 54n19